S0-AXS-174

Volatile Borderland:

Russia and the North Caucasus

The Jamestown Foundation
Washington, DC

THE JAMESTOWN FOUNDATION

Published in the United States by
The Jamestown Foundation
1111 16th Street NW
Suite 320
Washington, DC 20036
http://www.jamestown.org

Copyright © 2011 The Jamestown Foundation

All rights reserved. Printed in the United States of America. No part of
this book may be reproduced in any manner whatsoever without
written consent. For copyright and permissions information, contact
Jamestown Foundation, 1111 16th Street NW, Suite 320, Washington,
DC 20036.

The views expressed in the book are those of the contributing authors
and not necessarily those of the Jamestown Foundation.

For more information on this book of the Jamestown Foundation,
email pubs@jamestown.org

ISBN 978-0-9830842-1-1

Cover art provided by Peggy Archambault of Peggy Archambault
Design

Jamestown's Mission

The Jamestown Foundation's mission is to inform and educate policy makers and the broader policy community about events and trends in those societies which are strategically or tactically important to the United States and which frequently restrict access to such information. Utilizing indigenous and primary sources, Jamestown's material is delivered without political bias, filter or agenda. It is often the only source of information which should be, but is not always, available through official or intelligence channels, especially in regard to Eurasia and terrorism.

Origins

Launched in 1984 after Jamestown's late president and founder William Geimer's work with Arkady Shevchenko, the highest-ranking Soviet official ever to defect when he left his position as undersecretary general of the United Nations, The Jamestown Foundation rapidly became the leading source of information about the inner workings of closed totalitarian societies.

Over the past two decades, Jamestown has developed an extensive global network of experts – from the Black Sea to Siberia, from the Persian Gulf to the Pacific. This core of intellectual talent includes scientists, journalists, scholars and economists. Their insight contributes significantly to policy makers engaged in addressing today's new and emerging global threats, including that from international terrorists.

VOLATILE BORDERLAND:
RUSSIA AND THE NORTH CAUCASUS

A Collection of Speeches and Papers from The Jamestown
Foundation's conference on the North Caucasus

TABLE OF CONTENTS

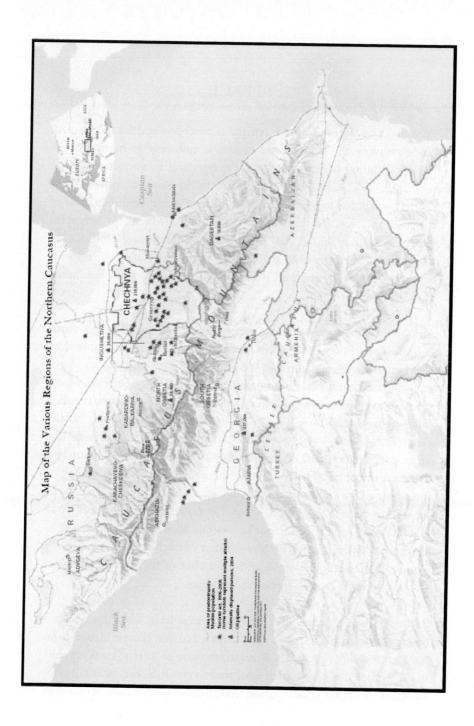

Map of the Various Regions of the Northern Caucasus

PREFACE

Books on the North Caucasus remain at best, few and far in between. Understanding this complicated region is not easy as many experts possess differing perspectives on the causes and consequences of the second Russo-Chechen war that began with the Russian invasion of its rebellious republic in September 1999. Since then an unending cycle of violence has engulfed the Northeast Caucasus with major surges in violence and instability that has seen a conflict once confined to Chechnya proper spread to the Caspian shores of Dagestan and now extend westward toward the Circassian regions of the Black Sea, home of the 2014 Sochi Olympics.

The bulk of the material contained in this collection of essays stems from two successive conferences on the North Caucasus organized by The Jamestown Foundation in 2006 and 2007. Few conferences of this scale and magnitude have been organized in the United States in recent years. Many of the world's leading experts on the Caucasus attended these conferences, including Paul Goble, Maria Bennigsen, Moshe Gammer, Mairbek Vatchagaev, and many other prominent specialists. Their participation and the papers they presented offer a unique and diverse array of perspectives that fill the gaps in our understanding of the nature of the conflict in the North Caucasus and the role that ethnic separatism plays in those wars. We at The Jamestown Foundation hope that this book will fill gaps in our knowledge about the region, as well as deepen our understanding of the evolution of the North Caucasus, both from an historical perspective and from that of the prism of conflict and instability in Russia's turbulent borderland.

For more than a decade, the North Caucasus have undergone several cycles of violence, first with Chechnya's bid for independence from 1994 to 1999, followed by the Russian invasion of its rebellious republic in September 1999 that started what many refer to as the second Russo-Chechen war. No other person has followed the role of Russian

2

nationalities closer than Paul Goble. His insight and knowledge of the ethnic groups that made up the Soviet Union was instrumental in helping U.S. policymakers react to its break up in 1991. In many cases his advice was ignored as a wave of Soviet republics broke free leading to one of the greatest geopolitical developments to affect Eurasia since the sacking of Moscow by the Golden Horde in 1380. Goble's timeless insight continues to offer the policy making community a glimpse into the future direction of Russia's nationalities and the hidden nations that continue to make up the Russian Federation. Paul Goble has been the keynote speaker at many Jamestown events and his keynote address at our conference in 2007 has served usefully as the formal introduction to this volume.

In many areas this book seeks to fill the gap of our understanding on key topics and regions of the North Caucasus that remain little understood in the corridors of U.S. policymaking on Russia. Hopefully one day some enlightened U.S. policymaker will turn to this volume to seek a deeper understanding of some unknown aspect of the North Caucasus imbroglio. Until then this book hopes to fill the void in several important areas. Each chapter in this book addresses certain key aspects of the political and military developments that have shaped the region up until 2007, examining the state of affairs in the little known and poorly understood republics that make up the Circassian areas of the Northwest Caucasus to the Northwest Caucasus republics of Dagestan, Ingushetia and Chechnya.

Several unique essays make up this volume. The doyen of Caucasian studies today, Moshe Gammer, has provided a masterful examination of the history of separatism in the North Caucasus that is a valuable contribution to this volume. No historian or analyst knows more about the Chechen nationalist movement that Mairbek Vatchagaev. His essay provides a unique discussion of the past, present and future of the Chechen nationalist movement as he charts the evolution of the movement to the untimely death of Chechnya's democratically elected President, Aslan Maskhadov in February 2007.

3

In the area of Russian policy toward the region, John Dunlop has skillfully traced the origins of Russian policy toward the North Caucasus that takes us to mid-2007, where the majority of the essays in this volume end. Dunlop addresses the efforts of the Russian polpred, Dmitri Kozak to chart a different approach toward the North Caucasus than the guns and roses approach taken by former Russian President, Vladimir Putin. Ultimately Kozak failed to provide an enlightened form of governance in the North Caucasus and Dunlop fills a very valuable gap in re-tracing Russian efforts to formulate a policy toward the restless North Caucasus.

Helping us understand Russian military strategy in the campaigns being waged in the North Caucasus is the excellent essay by Maria Bennigsen Broxup – a historian and expert who I admire deeply and can only be likened to be the Gertrude Bell of the Caucasus. Her contribution artfully assesses the history of Russian counter-insurgency strategy that originated in Russia's war against the Chechens in the 19th century, which later evolved after the Soviet intervention in Afghanistan, and finally followed another round of evolution again following Russia's renewed campaigns against the Chechens in both the first Russo-Chechen war in 1995 to the present. Her essay is invaluable in terms of the historical perspective it offers on the continuity of Russian policy whether it be under Tsarist or Soviet rule. In other military matters, this volume is graced by the analysis of one of Russia's leading strategic thinkers, Pavel Baev. He has offered two excellent pieces for this volume. One is an assessment of the Russian military campaign in Chechnya and the other is a careful retracing of the Kremlin's counter-terrorism strategy in the North Caucasus up until mid 2007.

Obviously the face of militancy in the North Caucasus has been strongly shaped by the rise of the Jammats in the region as their unique secretive structures have proven impossible to eradicate as they have become the backbone of the regional guerilla insurgency. Once limited to Chechnya, the Jammats have spread to Dagestan, Ingushetia and finally now have penetrated the Circassian heartland of Kabardino-Balkharia. Andrew McGregor provides an excellent description of the

4

role played by these religious-military units in the North Caucasus, particularly in Kabardino-Balkharia.

In regard to the Arabs who fought in Chechnya no other analyst is better qualified to discuss the rise and fall of Chechnya's Arabs than Murad Batal al-Shishani. His Chechen ancestry, command of Arabic, and a first hand knowledge of the Caucasian diasporas who migrated to the Middle East, make his chapter invaluable in understanding how a handful of Arab fighters transformed the Chechens struggle for independence into a trans-national threat. In regard to the pivotal role played by Islam in the North Caucasus, no region is more important than Dagestan. To help us understand the important role played by Islam in Dagestan we are indebted to have a contribution by the noted Russian expert on the North Caucasus Mikhail Roshchin who has written an interesting assessment of the important role that Islam plays in Dagestan.

Perhaps one of the most valuable insights contained in this collection of essay is the assessment of developments in the Northwest Caucasus. Until recently western analysts and even historians had rarely used the term Circassians. However, their nationalist awakening is truly becoming one of the major strategic issues affecting the Caucasus as we move closer and closer to the 2014 Sochi Olympics. By and large most of what we know in the West about the North Caucasus has been confined to the Northeast Caucasus and the struggle of the Chechens with some body of knowledge about Dagestan. The Northwest Caucasus, however, is rapidly emerging as a new area of research among scholars and activists, particularly those making up the seven million strong Circassian Diaspora. Instrumental to helping us understand this important region is Fatima Tlisova, a noted Circassian journalist who has offered two brief overviews of the important republics of Karachai-Cherkessek and the republic of Kabardino-Balkharia based upon her inside knowledge of the region. Rounding out our analysis of developments in the Northwest Caucasus is Jamestown analyst Andrei Smirnov who has written a description of the internal politics of Adyghea. Finally we have a rare and valuable analysis of political trends in the Russian region of Krasnodar by Matthew A. Light.

In sum, this collection of essays is designed to assist western policymakers understand the North Caucasus for an important time period and serve as a reference tool for helping analysts and experts on Russia and the Caucasus learn more about the movements and peoples that have shaped the region and which truly make the North Caucasus Russia's volatile borderland.

Glen E. Howard
President, The Jamestown Foundation

1990 – 1993 Post-Independence

November 1990

On November 25, a Chechen national conference declares independence for Chechnya and requests separation from the Soviet Union. The Chechen-Ingush Autonomous Soviet Socialist Republic becomes the sovereign Chechen-Ingush Republic.

September 1991

The declaration for Chechen independence is unanimously ratified by the All-National Congress of the Chechen People (OKChN) on September 6, 1991.

October 1991

An October 27 referendum approves of Chechnya's formal separation from the Russian Federation and elects General Djokhar Dudaev first president of the independent Chechen Republic. The USSR declares the election illegal and invalid.

November 1991

President Dudaev declares Chechnya's independence from the Soviet Union on November 1, 1991. Russian President Boris Yeltsin temporarily enacts emergency rule in Chechnya, later withdrawing forces on the order of the Supreme Soviet.

Shamil Basaev hijacks a Russian passenger plane on November 9 and holds a press conference upon landing in Ankara, Turkey demanding an end to emergency rule. Basaev becomes a hero overnight in his Chechen homeland.

7

December 1991

On December 31, the Russian Supreme Soviet dissolves itself, formally marking the end of the Soviet Union. The Chechen Republic refuses to recognize itself as a territory of the new Russian Federation. By 1994, Chechnya remains the only autonomous republic to abstain from the Russian Federation treaty.

June 1992

The Chechen-Ingush Autonomous Republic is formally dissolved by the Russian Federation.

November 1992

After days of open warfare between Russian-backed North Ossetian guards and ethnic Ingush militiamen, Russian President Boris Yeltsin decrees on November 2 that the Prigorodny Raion east of the Terek River remains formal territory of the North Ossetian Autonomous Republic. Nearly 600 people were killed with over 65,000 ethnic Ingush forced to flee from their homes in North Ossetia.

April 1993

Following a vote of no confidence by the Chechen Parliament, Dudaev dissolves the legislature, Constitutional Court, and the Grozny Municipal Assembly and unilaterally takes charge.

June 1993

Dudaev orders the military to interrupt a June 5 presidential referendum enacted by the dismissed parliament. The following months lead to an escalation in animosities between Dudaev's forces and Russian-supported opposition.

June 1994

Fighting breaks out in the streets of Grozny between pro-Dudaev militia and Russian-supported opposition forces.

November 1994

The opposition to Dudaev mounts a major offensive on November 26 with the covert support of Russian elite forces. Despite several efforts, the operations fail to unseat Dudaev from power.

December 1994

On December 11, two weeks after Russian forces launched a bombing campaign against Djokhar Dudaev's forces, President Boris Yeltsin orders the Russian military to seize Grozny to restore constitutional order in Chechnya.

January 1995

Known as 'The Battle for Grozny' the Russian army gradually takes control of the capital through a devastating urban warfare campaign. On January 19, Russian forces take over the Presidential Palace and General Dudaev's headquarters.

February 1995

A truce is declared on February 8 and remaining Chechen fighters retreat from Grozny. The Chechen capital is reduced to rubble during the assault with civilian casualties estimated around 30,000 in the first month of fighting. Some estimates indicate that over 100,000 Chechens were killed during the First Chechen War.

Russian troops claim to control two-thirds of Chechen territory and to have captured key cities.

June 1995

On June 14, Shamil Basaev leads a unit of 80 Chechen fighters to raid the Russian town of Budyonnovsk, resulting in a six day hostage standoff in a local hospital. After days of negotiations, Russian Prime Minister Viktor Chernomyrdin agrees to Basaev's demands to temporarily cease military operations in Chechnya. On June 19, Basaev escapes under hostage cover and flees across Chechnya's border. 147 people were killed as a result of the attack, 105 of which were civilians.

December 1995

After brokering a deal with Chernomyrdin, Chechen Prime Minister Dokku Zavgaev is elected president of Chechnya in December 17, 1995. Separatist forces unsuccessfully attempt to disrupt the election in an offensive on Gudermes and Dudaev goes on to declare the results invalid.

March 1996

Dudaev's rebel forces launch a surprise raid on Grozny on March 6, one of many humiliating offensives during Spring 2006, although they fail to capture the city.

April 1996

On April 21, Djokhar Dudaev is killed by a Russian guided missile attack, and is succeeded by Chechen resistance leader Zelimkhan Yandarbiev.

<u>May 1996</u>

Acting president of the Chechen resistance, Yandarbiev brokers a ceasefire with President Yeltsin on May 27, 1996. The short-lived agreement is violated by Russian troops.

<u>August 1996</u>

Chechen rebel units, under the command of Chief of Staff Aslan Maskhadov, launch a new Grozny offensive on August 6, dividing and surrounding a much larger Russian garrison. Weeks of hostilities and temporary ceasefires ensue, with Chechen forces having taken over most of the capital with separate offensives in Argun and Gudermes.

On August 22, a final ceasefire is brokered between Aslan Maskhadov and General Aleksandr Lebed.

A peace accord is signed on August 30 in Khasavyurt, Dagestan leading to Russian military withdrawal from Chechnya and a provisional settlement of Chechnya's formal independence until December 31, 2001.

1997 – 1999 INTER-WAR INDEPENDENCE

<u>January 1997</u>

Former Chechen Chief of Staff Aslan Maskhadov emerged victorious in the January 27 Chechen presidential election, garnering 64.8% of the vote. The runner-up, Shamil Basaev, won 22.7% of the vote, while the third-placed finisher, acting President Zelimkhan Yandarbiev, secured only 10.2%. OSCE mission head Tim Guldiman pronounced the elections "democratic and legitimate" on January 28, an opinion shared by monitors from the Council of Europe.

May 1997

On May 12, Maskhadov meets with Boris Yeltsin and agree on a "Treaty on Peace and the Principles of Relationships between the Russian Federation and the Chechen Republic of Ichkeria." The treaty established a peaceful framework for future bilateral agreements, followed by economic agreements signed by Prime Minister Chernomyrdin.

August 1997

In a second meeting between Yeltsin and Maskhadov on August 18, 1997, both sides agreed to build common spheres for cooperation on economic and defense issues. A political settlement is never brokered, and previous economic agreements were not initiated by Russia.

May 1998

Valentin Vlasov, Russia's presidential representative in Chechnya, is kidnapped on May 1, 1998 and held for six months. Later in the year, four engineers from Britain and New Zealand are kidnapped and murdered.

June 1998

President Maskhadov declares a state of emergency on June 23, following months of lawlessness and growing ideological rifts within his own government. The state of emergency lasts for five weeks.

July 1998

On July 3, acting Prime Minister Shamil Basaev tenders his resignation from Maskhadov's government. Days later, Maskhadov provisionally assumes the duties of premier.

September 1998

Lead by then Vice President Vakha Arsanov and leading field commanders, including Shamil Basaev, a September 29 national congress of opposition groups on issue a vote of no confidence in President Maskhadov. Maskhadov dismisses his entire cabinet a week later.

January 1999

On Januay 9, President Maskhadov announces that a new commission will be tasked with drafting the concept for a new Islamic state and constitution based on the Koran.

February 1999

Maskhadov formally dismisses the Chechen parliament on February 3 and orders an immediate transition to Shariah law and the drafting of a new Islamic constitution. Leading field commanders issued their support for Maskhadov under the conditions that the proposed reforms were enacted.

March 1999

Kremlin envoy Major General Gennadiy Shipgun was abducted on March 5 from an aircraft set to depart from Grozny. Despite numerous rumors and allegations into his kidnapping, Shipgun's body was later discovered in Chechnya in March 2000.

April 1999

On April 10, President Maskhadov survives the sixth attempt on his life over a four-month period of time.

<u>August 1999</u>

A group of Chechen fighters, lead by Shamil Basaev and Amir Ibn al-Khattab, launch an incursion into neighboring Dagestan on August 7, capturing several mountain villages in the name of Dagestani independence and the imposition of Shariah law. By August 25, the majority of the insurgents had been forced out of Dagestan by Russian Interior Ministry troops.

<u>September 1999</u>

A string of civilian bombings begins on September 4, 1999, starting with an explosion at a Russian military housing unit in Dagestan. Over the next two weeks, the attacks target two apartment buildings in Moscow and another in the town of Volgadonsk. Nearly 300 people are killed from the attacks, which are blamed on Chechen separatists and international mercenaries by then Prime Minister Vladimir Putin. Basaev denies involvement in the attacks. Mystery and conspiracy surrounds the apartment bombings, as responsibility for the explosions has never been established.

Chechen fighters launch a new offensive on four Dagestani villages on September 5, leading to a second retreat from Russian aerial bombardments over the span of a few weeks.

Russian fighter jets continue to launch aerial bombings against separatist strongholds along the Chechen-Dagestani border, and begin hitting targets in Grozny on September 23. It is reported that hundreds of civilians were killed by the bombings with 78,000 having fled to neighboring Ingushetia by Russia's own figures.

14

October 1999

On October 1, Prime Minister Vladimir Putin, under the pretext of the apartment bombings and incursion into Dagestan, ordered a land invasion into Chechen territory. Chechen President Maskhadov offered a peace settlement on October 10 offering to crackdown on rogue field commanders, such as Basaev. The offer was rejected.

On October 12, Russian military personnel crossed the Terek River and advanced towards positions outside of Grozny, where they coordinated months of conventionally artillery attacks on the capital and its surrounding cities, in an attempt to oust the Maskhadov government.

December 1999

President Yeltsin resigns on December 31, leaving Vladimir Putin as acting Russian President by constitutional procedure.

February 2000

After two months of direct assaults on Grozny, the Russian military seizes control of the Chechen capital on February 2, 2000 and razes the city. Although Chechen guerrillas continue fighting, taking Grozny is a military and political victory for Putin, whose popularity soars ahead of the presidential election.

March 2000

Vladimir Putin wins in the first round of the March 26 Russian presidential election.

June 2000

Chechnya experiences its first suicide bombing attack on June 6 when two young females drive a truck full of explosives through a Russian military checkpoint in Alkhan-Yurt. Similar attacks continue over the next few years, often times carried out by ethnic Chechen women, who have become characterized as Chechnya's Black Widows.

Moscow establishes direct rule of Chechnya, through a June 8 presidential decree giving temporary authority to Kremlin-loyal Chechen Mufti Akhmad Kadyrov. The order renders Aslan Maskhadov's government illegitimate by Russian law, and separatist ceasefire offers are dismissed.

August 2000

A bomb rips through a subway station in central Moscow on August 8, killing nine people. The attack is blamed on Chechen militants.

January 2001

Moscow transfers control of "anti-terrorist" operations in Chechnya to the Russian Federal Security Service (FSB). Human rights organizations continue to express sharp concern about violations in Chechnya and report on the alleged detainment and torture of Chechens by Russian troops and the discovery of mass graves in Grozny.

September 2001

On September 17, Chechen rebels launch a major offensive temporarily seizing control of Gudermes, Chechnya's second largest city with 40,000 inhabitants. Russian forces restore order the following day, detaining some 400 people suspected of aiding the rebels.

Putin declares on September 24 Russia's five-point plan to support an American-led war on terror, noting that "Chechen developments ought not to be regarded outside the context of efforts against international terrorism."

November 2001

Russian officials hold meetings with Maskhadov's official representative Akhmed Zakaev on November 18, 2001 -- the first formal talks with a Chechen separatist representative since 1999. Zakaev and Putin's southern envoy, Viktor Kazantsev, discuss a possible peace settlement on a secret government estate in Moscow.

December 2001

Chechen rebel field commander, Salman Raduev is sentenced to life imprisonment. He is reported to have died one year later in a Russian prison due to internal bleeding.

May 2002

An explosion during a Victory Day military parade in Dagestan kills at least 35 people, including 12 children. No groups claim responsibility for the bombing, but Chechen militants are widely suspected.

July 2002

With the exception of water distribution in Grozny, the UN halts aid operations in Chechnya for six weeks after a Russian aid worker is kidnapped.

August 2002

Chechen militants down a Russian military helicopter on August 18 using a Russian-made shoulder-held missile. The large personnel chopper crashed into a minefield outside of Russia's main military base in Chechnya, killing more than 100 servicemen.

October 2002

Militant Chechen separatists, led by 25-year-old Movsar Baraev, seize a Moscow theater on October 23 and hold some 800 people hostage, demanding that Russian troops withdraw from Chechnya within one week. Nearly 130 hostages and 41 of the 50 hostage-takers are killed when Russian forces storm the building three days later with a mysterious gas later determined to be an opiate-based compound.

November 2002

In a November 10 meeting with representatives of Moscow's Chechen community, President Putin contends that Chechnya should move forward with a new political referendum for peace, including the staging of new elections and the drafting of a new constitution, but refuses to negotiate directly with separatist leaders.

According to media reports, Russian authorities begin to close refugee camps on the border of Chechnya and Ingushetia, forcing thousands of Chechens to return to cities many believe are still unsafe. Russian officials deny that anyone is being forced to return to any particular area.

December 2002

On December 27, suicide bombers drive a truck full of explosives into a Russian government office building in Grozny killing more than 80 people. Despite the violence, Putin says the peace referendum will move forward as planned.

March 2003

Voters in Chechnya participate in a Moscow-backed constitutional referendum on March 23, approving a draft constitution and cementing Chechnya's place in the Russian Federation. The referendum passes with 96 percent of the vote but separatist leaders warn the move will not bring peace. Analysts consider the referendum a first step in Moscow's "Plan for Normalization" in Chechnya.

April 2003

The United Nations Human Rights Commission rejects the latest bid by the European Union to formally censure Russia for alleged human rights violations in Chechnya. The EU had encouraged the U.N. to declare "deep concern at the reported ongoing violations ... including forced disappearances, extrajudicial, summary or arbitrary executions, torture, ill-treatment ... as well as alleged violations of international humanitarian law" by federal Russian forces in Chechnya.

May 2003

Two suicide bombings rock Chechnya within days of each other in the largest flare-up in violence since the constitutional referendum. A truck loaded with explosives ripped apart a compound of government buildings in northern Chechnya on May 12, killing at least 59 people and wounding dozens more. The next day, a second suicide attack near Grozny killed at least 16 and wounded dozens when at least one woman detonated explosives strapped her body as thousands of Chechens, including the pro-Moscow administration leader Akhmad Kadyrov, gathered for a religious festival.

July 2003

On July 5, two female suicide bombers detonate belts laden with explosives and scraps of metal outside a rock concert at the Tushino airfield in Moscow. Authorities immediately accused Chechen separatists of carrying out the bombings, which killed 15 people and injured more than 50 others

August 2003

A powerful vehicle bomb blast destroys a Russian military hospital near Chechnya on August 1, killing at least 50 and wounding some 70 others. The military hospital is located in the North Ossetia town of Mozdok, considered the headquarters for Russian forces combating separatist Chechen fighters.

On August 8, 2003, U.S. Secretary of State Colin Powell designates Shamil Basaev, Amir of the Riyadus-Salikhin Reconnaissance and Sabotage Battalion of Chechen Martyrs (RSRSBCM), a terrorist. Under Executive Order 13224 on terrorism financing, the U.S. government imposes a blockade on Basaev's financial assets.

October 2003

Akhmad Kadyrov, the Kremlin-backed candidate for the leadership of Chechnya, wins the republic's October 19 presidential election by a considerable margin. International observers, such as the Council of Europe and the Organization for Security and Cooperation in Europe, declined to send monitors to the election, citing the tenuous internal security situation.

2004 – 2008 CONFLICT TRANSFORMATION

February 2004

On February 13, former Chechen separatist leader Zelimkhan Yandarbiev is assassinated in a bomb attack on his car in Qatar, where he had been living in exile for three years. The Qatari government arrested two Russian security service agents shortly after the attack. After intense months of negotiations with Russian authorities, the two agents were extradited to Moscow on December 23, 2004, where they were welcomed as heroes and were never prosecuted.

March 2004

Vladimir Putin wins re-election on March 14 with 71 percent of the vote.

<u>May 2004</u>

Chechen President Akhmad Kadyrov is assassinated on May 9 during a World War II Victory celebration. A bomb was hidden within the structure of a VIP stage and killed Kadyrov and a dozen others attending the festivities. Chechen militants claimed responsibility in the attack. Prime Minister Sergei Abramov becomes acting Chechen President, and Kadyrov's son Ramzan is named to the post of Vice Premier.

<u>June 2004</u>

The Russian authorities close Satsita, Ingushetia's final refugee camp, on June 1, 2004. Observers note that few of the thousands of refugees forced to return to Chechnya have proper economic and personal security guarantees.

On June 22, a group of 200-300 insurgent fighters launch a series of raids on the former Ingush capital Nazran, targeting 15 administrative buildings. The incursion, reportedly dominated by ethnic Ingush rebels, resulted in the deaths of some 90 people, most of whom were government and security service personnel. Chechen separatist leader Aslan Maskhadov claimed responsibility in coordinating the assault.

<u>August 2004</u>

Insurgent fighters enter Grozny on August 21 and coordinate a series of assaults on government installations, killing some 60 security service personnel. The group also targeted polling stations just one week before Chechnya's presidential elections.

On August 24, Russian media report two airplane crashes from flights leaving Moscow's Domodedovo Airport, killing a combined 89 passengers and crew. Investigations reveal that the crashes were caused by near-simultaneous detonations of a hexogen explosive. A group identified as the al-Islambouli Brigades immediately claims responsibility for the attacks, although Shamil Basaev later admitted

21

culpability following evidence that implicated two ethnic Chechen female passengers for carrying out the bombings.

Chechen Interior Minister Alu Alkhanov wins the August 29 Presidential election in Chechnya, replacing interim chief Sergei Abramov. Alkhanov, the only candidate endorsed by Moscow, won the vote with 74% of the vote. International observers abstain from monitoring, citing security concerns, but foreign journalists note fraud and an almost non-existent voter turnout.

On August 31, a suicide blast kills 11 outside a northern Moscow subway station. The attack is attributed to a Chechen female bomber.

September 2004

On September 1, a group of 32 heavily armed militants takes over Beslan School Number One, just 15 kilometers north of Vladikavkaz, North Ossetia. Gathering all over 1,200 hostages in the school gymnasium, the attackers rig the building with explosives and demand a political settlement to the conflict in Chechnya. After two days of unsuccessful negotiation efforts, including the alleged poisoning of prominent journalist Anna Politkovskaya, a gun battle broke out between Russian special forces and the hostage takers (it is still disputed who instigated the firefight) that resulted in the deaths of 344 civilians, over half of them children, as well as 31 of the 32 fighters. Chechen field commander Shamil Basaev claimed responsibility for the terrorist attack, although the operation was led by Ingush militant Magommed Yevloev. The participation of ethnic Ingush in the attack intensified historic animosities between rival Ossete and Ingush populations, although few reprisal killings were noted since Beslan.

October 2004

Commemorating the five-year anniversary of the start of the Second Chechen War, a large anti-war protest gathers in Pushkin Square in central Moscos on October 23. The largest demonstration in years, an estimated 2,500-3,000 people participate, led by the Russian Soldiers' Mothers Committee.

February 2005

Chechen separatist leader Aslan Maskhadov initiates a unilateral ceasefire, lasting from February 3-28, in an attempt to bring Moscow to the negotiating table. The Russian Soldier's Mothers Committee sends a delegation to meet separatist envoy Akhmed Zakaev in London, and agree on basic principles for a political settlement of the conflict. The peace initiatives are dismissed by the Kremlin and its Chechen administration, led by Alu Alkhanov.

March 2005

Aslan Maskhadov is killed on March 8, 2005 in a Russian special operation on the village of Tolstoi-Yurt. The next day, Shamil Basaev announces a pre-determined successor, Sheikh Abdul-Khalim Sadulaev, chairman of the separatist Supreme Sharia Court. The identify of Maskhadov's successor is confirmed by international envoy Akhmed Zakaev.

Acting separatist leader, Sadulaev, releases his first public statement on March 14 indicating that he would follow Maskhadov's line of advocating a political solution to the Russo-Chechen conflict.

May 2005

On May 16, Sadulaev announces the formation of a new "Caucasus Front" of the separatist Chechen government, appointing various field commanders across the North Caucasus' republics. Despite pleas from the West, the move indicates an unequivocal shift in Maskhadov's efforts to negotiate a cessation of hostilities.

June 2005

Chechen separatist leader, Abdul-Khalim Sadulaev, appoints field commander Dokku Umarov to the post of Vice President on June 17, signaling closer relations with renowned warlard Shamil Basaev.

October 2005

Heavy fighting erupts on October 13 in Nalchik, the capital of Kabardino-Balkaria, following a raid by over 200 armed militants. Apparently a reprisal for growing ethnic and religious persecutions, the attacks killed over 100 people including at least a dozen civilians. According to rebel news agency, Kavkaz Center, the raid was carried out by Ilyas Gorchkhanov, an ethnic Ingush commander of the new Kabardino-Balkarian Sector of the Caucasian Front, comprised primarily of ethnic Balkars.

November 2005

Chechnya holds Parliamentary elections on November 27, with over half the seats won by pro-Kremlin candidates from the United Russia party. The Chechen separatist leadership insists that the results are illegitimate, and rights groups continue to cite egregious human rights violations, particularly those committed by paramilitary forces loyal to Deputy Prime Minister Ramzan Kadyrov.

March 2006

Chechen Prime Minister Sergei Abramov steps down on March 1, paving the way for Ramzan Kadyrov to lead Chechnya's newly elected legislature.

June 2006

Chechen separatist president Sheikh Abdul-Khalim Sadulaev is killed on June 17 in a firefight in Argun, just outside of Grozny. On June 21, field commander Dokku Umarov is pronounced successor chief of the separatist Chechen Republic of Ichkeria, naming Shamil Basaev as his Vice President and future successor in a statement on June 27.

July 2006

Notorious Chechen warlord, Shamil Basaev, is reported killed on July 10 in neighboring Ingushetia. Russia claims that Basaev was fatally wounded in an accidental explosion while militants were loading a truck full of explosives in preparation for an attack.

Exiled Chechen Foreign Minister, Akhmed Zakaev, pronounces a "Manifesto for Peace" on July 13 seeking peaceful negotiations with Russia, without preconditions. Days later, the manifesto is harshly criticized by separatist President Umarov, who instead claims to have founded two new Caucasian fronts.

FSB Director Nikolai Patrushev announces a new amnesty initiative on July 15 for rebels to lay down their arms. Nearly 100 rebels were reported to surrender in subsequent weeks.

October 2006

Prominent critic of Russia's war in Chechnya, journalist Anna Politkovskaya, was found murdered in the elevator of her Moscow apartment flat on October 7, 2006, just days before she was to release an article exposing the torture practices of the *Kadyrovtsy*. Bearing the hallmarks of a contract killing, the murder has yet to be solved despite international outrage. The Kremlin suggests that exiled Russian tycoon Boris Berezovsky planned the killing, in addition to that of poisoned former FSB agent Alexander Litvinenko who died November 23, in an attempt to discredit President Putin. Some insiders have pointed to forces close to Ramzan Kadyrov, alleging that he personally ordered the assassination to silence his biggest critic.

<u>January 2007</u>

FSB Director Nikolai Patrushev's amnesty offer expires on January 15. Final numbers on amnestied rebels differ among news agencies, although it is generally reported that between 450-500 rebels laid down their arms over the six-month period.

<u>February 2007</u>

Alu Alkhanov is forced to resign as Chechnya's president on February 15, following an appointment to federal deputy justice minister. In a move that had been anticipated for months, Ramzan Kadyrov is named acting Chechen president until formal legislative approval.

<u>March 2007</u>

President Vladimir Putin announces on March 1 that he is nominating Ramzan Kadyrov, Chechnya's acting president, as the republic's new president. Kadyrov is overwhelmingly confirmed by the Chechen parliament the following day. On March 3, separatist leader Dokku Umarov appoints Supyan Abdullaev as Vice President and future successor leader to the Chechen Republic of Ichkeria.

<u>April 2007</u>

Ramzan Kadyrov is officially sworn-in as Chechnya's president on April 5 in his hometown of Gudermes. According to Russian news agencies, Kadyrov recited the oath of office in Russian, swearing on copies of the Russian and Chechen constitutions and the Koran. More than 2,000 guests and journalists gathered for the ceremony. Analysts view the transfer of power as a long-awaited Kremlin victory in consolidating the "Chechenization" of the conflict.

June 2007

A military court in southern Russia sentences four soldiers to prison terms for the murder of six Chechen civilians, a rare ruling against Russian troops.

2008 – 2010 NORMALIZATION

February 2008

Dmitry Medvedev wins 89% of the vote in Chechnya on a turnout of 91%.

April 2009

Russia declares the decade-old "counterterrorism operation" against separatist rebels to be over

July 2009

Russian human rights activist Natalia Estemirova, who had been investigating alleged abuses by government-backed militias in Chechnya, is abducted and killed.

January 2010

Alexander Khloponin named Vice-Premier and Envoy to the North Caucasus Federal District on January 19, 2010.

April 2010

Rebel leader Dokku Umarov claims responsibility for deadly suicide attacks on Moscow Metro on March 29, 2010.

Dokku Umarov announces his retirement and names Aslambek Vadalov as his successor. Days later, he declares that his resignation statement was "falsified" and that he remains the head of the Chechen militant movement.

October 2010

Chechen gunmen attack the Parliament in Grozny on October 19, 2010.

The Future of the North Caucasus

Introduction by Paul Goble[1]

As I reflect back on my career in writing about the nationalities of Russia and the former Soviet Union I can recall the days that when you tried to assemble all the people in the Washington, D.C. policymaking community who knew about all the nationalities of what was then the Soviet Union. At that time in the early 1980s you could gather them all together in to a small corner office in the Bureau of Intelligence and Research (INR) at the State Department and still have extra space. Times have changed though and now we are increasingly being forced to consider the future of the North Caucasus.

When asked to write an introduction to this important book on the volatile borderland between Russia and the North Caucasus, which explores in detail the region we call the North Caucasus, I wonder what the Caucasus may look like in 2050 which allows me to recall an event which some experts may remember. In 1981, an American novelist prepared a book called The End of the Russian Empire. A number of the U.S. book clubs saw the title, The End of the Russian Empire and assumed it was a history of the events of 1917 and wanted to buy it. But when the novel actually appeared, it was obvious that it was a work of fiction and it was not about events of 60 years earlier but rather of events ten years later; namely, the coming apart of the Soviet Union and the coming apart of the Russian state thereafter. Now, all of us who have lived in Washington for any length of time know that there are a large number of books that are listed on the nonfiction side that contain a great deal of fictional information. Indeed there have been a number of memoirs that I was quite prepared to see on the fiction bestseller list.

---

[1] From a speech given at The Jamestown Foundation on September 14, 2006

But I would like to make another argument in this introduction and that is that there have been a large number of works of fiction that have been instructive about the facts of the case, especially with respect to developments during periods of rapid change. That reflection is prompted by the amazing success in the last year of a novel by Elena Chudinova in the Russian Federation called <u>The Mosque of Notre Dame de Paris</u>. This has been a book that has gone now through eight different editions, has been a bestseller among many groups of people. It poses the Shariat Islamic takeover of the European Union by 2048 and the remodeling of the cathedral of Notre Dame in Paris into a mosque. And then a terrorist underground led by the daughter of an oligarch, a dissident Catholic cardinal, a Serb who hates Europeans, and someone from Israeli intelligence that decide that the way to overthrow Shariat control of Europe is to blow up the Mosque of Notre Dame de Paris.

Chudinova is a Russian Orthodox children's author whose views have unfortunately now surfaced. Her views about the way in which that country should be organized are truly frightening. But her novel has provided an occasion in the Russian media for the discussion of what is likely to happen in what we call the Russian Federation today over the next half century. Because what people are increasingly appreciating in Russia, but which many of us do not, is that we are still in the midst of a period of enormous change; that there is a turning point of history – there are several turning points of history that are not simple right angles, but rather a long trend line that we need to understand.

This is not unusual of course in the history of the world. It has frequently been the case that when individuals have been confronted by periods of massive change they have turned not so much to scholarship but rather to novels, to distopian novels or anti-utopian novels to try to come to grips with these changes. It was certainly true in the Soviet Union in the 1920's, it was true in the late 1940's and into the 1950's in Britain and the United States as we attempted to come to terms with things.

30

Now, I think there are three big reasons why this is the case. First, fiction novels provide a possibility for exploring periods of radical unsettled change for which there is no clearly defined set of categories in the standard academic or political literature. And it also provides the possibility of exploring both sides of these debates because all too often much of the discussion of people opposed to the Russian Federation sounds to me like a meeting of the Vatican in the twelfth century discussing heresies rather than an examination of problems which we make judgments about what the opponents think on the basis of what the Russians say. As I like to point out, you can cover Israel from Damascus, but it would be wrong. And in these periods which Thomas Kuhn talks about as a scientific revolution, fiction often allows us to get at those things.

The second thing is that fiction can provide a plausible explanation, allow you to explore things that have happened. When I look at the various distopian novels about the end of Soviet Union that appeared in the 1970's and 1980's, I am struck by how much they got right as opposed to some of the scholarly literature at the time. They were able to take risks because the normal standards of evidence were relaxed and the possibility of exploring multiplicities was increased.

And the third reason that I think distopias are so useful is that they allow us to extend our discussion and understanding of time, space and identities. When we talk about the Caucasus – the North Caucasus – we rapidly fall in to the trap of talking before the Soviets came, while the Soviets were there, and after the Soviets left, as if those were the most relevant periods for the people on the ground. In fact, that either argues for a return to the pre-Soviet past or it implies that it is all about escaping from what the Soviets did. That periodization does not capture, as I will argue in a minute, what is going on in the Russian Federation, in the Russian areas, or what is happening in the North Caucasus.

Second, fiction allows us to escape from our rigid geographic definition. Americans, as you probably know, are among the most geographically illiterate people on Earth. I like to say that we are prisoners of the

31

Mercator projection. You know the map of the world I have in mind which the United States sits in the middle as God intended, protected by two large blue bodies of water and a large number of vowel and consonant challenged countries on the edge ready to fall off. If you doubt that isn't hardwired, try briefing a senior official with a map that has anything else in the middle of it. When the Karabakh War started in the late 1980s, I briefed some people on the seventh floor at the State Department and I had a map put in ginned up by the geographer's office that put Nagorno-Karabakh in the middle. When you do that the United States is in four pieces. A certain now retired professor at Stanford University did not hear a single word I said but I watched his face go like a clock.

I think it is a real problem calling this the North Caucasus. I think of the question of what that includes. We have not talked about the extent to which demography is changing the boundaries of that to the north, nor the extent to which the Caucasus to the south is also part of a Caucasian world. Trying to exclude those things or allowing them to be excluded by definition gets in the way of a proper understanding of this region.

Finally, one of the things that fiction does for us is that it encourages us to understand other people the way we understand ourselves. We are as any number of people have observed like those Russian wooden nesting dolls, the matryoshka doll, we are a set of identities and personalities and the issue is which identity is exposed at any particular time and who makes the choice as to which identity is exposed? All too many of the discussions about the Caucasus act as if there are a series of discrete choices for people who will shift from talking about being either loyal Russians, being separatists, being Muslims, being terrorists, being whatever, as if these were things that people change completely overnight.

In fact, many characteristics are things people have in common and therefore it is terribly important. And if we are going to understand what is going to happen in this region by 2050, I think we need to do that. Now, many of you who I have known for years have heard me say before that one of the reasons that many of us who engage in Sovietology have taken refuge in futurology is that this is what we were trained in: a discipline that dose not require too many facts but a great deal of ideas.

And there are three major ideas I would like to focus on. First of all I would like to look at the changes in the three major outside actors around this region; not so much the chess moves, some of which have been described, but rather the broader trends of development in the Russian Federation, the world of Islam, and what we can call the global world. I think that we need to look at these because in many cases what these places do and how they act will determine which layer of the matryoshka doll in Grozny or Makhachkala is exposed.

Second, I would like to look at what I think are the incredibly rapid set of changes in what we are calling the North Caucasus in regards to demographics, religion, politics, and ideas.

Finally, because this is Washington I would like to talk about the challenges all of this presents for the United States, challenges which so far at least I do not think we have met very well. The Russian Federation – what we chose to call the Russian Federation is just as much an artificial formation as was any region within the North Caucasus. It was drawn with a specific intention. In fact, it is more artificial than anything in the North Caucasus because it was drawn by negation; to wit, Stalin drew everything else first and what was left was the Russian Federation. That tends to be forgotten because we tend to act as if Russia is a reality and all the others are simply made-up things. Moreover, it is true as we will see in a minute, Russian national identity is far more fragile, far less certain and with much shallower historical roots than the identities of the peoples of the Caucasus and elsewhere around the edges of what used to be the Russian and Soviet empires. However I want to make two arguments in particular on this point because of time.

The first is the argument that at least since the end of the nineteenth century we have been at a period in which the Russian state has been in a rather rapid and accelerating state of decline and disintegration. We have watched the empire be at least temporarily saved by the Soviet Union. The Soviet system saved the empire by changing the ideological formulation. It was about empire saving; it was not about empire transformation, and that tends to be forgotten. What happened in 1991 was tragically delayed by 74 years. Had Anton Denikin taken Moscow, which given how incompetent he was, this was unlikely, but had he taken Moscow you would have seen the disintegration of the Russian empire proceed 75 years earlier and you would have seen Russia emerge as a kind of East European state of one kind or another.

What we are currently witnessing is the downturn of Russian history. Until the early part of the twentieth century, Russia developed by having Russians assimilate other peoples. Now the pattern of assimilation has gone the other way in that these peoples are attempting to foster their own national identities. When that happens in a nation that is built on assimilatory pressures, you know that the end is near.

We are watching also the Russian state today fall into much the same trap that Alexander III and Nicholas II did. Nicholas I understood very well that you do not play the Russian nationalist card because it will destroy everything. Nicholas I classically said, there are no bad Germans and good Russians, there are only good subjects and bad ones. By the time of Alexander III and Nicholas II, we saw an attempt to play the Russian card and the country came apart. We saw again the attempt to play the Russian card with Boris Nikolayevich Yeltsin in 1989, 1990 and 1991 as the country came apart. This has not stopped. It may have started as a small thing, but as I write this introduction there have been killings in Saratov and in several towns in Omsk Oblast – and this is just in the last 48 hours. Just because it is not being reported in the West does not mean it is not happening. That is a general historiographic issue. We are watching some – you do not have to be a follower of Lev Gumelev, and I certainly am not, to buy into the notion that we are watching the end of some kind of huge cycle in Russian history.

But there is a more immediate, policy-relevant, if you will, issue of Russian imperial decay, which we need to focus on a little bit. After the Soviet Union came apart in 1991, the West, and the United States in particular, was terrified about the fact that more disintegration was likely. There was a fear that if more disintegration happened, it would lead to loose nukes, and therefore the United States became the last guarantor of Soviet borders announcing on February 6th, 1992, that there would be no secession from secession in the Russian Federation; not only trivializing what had happened the year before but having the effect of putting the United States on the side of the police and not the people. It slowed things down, but it did not stop them.

But what is worse, it means that the United States and most American analysts are refusing to acknowledge what is actually happening on the ground in a place we call the Russian Federation. What is actually taking place is not so much the end of an empire, although that is happening, but rather the death of a state and the subsequent attempts to revive this state.

The Russian Federation in the 1990s was very much a failed state. Mr. Putin has succeeded in recovering some of it, but far from all. And we were unwilling to look at that I think for three reasons. First, if you said it was a failed state, someone would say who controls the nukes? And the answer was that is not always clear. Second, if you said it was a failed state, you would have to confront the reality that we do not know of a single case of a failed state that has recovered without inflicting violence on its own people or on its neighbors. Indeed, it is arguable that what Mr. Putin did by blowing up the apartment buildings in 1999 and starting the Chechen War was an effort to recover state power, as ugly as that is.

But the third reason we did not want to talk about Russia as a failed state is that if we talked about Russia as a failed state we would have to confront this reality: while states fail all the time – and please understand a failed state is not one that has no powerful institutions on its territory, but rather no single controlling legal authority. Americans did not get chased out of Somalia because there was not anyone with power on the ground in Somalia.

When was the last time a major power's state disintegrated? The answer is Germany in November of 1918 and we all know how that story ended 15 years later. And the idea that the default setting of the end of the Soviet Union and the emergence of the Russian Federation might not lead to a liberal democratic free market ally of the United States, but to something else, was not something people wanted to be faced with.

Now, as I say, Mr. Putin is attempting to wrestle with this and he is addressing it by focusing on a whole variety of things, although I am not sure he entirely understands the issue. Let me very briefly say what I think the challenges are. And the way to do that is to recall to you Voltaire's observation about the Holy Roman Empire. You remember he said it was not holy, it was not Roman, and it was not an empire, but other than that it was a very good name. Well, I believe that the Russian Federation is the Holy Roman Empire of today; to wit, it is not the Soviet Union, it is not Russia, and it is not a federation. Other than that, calling it the Russian Federation works fine.

But it is not the Soviet Union which seemed to benefit because the Russian Federation is technically somewhat more homogenous than was the Soviet Union at the end, although not nearly as much as the Russians claim. They falsified the 2002 census only slightly less than Stalin did with the 1939 census. And we now have a situation where the birth rates of non-Russians are staggeringly higher than the Russian populace. Not only is Moscow already the largest Muslim city in Europe, but last year in the Russian capital the average fertility rate of ethnic Russian women was 1.1, while the average fertility rate of Khazan-Tatar women living in Moscow was six, and the average rate of Chechens and Ingush living in Moscow was ten. Given those numbers, it will not take many generations to change who's going to be in control.

It also helps that the United States has changed the rules and the non-Russians have fewer places to go. But the disadvantages of it not being the Soviet Union are far greater. First, the sense of loss that Russians feel is very great. We fought two world wars to convince one nation in Central Europe that its borders were to be respected. We have a government in Moscow now that thinks that its borders are to be respected, unless they can be expanded. That is a very dangerous thing when people have that problem, so this is one area.

The second is it is not Russia. No Russian that I have ever met thinks the borders of the Russian Federation are the proper borders. A poll in the spring of 2006 found that 74 percent of high school graduates in the city of Moscow think the proper borders of the Russian Federation are those of the Russian Empire in 1914. Which means Poland, Finland, the Baltic countries, and part of Turkey, and there are several people in the Russian Duma who want negotiations restarted about Alaska.

Countries that are not comfortable with their borders are a problem, as we know. I keep thinking of Tom Lehrer's song about Germany: he said we taught them a lesson in 1918 and have not had any problems since. Well, we shall see.

And the tragedy of it not being Russia is magnified by the fact that Russian identity is focused on the state. The tragedy of Russia, and this is something that is really a whole lecture in itself, is that the Russian state became an empire before the Russian people became a nation and as a result the Russian state has never been a nation-state, but the Russian nation has always been a state-nation. Which means that when state power is weak, nationalism is not a counterbalance; it becomes weak. When state power starts gaining, you see nationalism taking off as well. And it is not a federation, not only is there no agreement on who does what, there are not the instruments to link it together.

Many of you will have read the gushy articles in the American press about Mr. Putin opening the first trans-Russia highway in 2006 from Vladivostok to Moscow, all 6,600 miles. I would have been as impressed as the *New York Times* was at the time had I not known three things. First, that project was started in 1903. Second, of the 6,600 miles only 3,800 are paved and only 5 percent are more than two lanes wide. The highway connecting the two largest cities of Russia, St. Petersburg and Moscow, is paved, but it is two lanes wide. And this week the editor of the car magazine of the Russian Federation urged that the Russian Federation come up with a new international car sign: the end of the road. Because he had just gone on a federal highway which ran out into a track and provided absolutely no indication of how to get from here to there. And that was in between Irkutsk and Krasnoyarsk. So we have a problem in this respect.

If the Russian Federation is at a turning point, and I believe that it is and I believe that the borders will change in a variety of ways, and I think they will change largely due to the actions of the Russians and Russian desires, as we will see. And this leads me to my one good piece of advice to the people who monitor affairs in this region: do not buy any maps. Buy stock in companies that print maps and you will make a lot of money.

But it is equally important that Islam, too, is at a turning point. Indeed, if you understand the Muslim view of what happened in the Soviet Union in 1991, you can see a direct line from there to September 11th and you can understand why Muslims who were ethnic Muslims who did not know very much about their identity and what their faith was about turned to Islam in the ways that they did.

The collapse of the Muslim project after the French Revolution and the colonization of the Muslim world, which was more or less complete except for Egypt and Afghanistan by 1922, left the Muslim world with the question: if we are right, how come we are losing? And there were three answers. God's time is not our time so we wait it out. The second answer was, we are wrong; we have got to be radical secularists. And the third is, back to basics: Allah, Sharia – the people who become the fundamentalists.

As long as there was a Soviet Union supporting the radical secularists, and please remember it was the Soviets who were doing that, the third

category were in jail. Once the Soviet Union could not do that, those people emerged. And with the Muslims reading, or some Muslims reading anyway, of 1991 you saw a very different set of messages for people who were Muslims. These were in many ways – and this is another argument, different, but just to point it out for you – I believe that Central Asia and parts of the Caucasus will be over time the prime recruiting area
for a radical fundamentalist Islam. Why? Because people there know they are Muslims, but do not know exactly what it means and therefore they are prepared to listen to people who tell them exactly what it means.

I remember a conversation I had with Dzhokhar Dudaev, the first president of Chechen Ichkeria. Mr. Dudaev said to me, "Mr. Goble, I'm a good Muslim I pray three times a day." Well I was very polite and deferential to this senior officer and did not point out that a good Muslim prays five times a day. After all, he had been in the Communist Party since the age of 18 and was a major general in the Soviet Air force.

Therefore with the rise of Islam and the collapse of the Soviet Union, what was the message that the Allah-Sharia Muslims took with them at the collapse of the Soviet Union? From their point of view the USSR came apart overnight as a result of a single small set of shocks. For Americans the Soviet Union came apart because we had stood tall against communism for 40 years. But the people who thought it came apart overnight assumed that the Soviet Union, the most radical expression of Western secularism would come apart in the same way with a few good kicks. September 11th flows directly from that logic of 1991. It is wrong, but it has to be understood.

And the third turning point is the West. We are witnessing a number of changes to what the West or the international system means. Let me just list three. First demographically, 40 years ago there were twice as many people living in Europe and Anglo-America as there were living in the world of Islam. Today that number is approximately equal. In

2030, there will be three times as many people living in the Muslim World as living in Europe and Anglo-America. That is a huge shift.

Second the relationship of state power and violence has changed as we all know. Third the meaning of borders has changed. There is another example of a word that we invoke routinely, border, as if it were a fixed thing. Borders are a socially constructed reality and they keep changing in meaning. I live in Estonia very near the Latvian frontier. The Latvians do not have borders; they have frontiers. I torture my students by forcing them to write essays about the difference between a frontier and a border, but never mind.

Now, what is all this going to mean for the North Caucasus? Let me just discuss a couple of quick points. First the demographic realities are not just that there are getting to be more people who are in the North Caucasus – what we call the North Caucasus, but those people are leaving and they are moving elsewhere. At present, the number of North Caucasians living in Moscow is 700,000. The number of Caucasians living in Kondopoga is several thousand. The number of North Caucasians living in Omsk Oblast is in the tens of thousands. It is not just the demography there; it is the demography that is leading the spread.

In fact, there is now an argument in Russian national circles that we should give these people independence and then declare it a state border and keep them on the other side of it. One of the things people have not thought about is that people who may secure the independence of the North Caucasus are Russian nationalists who want to exclude them. If you doubt this, please go to the DPNI.ru website which is the movement against illegal immigration. These are the people who are fascists but wear good clothes. However, these people are some really ugly folks.

Within the North Caucasus, it is important to understand that the meaning of Islam is highly variable within all these republics we have been discussing. And the meaning of Islam for the actions of people politically is highly variable. We should not be surprised. Instead we treat Muslims as if they were automatons who would do certain things because they are Muslims no matter what. It does not work that way. We are, as I said, we have to look at people as matryoshka dolls with multiple layers and that is critical.

A third point about the North Caucasus is especially interesting. It is why people like me keep looking at it despite my Baltic obsessions of recent years because it is precisely at the point where these three huge trend lines are coming together: the changes in the world, the changes in Russia, and the changes in Islam. In essence, it is a fault zone, it is a fracture zone in which the outside actors are doing certain things and which inside actors are responding, and the other way around.

Now, looking out the next 50 years I see a huge range of possibilities. I would like to make one general comment and I am simply going to give you the three broad trends I see. We are very good in the West in studying one kind of nationalism and we are atrociously bad at studying another. We are good at studying pessimistic nationalism.

The Estonian version is, if we do not get those damn Russians out of here, there will not be any Estonians in a generation. The American version is Lexington and Concord: we have to stand here or else. We are very good at analyzing Chechnya that way. What we are not good in analyzing Chechnya or the North Caucasus or elsewhere is optimistic nationalism – the nationalism of people who think they are going to win because they are on the winning side of history. Those people behave differently. Some of you may have seen one of my favorite movies, "The Lion in Winter," with Katharine Hepburn playing Eleanor of Aquitaine. And at one point Henry II, played by Peter O'Toole, tells the young king of France, "Do not push me, boy. If you do any more, England will declare war on France." And the young teenage French king responds, "And France will surrender because we can't lose, old man." That kind of nationalism, that kind of view is something we rarely factor in to our understanding in the Caucasus or Central Asia and it is there.

There are so many people who because they were exposed to the world of Islam when they did and because they can see the Russian state dying are optimistic despite any particular defeats. I am not saying it is the only thing out there; I am only saying it is an issue we do not tend to examine.

I see three broad patterns ahead. One is this whole area could remain chaotic, unstable and a backwater with intermittent violence, a lot of corruption and increasing desires on the part of neighboring countries to build walls and keep the people behind them.

The second is the one solution the Russian government claims not to want and it is currently doing what it can to make happen, and that is a unified North Caucasus based on Islam that will resist being part of the Russian Federation and will demand independence as such. They will demand that unity precisely in response to Russian nationalism. Sergei Markedonov's writings were already mentioned by John Dunlop in his essay in this book. Markedonov has written a series of articles in the Russian press over the past couple of years in which he has said the real danger to Russian control of the borderlands is Russian nationalism, not the nationalism of the non-Russians.

Any number of people know that a number of the countries that emerged in 1991 did so less because their populations wanted to go than because they did not want to see what might happen if they were ruled by a Russian or at least Slavic-dominated state. So that unity could happen if Russia continues on its way, and given that empires on the way down tend to behave badly I do not think we can exclude that possibility.

And the third is something that I would ask you to consider in more detail than we have so far. And that is that as the peoples of the North Caucasus move out of the region and develop there will be competition with Russians. The ethnic Russian area is being pushed north, and the Terek River is no longer a border. The Caucasians are on both sides and they are moving north. And I find it very interesting that now we see maps being produced in some parts of southern Russia which do not refer to Saratov but Saritao, as the Mongols did 800 years ago.

If that happens, then we are talking about a fragmentation of the Russian Federation that will not be so much Muslim or Turkic, but will be part of a general fragmentation of Eurasia. I personally think that those who believe that the North Caucasus will lead the parade of new sovereignties are wrong. I think the people who will lead it will be the Sibiriaki, the people of Siberia and the Far East, because I think we have made a huge mistake in the West in assuming that Russian identity is strong and that everybody else's identity is weak. Russian identity is more artificial and weaker by any measure you care to name than the identities of the Avars or the Chechens or the Circassians. I say that not to dump on the Russians, but simply to correct what it is unfortunately the tendency to act as if Russia is a real place and these places are not, Russians are a real nation and these people are not. That is purely nonsense.

Now, to conclude the United States has three challenges. There are three possible responses we can use to what is going on. The first is we can encourage these people. I wish we would, but we will not and there are good reasons for this because our encouragement could be the kiss of death.

Second, we could do what we have done up until now and oppose them. Let me tell you that our track record of opposing the national right of people's self-determination has led to the kind of racist regime we currently see in the Russian Federation. Do not forget that on October 5th, 1993, after Boris Yeltsin had used that highly democratic method of dispersing his parliament; namely, using tanks, the mayor of Moscow, Mayor Yuri Luzhkov, issued a decree expelling people of Caucasian background from the city. Instead of denouncing that, we not only did not denounce it but we told our European allies to keep their mouths shut as well. Now there are similar regulations in every Russian city over 100,000 and in many smaller ones as well. In short, we set a train in motion by supporting something that is really frightening and morally reprehensible.

Finally we can watch; we can pay attention to what is going on. I commend The Jamestown Foundation for publishing this book because I think watching and developing expertise is critical so that we will be able at the margins to, one, know what is going on and, two, maybe be able to do something useful.

But let me end, since I began by talking about fiction and its role, by citing a name that should be present in the minds of everyone who does research on the Caucasus. I was thinking and mentioned to Paul Henze, who agreed this is the largest gathering we have seen in this area in a long time on this subject. I was thinking of President Kennedy's observation in 1962 or 1963 when he assembled the American Nobel Prize winners, and said there was more intelligence assembled in that room tonight except perhaps when Thomas Jefferson dined alone.

The person I am thinking of in terms of this subject is the late Alexander Bennigsen, the father of one of our participants, the direct teacher of a number of us and, in a larger sense, the teacher of all of us in this field. And I wanted to end by mentioning something that Alex used to say in his seminar at the University of Chicago, which we students did not understand at the time. Professor Bennigsen used to say that when he finally retired he looked forward to the day that he could write a book where he invented all the facts, all the footnotes, and all the bibliography. And most of us at the time assumed that he had already done that. But now I recognize that it was precisely another form of understanding; to wit, that if we are going to go beyond the day-to-day, incremental approach to a period of revolutionary change we are going to have to turn to a more imaginative direction, one that fiction may do more than what we call non-fiction most of the time.

Putin, Kozak and Russian Policy toward the North Caucasus

John Dunlop

Introduction

In an article entitled "From What is the Homeland Being Constructed?" that appeared in the magazine *Profile*, the authors posed a key question. "Will Russia," they asked, "be preserved within its borders fifteen years from now?"[1] The region of the Russian Federation singled out as being the most vulnerable was, not surprisingly, the North Caucasus, and, specifically, that region's "Muslim" autonomous republics.

Among the threats facing the North Caucasus, the *Profile* authors observed, were: "The fantastic, even by Russian standards, scale of corruption; the clan organization of politics and economic life; unemployment... and the collapsing social sphere." The poverty and the marginalizing of broad segments of the populace were said to represent, "a nutritional bouillon for the spreading of radical Islamic identity and filling up of the ranks of the terrorist underground," in the Russian South.

In the period antedating the horrific terrorist attack on a school in Beslan, North Ossetia in September of 2004 in which 330 hostages—186 of them children—lost their lives, the Russian leadership's approach to the North Caucasus region could have been summarized as being an unwieldy combination of coercion (including, at times, the use of massive police and military force), "Chechenization" (the empowerment of pro-Moscow Chechens headed up by representatives of the Kadyrov family) and heavy doses of "PR" (or "spin"). While this

---

[1] Evgenii Verlin, Dmitrii Mindich, Vladimir Rudakov, "S chego sobiraetsya Rodina," *Profil'*, 26 June 2006. I am grateful to Robert Otto for bringing this piece, as well as several other items cited in this article, to my attention. This essay updates and expands upon material contained in: John B. Dunlop and Rajan Menon, "Chaos in the North Caucasus and Russia's Future," *Survival*, Summer 2006, pp. 97-114.

approach yielded occasional successes, it was not working particularly well or effectively in the period leading up to the Beslan tragedy; largely because it failed to address the harsh economic and social realities besetting the region. It also failed to address the plague of all-pervasive corruption, especially police corruption.

The existence of this web of difficulties identified by the *Profile* authors undoubtedly helped convince President Putin in the early autumn of 2004 that a change in Russia's approach to the region was needed. A major change in Russia's approach to the North Caucasus was signaled in September 2004 when Dmitrii Kozak was named *polpred* (plenipotentiary presidential representative) of the Southern Federal District.[2] The appointment of this vigorous lawyer and seasoned bureaucrat, who had played a major role in organizing Putin's 2000 and 2004 presidential election campaigns and had occupied top posts in the Russian presidential administration, suggested that President Putin had become serious about tackling the manifold problems afflicting the region.

Despite periodic setbacks and defeats at the hands of local republican leaders and their allies, Kozak has, over the past two years, persevered and has succeeded in ousting—with Putin's backing—key leaders of the corrupt and deeply entrenched ruling clans of certain republics in the region. To the extent that it has proved possible, he has also sought to foster the rule of law in the Russian South. In July of this year, it was reported, for example, that Kozak was insisting upon an improvement of the work of the procuracy in the Southern Federal District: "Only last year [2005]," he noted acidly, "the courts returned about 4,000 cases to the procuracy [to be reworked and improved]. This is not something the procuracy should be proud of."[3]

One admirer and vigorous supporter of Kozak's approach has been Yuliya Latynina, a leading Russian journalist who has transformed

---

[2] For Kozak's biography, see Aleksei Mukhin, Praviteli Rossii: Staraya ploshchad' i Belyi dom (Moscow: Algoritim, 2005), pp. 55-58.
[3] "Dmitrii Kozak potreboval ot prokuratury YuFO bolee tshchatel'nogo rassledovaniya gromkikh del," Vek, 20 July 2006, also in compromat.ru, 20 July 2006.

46

herself into a specialist on the North Caucasus, which is a region she frequently visits. Her detailed reports—large segments of which often concern the North Caucasus—appear during her highly popular Saturday broadcast carried by Ekho Moskvy Radio (transcripts of the broadcasts are posted the following day on the radio's website) as well as infrequent columns that she publishes on the pages of *Novaya gazeta* or posts on the websites of Ej.ru and Gazeta.ru. Latynina, who is often sharply critical of the policies of the Putin regime, recently had this to say about *polpred* Kozak: "We have seen definite achievements in the state of our politics. One man—Dmitrii Kozak—the man who is now in the North Caucasus appointing responsible presidents there and is showing that the response to the anarchy [*bespredel*] which was created by previous Russian authorities and presidents is not for people to join the rebels but is rather to follow the law."[4]

"I am prepared to support any president appointed by Russia who does something useful in the Caucasus," Latynina observed during another Ekho Moskvy broadcast. "I will never cast a stone at Mukha Aliev, the new president of Dagestan, nor at Taimuraz Mamsurov, the president of [North] Ossetia, nor at Arsen Kanokov, the president of Kabardino-Balkariya; those presidents who under the most complex circumstances have come to help their people. Yes, they do not succeed in everything, and from the point of view of a true democrat I could point my finger a them...but I understand perfectly that these people are working under inhuman conditions."[5]

In another broadcast, Latynina provided several examples of the type of lethal Russian *bespredel* that threatens the work of Kozak and of the reformist presidents that Putin has been appointing in the region: "There exists conditions that give birth to the rebels...These conditions are called stupidity and anarchy. There is, for example, the situation in Ingushetia when after 22 June [2004] they introduced troops there and complete chaos [*bardak*] ensued. A [Russian] soldier came up to an open-air shop and asked for vodka. They gave him vodka and then

---

[4] "Yuliya Latynina," echo.msk.ru, 15 July 2006.
[5] Ibid.

asked, 'Where is your money?' He opened fire on the shop. In another incident, some drunken [Russian] paratroopers were eating a lamb in the mountains... Some shepherds came up to them and asked them, 'Where is our lamb?' The paratroopers then shot them and burned their bodies."[6]

"So," Latynina concluded, "I will never cast a stone at such people [the newly appointed reformist presidents]. To the contrary, I feel that they are making an enormous effort, and that they and *polpred* Kozak are trying to ensure that the [North] Caucasus will remain in Russia."[7] "Without Dmitrii Kozak," Latynina warned, with a touch of hyperbole, in early June of this year, "we would lose the Caucasus by the fall [of 2006]. I am completely serious."[8]

Of course, it is Vladimir Putin and not Dmitrii Kozak who has the most influential say in determining what Russia's policies toward the North Caucasus should be. Kozak's recommendations constitute only part of a mix of advice that Putin hears from his numerous counselors; on occasion Putin appears to prefer the advice of other more hard-line or more cynical aides. The Russian president's predilection for coercion and "PR" rather than for strenuous and costly economic, social and legal reform is often evident.

The "Patrushev Amnesty"

The recently announced "Patrushev amnesty" represents one example of such an alternative approach to the problems of the North Caucasus. FSB director Nikolai Patrushev, who is also the head of the Russian National Anti-Terrorist Committee, is, like Kozak, in a position to significantly influence events. On 15 July, following the killing of rebel leader Shamil' Basaev, and during the run-up to the G-8 summit in St. Petersburg chaired by Putin, Patrushev announced what impressed some commentators at the time as a genuine amnesty for Chechen

---

[6] "Yuliya Latynina," echo.msk.ru, 15 July 2006.
[7] Ibid.
[8] Ibid.

separatist fighters. "We offer you," he informed the rebels, "until 1 August 2006 to enter into negotiations with representatives of the legal authority of the Chechen Republic and the federal center."[9] (On 31 July, Patrushev extended the period of the amnesty until 30 September.)

Those who closely scrutinized Patrushev's statement, however, came to the conclusion that it was not in fact an amnesty but rather an exercise in "PR." "Publicly," journalist Tat'yana Stanovaya commented, "this sounds like an invitation to an armistice. But the word 'armistice' does not contain any political content."[10] It was noted by journalists that only those rebels who had committed neither crimes nor terrorist acts were eligible for Patrushev's amnesty. As Yuliya Latynia noted sardonically: "An amnesty is when a crime is forgiven... If they forgive those who are not guilty, that is called something else."[11] It was noted by reporters that of the 110 Chechen fighters who had contacted law enforcement organs, "essentially all of them had left the ranks of the Illegal Armed Formations a long time ago."[12] As for those who remained members of the armed separatists, according to one pro-Russian Chechen MVD official: "The rebels will come out of the woods only when the authorities forgive them not for an abstract participation in this illegal uprising but for serious crimes such as killings and terrorist acts."[13] Another commentator pointed out that no legal foundation whatever underpinned the FSB director's declared amnesty. "The words of Patrushev," he concluded, "constitute a guarantee only in words."[14] The Patrushev amnesty, thus, largely constituted an exercise in "PR," an approach apparently favored by Putin, but not, it would seem, by Kozak.

---

[9] Vadim Rechkalov, "Dukh Basaeva vyzvan na peregovory," mk.ru, 17 July 2006.

[10] Tat'yana Stanovaya, "Amnistiya ili smert'," politcom.ru, 1 August 2006.

[11] "Yuliya Latynina," echo.msk.ru, 5 August 2006.

[12] Vladimr Mukhin, "S povinnoi v Chechne prikhodyat boeviki, davno slozhivshie oruzhie," *Nezavisimaya gazeta*, 18 August 2006.

[13] Nikolai Sergeev, "Boeviki vydelili nomera v Sovete Federatsii," *Kommersant*, 1 August 2006.

[14] Igor' Plugaterev, "Amnistiya ob"yavlena no ne garantirovana," *Nezavisimoe voennoe obozrenie*, 11 August 2006.

Putin's Recently Announced "Withdrawal of Troops"

In similar fashion, on 8 August, the Russian government newspaper *Rossiiskaya gazeta* published excerpts from Putin's decree of 2 August that seemed to mandate a phased withdrawal of Russian forces in Chechnya over the next two years. Once again, those analysts who looked closely at the decree concluded that there was in reality little substance to it. Journalist Oleg Vladykin, for example, entitled his report, "A withdrawal of troops that will not happen,"[15] while a leading specialist on the North Caucasus, Sergei Markedonov, captioned his essay, "His Majesty PR."[16]

At present, there are approximately 70,000 *siloviki* based in Chechnya: 23,000 on permanent assignment from the Ministry of Defense; 24,000 from the Internal Troops of the MVD; 17,000 pro-Moscow regular police; 3,000 FSB border guards, plus FSB and Ministry of Justice units.[17] It is not at all clear that at the end of 2008 there will be less of them there. In the North Caucasus as a whole, Russia possesses approximately 250,000 *siloviki* throughout the Southern Federal District. Dmitrii Kozak has stipulated that the district has 1,180 *siloviki* per 100,000 people, making it among the most militarized regions in the world.[18] Despite this huge armed presence, Kozak has underlined the lack of effectiveness of these forces.

It seems fair to conclude that for Vladimir Putin, if not for Dmitrii Kozak, coercion and PR remain the cornerstones of Russia's approach to the North Caucasus. The divergent approaches of Kozak on the one hand, and of the *siloviki* and Russian Procuracy on the other hand, were highlighted at important meetings held on 25 August in Rostov-on-Don. Kozak, FSB director Patrushev, MVD chair Nurgaliev and the new Russian procurator general Yurii Chaika met with the thirteen

---

[15] Oleg Vladykin, "Vyvod voisk, kotorogo ne budet," *Moskovskie novosti*, 18 August 2006.
[16] Sergei Markedonov, "Ego Velichestvo PR," APN.ru, 14 August 2006.
[17] Vladimir Mukhin, "Ivanov raskryl voennuyu tainu," *Nezavisimaya gazeta*, 12 July 2006, and the same author's, "Moskva narashchivaet voennoe prisutstvie v Chechne," *Nezavisimaya gazeta*, 5 June 2006.
[18] "Prodaem Kavkaz," mk.ru, 16 June 2005.

heads of districts in the Southern Federal District.[19]   In his remarks, Kozak emphasized that, "over the past two years the number of terrorist acts has decreased in Southern Russia by 300 percent." He added that, according to polls, for local residents, corruption among the representatives of the Russian government was the second most significant problem after unemployment. The issue of security, he said, should be solved not by, "spewing out slogans," but by creating, "a system of administration that is understood by everyone."

The Russian procurator general, by contrast, emphasized at these meetings that the number of terrorist acts over the first seven months of 2006 was at the same level as for the same period in 2005. He said that crime was up in the federal district by ten percent, with Rostov Oblast' leading the way, followed by Dagestan, Ingushetia, North Ossetia and Chechnya. Kozak's relative optimism contrasted rather starkly with the procurator general's gloomy pessimism.

For the remainder of this paper we shall examine how Putin and Kozak have been seeking to cope with the manifold problems besetting the "Muslim" republics of the North Caucasus.

Chechnya

The situation in this unsettled region remains charged and difficult. On the one hand, "Chechenization" has, to a considerable extent, represented a success for the Russian leadership. The pro-Moscow leadership under President Alu Alkhanov and the de facto dominant figure in the republic, Prime Minister Ramzan Kadyrov, has quite successfully been taking the fight to the rebels. Today, Chechnya is no longer the most at-risk republic in the North Caucasus.

In accomplishing this, Moscow has, however, acquired a difficult-to-control proxy leader, Ramzan Kadyrov, son of the "martyred" former president of Chechnya Akhmad Kadyrov, who, especially in the time since he was made prime minister in early 2006, has sought to take the

---

[19] Ivan Sukhov, "Terror v tsifrakh," vremya.ru, 28 August 2006.

51

republic and its finances under his personal control. While the appointment of Ramzan as prime minister appears to have represented Putin's personal choice, and not Kozak's (who is clearly repelled by corrupt leaders), in order to help the consolidation of Russia's hold over the republic, it remains unclear how much longer the Russian president and his *siloviki* allies will be able to tolerate the excesses of the ambitious Chechen premier. Early next month Ramzan will turn thirty, which will make him eligible for appointment by Putin to the post of Chechen president. It will be difficult for Putin to keep Ramzan reasonably content while at the same time denying him the Chechen presidency. Ramzan's supporters in Chechnya, however, are currently ratcheting up the pressure to force Putin to name Kadyrov president right now. The speaker of the lower chamber of the Chechen parliament, Dukvakha Abdurakhmanov, recently asserted, "The people do not ask whether or not he [Ramzan] wants to head up the republic but desire that he should be president [now]."[20] On 5 October—Ramzan's birthday—Abdurakhmanov announced that a World Congress of the Chechen People will open in Grozny. This Congress's chief task will be to push for Ramzan's appointment as Chechen president.

Putin, who has historically been a highly skilled mediator of ambitious subordinates, is evidently attempting to use President Alu Alkhanov and several pro-Moscow police leaders as a political counterweight to Ramzan. If, however, Ramzan were to be sacked from his post or, as some have speculated, to be given a prestigious administrative post elsewhere in Russia, it seems likely that a number of his recent successes against the rebels could unravel. Indeed many members of his police force are former rebels who could once again decide to turn against Russia. President Alkhanov, in contrast to Ramzan, appears to be a loyal servant of the Russian state and its interests. His biography makes this clear: "Alkhanov is a graduate of the Academy of the MVD of the USSR. He occupied various positions in the Ministry of Internal Affairs of the Checheno-Ingush ASSR. After the rise to power in the republic of Dzkhokhar Dudaev he was one of the leaders of the opposition... In

---

[20] Ivan Sukhov, "Prigovoren k vyshei vlasti," vremya.ru, 21 August 2006.

1996 he personally confronted the rebels who seized Grozny. In 1997-2000 he was the head of a department of the police in the city of Shakhty, Rostov Oblast'."[21]

When Kadyrov, in an overt attempt at intimidation, ordered Alkhanov's office surrounded by armed followers at the time that the Chechen president was meeting with the head of the Russian Auditing Chamber, former Russian premier Sergei Stepashin, Alkhanov became so incensed that he traveled to Rostov and informed Kozak that he wanted to resign. "Kozak," Yuliya Latynina has recalled, "persuaded the president of Chechnya not to resign. Then Putin reconciled Alkhanov and Kadyrov [at a meeting in Moscow]. They both returned to Chechnya, and Kadyrov began to restore Grozny so as to show that he is better than Alkhanov. Since the federals had forgotten to put money into a special program for the restoring of Grozny...Kadyrov had to pay with his own money."[22]

Ramzan Kadyrov, in contrast to Alkhanov, is a Chechen nationalist who has sought to identify himself, despite egregious behavioral lapses, with the traditional religion of Chechnya, Sufi Islam. His feelings toward ethnic Russians are not warm. On one occasion, when he was in the reception room of Kozak's office, Ramzan reportedly confided, "I killed my first Russian when I was sixteen years old."[23] A Western journalist who recently spent time with Ramzan has written: "In private, Kadyrov is said to despise the Russians, admitting to one interviewer: 'We should keep away from them.'... He troubled Moscow earlier this year by banning gambling, calling for women to wear headscarves and promising that polygamy would be tolerated in the republic, which is a clear breach of Russian laws."[24] Ramzan's

---

[21] Sergei Markedonov, "Kadyrov protiv Alkhanova: prezidentskie spory," politcom.ru, 15 August 2006. On the intensifying power struggle between Alkhanov and Kadyrov, see also: Anna Politkovskaya, "Slozhenie oruzhiya, vychitanie Kadyrova," *Novaya gazeta*, 14 August 2006, and Musa Muradov, "Alu Alkhanov ukazal Ramzanu Kadyrovu na konstitutsiyu," *Kommersant*, 26 August 2006.

[22] Yuliya Latynina, "Kto prodlit srok prezidenta," ej.ru, 4 August 2006.

[23] "Yuliya Latynina," echo.msk.ru, 15 July 2006.

[24] Tom Parfitt, "The Republic of Fear," *The Sunday Times*, [UK], 20 August 2006.

disrespectful attitude toward Russians even while he heaps praise on Russian president Putin and urges that he serve at least two more terms, earns him points with elements of the Chechen populace. Like Ramzan's late father, specialist Sergei Markedonov has noted, "Kadyrov positioned himself not as a pro-Russian politician but as a person who is personally devoted to President Vladimir Putin."[25]

In the opinion of Yuliya Latynina, in seeking to rein in Ramzan, or especially by removing him from office, Moscow, could be making a critical error. In her view, Kadyrov constitutes, along with Dmitrii Kozak, "a very important achievement in our policy in the Caucasus."[26] Despite his self-evident flaws, Ramzan has accomplished much on behalf of the Russian state. "We see," she recently observed, "that Ramzan Kadyrov is indeed the chief person in Chechnya. He is someone who has managed to get Chechnya under control. In other words, he is someone who has accomplished what neither Dudaev nor Maskhadov succeeded in doing. Moscow is currently attempting to create a counterweight to Kadyrov in the person of Alkhanov, and with the detachments of Yamadaev and Kakiev. But this effort is repeatedly unsuccessful because Kadyrov turns out to be too strong. In addition, Kadyrov is now restoring Grozny…with his own money… Kadyrov is one of the few activists of the Putin epoch who has understood the chief secret of the Putin regime—if you say pleasant things to the regime but do whatever you want, then the regime is too weak to prevent you from doing what you want."[27]

In contrast to Latynina's appreciation for what Ramzan has accomplished on Russia's behalf, analyst Sergei Markedonov has emphasized the deleterious effects of Ramzan's political dominance: "Today one can speak of the concentration of all real power in the republic in the hands of the Chechen prime minister… This means that the institutionalization of power in the republic …has not been carried out." There has, in addition, he notes, occurred a "squeezing out

---

[25] Sergei Markedonov, "An Imperfect Amnesty," *Russia Profile*, 25 August 2006, in Johnson's Russia List, #194, 27 August 2006.
[26] "Yuliya Latynina," echo.msk.ru, 15 July 2006.
[27] "Yuliya Latynina," echo.msk.ru, 21 August 2006.

Russians from positions of control [the prime minister, for example, is no longer an ethnic Russian]...a minimalizing of Russian power structures; a 'Chechenization' of power and of the administration of the police; and an extension of this concept into the military."[28] Russia's hold on Chechnya has thus been weakened, not strengthened, by Ramzan's period of rule.

A key issue for the future is whether or not Russia will prove capable of carrying out the physical restoration of Chechnya. As Russian journalists have noted, Ramzan has been conducting a rather extensive restoration of the republic out of his own pocket. One way he has been doing this has been to withhold funds from the paychecks of pro-Moscow Chechen officials and police and then contribute those monies to the restoration effort. Ramzan and other pro-Moscow Chechen officials have complained bitterly that Moscow has contributed nothing to the restoration campaign. Dmitrii Kozak for one appears to understand the danger for Russia represented by such a perception among Chechens. In late July, he was accompanied on an inspection trip to Grozny by German Gref, the Russian minister for economic development and trade, Aleksei Kudrin, the minister of finance, and Andrei Fursenko, the minister of education, as well as other high-ranking Russian officials. According to the newspaper *Kommersant*, the inspection group confirmed that Kadyrov's home base of Gudermes had been completely restored but saw that Grozny manifestly had not. "Even the rubble had not been removed."[29]

According to a path-breaking report by journalist Anna Politkovskaya, Ramzan demanded to the visiting Russian ministers that Chechnya be reimbursed for the extensive restoration work that has already been carried out. Ramzan was, however, unable to provide the required documentation for this work.[30] According to Politkovskaya, Kudrin told Ramzan directly that he did not intend to go to prison because of

[28] Sergei Markedonov, "Chechnya ostaetsya na tretii srok," politcom.ru, 3 August 2006.
[29] Musa Muradov, Petr Netreba, "Pravitel'stvo inspektiruet Ramzana Kadyrova," *Kommersant*, 26 July 2006.
[30] Anna Politkovskaya, "Slozhenie oruzhiya, vychitanie Kadyrova," *Novaya gazeta*, 14 August 2006.

him. Given this impasse between Ramzan and several top Russian ministers, it seems unlikely that the Russian state—despite assurances to the contrary made by German Gref and others—will agree in the foreseeable future to give massive funds to a Chechnya that is de facto headed by Ramzan.

In similar fashion, the Russian Ministry of Defense has likewise made what has turned out to be empty promises. In December of last year the defense ministry was given the job of removing the rubble from Grozny.[31] An inspection visit by defense minister Sergei Ivanov in July of this year served, however, to only point out that almost nothing had been accomplished toward this goal. The financing of the restoration of Grozny, Ivanov hastily announced during his visit, "will begin next week."[32] It did not. What actual restoration is accomplished in Grozny will therefore likely be conducted by the Chechens themselves. If this turns out to be the case, then what perceived need will Chechens feel for a Russian state that is demonstrably incapable of keeping its promises?

Ingushetia

The situation in Ingushetia could, today, be the most critical within the entire North Caucasus region. The Putin-appointed president of Ingushetia, Murat Zyazikov, a former FSB general, represents an appointment made with Putin's blessing, but not Kozak's. (Zyazikov's name is conspicuously missing from Yuliya Latynina's list of "rational" presidents in the North Caucasus.) By failing to address the massive social and economic ills afflicting his republic, Zyazikov has allowed the situation there to markedly deteriorate.

In late June of this year, it was reported that over the past two months, "illegal armed units conducted more than twenty terrorist operations" in the republic. Among those assassinated by the terrorists were the

---

[31] See "Pod elochku Ivanovu polozhili Chechnyu," *Nezavisimaya gazeta*, 23 December 2005.
[32] Vladimir Mukhin, "Ivanov raskryl voennuyu tainu," *Nezavisimaya gazeta*, 12 July 2006.

deputy minister of internal affairs of Ingushetia, Dzhabrail Kostoev, the commander of the republican OMON of the Ministry of Internal Affairs, Musa Nal'giev, and the deputy head of the Sunzhenskii District in the republic, a woman named Gubina who had been in charge of a program to return ethnic Russians to Ingushetia. In fact, she had succeeded in returning a thousand of them. In August an attempt on the life of the procurator of Nazran' district also took place.[33] These terrorist acts were committed despite the presence of a regiment of Internal Troops and a motor rifle regiment from the Defense Ministry in the tiny republic.[34]

The assassination of Lieutenant Colonel Nal'giev, as well as the killing of his young children, was, the newspaper *Kommersant* observed, clearly intended to send a brutal message: "The terrorists sent the local OMON a clear message. He who cooperates with the federal center will be pitilessly destroyed together with his family, including his children." The murder of Gubina carried the additional message that "there is no place for ethnic Russians in Ingushetia."[35]

The deteriorating relations with ethnic Ingush and Ossetians within both the republics of Ingushetia and North Ossetia has, from the point of view of the Russian leadership, been even worse than such terrorist acts. It was reported in early August that Dmitrii Kozak had tried but failed to reconcile the presidents of the two republics.[36] The regime's attempt to return ethnic Ingush to the contested Prigorodnii District in North Ossetia, an effort apparently supported both by Putin and Kozak, has, not surprisingly, proven to be a destabilizing policy.[37]

In late August, General Nikolai Patrushev, the head of the National Anti-Terrorist Committee, reported that, as a result of Russia's

---

[33] "Ingushskomu prokuroru postavili stakan s granatoi," *Kommersant*, 11 August 2006.

[34] Vladimir Mukhin, "Ingushetiya prevrashchaetsya vo vtoruyu Chechnyu," *Nezavisiamya gazeta*, 26 June 2006.

[35] *Kommersant*, 11 August 2006.

[36] "Iz Kozaka ne vyshlo mirotvortsa," *Nezavisimaya gazeta*, 8 August 2006.

[37] On the return of ethnic Ingush to the Prigorodnii District, see Ol'ga Bobrova, "Lyudi iz obshchikh vagonov," *Novaya gazeta*, 10 August 2006.

successful counter-terrorist operation in Chechnya there had occurred a "transfer of terrorist activity into regions bordering on the republic."[38] He stipulated that of the 78 terrorist acts that took place in Russia during the first seven months of 2006, 18 of them occurred in Igushetia and 11 took place in North Ossetia. In addition, Patrushev said, the number of crimes committed with the use of illegal firearms had increased during that period in North Ossetia by 101% and in Ingushetia, by 20%.

The stated desire of Ramzan Kadyrov and his followers to reintegrate Ingushetia with Chechnya has also had a destabilizing effect upon Ingushetia. "De facto," one journalist, Vadim Rechkalov, has commented, "this idea [of Ramzan's] is little different from Basaev's idea of a 'Caliphate from the Black Sea to the Caspian.'"[39] (Ramzan's project, it should be noted, also foresees Chechnya's eventual integration with all or parts of Dagestan.[40])

North Ossetia

Given the deteriorating conditions in North Ossetia, a republic where the majority of the population is not Muslim but which is nonetheless heavily impacted by developments in adjacent Muslim areas, especially in Ingushetia, it has become evident that decisive action needs to be taken. On 29 August, it was announced that the republic's president, Taimuraz Mamsurov, had fired the republic's entire government.[41] The likely new head of government, Nikolai Khlyntsov, is an official with close career ties to Mamsurov. The attitude of Dmitrii Kozak toward Khlyntsov's candidacy remains unclear.[42]

---

[38] Sergei Kisin, Musa Muradov, "Terroristy razrelis' po Kavkazu," *Kommersant*, 26 August 2006.

[39] Vadim Rechkalov, "Na Ingushetiyu napali s trekh storon," mk.ru, 14 June 2006. See also Liz Fuller, "Analysis: Chechnya seeks to subsume, 'stabilize' Ingushetia," rferl.org, 13 June 2006.

[40] See Ivan Sukhov, "Ot separatizma k imperializmu: Chechenskie politiki mechtayut vernut' Ingushetiyu i pretenduyut na chast' Dagestana," vremya.ru, 31 August 2006.

[41] "Pravitel'stvo Severnoi Osetii otpravleno v otstavku," grani.ru, 29 August 2006; Ivan Sukhov, "Otstavka pered traurom," vremya.ru, 30 August 2006.

[42] "Osetinskii prem'er ne dostig sootvetsviya dolzhnosti," *Kommersant*, 30 August 2006.

Dagestan

As in Ingushetia, the large republic of Dagestan, which has a population of approximately 2.5 million, has also been destabilizing rapidly. "Dagestan," Sergei Markedonov has remarked, "has become the leader in terrorist activities. Just last year [2005] it surpassed Chechnya in terms of the number of terrorist acts."[43] According to police spokesmen, there could presently be as many as 2,500 rebels active in the republic, while there are perhaps several hundred active in Chechnya.[44] In early August, in the town of Buinaksk, the local procurator, Bitar Bitarov, was killed by a bomb. A second assassination attempt on the same day came close to killing the republic's minister of internal affairs, Adil'gerei Magomedtagirov.[45] There are Muslim villages in Dagestan, such as the highland village of Gimry, where Sharia law, not Russian law rules.[46]

Two key problems contributing to the destabilization of Dagestan and serving to empower the rebels are massive unemployment as well as police brutality and corruption. According to the former Russian minister of nationalities, Ramazan Abdulatipov, who is currently Russian ambassador to Tajikistan, "In my native Dagestan, for every employed person there are 160 who are unemployed."[47] "In Dagestan," journalist Ol'ga Allenova has stated flatly, "there are no jobs... If in Dagestan they promised work to those who would put down their weapons then a half of the informal formations would not remain."[48]

As for the corrupt and ineffective Dagestani police, they routinely resort to the use of torture, employing "needles under fingernails, the breaking of fingers, and beatings on the kidneys with rubber truncheons." Far worse torture than this is routinely used. "Not a

---

[43] "North Caucasus: Analyst warns of rising radical Islam," rferl.org, 5 May 2006.

[44] Sergei Markedonov, "Molchanie yagnyat," politcom.ru, 9 August 2006.

[45] "V Dagestane soversheno pokushenie na glavu MVD respubliki," newsru.com, 7 August 2006.

[46] "Yuliya Latynina," echo.msk.ru, 22 July 2006.

[47] "Ramazan Abdulatipov," *Rodnaya gazeta*, 4 August 2006.

[48] Ol'ga Allenova, "Dagestanskaya voronka," *Kommersant-vlast'*, 14 August 2006.

single man in the [North] Caucasus can forgive [such treatment],"
Allenova has commented.[49] Polls conducted by the government agency
FAPSI have shown, as Dmitrii Kozak recently underscored, that 88% of
the residents in the republic do not have faith in the Dagestani police.[50]

As soon as he was appointed to the post of *polpred* for the Southern
Federal District, Kozak began to pay close attention to the worsening
conditions in Dagestan. A special report on Dagestan was issued by a
working group attached to his office that, citing public opinion surveys
that it had commissioned, warned that poverty and broad-scale
corruption were serving to rapidly destabilize the republic.[51] On
Kozak's recommendation, Putin appointed Mukhu Aliev, an ethnic
Avar, as the new head of the republic. (Aliev figures prominently on
Latynina's list of "rational" presidents in the North Caucasus.) A key
point in Aliev's program has been that the highly corrupt and violent
siloviki who served under his predecessor, Magomedali Magomedov,
had to be removed; something that is, of course, easier said than done.
Aliev is said to believe that "the problem of extremism in the republic
will not be resolved by special operations alone ...Jobs have to be
created, unemployment has to be reduced, and the number of those
who go abroad to attend religious schools in Arab countries has to be
cut back."[52] Aliev has, like other reformist presidents in the region,
sought to make use of the "Patrushev amnesty" in order to offer the
rebels attractive incentives to disarm.

It has been noted by commentators that Aliev appears not to be
corrupt, that he does not give or take bribes, and that he is not part of
the republic's ruinous clan system. In Latynina's approving words,
"The president of Dagestan is in general a very rational man." "I am an

---

[49] Ibid.
[50] Madina Shavlokhova, "Dagestanskii lider razoblachaet vzyatichnikov v pogonakh,"
GZT.ru, 28 August 2006.
[51] "Kak budut vzryvat' Dagestan." mk.ru, 8 July 2005.
[52] Yuliya Rybina, "Dagestanskim boevikam predlozhili dialog po razoruzheniyu,"
Kommersant, 21 July 2006.

adherent not of [protest] meetings but of the law," Aliev told her in words that, perhaps intentionally, echoed the views of *polpred* Kozak.[53]

Kabardino-Balkariya

In October of 2005, a major assault by Islamic militants took place in the city of Nal'chik, the capital of Kabardino-Balkariya. Thirty-five representatives of the power ministries perished, as did ninety-two rebels and twelve civilians. The unexpected appearance of some 150 rebels represented a major surprise for the authorities, but it could have been worse—Shamil' Basaev reportedly watched the fighting from a nearby hilltop and chose not to commit 150-300 of his own fighters to the fray.[54]

The geopolitically key republic of Kabardino-Balkariya finds itself today enmeshed in the same harsh poverty as the rest of the North Caucasus. "The level of wages in the republic is two times lower than the average, while the percentage of those who are unemployed is 25%. In addition, not one of the large industrial enterprises in the republic is currently operating."[55]

In addition to such economic woes, Kabardino-Balkariya has been the victim of a plague of police corruption and brutality. The chair of the State Duma's committee on security, Vladimir Vasil'ev, has called the police in Nal'chik "the most corrupt system of the MVD [in Russia]."[56] Concerning the issue of police brutality in the republic, Yuliya Latynina has said,"I have said many times that the situation in Kabardino-Balkariya and in Ingushetia is typical in the sense that the main source of extremism in these republics is not so much the terrorists as much as it is the law-enforcement organs who behave, of course, as they

---

[53] Yuliya Latynina, "Odin den' prezidenta," *Novaya gazeta*, 10 August 2006.
[54] Andrei Soldatov, Irina Borogan, "Basaev brosil boevikov v bede," politcom.ru, 7 July 2006.
[55] "Prezident Kabardino-Balkarii izbavilsya ot proshlogo v litse prem'era," *Kommersant*, 20 June 2006.
[56] Sergei Varsavchik, "Militsiya Nal'chika priznana samoi korrumpirovanoi," *Nezavismaya gazeta*, 19 October 2005.

generally behave in Russia itself…When it [police brutality] happens in Blagoveshchensk [in the Russian Far East], no one reacts. However when such a thing occurs in the Caucasus… the man who has been beaten can very easily convince himself that he has to take up an automatic weapon and kill [ethnic] Russians in return…."

In Kabardino-Balkariya, Latynina recalls, the former head of the republican police, Colonel Shagenov, "unleashed a literal terror against the Kabardino-Balkariya Jamaat. Believers were dragged out of mosques, were beaten up by the hundreds, had [Orthodox] crosses shaved on their skulls, had their beards were set on fire, and kicked a pregnant woman [Elena Gaseeva] in the stomach with their shoes…saying, 'You will not give birth to another 'Wahabbi.'" To keep Gaseeva from identifying her police attackers, they seized her husband, warning, 'If you identify us, we will kill your husband.'"[57] Latynina's reference to the widespread corruption of the police throughout Russia, and not just in the North Caucasus, has been confirmed by recent polls conducted throughout Russia. According to one survey taken in January of this year, 70% of respondents stated that they did not trust Russian law-enforcement organs. Fifty-three percent maintained that they were poorly defended by the police, while 27% said that they were not defended at all.[58]

Dmitrii Kozak, supported by President Putin, has clearly seen the danger represented in Kabardino-Balkariya by the mix of harsh poverty, sky-high unemployment and police brutality and corruption. A reformer, Arsen Kanokov, who is on Latynina's list of "rational" republican heads, has been named republican president. Also just recently, a member of Kozak's own staff, Andrei Yarin, was appointed prime minister of the republic.[59] But is there sufficient time for the reformers to avert disaster? On 12 August, after a lull of some months,

---

[57] "Yuliya Latynina," echo.msk.ru, 29 July 2006. On police brutality in Kabardino-Balkariya, see also: Anna Politkovskaya, "Cheloveka ubili 'dlya profilaktiki,'" *Novaya gazeta*, 10 July 2006.
[58] Tat'yana Mashkova, "Obernis' neznakomyi v pogonakh," *Novaya gazeta*, 27 July 2006. The poll was taken by the organization "Obshchestvennyi verdict."
[59] "Prem'erom KB stanet chelovek Kozaka," GZT.ru, 20 June 2006.

rebels once again made their presence felt by opening fire on police in the town of Khasan'ya, a suburb of Nal'chik. The rebels were reportedly from the same group that had attacked Nal'chik in October 2005.[60]

Karachaevo-Cherkesiya

The Republic of Karachaevo-Cherkessiya is one in which Kozak has not yet succeeded in removing the republic's compromised president, Mustafa Batdyev, who has been in power since 2003. This is true despite the fact that Batdyev's (former) son-in-law orchestrated a gangland-style slaying in 2004 in which seven people were gunned down. The grisly murders sparked significant popular unrest.

Adygea

In the case of Adygea, an autonomous republic located within the confines of Karasnodar krai, Kozak (and Putin as well) appear to have suffered a noteworthy political setback. In an apparently ill-advised effort to "strengthen the vertical" they sought to remove the republic's Adyg president, Khazret Sovmen from office, and to do away with Adygea's autonomy and sovereignty, merging the region with the largely Russian and Cossack Krasnodar krai. This ill-considered move threatened to destabilize the entire western North Caucasus: "Adyg and Cherkess committees from across the North Caucasus warned that if Moscow continued to push the abolition of Adygea's status as a separate republic, these committees would in turn propose to unify the historic territories of Adygea, Kabarda, Cherkessia, and Shapsughia to create a far larger Adyg (Cherkess) republic."[61] This episode, as well as the efforts made by the regime to resettle Ingush in North Ossetiya and

---

[60] "V Nal'chike predotvrashcheny dva mashtabnykh terakta," newsru.com, 12 August 2006; "Vozobnovlena operatsiya v Kabardino-Baklkarii,"grani.ru, 13 August 2006.
[61] Liz Fuller, "North Caucasus: Adygea president, opposition assail presidential envoy [Kozak]," referl.org, 13 April 2006. See also Georgii Kovalev, "Sovmen vse-taki ukhodit?" politcom.ru, 12 April 2006. An effort is apparently also being made to "de-sovereignize" the Republic of Bashkortostan. See: "Vladimiru Putinu predlozheno izmenit' status Bashkirii," *Kommersant*, 31 July 2006.

63

ethnic Russians in Ingushetia, seems to demonstrate that Kozak, at least to a degree, shares Putin's relative blindness with regard to the acute dangers involved in shaking up the delicate and highly combustible ethno-religious balance in the region.

Conclusion

With the appointment of Dmitrii Kozak as *polpred* in the Southern Federal District, Vladimir Putin has for the first time chosen a "rational" man to spearhead Russia's efforts to keep the Russian South attached to Russia. This is despite the fact the overall record has been somewhat mixed. Kozak has, with Putin's approval, appointed "rational" regional leaders in certain key republics: Aliev in Dagestan; Kanokov in Kabardino-Balkariya; Mamsurov in North Ossetia. In other instances, the Russian president has not acquiesced to the removal of an incompetent or corrupt incumbent. The most notable of these is Murat Zyazikov in Ingushetia. In at least one instance, both Kozak and Putin, as we have seen, were rebuffed in an attempt to remove an entrenched incumbent: Khazret Sovmen in Adygea. Finally, both Kozak and Putin currently find themselves confronted with the intractable problem of what to do about the ambitious Ramzan Kadyrov in Chechnya—Kadyrov has to date served as a champion of Russia's interests in the region but he could represent a dire threat to those same interests in the future.

As to what will happen in the North Caucasus region in the near future, it remains unclear whether Kozak and Putin will prove capable of overcoming the endemic Russian *bespredel* and *bardak* highlighted by Latynina and other commentators. To do this, they need to set about bolstering the economy and infrastructure in the region's desperately poor "Muslim" republics with their stratospheric numbers of unemployed and heavily armed young men. If they should fail, then it will remain uncertain whether the North Caucasus, or at least sections of it, will remain part of Russia in 2015.

On 17 August, it was reported that Putin intended to soon meet with "the biggest businessmen in the country", Oleg Deripaska, Aleksei

Miller and other oligarchs, at his summer residence in Sochi in order to encourage them to invest in the North Caucasus. "The initiator and intermediary for this meeting," it was remarked, "was to be the _polpred_ Dmitrii Kozak."[62] While the leading Russian oligarchs will predictably listen carefully to the Russian president's exhortations, it remains unclear whether, even if the requested funds are offered, the Russian state will prove capable of carrying out the restoration of Chechnya and the bolstering of the economies and infrastructure of the North Caucasus republics.

While Putin and his press spokespeople are wont to indict Al-Qaeda and "international terrorism" for the monumental difficulties they currently face in the North Caucasus, it seems clear that this is little more than a red herring. A quarter of a million _siloviki_ stationed in the North Caucasus District should be sufficient to hold eight hundred (the figure provided by General Arkadii Edelev, deputy minister of internal affairs) rebels at bay.[63] Even if the actual number of rebels is four times as high, a quarter of a million armed men should be enough to do the job.

It seems clear that there is another key question. As Anton Danilov-Danilyan, the head of the Economic Working Group of the Russian Presidential Administration, recently put it: "If there are jobs and investments in the economy of Chechnya, Ingushetia and Dagestan, then there will be fewer of those willing to risk their lives for the sake of [Islamic] slogans."[64] The operative word here is "if." Will Kozak and Putin be able to get the job done, or will they fail?

Postscript

In the approximately nine months that have passed since this essay was completed, the regime has pressed ahead with implementing President Putin's strategy toward the North Caucasus region. This strategy, it

---

[62] "Putin predlozhit oligarkham vlozhit' den'gi v Chechnyu," newsru.com, 17 August 2006.

[63] "Spetssluzhby nashli sredstv protiv 'Al'-Kaidy,'" _Nezavisimaya gazeta_, 27 July 2006.

[64] "Teper' voina konchilas'!," _Kommersant-vlast'_, 17 July 2006.

should be noted, appears to owe considerably more to the convictions (and to the deep political cynicism) of the Russian president than it does to the views of his polpred in the Southern Federal District, Dmitrii Kozak. The Putin approach to the region, as was remarked earlier, combines heavy doses of coercion and of PR (or "spin") with the installing of local leaders who can be counted on to do Moscow's bidding. In pursuing such a strategy, the regime has self-evidently not been addressing the key socio-political problems of the region: sky-high unemployment, widespread poverty, inter-ethnic strife, and massive corruption of republican police and local bureaucracies.

In early February of 2007, a leading specialist on the region, Sergei Markedonov, published an essay entitled "Irony instead of a strategy" in which he awarded the regime low marks for its benighted and counter-productive approach to the North Caucasus.[65] During a recent Putin recent press conference devoted to the region, Markedonov commented, "The problems of the North Caucasus were simply not examined. Not the problem of Dagestan (where since 2005 terrorist activity has been intensively growing), not the unresolved Ossetian-Ingush conflict (which did not once attract the interest of experts and politicians during 2006), and not the situations in Kabardino-Balkariya (the results of the [October 2005] tragedy in Nal'chik) and Karachaevo-Cherkesiya (the growth of the activity of Islamic radicals). None of these issues were focused upon by journalists or by the President of the Russian Federation.... The president also did not say anything new [about Chechnya], limiting himself to the traditional 'high assessment' of...Ramzan Kadyrov."

As for the attitude toward the region of Dmitrii Kozak, Markedonov went on, the polpred has recently been asserting that the North Caucasus has become a stable and secure region. "The problems of security and instability," Kozak was quoted as maintaining, "now lie in the past.... With full certainty one can state that it is 40% safer to work here than it is in Russia as a whole." Markedonov wondered where Kozak could have come up with such a bizarre statistic. The "wahhabis"

---

[65] Sergei Markedonov, "Ironiya vmesto strategii," politcom.ru, 6 February 2007.

who are increasingly active in the North Caucasus, he pointed out, would beg to differ with Kozak's opinion. In Markedonov's view, an unjustified mood of triumph underlies the Putin-Kozak approach to the North Caucasus.

In an informative and stimulating April 2007 essay entitled "Beyond the Borders of Chechnya: The Emergence of Jamaats in the Northern Caucasus and their Radicalization," Emil Souleimanov of Charles University in Prague (a visiting fellow at Harvard during 2007) summed up recent developments in the North Caucasus thusly: "One thing is certain: over the last few years, [Islamic] jamaats have been springing up like dandelions all over the Northern Caucasus. More and more frequently these jamaats have a military agenda, while some (not all) established jamaats are becoming militarized. These jamaats are then gradually losing their ethnic character, are internationalizing, gaining contacts with the Chechen resistance and trying to draw the attention and appreciation of their colleagues with highly visible actions.... They are united, however, by the idea of the justness of their common cause: jihad, an effort to rid themselves of the corrupt local elite as well as Russian domination and to create an Islamic state based on the sharia."[66]

Souleimanov underscored one significant development that is currently taking place in the northwestern part of the North Caucasus: "Processes are underway that are similar to those experienced in Chechnya in the period between the wars [i.e., during 1996-1999]. Religious societies of (not only) ideologically devoted people are gradually becoming radicalized and militarized beneath the indiscriminate repression of the state apparatus.... Moreover, both in Karachaevo-Cherkesiya and in Kabardino-Balkariya, people are aware that (mono)ethnic separatism is, if not impossible, at least very complicated, taking into account the

---

[66] Paper presented at the 2007 World Convention of The Association for the Study of Nationalities (ASN), Columbia University, New York, NY, 12-14 April 2007. See also Akhmet Yarlykapov, "Separatism and Islamic extremism in the ethnic republics of the North Caucasus," Russian Analytical Digest, www.res.ethz.ch and wwww.ruslandanalysen.de, No. 22, 5 June 2007. Yarlykapov is a senior researcher at the Institute of Ethnology and Anthropology of the Russian Academy of Sciences in Moscow.

enormous numbers of local Russians. If the apologists of the jamaats are to succeed, it is vitally important to forget 'ethnic' wrongs and to stick together with 'Muslim brothers'…. The latest attacks against Islam and Muslims by the republic's law enforcement agencies, in which Russians play leading roles, are strongly resented by much of the local population, whether of Turkic or Adygean origin."

We now move on to a necessarily brief examination of the political situation in certain key republics of the North Caucasus region. Our main focus here will be on the charged situation in Chechnya and on the uncertain fate of the Chechen diaspora living in the Russian Federation. As is well known, Ramzan Kadyrov was appointed Chechen head of state by President Putin earlier this year. While repeatedly emphasizing his fealty to Putin and his personal concern for the well-being of ethnic Russians, Kadyrov has, at the same time, been sponsoring a campaign to take full control of all police, procuracy and economic levers in the republic. Through his close allies in the Chechen leadership, he has, for example, recently sought, to oust the republic's procurator, an ethnic Russian, Valerii Kuznetsov. Kuznetsov had earned the ire of Kadyrov and his colleagues by investigating cases of corruption among Chechen elites. Kadyrov has also been seeking to take control of the one remaining police entity in the republic that he does not yet control—the Operational Investigate Bureau (ORB-2)—currently subordinated to the Russian Ministry of Internal Affairs of the Southern Federal District.

Having only just been appointed as Chechen president, Kadyrov is already, through his republican allies, pressing to have his presidential term extended from four years to 5-8 years. If Putin follows through on his assurances to hand over power to a chosen successor in 2008—and especially if that successor is a silovik, such as Sergei Ivanov-- then Kadyrov's continued loyalty to the Russian state will be very much in question. At the least, he will predictably seek to freeze the Russian state out of all Chechen internal affairs.

Kadyrov's mounting difficulties with the Russian state are taking place, it should be emphasized, against a background of rising ethnic Russian

68

xenophobia directed toward ethnic minorities and especially toward Chechens. This sentiment has been documented in polls taken, for example, by the Levada Center in Moscow. One indication of such xenophobia was the recent effort by certain extreme Russian nationalists forcibly to obtain the renaming of Akhmad Kadyrov Street in Moscow (named, of course, after Ramzan's father) to "the Street of the Pskov Division of Russian Paratroopers."[67] Significant numbers of Moscow police had to be called out to keep the street sign from being torn down by angry Russian activists. A number of residents of the Russian capital, including those living on or close to the street, were reported by the press to be incensed that a street in the Russian capital had been named after a Chechen "bandit."

A far more serious sign of deteriorating Russo-Chechen relations was the severe ethnic riots that erupted in the city of Stavropol' in late May and early June of this year. Stavropol' Krai, it should be noted, borders on all of the "Muslim" republics of the North Caucasus (with the exception of Adygea). Several hundred ethnic Russians and Muslims from the North Caucasus clashed in a mass riot that saw the wielding by the rioters of knives and a threatened use of firearms. Three deaths marked these tumultuous events. On 24 May, a Chechen student was beaten to death, apparently by Russian police who had taken him into custody. On 3 June, two ethnic Russian students were found stabbed to death. Rumors, as are their wont, spread like wildfire, and local public opinion in Stavropol' concluded that the stabbings of the Russians had been payback for the killing of the Chechen (though no such connection has been demonstrated). The local police, many of them veterans of the two wars in Chechnya, openly sided with the Russian "side" in the melee.

According to some reports, approximately a thousand Russians paraded by the mayor's office in Stavropol' shouting "Glory to Russia!" (a well-known slogan of the neo-Nazi Russian National Union) and "A suitcase—a train station—Chechnya!" (a call to deport Chechens back

---

[67] "Kadyrova navestili pskovskie desantniki," APN.ru, 29 April 2007; "Ulitsa Kadyrova zhivet po zakonam voennogo vremeni," mk.ru, 4 May 2007.

to their home republic). Some demonstrators were reported to have marched by the local FSB headquarters "shouting slogans and extending their arms in a Nazi salute."[68] During the bloody mass slugfest, Muslim participants were said to have shouted: "Allah akbar!" and "Russian swine—get out of the Caucasus!"[69] Fifty-one individuals were taken into custody by the police, many of them reportedly Muslims, while nine criminal cases were subsequently opened by the procuracy in connection with the riots.[70] A number of those involved in the slugfest—thirty in all from both "sides"-- had to be hospitalized, some with quite serious injuries.[71] Reporters noted that many of the Russian and Muslim participants in the skirmish were unemployed.

Russian journalists and academic specialists chose to emphasize the regime's inadequate reaction to the incident. Polpred Dmitrii_Kozak was quoted as dismissing the incident as having been a "banal scuffle."[72] In similar fashion, the head of the Russian MVD, Rashid Nurgaliev, stresssed that the incident was "not connected with ethnic motives."[73] Specialist Sergei Markedonov pointed out that such a dismissive attitude by the authorities toward latent conflicts had in the past led to severe military-political consequences both in Russia and in post-Soviet space.[74] "During the 1950s-1980s," he recalled, "inter-ethnic clashes between Russians and Chechens, Russians and Ingush, and Chechens and Ingush were exclusively seen as common social conflicts." But, as one can see now, he added, such conflicts paved the way for the savage Russo-Chechen wars of 1994-1996 and 1999-present. In similar fashion, the Armenian pogroms that took place in Sumgait (1988) and Baku (1990) presaged an all-out Armenian-Azerbaijani war.

Journalist Yuliya Latynina made a similar point in her comments on the incident. "In answer to the question, 'What is happening?' the

---

[68] Ivan Sukhov, "Sumashedshie lzhepolitiki," vremya.ru, 7 June 2007.
[69] "Udastsya li predotvratit' novuyu Kondopogu na Stavropol'e," kp.ru, 5 and 6 June 2007.
[70] Yuliya Latynina, "Stavropol'," ej.ru, 8 June 2007.
[71] Sergei Markedonov, "Stavropol' zhivet po printsipu krovi," politcom.ru, 7 June 2007.
[72] "Kozak: V Stavropole net ekstremizma," grani.ru, 6 June 2007.
[73] Yuliya Latynina, "Stavropol'," gazeta.ru, 8 June 2007.
[74] Sergei Markedonov, "Stavropol zhivet po printsipu krovi," politcom.ru, 7 June 2007.

regime declares that nothing is happening...A crowd races down the streets [of a city] while the regime with white lips says that everything is in order. Under Yeltsin Russia lived worse than under Putin... But there were no pogroms.... The course that Russia is pursuing today dooms it to inter-ethnic fragmentation [razlom], and the most dangerous part of that fragmentation is the relations between Chechens and Russians. For the Russians this is a conflict between beasts and human beings, for the Chechens, between wolves and sheep. This conflict is developing under conditions of the complete absence of the [Russian] state...The regime denies the problem with a well-tested approach—by denying its existence. That is as effective as curing a stroke by asserting that a patient is healthy."[75]

In a detailed analysis of the Stavropol' riots that appeared in the mass circulation daily Komsomol'skaya Pravda, journalist Vladimir Voloshin warned: "In point of fact we are already witnessing the beginning stages of a disease in comparison to which the civil war [that pitted Reds against Whites] was a just a common cold. The viruses of Kondopoga, Sal'sk and now Stavropol' are capable of paralyzing the entire country which will then break apart...[Russia] needs to be healed immediately. Two heavy doses of medicine are needed—harsh punishment for the provoking of national conflicts and at least some kind of ethnic policy on the part of the state. At least something like the Soviet model, when in the USSR the authorities painstakingly constructed a 'melting pot of nations'... And now there is simply no choice—we have to construct that melting pot once again. Before it is too late..."[76]

Moving on very briefly to the key republic of Dagestan, one should note that it is not clear today that the Putin-Kozak effort to replace the republic's State Council as a ruling body with an appointed president (an ethnic Avar, Mukhu Aliev) will prove successful. Growing ethnic strains are already becoming visible.

---

[75] Yuliya Latynina, "Stavropol'," gazeta.ru, 8 June 2007.
[76] "Udastya li predovratit' novuyu Kondopogu na Stavropole'e," kp.ru, 6 June 2007.

In Ingushetia, the incompetent leadership of former FSB general Murat Zyazikov is failing to prevent an accelerating economic and social decline of the republic. In addition, Zyazikov is now being called upon to fend off efforts by Ramzan Kadyrov and his supporters to merge the two republics, with Chechnya, of course, being slated to play the dominant role.

Lastly, in the small but politically key republic of Adygea, the Russian imperialist approach being taken by Putin and Kozak threatens quite simply to blow up in their faces. A political client of the Russian president and of Kozak, Aslancheryy Tkhakushinov, a former rector of Maikop Technological University, was appointed republican president by Putin in January 2007. Like Murat Zyazikov in Ingushetia, Tkhakushinov seems likely to prove incapable of coping with the forces that and his sponsors have unleashed. His attempts to merge Adygea with Russian and Cossack Krasnodar Krai have already served to anger and stir up the Muslim populace of his republic. In December of 2006, Putin was forced by Adyg public opinion to rule out such a plan. But Kozak and Tkhakushinov are continuing to promote Adygea's rapid economic integration into Krasnodar Krai, even in cases where this is not to the economic advantage of Adygea. If pursued to the end—i.e., to the de facto merger of Adygea with its much larger neighbor--such a development could eventually produce a political explosion in the northwestern part of the North Caucasus where pan-Cherkess (pan-Adyg) sentiment is already strong and growing. This point was recently made to me by a Russian journalist who makes frequent visits to the North Caucasus region.

To sum up, the future of the North Caucasus remains murky and uncertain. The Putin-Kozak approach to the region has in many ways proved to be ineffective. Under Putin's successor—especially if he should prove incapable of forging a modus vivendi with the thrusting and unpredictable Ramzan Kadyrov—the situation in the region could deteriorate further, perhaps rapidly so. The worrisome growth of ethnic Russian xenophobia and in particular of the widespread detestation of dark-skinned "peoples of the Caucasus" could serve to threaten and significantly to weaken Russia's continued hold on the region.

Separatism in the Northern Caucasus

Moshe Gammer

Introduction

Western media and observers frequently call those Chechens fighting the Russian army "separatists". From the media's perspective this term is used for two reasons: it is accurate and at the same time does not convey sympathy with either side. Although the original definition of the word "separatism," is, "the advocacy or practice of separation of a [certain] group of people from a larger body on the basis of ethnicity, religion, or gender,"[1] it is nowadays limited mainly to ethnic/national groups striving for independence.[2] As such the term, "separatists," is practically synonymous to, "secessionists,"[3] but is far simpler to use, write and pronounce. Also, in many cases, "separatism," is interconnected with, "irredentism," which is defined as, "nationalist agitation in other countries, based on historical, ethnic, and geographical reasons, for the incorporation of territories under foreign rule."[4]

---

[1] *The Concise Oxford English Dictionary.* Similarly: *The New Oxford American Dictionary; The Oxford Dictionary of English* (2nd revised ed.).

[2] It is defined as "the ambition of a minority to form its own sovereign state" (*Dictionary of Geography*), "the idea of creating a separate and sovereign political entity" (*The Oxford Companion to Canadian History*) and "can involve secession from a state and the establishment of independent countries" (*Dictionary of the Social Sciences*).

[3] "Secession" is defined as the "formal withdrawal from an association by a group discontented with the actions or decisions of that association. The term is generally used to refer to withdrawal from a political entity; such withdrawal usually occurs when a territory or state believes itself justified in establishing its independence from the political entity of which it was a part. By doing so it assumes sovereignty." (*Dictionary of the Social Sciences*).

[4] *The Columbia Encyclopedia*, Sixth Edition (2002 – 2005). And see Naomi Chazan (ed.), *Irredentism and International Politics* (Boulder, Co., 1991).

It seems the phenomenon of separatism in its modern connotation is strongly connected to nationalism and nation-building.[5] After all, nationalism is an ideology that advocates the right of each national group to have its own independent state. Since World War I, nationalism has become the norm for international relations and the basis for the existence of the nation-state.[6] In the case of the Northern Caucasus, nation-building and nationalism were the products of and the end consequence of Soviet policies and practices with regards to ethnic minorities in the USSR.

Soviet Nation-Building and National Conflicts

Ethnically and linguistically, the Caucasus is one of the most diverse regions in the world. Several dozen ethnic groups inhabit this mountain range. The sizes of these ethnicities vary from the inhabitants of a single village to several hundred thousand. The people in the Caucasus were aware of their ethnic and linguistic divisions long before they had contact with Russia and the modern world, but these differences had no political overtones at that time. In spite of this ethnic, linguistic and even religious diversity all the "mountaineers" shared the same way of life, traditions, customs and even way of dressing.[7] In other words, while fully aware of their own peculiarities, all these groups also shared a common culture and identity.[8]

---

[5] There is, of course, a difference between nationalism and separatism. See, for example, Ekaterina Sokirianskaia, "Ideology and Conflict: Chechen Political Nationalism Prior to and During Ten Years of War," in: Moshe Gammer (ed.), *Ethno-Nationalism, Islam and the State in the Caucasus: Post-Soviet Disorder* (tentative title, to be published by Routledge).

[6] For nationalism as ideology, see Elie Kedourie, *Nationalism* (London, 1985, 3d. rev. ed.).

[7] The majority of the native people of the Northern Caucasus are Sunni Muslims, but there are also Christians and Jews (known as Mountain, Caucasus or Tat Jews). At the time of the Russian conquest some groups were still pagan.

[8] See Moshe Gammer, "Unity, Diversity and Conflict in the Northern Caucasus," in: Yaacov Ro'i (ed.), *Muslim Eurasia: Conflicting Legacies*, London: Frank Cass, 1995, pp. 163-186.

74

Ethnic demarcation was introduced into the Northern Caucasus by Imperial Russian ethnographers and administrators.[9] By 1917, these new boundaries were internalized, at least by the more educated strata in the Northern Caucasus. Thus, the short-lived "Independent Democratic Republic of the Mountaineers of the Northern Caucasus" (1918 – 1919) was planned as a federal republic of seven states based on the nationalities established in the previous century.[10] It was, however, the Soviet regime, and more precisely Stalin as Commissar for Nationalities Affairs, which created and shaped the current divisions of the existing peoples in the Northern Caucasus.

Soviet nationalities policy vis-à-vis the Muslims of the ex-Russian Empire (reassembled by the Bolsheviks) was motivated by a strong fear of pan-Islamism and pan-Turkism. It aimed, therefore, at, "dividing and ruling," these societies along three parameters:

1) To divide them by creating new peoples out of existing ethnic groups and by creating new literary languages to replace long established regional languages.

2) To keep the outside Muslim world out of the region through the methods described above as well as forcing a switch from Persian (Arabic) to Latin (and later on to Cyrillic) orthography.

To make them forget their unique histories through the application of these new languages and alphabets.

---

[9] For this phenomenon, see Austin Lee Jersild, "Ethnic Modernity and the Russian Empire: Russian Ethnographers and Caucasian Mountaineers." *Nationalities Papers*, Vol. 24, No. 4 (1996), pp. 641- 648.

[10] For the history of the Mountain Republic, see V. D. Dzadziev, *Ot soiuza ob"edinennykh gortsev Severnogo Kavkaza i Dagestana do Gorskoi ASSR (1917 – 1921)* (Vladikavkaz, 2003). G. I. Kakahasanov, A-H. S. Hajiev, S. Ch. Asil'darov, L. G.Kaimarazova and I. M. Musaev, (eds.), *Soiuz Ob"edinenykh Gortsev Severnogo Kavkaza i Dagestana (1917 – 1918 gg.), Gorskaia Respublika (1918 – 1920 gg.). (Dokumenty i materialy)* (Makhachkala, 1994) is a collection of documents on the subject.

In the Northern Caucasus the application of this nationalities policy started with the division of the region into two multi-ethnic Autonomous Soviet Socialist Republics (ASSRs) within the Russian Soviet Federated Socialist Republic (RSFSR). These two ASSRs were Dagestan and the Mountain Republic. Dagestan remained a single multi-ethnic republic. When this happened, more than 30 native ethnic-linguistic groups were redefined into 11 officially recognised titular "peoples". Three more ethnic groups were then lumped into Dagestan with these 11, with each ethnic group enjoying its own polity within the USSR. Dagestan is, thus, a unique state that is "owned" jointly by 14 peoples.

The Mountain Republic ASSR was divided into several separate autonomous regions within the RSFSR.[11] After some initial fluctuation the number of autonomous regions stabilized in the late 1950s at five: the Chechen-Ingush ASSR, the North Ossetian ASSR, the Kabardino-Balkar ASSR, the Karachai-Cherkess Autonomous Oblast (AO) and the Adyghe AO.[12] This is how three closely related Muslim ethnic groups were split into separate peoples and divided throughout two or three republics -- the Circassians were divided into the Kabartay, Cherkess and Adyghe peoples; the Vaynakhs into Chechens and Ingush; and the Karachai and Balkars were separated from each other by political boundaries.[13] Yet, at the same time, three of the autonomous oblasts were bi-national in their make-up. The exception, Adygea, was mono-ethnic but the Adyghes formed a tiny minority group surrounded by a Russian sea.[14]

---

[11] See A. Kh. Daudov, *Gorskaia ASSR (1921 – 1924 gg). Ocherki sotsial'no-ekonomicheskoi istorii* (St. Petersburg, 1997)

[12] In addition the Abkhaz ASSR and the South Ossetian AO were created and made part of the Soviet Socialist Republic (SSR) of Georgia.

[13] In all three cases, it seems the Soviets merely reconfirmed divisions made by the Tsarist authorities. And cf. Francine Hirsch, *Empire of Nations. Ethnographic Knowledge and the Making of the Soviet Union* (Ithaca, 2005).

[14] The other mono-ethnic unit – the North Ossetian ASSR could hardly be regarded an exception. A large portion of Ossetians are Christian (at least nominally) and were, therefore, measured by a different yardstick, especially since they had been the most loyal ethnicity to Russia in the Caucasus. However, even they did not escape division into the

All these new "peoples," in due time, developed their own identity (however partially-formed and imperfect these identities might have been) and nationalism (and under Soviet conditions even xenophobia and chauvinism) and proceeded along divergent paths. Thus, a large potential was created for "nationalist" strife and conflict between these newly-created peoples. The universal policy of creating national autonomous territories further enhanced this potential.[15]

First, these peoples did not have equal access (and in some cases did not have any access at all) to the state apparatuses and tools of rule accompanying the status of titular people. In a situation where a territory had more then one titular people it was rather natural for the largest one to monopolize power and resources. The smaller titular peoples, therefore, felt they were being discriminated and/or persecuted. Yet the attainment of status as a titular group was crucial for the advancement of political goals. Groups that were not defined as having titular status did not enjoy such opportunities and consequently were not able to develop nationalist and separatist demands. These groups that were not officially recognized as a titular group include the Avars and Darghins in Dagestan, the Abaza in the Karachai-Cherkes ASSR and the Shapsugs in the Krasnodar krai.

Second, the political-administrative borders diverged markedly from ethnic borders (if these even existed). These political-administrative borders were purposely set up in this fashion. Consequently, large portions of ethnic groups and peoples found themselves living outside their nominal territories as non-titular minorities with no national rights.[16] These disenfranchised groups included the Lezghins, Tsakhurs

---

North Ossetian ASSR within the RSFSR and the South Ossetian AO within the Georgian SSR.

[15] For Soviet nationality policies, see, in addition to the book mentioned in footnote 13 by Hirsch, Lubomyr Hajda and Mark Beissinger (eds.), *The Nationalities Factor in Soviet Politics and Society* (Boulder, Co., 1990); Alexander J Motyl, *Sovietology, Rationality, Nationality: Coming to Grips with Nationalism in the USSR* (New York, 1990); Bohdan Nahaylo and Victor Swoboda, *Soviet Disunion: A History of the Nationalities Problem in the USSR* (New York, 1990).

[16] The only exception is the Aki (Dagestani) Chechens who were recognised as a titular people of that ASSR

and Rutuls in Azerbaijan who were officially registered on their internal passports as Azerbaijanis, the Avars in Georgia as well as the Nogais in the Chechen-Ingush ASSR and Stavropol krai.

All the disputes associated with this political and administrative quagmire were kept under wraps during the Soviet period. Indeed, these frictions did not develop into serious conflicts during Gorbachev's glasnost' or even after the dissolution of the USSR. The only exception was the problem of the Lezghins and other Dagestani groups, who now found themselves divided by an international border between the Russian Federation and Azerbaijan. The serious conflicts that developed in the aftermath of the collapse of the USSR were the result of two actions that took place during the Soviet period.

One was Stalin's deportation, and even more so Khrushchev's subsequent "rehabilitation". During World War II several peoples were completely expelled from their homelands and forced to relocate to Central Asia and Siberia. Among them were four North Caucasian peoples – the Chechens, Ingush, Balkars and Karachai. Their autonomies were abolished and their territories were obliterated. Oftentimes, they were renamed and partly annexed by neighboring administrative areas thus ensuring that any sign or memory of their existence in their homelands left with them. In 1956, in what became known as the "Secret Speech", Khrushchev denounced, among other things, the deportations. Afterwards, these peoples were "rehabilitated", and were allowed to return to their lands and their autonomies were reinstated.[17] But the restoration was not complete, as a Karachai leader told a British reporter in 1991:

---

[17] For the "deportations" see, Robert Conquest, *The Nation Killers: The Soviet Deportation of Nationalities* (London, 1970); Alexandre M. Nekrich, *The Punished Peoples: The Deportation and Fate of Soviet Minorities at the End of the Second World War* (New York, 1978); and N. F. Bugai, *The Deportation of Peoples in the Soviet Union* (New York, 1996). For the "deportation" and "rehabilitation" of the Chechens and Ingush, see Moshe Gammer, *The Lone Wolf and the Bear: Three Centuries of Chechen Defiance of Russian Rule* (London and Pittsburgh, 2005), pp. 166 – 183.

It's not like in the United States where the Japanese-Americans who were put in camps during World War II were apologized to and given financial compensation. Or look at the Germans, the way they have apologized to the Jews and banned anything anti-Jewish.

Instead, our repressed peoples came back in the late 1950s either to have their oil exploited in the case of the Chechens, their best lands taken away in the case of the Ingush, their autonomous status removed in the case of the Karachai and, again, a loss of territory in the case of the Balkars.[18]

While there were reasons behind the lack of full restoration of these peoples, the fact that it was not done was the major cause for almost all of the acute conflicts in the Northern Caucasus, including the desire of these peoples for separatism.

The other Soviet deed which contributed to an acute conflict was more specific to Dagestan. Rapid economic development of the lowlands accompanied by sometimes poorly planned and massive resettlement and urbanization rapidly changed the ethnic balance in the lowlands. This process, combined with the results of the partial "rehabilitation" of the Dagestani Chechens, created the most complex conflict in the Northern Caucasus, as shall be described below.

Post-Soviet National Conflicts and Separatism

The current post-Soviet conflicts in the Northern Caucasus can be divided into two categories:

---

[18] Sebastian Smith, *Allah's Mountains: Politics and War in the Russian Caucasus* (London and New York, 1998), p. 91. The references exclude the Prigorodnyi *raiion*, which had been part of Ingushetia but were subsequently annexed to North Ossetia from the reinstated Chechen-Ingush ASSR, the unification of Karachai, which had been a separate AO before the "deportation" with Cherkesia, and the failure to reinstate the pre-"deportation" Balkar districts in the re-established Kabardino-Balkar ASSR.

(1) conflicts between mountain peoples, and (2) conflicts between mountain peoples and external actors. The latter conflicts tend to deteriorate into violent clashes more easily. With one exception, the conflicts between mountain peoples have not deteriorated into armed warfare. The mere fact that such conflicts had emerged at all proves that the Soviet (Stalinist) policy of "divide and rule" has worked beyond all expectations. Most if not all these conflicts in both categories involve either separatism, irredentism or a combination of both. However, with one notable exception no separatist movement has had full independence as its end goal.

Conflicts between Mountain Peoples

All of the conflicts between mountain peoples have their roots in the actions of the Soviet government during and after the Second World War. As was described above, this was the period of "deportation" and "rehabilitation" and the rapid economic development in the 1950s.[19] As mentioned above, the main problems and frictions resulted from an incomplete return to the status quo ante bellum. Gorbachev's liberalization brought all these problems and conflicts to the forefront

---

[19] No national movement in the Northern Caucasus objected – at least not openly – to the political structure and national divisions in the early Soviet period. Even peoples who were divided into two and three separate political entities, such as the Karachai-Balkars and the Circassians (who were divided into Kabartay, Cherkes and Adyghe groups, which had not previous existed) ,conducted their political activity within republican borders. The Circassian *Adyghe kh'ases* (Adyghe Councils), although cooperating with each other, addressed specific problems in its own republic, while the International Circassian Association defined its goal as "to serve the idea of the cultural and historical revival of the Circassian people" – B. Akbashev, "Prophet in his Homeland," *Circassian World*, No. 1 (Spring 1998), p. 7. See Chen Bram, "The Congresses of the International Circassian Association: Dilemmas of an Ethno-National Movement," in: Moshe Gammer (ed.), *The Caspian Region*, Vol. II: *The Caucasus* (London, 2004), pp. 63 – 103, from where this quotation is taken. Since the Balkars and Karachai still saw themselves as one people, they were rather reticient to cooperate. Only in 2000 – 2001 did the Balkar *Malkar Auzy* and the Karachai *Alan* organizations decide "to coordinate their activities, especially in the cultural sphere – the development of spiritual heritage, the preservation of national originality and the re-establishment of objective history" – Quoted in Julietta Meskhidze, "The Events of November 1996 in Kabardino-Balkaria and their Prehistory," in: Moshe Gammer (ed.), *Ethno-Nationalism, Islam and the State in the Caucasus: Post-Soviet Disorder* (tentative title, to be published by Routledge)..

80

when people used their newly established political freedom to create nationalist movements and parties. All of these conflicts – with one exception – reached their peak towards the mid-1990s, but were all self-contained and did not become violent.

The Karachais' main complaint, apart from the lack of personal compensation for their hardships, was the fact that the Karachai AO was not restored, but rather merged with the Cherkess AO. However, any separatist tendency was mitigated by the fact that the Karachai were the larger, and therefore the dominant people in the newly formed AO.

Unlike the Karachai, the Balkars were not given separate autonomy by the Soviets. Balkaria was a separate okrug in the Mountain ASSR. Once Kabarda was designated as an AO in 1922, however, Balkaria, contrary to the will of its populace, as well as some recommendations in Moscow, was forced to combine with Karbada to form the Kabardino-Balkar AO, which was later elevated in status to an ASSR. After the deportation, Balkar lands were partly annexed to Georgia and partly resettled by people from "kolkhozes short of land" in other parts of the republic. When the Balkars were "rehabilitated," the borders were not fully re-established. Another Balkar grievance was the failure of the Kabardino-Balkar authorities to allocate proper financial and other resources to the Balkars. Rather, they later claimed, the authorities treated them "as a 10% minority".[20]

As Gorbachev's perestroika and glasnost reforms began to affect life in the peripheral regions of the USSR in the late 1980's, "Töre – the Balkar Forum" was established in 1990 as a popular movement. Its stated aim was the "full political, legal and economic rehabilitation of the Balkar people." More precisely, this meant figuring out how to ensure the "survival and [the recovery from the] dire economic situation" of the Balkar people and re-establishing "the administrative-territorial integrity of Balkaria." On November 17, 1991 the First Congress of the Balkar People convened and declared the, "national sovereignty of the

---

[20] Ibid.

Balkar people."[21] Thus from the very beginning the Balkar national movement had in it an element of separatism, and to a lesser extant irredentism. However, this separatism was only a symptom of the Balkar nationalist demands to redress the consequences of the deportation and to complete the supposed "rehabilitation".

In March 1994, on the 50th anniversary of the deportation of the Balkars, President Boris Yeltsin publicly apologized for the "injustice" and signed a decree "on the Means for the Rehabilitation of the Balkar People and Statehood and to Support its Revival and Development".[22] Yet, next to nothing was done to implement this decree in the following years. It was only then that Balkar separatism truly surfaced and peaked on November 17, 1996, when the Congress of the Balkar People proclaimed the establishment of an independent Republic of Balkaria as part of the Russian Federation, suspended the Constitution and legislation of the Kabardino-Balkar Republic in Balkarian territory, and requested that the President of the Russian Federation and the Federal Council in Moscow install direct presidential rule in Balkaria.

As stated above, the most complicated conflict where separatism was present developed in Dagestan. The economic development and urbanization of the lowlands accompanied by the massive resettlement from the mountains had changed the old ethno-demographic balance there within a generation and transformed the Kumyks, the Nogais and the Azeris into minorities in their historical homelands. Of the three, the Kumyks felt particularly overwhelmed by this process. In comparison, only a small portion of the formerly nomadic Nogais lived in Dagestan – most of them lived in other parts of the Northern Caucasus – and were not historically attached to their territory in Dagestan. The Azeris in Dagestan represented but a tiny fraction of the titular nation across Russia's southern border. The Kumyks, on the

---

[21] This was but one in a series of such declarations following Yeltsin's call to the various peoples of the USSR to, "take as much sovereignty as you want."

[22] B. M. Zamukalov, *Reabilitatsiia balkarskogo naroda. Istoriia, problemy, resheniia* (Nalchik, 1998), pp. 4 and 184 – 186 (document 38).

82

other hand, felt that they were losing their ancestral lands and becoming a minority in their homeland in the process.

Once Gorbachev's policies of glasnost and perestroika reached the periphery of the USSR in the late 1980s, several Dagestani peoples were quick to establish their separate national movements. Among these were the Kumyks. Their national movement – Tenglik – demanded a cessation of further migration into the lowlands. It also demanded that Dagestan be restructured into a federal republic with full territorial autonomy for each nationality in its historical homeland, regardless of the demographic realities at the time. These demands have been fervently opposed by both the republican government and the Avar national front. This conflict reached a boiling point when it became intertwined the one involving the Aki Chechens.

The primarily Chechen district of Aki (Akinskii raiion) was annexed to the Dagestan ASSR in the 1920s. Its Chechen population was deported on February 23, 1944 along with their Chechen brethren across the border. Laks from central Dagestan were forcibly settled in most of the empty villages and the district was renamed the 'New Lak' (Novolakskii) raiion. To prevent the Lak settlers from returning to their homeland, their original villages – and more importantly, the elaborate system of terraces which enabled agriculture to flourish in the mountains – were destroyed. When the Chechens were "rehabilitated" in the late 1950s, the Aki Chechens were not allowed to return to their original villages and were forced to settle in the towns of Khasav Yurt and Kizil Yurt.

Nevertheless, the Aki Chechens never gave up the dream to return to their ancestral villages and the graves of their forefathers.[23] Under Gorbachev's glasnost they publicly voiced their claims again. This time the Dagestani authorities acknowledged their right to return to their ancestral villages. But in order to do so, a solution had to be found for

---

[23] According to a British observer, the Chechens, "consider ancestors as important as the living, [and] still rise out of their car seats in respect as they drive past cemeteries."— Smith, *Allah's Mountains*, pp. 1 – 2.

the Laks who had settled in this region. It was decided, therefore, to resettle the Laks in the vicinity of Makhachkala, Dagestan's capital city. But, such a massive resettlement threatened to diminish even further the percentage of the Kumyks in their homeland. Tenglik, therefore, warned that it would forcibly resist any such move. The Avar national movement threatened to use force against such steps by Tenglik. The conflict reached its peak in the early 1990's, when thousands of armed Avars and Kumyks confronted each other on several occasions.[24]

It was against this background that the extreme wing of Tenglik demanded separation from Dagestan and the creation of a separate Kumyk autonomous republic within the Russian Federation. Their claim was that the Kumyks had never been part of Dagestan until they had been annexed to the republic by the Soviets in the 1920's. Furthermore, the Kumyks had always had and autonomous and independent state since the times of the Khazars – whom they claimed as forefathers – up to the time of the Russian conquest of the Northern Caucasus in the 19th century.[25]

The Ingush - Ossetian conflict was an exception in several ways: it deteriorated into open warfare; it reached its peak in 1992; and one of its outcomes was a successful case of separatism.

Even before the Soviet era, relations between Ossetians and Ingush were strained.[26] Indeed, the current conflict between them goes back to the deportation. When the Ingush were deported in February 1944, the Prigorodnyi raion (across the Terek River from Vladikavkaz) was re-

---

[24] For these conflicts, see Moshe Gammer, "Walking the Tightrope between Nationalism(s) and Islam(s): The Case of Dagestan," *Central Asian Survey*, Vol. 21, No. 2 (June 2002), pp. 133 – 142 and Moshe Gammer, "The Road Not Taken: Dagestan and Chechen Independence," *Central Asian Survey*, Vol 24, No 2 (June 2005), pp.97- 108; Anna Matveeva, "Dagestan: Interethnic Tensions and Cross-Border Implications," in: Moshe Gammer (ed.), *The Caspian Region*, Vol. II, *The Caucasus* (London, 2004), p. 122 – 131.

[25] Hand-written historical sketch by a Kumyk nationalist leader submitted to the International Alert Fact-Finding Mission, Makhachkala, September 1994 (in author's possession).

[26] And see descriptions in John Frederick Baddeley, *The Rugged Flanks of the Caucasus* (Oxford and London, 1940).

settled by Ossetians and subsequently annexed to the North Ossetian ASSR. When the Ingush were allowed to return to their homeland, and the Chechen-Ingush ASSR was restored, the Prigorodnyi raion remained part of the North Ossetian ASSR and the Ingush were not allowed to return to it. Those who tried to return to their villages faced considerable animosity. Nevertheless, during the Soviet period a considerable number of Ingush managed to unofficially purchase and occupy their former houses but they were never recognized as official residents.[27]

Demands to return the Prigorodnyi raion to Ingush control were raised occasionally during the Brezhnev years.[28] It was natural, therefore, that during Gorbachev's last years, a campaign with that goal in mind unfolded. Encouraged by what looked as Yeltsin's positive stance and faced with growing Chechen threats to secede from (what was still officially) the RSFSR, an Ingush Congress declared on September 15, 1991 a separate Autonomous Republic of Ingusgetia within what would soon be the Russian Federation. Thus, a marginal separatist aim was achieved in what looked as a means to secure Moscow's support in an irredentist one.

However, if the Ingush were seeking to procure the Kremlin's support through this declaration, they were soon to be disappointed. In late October 1992 the Ingush-Ossetian dispute flared up into an armed conflict in which tens of thousands of Ingush were forced out of their homes in the Prigorodnyi raion into refugee camps in Ingushetia.[29]

---

[27] And see Anna Matveeva, "North Ossetia/Ingushetia: A History of the Expulsion and Resettlement of People," in: Paul van Tongeren, Hans van de Veen and Juliette Verhoeven (eds.), *Searching for Peace in Europe and Eurasia: An Overview of Conflict Prevention and Peace Building Activities* (Tha Hague, 2002).

[28] See for example, Gammer, *The Lone Wolf and the Bear*, p. 189.

[29] For the Ingush-Ossetian war, see Julian Birch, "Ossetia: A Caucasian Bosnia in Microcosm," *Central Asian Survey*, Vol. 14, No. 1 (1995), pp. 43 – 74; Human Rights Watch, *The Ingush-Ossetian Conflict in the Prigorodnyi Region* (New York and London, 1993); V. A. Tishkov, *The Mind Aflame: Ethnicity, Nationalism and Conflict in and after the Soviet Union* (London, 1997), pp. 155 – 182.

The Ingush accused Russian peacekeeping troops of siding with the Ossetians.

Conflicts between Mountain Peoples and Outsiders

These conflicts focused on disputes arising from the borders that were demarcated by the Soviet Union in the North Caucasus region in the 1920s. The multi-layer structure of the Soviet Union, in which ASSR's and AO's were created within (and as a part of) constituent republics of the USSR, the Soviet Socialist Republics (SSRs), created what nationalists in the post-Soviet space called "mini-empires." In other words, these were regions in the SSRs that, under the pressure of Russification, developed strong nationalist tendencies and attempted, many times forcefully, to assimilate the minorities of these regions into their own culture and language. Such minorities included both groups given their own autonomies within union republics and groups who were separated from their brethren across SSR borders. In most, if not all cases, this nationalist pressure often had the opposite effect of what was intended. The minorities clung to their own culture(s) as far as possible. When the USSR dissolved, all these minorities found themselves in new states bound on forging cohesion with regards to national identity and homogeneity. In many cases this was a prescription for conflict.

The Lezghin problem involves groups with no autonomous status in Azerbaijan. That might be one reason to why it has not become a violent conflict. The borders drawn in the 1920's divided some of the titular nationalities of Dagestan, making it so that some nationalities' homelands straddled the borders. Included among such affected nationalities were the Avars in Georgia and in Azerbaijan as well as Lezgins, Tats and Tsakhurs in Azerbaijan. While the Avars living across the border constituted only a small portion of their nation, the Lezghins in Azerbaijan accounted for more then a third of the Lezghins and the Tsakhurs and Tats were to be found in larger numbers in Azerbaijan than in Dagestan.

As long as the Soviet Union existed, this divide caused few problems since the borders between Azerbaijan and Dagestan were meaningless. Once the USSR was dissolved, however, all these groups faced national as well as personal daily problems. Overnight, they became cut off from their national, cultural and educational centers. Personally, thousands of people suddenly needed a visa to visit their families, ancestral lands, places of work, markets, etc., which, in many cases, they had previously done on a daily basis.

Of the peoples affected, only the Lezgins had the political clout necessary to solve this problem. The Lezgin national movement, Sadval, demanded a solution to the problems emanating from these new realities. If no satisfactory solution could be found within the existing borders, its moderate wing demanded border changes be made to include all the territories inhabited by Lezgins within Dagestan (and thus within the RF). The more radical wing of Sadval added a separatist dimension to the irredentist demands of its moderate wing: it demanded the establishment of an autonomous republic of Lezginistan, separate from Dagestan, which would include all Lezghin-inhabited territories in both Dagestan and Azerbaijan, within the RF.[30]

The conflict in South Ossetia carried also irredentist as well as a separatist elements, but unlike the case of the Lezghins, the Ossetians were a titular nation in that territory.

The AO of South Ossetia was established in April 1922 as part of the Georgian SSR. In the late Gorbachev years, in response to growing Georgian nationalism, the Ossetian national movement Ademon Nykhas (Popular Front) was formed. It initially demanded greater autonomy for the AO. Afterwards, it sought unification with the North Ossetian ASSR. On September 20, 1990 the South Ossetisan AO declared its independence from Georgia as the South Ossetian Democratic Soviet Republic and requested Moscow's recognition of it

---

[30] For the Lezghin problem, see Anna Matveeva, "Dagestan: Interethnic Tensions and Cross-Border Implications," in: Moshe Gammer (ed.), *The Caspian Region*, Vol. II, *The Caucasus* (London, 2004), pp. 131 – 136.

as an SSR within the Soviet Union. The self-proclaimed republic boycotted the October 1990 elections in Georgia and held its own elections on December 10, 1990. On the following day the Supreme Soviet of the Georgian SSR annulled the elections and abolished the autonomous status of South Ossetia. Georgian police and National Guard units were also sent to South Ossetia, which provoked a war which has continued intermittently to this day.[31]

The conflict in Abkhazia, on the other hand, was purely separatist in nature. The Abkhaz, who inhabit the southwestern area of the Caucasus range are closely related to northwestern Caucasian ethnic groups such as the Circassians, Abaza, Shapsugs. Whether they are native inhabitants of the land or migrants who were preceded by "Georgian tribes" is a matter of dispute between historians on both sides of the divide.[32] In the 19th century, the principality of Abkhazia was peacefully annexed by Russia, but following its abolition in 1864, some 60% of Muslim Abkhaz emigrated to the Ottoman Empire. Between then and 1917 many Armenians, Russians and Georgians subsequently settled in the area.

In 1921 Stalin created a special status for Abkhazia. He turned it into a Soviet Socialist Republic (that is a union republic) associated to the Georgian SSR. However, in 1931 Abkhazia was demoted to an ASSR within the Georgian SSR.[33] Between 1931 and Stalin's death in 1953, many Georgians were encourages to immigrate to Abkhazia. Many Russians settled there as well. Finally, in the 1950s and 1960s the Armenian Church supported a massive migration of Armenians. As a

---

[31] For the conflict, see Jim Potier, *Conflict in Nagorno-Karabakh, Abkhazia and South Ossetia* (The Hague, 2002).
[32] See, for example, M. Lortkipanidze, *The Abkhazians and Abkhazia* (Tbilisi, 1990) on the one hand and O. Bgazhba, "History: First - 18th Centuries", and S. Lakoba, "History: 18th Century – 1917," in: George Hewitt (ed.), *The Aphsuaa Abkhazians: a Handbook* (London, 1999).
[33] The reason behind Abkhazia's special status of Abkhazia was Stalin's personal friendship with Abkhazia's first Soviet leader. When Beria became the party "boss" of Georgia he managed to get in the way of that relationship. From that time until Stalin's death and Beria's execution Abkhazia was controlled personally by Beria even after he moved to Moscow.

result, the Abkhaz became a small minority in the republic named after them.[34]

In the perestroika years, as Georgia moved towards independence, tensions between the Abkhaz and the Georgians grew and Abkhaz nationalists demanded separation from Georgia and the restoration of Abkhazia's pre-1931 status as a union republic. On February 21, 1992, Georgia reinstated its 1921 constitution. Abkahazia declared its independence from Georgia two days afterwards. In response, Tbilisi sent in troops, thus starting a two year war. Aided covertly by Russia and overtly by other North Caucasian peoples, the Abkhaz separatist gained control of the country.[35]

All the above cases have quite a few common features. In none of them did the separatist party aim at establishing an independent state. To the contrary, they wanted to detach themselves from another entity and either join, or remain part of, Russia. In this sense they were all pro-Russian. Furthermore, they all depended on Moscow's goodwill. They all were, therefore, contained, though not solved, through this dependence on Russia.

The conflict in Chechnya is in a category of its own. First, while it was a conflict between mountain peoples and outsiders, its immediate roots were the same as in conflicts between mountain peoples. In other words, the main grievances of the Chechens were in the result of "deportation" and "rehabilitation", not in the national and territorial delimitation of the 1920s.[36] Second, unlike other cases of separatism aimed at external (that is non-Mountain) political units, Chechen separatism was aimed against Russia. Furthermore, Chechen separatists

---

[34] See Daniel Müler, "Ethno-Demographic History: 1886 – 1989," in Hewitt (ed.), *The Aphsuaa Abkhazians*.

[35] For the conflict see, for example, Potier, *Conflict in Nagorno Karabakh, Abkhazia and South Ossetia*.

[36] Indeed, the Chechens in Chechnya have been extremely cautious not to address the problem of the Chechens in Dagestan so as no to arouse suspicions of irredentism, while the Aki Chechens have always referred to their problem as an internal Dagestani matter for the very same reason.

demanded full independence. Finally, Chechnya is the only conflict in the Northern Caucasus to go through two full-scale wars with Russia, the second of which is still not over.

To understand these grievances one has to remember that while not always allowed to resettle in their native lands, on the whole, the Chechens as a whole had a larger territory after their "rehabilitation" in 1958 than in the original, pre-1944 republic. Therefore, on the surface, the Chechens had no territorial grievances. However, there were still two reasons behind their alienation from the Soviet state.

First, although they were publicly "rehabilitated" and their "deportation" declared a crime, the authorities continued to express doubts concerning Chechen loyalty and considered them as having been "pardoned rather than politically rehabilitated."[37] "The deportations were considered non-events. No memorial monuments were erected and there was certainly no mention of what had happened."[38] "People kept quiet as if the tragedy were some sort of collective stigma for which they had to pay," and "middle-aged Chechens, particularly those who had attained prominent administrative posts, curiously referred to their exile period as work on the 'virgin lands'".[39]

The second grievance, which follows from the first, was that Russian dominance in the Chechen-Ingush ASSR was much stronger and more manifest then in any other nominally non-Russian portion of the Soviet Union. In these other regions, a member of the titular nationality was always a figurehead first secretary even though real power rested in the hands of the second secretary, who was almost always a Russian national. For 32 years, the first secretary of the party obkom was a Russian.[40] Only towards the end of Gorbachev's rule, in 1989, and after strong Chechen pressure, was a Chechen nominated as first secretary. The result was that there was no Chechen political elite (other than a

---

[37] Jabrail Gakayev, *Ocherki politicheskoi istorii Chechni (XX vek)* (Moscow, 1997), p. 107.

[38] Smith, *Allah's Mountains*, p. 67.

[39] Valery Tishkov, *Chechnya: Life in a War-Torn Society* (Berkeley, 2004), pp. 25, 26.

[40] For details, see Ibid., pp. 35 – 40.

few individuals) capable of running the country. The detrimental consequences of this fact were revealed in the post-Soviet period.

In Chechnya, unlike in the other republics of the Northern Caucasus, but very similar to what transpired in neighboring Georgia and Azerbaijan, the ex-Communist political elite was replaced by nationalists. In both Azerbaijan and Georgia, the inexperience of the new leadership resulted in considerable damage to their countries and they were soon replaced by the partokratiia. In Chechnya, this did not happen because there was no Chechen partokratiia. Furthermore, the new Chechen leadership lacked not only experience, but also a common language with the Russian (ex-nomenklatura) leadership. This political experience and a common language with Moscow were two important components in the success of the partokratiia in the neighboring autonomous republics to contain their local conflicts. The lack of both experience and a common language were major factors which contributed to the escalation of the Chechen nationalist leadership to supporting full separatism and its inability to find a compromise with Moscow that would prevent war.[41]

The First war in Chechnya (1994 – 1996) ended with a pyrrhic victory for the Chechens. The political, economic, social and cultural infrastructure of the country lay in ruins while, and even more important, the moral structure of its people was destroyed. The chaos during the inter-war period and the second war (1999 – present) only added to the general environment of lawlessness. More important, this ambiance and Russian actions against the (moderate) nationalists only served to enhance the strength of the Islamists, or the "Wahhabis" as they have been called in the post-Soviet space.[42]

From National to Islamic Separatism?

The "return of Islam" began in the Northern Caucasus under Gorbachev's glasnost and was part of the general religious revival in the

---

[41] See Gammer, *The Lone Wolf...*, pp. 206 – 208.
[42] For further details, see Ibid., pp. 208 – 218.

USSR.[43] This was also the first public appearance of foreign extremist Islamic currents, dubbed all over the former Soviet Union as "Wahhabis." In the ideological and legitimacy void that followed the banning of the Communist Party of the Soviet Union and then the dissolution of the USSR itself, one could observe a growing Islamization of politics as both the authorities and some opposition groups turned to Islam for political mobilization and legitimization. This was especially true in Chechnya and Dagestan. Still, Islam played second violin to nationalism.[44]

The first war in Chechnya accelerated the Islamization of Chechen politics and policies.[45] The arrival of foreign – mainly Arab – "Jihadists" played its role in Islamizing Chechen resistance, or at least the language of the resistance, and directing it in the "Wahhabi" direction.[46] But it was the second Chechen war that propelled Islamism into dominating the resistance. More importantly, Chechen leaders who embraced "Islamism", such as Shamil Basayev, were now successful in exporting "Russian decolonization" to other parts of the Northern Caucasus. Thus, Islamic organizations bearing various names have popped up, first in Dagestan and then in other autonomous republics, including Ingushetia, Kabardino-Balkaria, Karachai-Cherkesia and even North Ossetia.

Most of these organizations have called for the establishment of an Islamic state in their republic. Many of these have called for an Islamic state comprising the entire Northern Caucasus. In either case, the establishment of an Islamic state means separation from Russia, unless, as some organizations have noted, Russia embraces Islam. Furthermore, some of these organizations have maintained that they

[43] Bernard Lewis, "The Return of Islam", *Commentary*, January 1975, pp. 39 – 49.

[44] See Gammer, "Walking the Tightrope between Nationalism(s) and Islam(s)."

[45] See Moshe Gammer, "Between Mecca and Moscow: Islam, Politics and Political Islam in Chechnya and Dagestan," *Middle Eastern Studies*, Vol. 41, No. 6 (November 2005), pp. 833 – 848.

[46] See Brian Glyn Williams, "Allah's Foot Soldiers: An Assessment of the Role of Foreign Fighters and Al-Qaeda in the Chechen Insurgency," in: Gammer (ed.), *Ethno-Nationalism, Islam and the State in the Caucasus.*

are connected to the Chechen Islamic resistance and have claimed responsibility for attacks on Russian and local government targets as well as military targets and personnel. They have also not shied away from civilian casualties and acts of terrorism.

The reasons for the proliferation of Islamic opposition groups are rather clear. First is the successful containment of nationalism all over the Northern Caucasus. In Chechnya Moscow crushed it; in the other republics the partokratiias emasculated it by co-optation and other means. The nationalist alternative has, thus, become obsolete. Second is the new Russian policy of re-centralization since the accession of Putin, which has strongly curtailed local autonomy and "elbow room". Third is the targeting of Islam as "the enemy" by republican and central authorities.[47]

The interest of both Moscow and the local authorities in the Northern Caucasus in portraying any opposition as part of a single, unified movement connected to international Islamic terrorism is evident. So is the interest of the Chechens and many of these groups themselves to do so.[48] Does this however, reflect reality? Have all these groups overcome their local, ethnic, national and social interests and grievances? Are they really strongly committed to an Islamic ideology,

---

[47] See Walter Richmond, "Russian Policies towards Islamic Extremism in the Northern Caucasus and Destabilization in Kabardino-Balkaria," in: Gammer (ed.), *Ethno-Nationalism, Islam and the State in the Caucasus*; Chen Bram and Moshe Gammer, *Radical Islamism, Traditional Islam and Ethno-Nationalism in the Northern Caucasus* (to be published by the Hudson Institute, Washington DC).

[48] "The reason for such behavior could perhaps be found in the fact that in a world where 'fundamentalist Islam' is a (if not *the*) major enemy, to be a 'fundamentalist Muslim' is, surprising as it may seem, second best. Admittedly the ticket to join the club is to appear to fight the 'baddies,' (i.e. 'fundamentalist Islam'). This is the position to strive for. However, if one is rejected from, or unable to join the club there are still advantages to be reaped from being a 'fundamentalist,' if one does not overplay one's hand. Such a label carries with it notoriety, nuisance value and a certain amount of bargaining power, since the most obscure group once called by its opponents 'Wahhabi,' or 'fundamentalist' is immediately promoted to the status of the West's enemy No. 1. Perhaps this should not be as surprising as it looks. After all, in a world where 'market economy' is the ideal, this is merely the translation into politics of the laws of supply and demand." – Gammer, "Between Mecca and Moscow," p. 848.

and if so to which one exactly? Have they the same vision of the future? Can one really speak of an Islamic separatism in the Northern Caucasus? Only the future will provide the answers to these questions and many more.

Appendix: The Titular Nationalities in the Northern Caucasus According to the 2002 Census

Republic/Nationality	No. (in Thousands)	% of Population
DAGESTAN		
Avars[49]	815	31.6
Dargins[50]	425	16.5
Kumyks	366	14.2
Lezgins[51]	336	13.0
Laks	140	5.4
Tabasaranians	110	4.3
Nogais[52]	38	1.6
Rutuls	24	0.9
Aguls	23	0.9
Tats[53]	3	0.1

---

[49] Thirteen additional ethnic groups have been officially registered as Avars: Akhvakhs, Andis, Archis, Bakgulals, Botlykhs, Chamals, Didois, Godubers, Kapuchins, Karatais, Khunzalis, Khvarshis and Tindis.

[50] Two additional ethnic groups have been officially designated as Dargins: Kaitaks and Kubachis.

[51] Only less than half of the Lezgins live in Dagestan. The majority of them live in the adjacent areas of northern Azerbaijan.

[52] Only about 42% of the Nogais live in Dagestan. An equal number live in the Stavropol krai, and almost all of the rest – (3,572 according to the 2002 census) in the Chechen Republic.

[53] Tats, particularly in Dagestan, are Caucasian (Mountain) Jews (*gorskie evrei*). Almost all respondents of the 2002 census preferred to designate themselves as "Mountain Jews" or simply as "Jews." Another major concentration of over 1,000 Mountain Jews (Tats) lives in Kabardino-Balkaria according to the census. A great number of Tats live in areas adjacent to Dagestan in northern Azerbaijan, where this name is applied not only to Mountain Jews but also to Muslim (mainly twelver Shi'ites) and Christian (belonging to the Armenian church) speakers of Tat dialects. See Mark Tolts, "Demography of North Caucasian Jewry: A Note on Population Dynamics and Shifting Identity," in Moshe

Tsakhurs[54]	8	0.3
Azeris	111	4.3
Chechens	88	3.4
Russians	121	4.7
Total	**2,576**	**100**

CHECHNYA		
Chechens[55]	1,031	93.5
Total	**1,103**	**100**

INGUSHETIA		
Ingush[56]	361	77.3
Total	**467**	**100**

NORTH OSSETIA-ALANIA		
Ossets[57]	446	62.8
Total	**710**	**100**

KABARDINO-BALKARIA		
Kabartay[58]	500	55.5
Balkars[59]	106	11.8

Gammer (ed.), *Ethno-Nationalism, Islam and the State in the Caucasus: Post-Soviet Disorder* (tentative title, to be published by Routledge).

[54] Only about 34% of the Tsakhurs live in Dagestan. About 63% of them live in Adjacent areas in northern Azerbaijan.

[55] The number of Chechens in Chechnya is clearly inflated while their numbers in neighboring Ingushetia (some 95,000) and Dagestan (about 88,000) are strongly depleted. For the falsifications of the census results in Chechnya, see "Naselenie Chcchni: prqava li perepis'?" *Demoscope Weekly*, September 7, 2005, http://www.polit.ru/research/2005/09/07/demoscope211.html.

[56] There are other Ingush concentrations, including some 21,000 in the Prigorodnyi raiion of North Ossetia as well as another 3,000 that live in Chechnya.

[57] Many more Ossetians live across Russia-Georgia border in South Ossetia.

[58] All three 'Circassian' groups – Adyghe, Kabartya and Cherkes – were grouped together in their three titular republics.

95

Total	901	100

KARACHAI-CHERKESIA

Karachai	169	38.5
Cherkes[60]	51	11.6
Total	**439**	**100**

ADYGEA

Adyghe	109	24.4
Total	**447**	**100**

---

[59] The Balkars and Karachai were grouped together in both their titular republics.

[60] This should also include 32,346 Abaza, a non-titular nationality closely related to, though distinct from the Cherkes. Together they represent some 83,000 people, and account for about 19% of the population.

The Russian Experience with Muslim Insurgencies:

From the North Caucasus in the 19th Century to Afghanistan and Back to the Caucasus

Marie Bennigsen Broxup

Introduction

Moscow is congratulating itself on its resurgence as a world power. The economy is booming thanks to spiraling oil and gas prices; political opposition has been muted, and the press has been effectively gagged. In one year the leadership of the Chechen resistance has been eliminated and the situation, we are assured, is so quiet that Russian troop levels are currently only a mere 45,000 men.[1] Dimitri Kozak, Putin's new henchman in the North Caucasus, is successfully replacing corrupt leaders with efficient technocrats. In short, Chechnya is being thoroughly reconstructed although Western observers have yet to be allowed to witness this transformation first-hand. Of course, all these achievements by the Russian government stand in sharp contrast to the floundering of the USA and the UK, which are bogged down in increasingly violent conflicts in Iraq and Afghanistan.

Barring a few hiccups here and there, we are led to believe that once banditry has been finally curtailed in the North Caucasus, Russia will resume the march towards democracy and the rule of law. But is this positive image realistic? Is the war in Chechnya truly over? Is the

---

[1] These include the Internal Ministry 46th Brigade, which is permanently stationed in Chechnya and the 42nd Division of the Defense Ministry. See Rogozhin's interview in *Rossiiskaia gazeta*, January 20, 2007 and Sergei Ivanov's, Minister of Defense, comments to RIA Novosti, chechnya-sl@yahoogroups.com, Saturday, August 26, 2006: RIAN: "Federal Troops in Chechnya Cut to 20,000: Defense Minister".

country pacified for good and ready to return to the bosom of Mother Russia? Is the unrest in the neighboring republics of Dagestan, Ingushetia, Kabardino-Balkaria and Karachai-Cherkessia merely due to inefficient and corrupt administrations which are being replaced by the pragmatic Putin-Kozak team?

To answer these questions and to assess the future of the Chechen conflict and its impact on the region, we must look at Russia's experience during the conquest of the North Caucasus in the 18th and 19th centuries as well as the numerous insurgencies that followed in this region. A good way to assess this is to look at the situation in this region over the past few centuries in comparison with the more recent Soviet adventure in Afghanistan.

From the Conquest to the End of the Soviet Era

We can distinguish several phases in Russian-North Caucasian relations:

1783-1824

This period saw the beginning of a systemic Russian offensive against the North Caucasus. The fall of the Crimean Khanate and the retreat of the Ottomans after the capture of Azaq in 1783 opened the way for direct confrontation between Russia and the North Caucasus. Totally divided linguistically and socially, the North Caucasians nevertheless vigorously reacted in a unified fashion against Russian incursion. Sheikh Mansur Ushurma, a Chechen Naqshbandi, managed to unify the resistance of the North Caucasus and to inflict the worst defeat ever suffered by the armies of Catherine II in 1785 when a large Russian force was encircled on the bank of the Sunja River and completely annihilated. Mansur was finally defeated and captured during the fall of the Ottoman fortress of Anapa in 1791. His legacy, however, is important to this day; particularly the notion that unity based on the shared Islamic background of the peoples of the North Caucasus was possible.

The Russian offensive continued after the victory at Anapa in 1791, during which time the piedmont was occupied and inroads made into the mountains. The resistance offered by local feudal lords was weak and ruthlessly suppressed by General Ermolov. It was during this time when genocide tactics were first applied against the North Caucasians.

1824-1920

This period was the century of the Ghazawat, the holy wars, which were led by the Dagestani and Chechen Sufi brotherhoods. The period of *muridism* and Shamil's imamate from 1824 to 1859 represents the longest and most heroic military resistance of any small nation against a colonial power. Shamil surrendered in 1859, although his Chechen *naib* (deputy), Baysangur, refused to submit to Prince Bariatinski. He escaped from the defeat at Gunib with a force of 500 men and continued the struggle for another three years in Chechnya.[2] Throughout his rule, and despite his remarkable military and political talents, Shamil never managed to break through the Christian barrier of Ossetia to join forces with the Circassian resistance in the northwest Caucasus.

After Shamil's defeat, Bariatinski was able to turn his attention west where the Cherkess tribes – the Shapsugs, Abadzekhs, and Ubykhs – had been fighting the Russian incursion since the retreat of the Ottoman Empire from the Black Sea in the 1830's.[3] In March 1864, the Ubykhs, the most warlike nation in the northwest Caucasus, were given the choice of being expelled to the Ottoman Empire or to be allowed to resettle outside their native land, a choice that many Cherkess tribes already had to face. In response, the Ubykhs burned their villages before departing from the shores of the Black Sea. The whole Ubykh nation, some 50,000 people who had lived in the Caucasus since antiquity, left for Turkey, resulting in a complete and successful ethnic

---

[2] It is interesting to note that Shamil Basaev claimed to be a descendant of one of the "five hundred" of glorious memory in Chechnya. This was obtained in a communication to the author in April 1996.

[3] The turning point for the Cherkess people and the Northwest Caucasus was the signing of the Treaty of Adrianople between the Ottoman Empire and Russia in 1829.

cleansing.[4]   The Cherkess, the largest nation in the North Caucasus prior to the Russian conquest, were also victims of ethnic cleansing. The majority left for the Ottoman Empire, leaving only a small populace behind.   Thus on May 21, 1864, the Governor General of the North Caucasus, Grand Duke Michael, was able to announce the "official pacification" of the North Caucasus to St. Petersburg.[5]

The North Caucasus was thus devastated and occupied by an army of a half million. Logically this should have been the end of history for this turbulent region.   However, this was not to be and the announcement that Chechnya and the rest of the North Caucasus was "pacified" would come to haunt the Russians for decades.   The harshness of Russian rule in Chechnya and Dagestan with its attendant executions, deportations and religious persecutions had a logical outcome.   In 1877 and 1878 Dagestan and Chechnya were aflame again.   Once more the Sufi brotherhoods – the Naqshbandia and Qadiria – led the insurrection. When the rebellion was crushed all the leaders were executed and thousands of *murids* were exiled to Siberia.   The relative generosity shown to Shamil by Alexander II, in a pale imitation of the French treatment of Abdel Qadir, was no longer the flavor of the day.

The 1917 Revolution gave the North Caucasians hope of overthrowing colonial rule.   For a short time the nationalist elites took the lead in joining forces to create a confederate state – the Mountain Republic. The Republic, however, was short lived for it was engulfed in the Russian Civil War, which was as ferocious and confusing in the North Caucasus as anyplace.   Four adversaries faced off against each other: the Bolsheviks (primarily composed of ethnic Russians and native peoples), Caucasian nationalists, the White armies (primarily consisting of Denikin, Kuban and Terek Cossacks), and the Sufi brotherhoods. Several outsiders also took part in the conflict, including Lazar Bicherakhov's army, which was equipped by the British, the Turks, the

---

[4] The Ubykhs were a nation related to the Cherkess. They formed a military alliance with the Shapsugs and Abadzekhs and were the leaders of the resistance in the Northwest Caucasus.

[5] Georges Dumezil, *Documents anatoliens sur les langues et les traditions du Caucase*, Paris, Institut d'Ethnologie Musée de l'Homme, 1965, 269 pp.

Azerbajani Mussavatists (nationalists), the Georgians and Armenians. In spring 1920 Azerbaijan and Georgia fell to the Soviets and the White Army was defeated. Only two adversaries were left: the Russian Bolsheviks and the Sufi brotherhoods. The war that erupted in August 1920 was short (it ended in May 1921) but extremely brutal – no quarter was given and there were no survivors on the Caucasian side. This was the last uprising to be led jointly by the Chechen and Dagestani Sufi brotherhoods.

1922-1991

This was, of course, the Soviet period. From 1922 to 1944 the history of Chechnya and Dagestan was an almost uninterrupted succession of rebellions, punitive reprisals and individual terror campaigns culminating in two serious uprisings in Chechnya-Ingushetia in 1940 and 1942, led respectively by Hassan Israilov, a Communist-educated journalist, and Mairbek Sheripov, the brother of famous Chechen revolutionary, Aslanbek Sheripov. These two uprisings, of which we know very little, were important enough to prompt the Soviets to savagely bomb Chechen mountain villages. By spring 1942 the villages of Shatoy, Itumqala and Galanchozh had more dead citizens than living ones.[6]

On February 23, 1944, the Chechens and Ingush were deported en masse in appalling conditions to Kazakhstan. Nearly a third of those deported died en route.[7] Even after Stalin's death and the subsequent partial rehabilitation of the Chechens, which allowed them to return to Chechnya from Kazakhstan, the Chechens were still forbidden to settle in Grozny, which remained a Russian city. There was no *korenizatsia* in Chechnya-Ingushetia – the leadership of the republic and of the Communist Party was kept firmly in Russian hands. The Chechens remained second-class citizens in their own homeland. (It was only in

---

[6] Abdurahman Avtorkhanov, "The Chechens and Ingush During the Soviet Period and its Antecedents", in: Marie Bennigsen et al, *The North Caucasus Barrier: The Russian Advance Towards the Muslim World*, Hurst & Co, London, 1992, p. 183.

[7] Also deported as whole nations were the Crimean Tatars, Karachays, Balkars, Volga Germans, the Kalmyks, and the Meskhetian Turks.

1989 that a Chechen was finally nominated First Secretary of the Communist Party of the Chechen-Ingush Autonomous Republic.) At the same time that this political apartheid was taking place, an anti-religious campaign was launched to eradicate Islam in the region.

A notable feature of tsarist rule in Chechnya was the maintenance of an occupation army and a military administration even after the nominal pacification in 1864. Similarly the Soviets were obliged to garrison an army in Chechnya until the deportation of 1944. Many Chechen separatists pride themselves that every generation since the conquest has continued their struggle against the Russians. After a 50-year interregnum from 1944 to 1994, the bloody cycle of rebellion and repression is being re-enacted.

Several significant changes occurred after the Russian Revolution:
1) After 1921 there were no concerted efforts by the North Caucasians to throw off Russian rule (except the short-lived action of the Assembly of North Caucasian Peoples in Abkhazia in 1992). This has since been changed with the recent espousal of the military *Jamaat* sponsored by Abdul Halim Sadulaev and Shamil Basaev before their deaths. The deportation created a subsequent wedge between the Chechens and their traditional Dagestani allies. During and after the deportation the Soviets encouraged the fomenting of old enmities in North Caucasian society. The Chechens were depicted as people who deserved deportation for their many crimes. The negative depiction of Chechens in Russian society had not changed since a civil servant, Platon Zubov, wrote in 1834 that Chechens were a nation "remarkable for [their] love of plunder, robbery and murder, for [their] spirit of deceit, [their] courage, recklessness, resolution, cruelty, fearlessness, [their] uncontrollable insolence and unlimited arrogance... The Chechens spend their lives plundering and raiding their neighbors who hate them for their ferocity..."[8] For good

---

[8] Platon Zubov, *Kartina Kavkazskogo kraia prinadlezhashchego Rossii i sopredel'nykh emu zemel*, St Petersburg, A. Vingeber, 1834, 2 volumes.

measure he added: "The only way to deal with this ill-intentioned people is to destroy them to the last…" After the Chechen victory of August 1996, even prior to Basaev's ill-fated expedition into Dagestan in summer 1999, the Russian government was particularly active in sowing discord between Chechnya and Dagestan. Between 1997 and 1999, if one was to believe Dagestani newspapers and public opinion, thousands of Dagestanis, mainly women of all ages, were kidnapped by Chechen bandits and detained in various cellars across Ichkeria.

2) In the 19th century the mountains of Dagestan and Chechnya were renowned throughout the Muslim world for their theologians and Arabic scholars. Generations of anti-religious propaganda have since left the large majority of the peoples of the North Caucasus without any kind of classical religious education. As a result they are easy prey to any charlatan with a smattering of Arabic and a wife in a *hijab* who claims to educate them in "proper" Islam. The danger that Abdul Halim Sadulaev presented Moscow, unlike his predecessors Dudaev and Maskhadov, was the fact that he was an *alim* and thus able to provide the impetus for a pan-Caucasian religious movement.

The Character of Past Conflicts: Policies and Ideology

After crushing the Basmachi Revolt in Central Asia and defeating the North Caucasians in the 1920s, the only serious Soviet military adventure in a Muslim country was the invasion of Afghanistan. Are there any new dimensions in this present conflict in the North Caucasus that were not present in the other conflicts with Muslim nations? Do today's Russian leaders have any reason to assert that, contrary to all other colonial powers and their Soviet predecessors in Afghanistan, they have a magic recipe to convince the Chechens to become docile Russian Federation citizens after 13 years of war? What conditions existed that allowed Tsarist Russia and the Bolsheviks to win the long war against Imam Shamil and the insurrection of 1920? And what was the cost of the victory to the Empire?

Throughout its history Russia has used certain strategies in dealing with its Muslim dominions. Some were more successful than others:

1) *Settlement of peasant colonies, such as the Cossacks into the disputed region.* Often the colonization preceded the military conquest. In the past this process was meant to be irreversible. Today this is no longer possible due to the dramatic demographic decline of the Russian population. Even long-established Cossack colonies are today leaving the North Caucasus.

2) *Assimilation through Russification or Sovietization.* Assimilation only worked with the Tatars, although after 400 years of co-habitation it can hardly be called a full-fledged success – at least half of the Kazan Tatars still speak their native language, are conscious of their different ethnic identity and have remained at least nominally faithful to Islam. In the case of Chechnya, Dagestan and Ingushetia there was no attempt at assimilation. In Chechnya a new generation is growing up without speaking Russian. When compounded with the xenophobia currently exhibited by the Russian populace, co-habitation no longer seems like a viable option. Even Russians who had lived in Grozny and then returned to Russia have found it difficult to readjust and to be accepted by their fellow countrymen – they are often considered to be "tainted" by the Chechens.

3) *Co-opting the elites.* In the North Caucasus, this stratagem worked with the Kabardian aristocrats, although they frequently shifted allegiance between the tsars, the Crimean khans and Ottoman sultans.[9] This option is still possible in

---

[9] Chantal Lemercier-Quelquejay, "Co-optation of the Elites of Kabarda and Dagestan in the Sixteenth Century", in Marie Bennigsen et al, opus cit., pp. 19-44.

many parts of the North Caucasus, as Dimitri Kozak is currently proving, although it is less effective in Chechnya where most of the elites have been killed or are in exile (the *Kadyrovtsy* can never be categorized as elite). But is this strategy durable? What incentives are the Russian state willing to offer in terms of power sharing? Economic benefits alone have seldom proved sufficient.

4) *Expulsion, deportation and genocide.* Although attempted several times in the North Caucasus, genocide and expulsion has never worked in the case of the Chechens. Even Stalin failed to solve the "Chechen problem."

The Russian officers sent to conquer the North Caucasus in the 19th century were the elites of their time: grand dukes, generals haloed by victory over Napoleon, the most famous poets and writers. They had no ideology nor any viable economic incentive to offer the native peoples as they were too poor and Chechen oil was not an issue then. They had, however, the conviction that Russia had a divine right to impose its rule and superior way of life upon what were seen as savage natives.

The ideology of the North Caucasians in the 19th century was that of Ghazawat, or Jihad, and freedom, which they deemed an inalienable right. This ideology has survived to this day. Every North Caucasian knows what it stands for although it bears little resemblance to present day "Jihad" as interpreted by Mowladi Udugov. It was propagated by the free (*uzden*) mountain communities that had not known, or had rejected, feudal rule. A Dagestani scholar described it recently in this manner, "The aim of this great war had been based on the unconditional recognition of the right of each people to sovereignty and the right of each person to freedom."[10] Muhammad Al-Yaraghi,[11]

---

[10] Dibir Mahomedov, "On the Social Aims and Spiritual Ideals of the Mountaineers During the Caucasian War", *Central Asian Survey*, 2002, vol. 21, No 3, pp. 245-248.

[11] He was the teacher of the first three Imams – Ghazi Muhammad, Hamzat Bek and Shamil.

the first Naqshbandi sheikh to call for Jihad in the North Caucasus, preached:

> "As long as we remain under the rule of the infidels we are covered with shame. The prayers of the slaves are not heard in Heaven… All your ablutions, prayers and pilgrimages to Mecca, your repentance and sacrifices, all your holy deeds are invalid as long as the Muscovites supervise your life…"[12]

The Sufi sheikhs who led the 1920-1921 uprising espoused the same ideals of Ghazawat and freedom. Najmuddin Samurskii, First Secretary of the Communist Party of Dagestan and a fierce opponent of the Sufi leaders, described the Sufi leaders in this way:

> "These men were among the most famous scholars of the entire Muslim world…They were haloed by the glamour of a deep learning and their words were as sacred as the law itself…but at the same time they belonged to the people… they were armed with the same sword and rifle and in battle they were the leaders fighting in the forefront; they were the bearers of a certain democracy…which was the very essence of Shamil's rule; they were the defenders of national independence…"[13]

During the Soviet *reconquista* of the Caucasus in the 1920s, the Bolsheviks were fired up by revolutionary zeal. Furthermore, they had the support of some of the Chechen and Dagestani population and elites. The Red Armies fighting against the rebels in 1920 (the 11th Army from Astrakhan and part of the 9th Army) were entirely Russian

---

[12] Anna Zelkina, "Jihad in the Name of God: Shaykh Shamil as the Religious Leader of the Caucasus", *Central Asian Survey*, 2002, vol. 21, No 3, pp. 249-264, quoting F. von Bodenshtâdt, *Die Volker des Kaukasus und ihre Freiheitkâmpfe gegen die Russen*, Berlin, 1855.

[13] Najmuddin Samurskii, *Dagestan*, Moscow and Leningrad, 1925, p.128.

but Caucasian partisans acted as scouts in difficult and unknown terrain which played a role in the rapid victory.

Those North Caucasians who sided with the Bolsheviks, including nationalists like Najmuddin Samurskii or religious leaders like the Sufi sheikhs Ali of Akusha and Ali Mitaev,[14] were swayed by Lenin's promises of independence and were convinced that the freedom they longed for would be achieved through the Revolution. Thus, they were different than Chechens today who back Moscow and do not seem to care for independence. Anna Politkovskaia, in one of her last articles, had these damning words to describe the partisans of Ramzan Kadyrov, the pro-Russian Chechen prime minister:

> "We can say that for most of the Kadyrovtsy... the decision to side with the federal forces in the war is not politically motivated. It is a convenient way of achieving their own objectives with the state's assistance, ensuring their own security and providing them with a guaranteed income for a while. Members of these detachments are involved in abductions; they murder and torture people, and their cruelty has long since rivaled that of the 'death squads' made up of federal special service members. A substantial number of Chechnya's so-called security and law enforcement agencies these days have been established with the participation, and under the direct leadership, of people who have committed premeditated murder and abduction."[15]

---

[14] Respectively Dagestani Naqshbandi and Chechen Qadiri. In the case of Ali of Akusha it was his enmity with Najmuddin Gotsinski that prompted him to side with the Bolsheviks. Ali Mitaev was a member of the Chechen Revolutionary Committee – Revkom. Both men were executed in 1925 and 1926.

[15] Anna Politkovskaia, "The Real Nature of Chechnya's Security and Law Enforcement Agencies", Novaia gazeta, No 74, September 28, 2006, translation by chechnya-sl@yahoogroups.com, September 29, 2006.

The decision not to engage any respected Chechen personality or group in a political dialogue is one of Russia's many failures today. The only figure in Moscow with any influence in Chechnya is Ruslan Khasbulatov, the former speaker of the Duma. Although he opposed Dzhokhar Dudaev and the independence movement during the mid-1990's, he has since distanced himself from the various Chechen "lobbies" in Moscow and has accused Putin's regime of "deliberately turning Chechnya into a military-police enclave under a mini-Saddam Hussein."[16] (referring to the late Ahmad Kadyrov, who was milder than his son, Ramzan)

The emphasis put on Ramzan Kadyrov's Chechen militias and the "Chechenization" of the conflict is more reminiscent of the policy used by the Soviets in Afghanistan rather than that used by Russians in previous Caucasian wars.

What Comparisons with Afghanistan?

The Soviet intervention in Afghanistan brought mayhem and devastation which has continued long after the end of the war. Could this happen in Chechnya after the end of the current conflict? Many comparisons have been made between Afghanistan and Chechnya, including the warning that the withdrawal of Russian troops would precipitate civil war and a Taliban style regime in the republic. Many of these comparisons, encouraged by Kremlin spin-doctors, are absurd but they have given rise to a certain myth about what could happen after the end of the war. What are the similarities and differences between Chechnya and Afghanistan that could justify this myth?

Society

The most important distinctions are found in the social and ethnic structures of the two countries. Afghanistan is a multi-national country made up of Pushtun, Tajik, Uzbek, Turkmen, Hazara, Nuristani, and so

---

[16] Interview conducted by Andrei Riskin for *Nezavisimaia gazeta*, "Peace in Russia Requires the Intervention of the International Community", April 10, 2003, Johnson's Russia List, No. 7140, April 10, 2003.

forth. Afghanistan is dominated by the Pushtuns, who are themselves divided into two main tribal units that often compete with each other (the Durranis and Ghilzais). There are two official languages, Pashto and Dari, not to mention many other unofficial ones. There are several religious factions, with the majority being Sunnis but with important Shia and Ismaili minorities. Afghan society is usually endogamic, especially the Pushtuns.

On the other hand, the Chechens are one nation with one religion and one language. They have extremely strong taboos about marrying within the same clan. This exogamic tradition is still so strong today that it is even frowned upon to marry within the same village, even if the bride and groom belong to different clans. Although clan (*taip*) obligations, such as vendetta, are strictly patrilineal, most clans are maternally related. This helps to forge loyalties and solidarity across society and clans, and encourages channels of communication between Chechens, even those who are on opposite sides, politically and militarily. The sense of national unity was reinforced in the past by the Sufi brotherhoods and by the common tragedy of the deportation. One of the many tragedies of this latest war is that this social fabric that has helped the Chechens survive generations of national strife is in danger of disintegrating.

Despite these basic differences between Afghans and Chechens, there are some similarities. Chief among these is the survival of blood feuds and strong customary law, *adat*, often prevailing over Sharia law, as well as the presence of powerful Sufi brotherhoods. In Afghanistan as in Chechnya, religious authority belonged to the Sufi families. Both the Afghans and the Chechens live in rugged, mountainous regions and can be described as "martial races" with a strong code of honor (Pukhtunwali). Both nations were (and still are) renowned for their "insolence" and refusal to bow to colonial power.

Religious Movements

After the April 1978 coup, the Communist government of Nur-Muhammad Taraki and Hafizullah Amin began a wholesale slaughter

109

of religious families, Shia clergy and young fundamentalists. In January 1979, presumably on the advice of the Soviets, all the men of the Mojaddidi clan (the most important Naqshbandi family of Afghanistan) were secretly assassinated in one night and all the women and children rounded up and sent to Pul-e Charki Prison. The Soviets did not try to co-opt the tariqat as they did in the North Caucasus. They believed that Afghanistan was ripe for communism. They were confident that they did not need unreliable allies because they effectively controlled the Afghan army, which was trained in the USSR.

Despite the predominance of the Sufi brotherhoods, there was an important difference in the religious development of the two countries. Unlike Afghanistan, at the beginning of the war in 1994, Chechnya did not have an indigenous fundamentalist/Salafi movement. Sharia was never really a factor in Chechnya. The first small Wahhabi groups appeared in Chechnya around 1990, having been "imported" from Dagestan, and were led by a Jordanian Chechen, Fathi, a former companion of Gulbuddin Hekmatyar. Between 1991 and 1994 the movement made no inroads whatsoever. With the onset of the war the situation changed. In 1995, Khattab, a Saudi Salafi jihadist, arrived in Chechnya to form and train a battalion of foreign volunteers. Flush with money, he was able to attract young Chechens in search of weapons and ammunition, not to mention those looking for some sort of glory or other deeper meaning in their participation in this national liberation movement. The spectacular ambush of a Russian column in the mountains in Yaryshmardy in April 1996, which killed some 100 soldiers, increased Khattab's, and therefore the Wahhabis', prestige out of all proportion to their military achievements.[17]

In the inter-war period (1997-1999), Chechen Wahhabis were more interested in seizing power from Maskhadov's government and

---

[17] Khattab and his Wahhabi companions gained a lot of prestige because of this operation. This, combined with the money they had at their disposal, facilitated their nefarious activities in the inter-war period. It is the belief of many people in Chechnya that it was Shamil Basaev who planned this operation, which was typical of Chechen tactics. This is likely as it was the one and only successful military operation conducted by Khattab against the Russians.

wreaking havoc than in any true religious discourse or in strengthening Chechen independence. Their real priority was the establishment of a Sharia state that they could control. They nearly achieved their goals. However, their excesses and arrogance combined with attacks on the Sufi *tariqat* and their rejection of nationalism quickly alienated the majority of the populace. The public execution of an adulterous couple in Grozny in 1997, imposed by young Wahhabis in a Sharia court, shocked many. The assassination attempts on Maskhadov, the violent clashes in Gudermes with government forces in summer 1998, and the disastrous summer 1999 expedition into Dagestan convinced many Chechens that the interests of the nation and those of the Wahhabi faction were not the same. Their conduct during the present war has done little to revive their prestige. Wahhabi politicians were the first to flee the ferocious bombing of the country. None of the Wahhabi units participated the long and desperate siege of Grozny between October 1991 and February 2000. When the Chechen forces were finally forced to withdraw from Grozny, the Wahhabis failed to appear at the rendezvous point to re-supply and assist the retreating troops. As a result of this betrayal, Chechen forces suffered their worst casualties since 1994 when 847 fighters died in the battle of Komsomol'skaia. The Chechens like to joke, "they are leaving Chechnya because it was not Jihad but suicide!"

Afghanistan on the other hand had a long established Wahhabi tradition going back to the 17th century, which was a reaction to Akbar's syncretism, and grew considerably in the early 19th century during the struggle against the British. The period from 1963 to 1973 was marked by a growth of left-wing ideology within Afghanistan. This led to inevitable conflict between fundamentalist and communist factions. Left-wing parties, led by Khlaq, took advantage of the freedom of activity allowed by the Afghan Constitution of 1963 to publicize their anti-religious views. This soon provoked an obvious reaction, initially among intellectuals in Kabul University, which sparked a fundamentalist movement comparable to that of the Ikhwan al-Muslimin. By the time Taraki and Amin came to power, this movement was already well-organized and its leaders were able to establish resistance parties from Peshawar where Gulbuddin

111

Hekmatyar and Professor Rabbani had fled. The Taliban movement therefore arose in a terrain that was already well prepared by fundamentalists like Hekmatyar and his ilk. All it needed was the additional leavening of rural Pushtun conservatism and illiteracy.

The Resistance

Afghan resistance was divided, geographically and ethnically. The six official resistance parties in Peshawar never managed to form a real alliance. In Afghanistan itself, fighting techniques, organization and capabilities varied from one front to another on the basis of tribal or ethnic affiliation. A Western observer, Edward Girardet, noted that a bombing, a Soviet offensive or the death of a guerrilla commander could change the situation of one particular region in a matter of days.[18] The resistance never formed a coherent strategy. There were few large-scale operations. The Mujahidin were usually organized in small and highly mobile hit-and-run units that proved effective against the Soviet forces. They concentrated on ambushes, the mining of roads, assassinations, and rocket attacks on enemy positions. To use the terminology applied to Chechnya today, it was a "low intensity" conflict until the resistance was supplied with Stinger missiles in 1986.

Numerous bloody clashes occurred among the Mujahidin, usually involving the most radical party, Gulbuddin Hekmatyar's Hezb-i Islami, and other groups. Afghans frequently accused Hekmatyar of undermining the resistance and suspected him of working with the Soviets. After the withdrawal of the Soviet troops when the Mujahidin tried to establish a government in Kabul, Hekmatyar showed no compunction in ordering the bombardment of Kabul to force his government colleagues out.[19]

The Chechens, despite Russian misconceptions and disinformation about their lack of unity, have always adhered to strict military

---

[18] Edward Girardet, "Russia's War in Afghanistan", *Central Asian Survey*, 1983, volume 2, No 1, pp.83-109.

[19] It is interesting to note that Chechens often assume that the most radical Wahhabis are working for the Russians.

discipline in wartime. Aslan Maskhadov was the commander-in-chief, subordinates swore allegiance, followed his orders and coordinated with him. It was Maskhadov, a better general than politician, who planned the brilliant recapture of Grozny in March and August 1996, and the later defense of the city in 1999-2000. His strategic thinking was evident in the development of the war, from conventional warfare to sophisticated urban guerrilla tactics. The Chechen forces had one strategy and a unified leadership although tactics varied between individual commanders and units. Generally they remained true to the traditional approach of Caucasian warfare, "unseen but everywhere," that denied the Russians any lasting control of the territory.

Whatever the political differences between Maskhadov and Basaev, they were put aside during the war. Their ultimate goal was the same: independence for Chechnya. They diverged only in their thoughts on how this could be best achieved. The same unity and authority was obvious in the short-lived leadership of Abdul Halim Sadulaev, but is too early to say whether Doku Omarov will have the same sway. His task is daunting given the loss of his best commanders.

Soviet Tactics in Afghanistan

Russia's military and political tactics rarely change. As in Chechnya today, the Afghan civilian population suffered the heaviest from bombing, heavy artillery offensives, anti-personnel mines and massacres in areas where the resistance was active. Villages were also razed. Cattle and crops were destroyed. The following are just a few examples of these hideous tactics. In early 1982, in Shomali, north of Kabul, hundreds of men, women and children were gunned down or executed. Also in 1982, a combined Soviet-Afghan offensive in Logar province resulted in 2,000 dead, the majority of whom were civilians. In an event in September 1982 that resembled the massacre of Khaibakh in 1944 and Samashki in April 1995, Soviet troops burned 105 people alive in an irrigation tunnel in Logar province. Approximately one million Afghans died during the war and the refugees numbered over five million as its peak. One has to remember that Afghanistan has a population estimated at 15-20 million at the beginning of the war. The casualty and emigration figures are proportionally similar in Chechnya.

Since the days of Stalin, Moscow has distrusted its military. In Chechnya this distrust has resulted in a competition between troops of the Ministry of Defense and those of the Ministry of Internal Affairs (MVD). This mistrust has also resulted in a lack of communication during operations not to mention sabotage between forces. In Afghanistan many reports indicated that, from the start of the campaign, the KGB disagreed with the army on how to handle the resistance. By 1981 the KGB gained at least a major role in determining which tactics to use, including use of informers, agents provocateurs, financial payoffs, and other means to attract tribes, political parties, and guerrilla commanders. KHAD (the Afghan KGB), directed by Soviet advisers, also tried a tactic later favored by the Russians in Chechnya. They used volunteer militias composed of unruly youths and thugs masquerading as mujahadeen in order to bring chaos to the countryside and discredit the resistance. As the war progressed and the military campaign faltered, the Soviets came to rely increasingly on KHAD as opposed to the Afghan army.

How Many Troops to Subdue Chechnya?

In Afghanistan the invading Soviet force numbered 85,000 troops, a figure which increased to approximately 105,000 later in the war. It was backed up by the Afghan army, which had some 35,000 or 40,000 troops at the beginning of the conflict. Very soon, however, with increasing defection to the mujahadeen, the Afghan army had shrunk to 20,000 or 25,000. The Soviets understood quickly that they could only count on the Afghan army to act as cannon fodder. It is impossible to give an exact estimate of the number of full-time Afghan fighters against the Communist forces. Figures vary between 100,000 to 150,000, but these do not include the hundreds of thousands of civilians and refugees who took part in the war on a part-time basis. One could therefore say that forces were rather evenly matched against each other.

By contrast Russia has never spared military manpower in the North Caucasus. Prince Bariatinski deployed 40,000 men to force Shamil's surrender and capture Gunib, a small mountain village on a rocky promontory. Precise estimates for the contingent in 1994-1996 and after 2000 in Chechnya are difficult given Russia's penchant for secrecy and contradictory official statements. In 1994-1996 Russian invading troops numbered between 38,000 and 45,000 but the Chechen high command reckoned that the Russians had approximately 200,000 men at their disposal taking into account the total number of troops in the North Caucasus Military District who could be called up at short notice, including various forces of the MVD, spetnaz, FSB, OMON, FSB, ALPHA group, as well as ordinary militia units.

In January 2000, after three months of heavy bombing, Russia launched another ground offensive against Grozny with, according to the Kremlin spokesman Sergei Iastrzhembski, 93,000 men (57,000 of which came from the Defence Ministry and the remaining 36,000 from the MVD). The population of Chechnya numbered approximately 800,000.

At the height of the 1994-1996 war, Maskhadov never had more than 6,000 armed men, not for lack of volunteers but of weapons and ammunition. In 2000, Maskhadov claimed that he had an "active reserve" of 15,000.[20] Present figures from the resistance are not available, but there can be little doubt that the number of "regular" fighters has dramatically declined given the overwhelming Russian military presence. (Some weapons used by these Russian forces include not only heavy flamethrowers which are strictly forbidden by the Third Protocol of the 1980 Geneva Convention against military targets in populated areas, but also "Tochka" and "Tochka-U" ballistic missiles.) The use of suicide commandos in July 2000 in an operation against an MVD base was the first sign of growing desperation among the resistance.

---

[20] Personal communication to the author.

It is difficult to give accurate estimates of the losses suffered by the Soviet army in Afghanistan. At the end of the war, the Soviet military hinted that there were around 15,000 troops killed, which seems to be a rather unrealistic figure due to the fact that Western observers had been reporting that figure in the early 1980's. Similarly, Western diplomats in Moscow, referring to unofficial Soviet sources, were quoting 30,000 dead by 1983.[21] Other estimates mentioned that 100 Soviets died per week. The casualty ratio was reckoned to be 20 dead Soviets for every dead guerrilla. In Chechnya we can only guess at the total Russian military casualties but some Russian sources postulate that they have been as heavy as in Afghanistan. Estimates fluctuate widely between 15,000 and 40,000 men or more. All we know for certain is that two brigades and a full regiment ("Maikop", "Volgograd" and "Samara"), totaling some 4,000-5,000 men, were wiped on the night of on December 31, 1994 in Grozny after the then-Minister of Defense, Pavel Grachev, boasted that he all he needed to conquer the city was a regiment of paratroopers and two hours.

What Future for Chechnya?

After the capture of Grozny in February 2000 the Kremlin announced that it had quashed the resistance. Only some 1,000 men supposedly remained in ragtag groups of 10 to 30 fighters. Over the past seven years, similar statements have regularly been made with only slight variations. For example, on December 1, 2006, General Nikolai Rogozhkin announced that, "there are between 800 and 1,000 members of illegal armed groups in Chechnya...They could be operating from either the mountains or the plains. They are moving all the time and many militants are trying to register in villages and cities."[22] Two months later, Russian Deputy Interior Minister and Chief of Staff of the federal forces in the North Caucasus, General Arkadi Edelev, claimed

---

[21] Edward Girardet, opus cit.
[22] Interfax, December 1, 2006, quoted by chechnya-sl@yahoogroups.com, December 2, 2006.

116

that there were only 450 militants operating in Chechnya (including 30 foreigners), and that their number was decreasing all the time. He optimistically assumed the forthcoming demise of the new Chechen leader, Doku Omarov, but added that it was very hard to tack him down, "because he hides in places that are difficult to access, where any major troop movement is difficult to see."[23]

These insignificant figures and the daily declarations that scores of Chechen fighters have been killed or have taken up government offers of amnesty have prompted the Defense Minister, Sergei Ivanov, to announce a withdrawal of troops at some unspecified future date. Only those units "permanently" quartered in Chechnya will remain, which will include 23,000 men of the Defense Ministry 42nd Division, 24,000 men of the 46th Interior Ministry (MVD) Motor Rifle Brigade, and some 17,000 Chechen pro-Russian militia, the majority being Kadyrov's partisans, who do not show the same reluctance in pounding their own people as the Afghan army did.[24] The number of troops on "temporary" service in Chechnya has not been revealed for some time.

Moscow now states that Chechnya is the quietest region of the North Caucasus. Grozny is being reconstructed. Indeed the façades of the main streets are being repainted, and the peace-loving younger Kadyrov is shown to be endowing schools, hospitals, building fountains, and so on, in a display that Prince Potemkin would have admired. Dimitri Kozak now claims that the main factor destabilizing southern Russia today is corruption as nobody is concerned about terrorist activity and crime levels.

This rosy picture is similar to that painted by Russian generals on the eve of the capture of Grozny on August 6, 1996. On July 28, 2006, General Pulikovski, commander-in-chief of the Federal Forces in Chechnya, declared on "Russia TV" that, "there was little fighting because there are too few Chechen rebels." He was supported by the

---

[23] Interfax, February 1, 2007, quoted by chechnya-sl@yahoogroups.com, February 2, 2007.
[24] See among others *Nezavisimaia gazeta*, July 12, 2006, p. 5. Although the Russians are regularly talking about troop withdrawal, the figures of those deployed have not changed from those announced in 2001.

then-Minister of Defense, Igor Rodionov, who claimed that, "important battles are not occurring anymore. Our work consists of identifying isolated bands and giving them an ultimatum to surrender."[25] Three days later, as Shamil Basaev proclaimed that he controlled Grozny, ITAR-TASS "World Service" was quoting General Kvashnin, Commander in Chief of the North Caucasus Military District, as saying, "small groups of fighters must be neutralized by special operations but it is not necessary to hurry because we the situation is under control."[26]

Today the Kremlin is relying on two primary tactics to control Chechnya: 1) "Chechenization", i.e. having Ramzan Kadyrov's units police the country and destroy the resistance. Thus any mistakes, war crimes and atrocities can be blamed on the Chechens and the conflict can be presented as an internecine one. A similar policy was attempted without success in Afghanistan under Babrak Karmal and Najibullah; 2) reverting to Stalin's days of "*chekist*" operations, which were used successfully against nationalist insurgencies in Ukraine, the Baltic republics and Chechnya-Ingushetia. This means giving overall command to the FSB rather than the military, and then installing permanent garrisons in Chechen villages (in 1994-1996 Russian troops avoided entering villages) with the FSB leading the troops and designating the targets.

Both tactics are a sign of political and military failure. If only 450 rebels are left, why arm an extremely unreliable 17,000 strong native militia to back an army of over 50,000 men? Moscow may be using Stalinist tactics in Chechnya, but it lacks Stalin's ruthless determination. There is more style than substance in Mr. Putin's nostalgia for the days of Uncle Joe. As coined by Pavel Felgenhauer, "Stalin would have no doubt swiftly ended the present conflict by sending all Chechens, loyal or not, to freeze in Siberia."[27] But Stalin's policies were counter-

---

[25] NTV, July 28, 1996, 17:00 GMT. Rodionov commanded the 40th Army in Afghanistan in 1986 and was a fervent proponent of Soviet withdrawal.

[26] ITAR-TASS World Service, August 11, 1996, 15:54 GMT.

[27] "The Russian Army in Chechnya", paper presented at a conference "Tchétchénie: après seize mois de guerre, quelles perspectives politiques et militaries?", held in Paris on January 29, 2001.

productive.. When Mikhail Gorbachev tried to reform the Soviet Union fifty years later, the strongest separatist movements emerged in the Baltic Republics, Chechnya and Western Ukraine.

The present conflict started in November 1991 when Chechnya unilaterally declared independence. Since then Russia has lost several chances to negotiate a political solution. Among these lost solutions were: in 1994, when many Chechens became disillusioned with Dudaev's rule; in September 1996 when Aslan Maskhadov and, on behalf of Russian, Alexander Lebed, signed the Khasav Yurt Agreement; on numerous later occasions when Maskhadov offered to negotiate a face-saving accord with Moscow.

The resistance today has undoubtedly suffered heavy blows with the death of so many of its leaders. Yeltsin's promise to bomb Chechnya back into the stone age has been achieved by Putin. The population needs to lick its wounds and recover its strength. Healthy signs of recovery are already present, such as a baby boom to compensate war losses. The Chechens and the Russians could probably sustain the present status quo of relatively low-intensity warfare indefinitely until a Russian leader whose political career is not determined by promises of thumping Chechen "rebels" can bring about a political settlement. Russia, however, must prevent the conflict from spilling over to other regions in the North Caucasus. One of the official explanations of the 1994 and 1999 campaigns was the need to avert the spread of separatism in neighboring Muslim republics to safeguard Russia's "territorial integrity". For ten years the scenario of an all out war in the North Caucasus seemed improbable. Now the situation is changing dramatically. The struggle is spreading from Chechnya across the entire region. Russian response in other republics of the North Caucasus has been as heavy-handed as in Chechnya. It is unlikely that the Chechens will be fighting alone in the future. They will continue to fan the flames throughout the North Caucasus until a political solution is found that takes national aspirations into account.

Wars in the North Caucasus and in Afghanistan, whether victorious or not, were not lucky for Russia. The brutality of the 19th century

119

conquest discredited the Romanov dynasty, exhausted Russian forces and helped towards defeat in Crimea. During the Russian Civil War, Denikin wasted his chances by fighting the North Caucasians. The Afghan war heralded the demise of the Soviet empire. No cosmetic reconstruction of Grozny, no pseudo-amnesty will ever win the hearts of the Chechens after the holocaust of the last decade, coming as it does after two and half centuries of warfare. They are forever lost to Russia as docile subjects. The sooner Moscow acts on this assumption, rather than reviving policies that have failed in the past, the sooner it can pick up the pieces and save some of its influence in the North Caucasus. However, it may well be that Russia has already completely squandered the chance to exert its will over the North Caucasus.

The Russian Military Campaign in the North Caucasus:

Is a Victory in Sight?

Pavel K. Baev

Introduction

At the beginning of 2005, propositions about a possible Russian military victory in Chechnya and a military-political victory in the struggle against terrorism in the North Caucasus would have been truly hypothetical, unless sponsored by Moscow's propaganda machine. In mid-2006, they might still have appeared far-fetched – but nevertheless deserving of a serious assessment, providing that the sponsorship of the abovementioned kind is not a factor. The trajectory of the conflict-generating political transformations in this region has never been straight in the last 15 years, since Chechnya proclaimed its independence in September 1991. In the few years, perhaps starting with the Beslan tragedy, the sum total of the outcomes of continuing violent clashes and incremental political steps has amounted to a quite significant shift of momentum that has acquired a pronounced de-escalatory character. It remains uneven and uncertain, and during the first post-Beslan year it was barely distinguishable as political attention was focused on the spectacular political crises known as the 'colored revolutions'. The attack on Nalchik, Kabardino-Balkaria on 13 October 2005 marked an intersection of the Islamic guerilla and popular uprising, which could have opened new avenues for both across the region but in fact has narrowed the paths of resistance. The situation, nevertheless, remained quite volatile and many experts, including this author, warned about the hidden tensions that could have resulted in new explosions.[1]

---

[1] See, for instance, John B. Dunlop & Rajan Menon, 'Chaos in the North Caucasus and Russia's future', *Survival*, vol. 48, no. 2, Summer 2006, pp. 97-114. My recent analysis is in

The real explosion, however, happened on July 10 when, among a dozen or so victims was Shamil Basaev, the legendary elusive terrorist who had become not just a source of inspiration but also the main driver for, and the crucial connection between multiple North Caucasian Islamic/terrorist/criminal networks.[2] His death, probably accidental, reinforced the trend of declining terrorist activity and de-escalation of overlapping conflicts, which now requires a new evaluation.

The Decade of Patience and Resilience

The reference point in analyzing the security developments in the North Caucasus is inevitably the violent turmoil of the early 1990s when the region was engulfed by instability: Chechnya effectively seceded in September 1991; North Ossetia was deeply involved in the armed clashes in South Ossetia from the start of 1990 to June 1992 and in the ethnic cleansing in its own Prigorodny district in October-November 1992; Abkhazia was rescued from an attack by Georgian para-militaries by volunteers organized by the Confederation of Mountain Peoples of the Caucasus in September 1992 and achieved a decisive victory in October 1993.[3] Russian military interventions in South Ossetia, Prigorodny district, and Abkhazia were more impromptu responses rather than elements of a pro-active strategy, while Chechnya, remarkably, was left alone.

The situation started to change in late 1993, after President Yeltsin had established his grasp on power with the help of several tanks; at that time, most Caucasian conflicts were 'frozen' by ceasefires and Russian

---

Pavel K. Baev, 'Contre-terrorisme et islamisation du Caucase du Nord', *Politique Etrangere*, vol. 70, no. 1, pp. 79-89.

[2] For an incisive portrait, see Thomas de Waal, 'Basaev: From Rebel to Vicious Extremist', *IWPR Caucasian Reporting Service*, 11 July
(http://www.iwpr.net/?p=crs&s=f&o=322196&apc_state=henicrsf0b0dd69d4b41e3718df
38e196f8e8ce).

[3] Excellent sociological analysis of these turbulent developments with a particular focus on the role of the Confederation can be found in Georgi M. Derluguian, *Bourdieu's Secret Admirer in the Caucasus*, Chicago: The University of Chicago Press, 2005.

peacekeepers, while the unruly Confederation was dissolved.[4] Chechnya emerged as the major source of regional instability spread by smuggling and banditry, kidnappings and plane hijackings. The Russian military invasion in December 1994 was certainly a huge political mistake, but it did help in stabilizing the region and, in retrospect, it appears quite remarkable how little direct spill-over was produced by the high-intensity military operations of 1995-1996. Even the penetrating rebel raids in June 1995 and January 1996 were aimed at civilian 'soft targets' and not at disrupting the vulnerable rear echelons of the 50,000-strong grouping of federal forces in Chechnya.

The end of the First Chechen War in the last day of August 1996 provided a short respite in the hostilities but in a few months the drivers of instability re-emerged resembling quite closely the pattern of 1994. It was perfectly possible for Moscow to cut Chechnya out as an unpleasant reminder of a humiliating failure but the North Caucasus was left exposed to the enterprises of the victorious warlords. The incursion of Basaev's 'mujahideens' into Dagestan in the summer 1999 generated, clearly against his newly-born Islamic vision, a remarkably strong defensive response among Dagestani society. That response went beyond expelling Basaev's units and determined the interruption of most channels that could have transmitted the resonance from the Second Chechen War.[5] That made it easier for Moscow to implement its strategy for isolating the war zone and cutting Chechnya out of all regional interactions, so that it could be dealt with inside a carefully maintained 'black hole'.

At that time, Moscow had only limited resources to invest in enhancing political stability in the republics of the North Caucasus, so the main emphasis was placed on securing dependency of their presidents who were seen as 'guarantors' of loyalty of local elites. Combined with

---

[4] My first assessment of these applications of military power was in Pavel K. Baev, 'Russia's Experiments and Experience in Conflict Management and Peacekeeping', *International Peacekeeping*, Autumn 1994, pp. 245-260.
[5] For a thoughtful comparison, see Enver Kisriev, 'Why is there stability in Dagestan but not in Chechnya?', in Christoph Zürcher & Jan Koehler (eds), *Potentials of Disorder*. Manchester: MUP, 2003.

gradually increasing subsidies and transfers from the federal budget, that strategy initially appeared successful and provided for minimizing the impact of occasional terrorist attacks and other 'disturbances' emanating out of Chechnya. Following that approach, President Ruslan Aushev, who managed to keep his Ingushetia out of the harm's way during a turbulent decade, was forced out of office in late 2001 and a more controllable Murat Zyazikov was installed through a shamelessly rigged presidential election in May 2002.[6] In Dagestan, Moscow became reluctant to accept the traditional way of balancing interests in the State Council where political clans representing various ethnic groups engaged in delicate bargaining, and put the stake on this Council's chairman Magometali Magomedov, treating him as de-facto president. Both choices appeared entirely logical and rational, and both had disastrous consequences.

The Insecurity Complex Takes Shape

The significant increase of terrorist attacks across the North Caucasus since 2002 (the attached Table provides some data on that) did not alarmed Putin's team since the priority issue was the threat to Moscow exemplified by the *Nord-Ost* hostage drama in October 2002. Putin demanded from the High Command to concentrate on countering terrorism, a task for which the Russian Armed Forces were quite unsuitable.[7] The 'top brass' suggested instead to the inexperienced Commander-in-Chief to focus on the operations against terrorist bases outside Russia's territory, for instance, in the Pankisi Gorge in

---

[6] On Aushev's outstanding performance see Georgi Derluguian 'A Soviet general and nation-building', *Chicago Tribune*, 28 October 2001; Matthew Evangelista described the intrigue around his removal in Chapter 6 of his excellent book *The Chechen Wars: Will Russia Go the Way of the Soviet Union?* Washington: Brookings Institution, 2002.
[7] I examined that problem in Pavel K. Baev, 'The Challenge of "Small Wars" for the Russian Military', in Anne Aldis & Roger McDermott (eds), *Russian Military Reform 1992-2002*. London: Frank Cass, 2003; for a more recent analysis, see Roy Allison, 'Russia, regional conflict, and the use of military power', pp. 121-156 in Steven E. Miller & Dmitri Trenin (eds), *The Russian Military: Power and Policy*. Cambridge MA: The MIT Press, 2005.

Georgia.[8] They promised to minimize high risks of such operations by deploying long-range high-precision missiles, an idea that clearly captured Putin's imagination.[9]

As for the North Caucasus, the key point was to reduce the spill-over from Chechnya and the newly-adopted policy of 'Chechenization' was supposed to provide for that. The spill-over actually increased, not as a result of any escalation of combat operations but primarily because of the gradual but accumulating growth of the explosive potential in the region itself. That trend involved two main elements – the degradation of the ruling regimes and the spread of discontent in the societies. The first one was directly related to the Kremlin's stake on loyal rulers who were materially rewarded with resources to be distributed among their clans. The rapidly maturing neo-patrimonial regimes not only featured staggering levels of corruption but also expanded their control over illegal activities so that local law enforcement structures became undistinguishable from criminal groupings.

The second element was less visible and hidden by official 'life-is-good' reporting, but manifested itself in the growth of various self-help networks that often acquired Islamic character and resulted in the spread of 'alternative' and, in many cases, radicalized Islam. Ingushetia, where President Murat Zyazikov failed to build any support base, and Dagestan, where Magometali Magomedov presided over a spectacularly corrupt system of clan patronage, had the worst combination of destabilizing factors and formed one 'insecurity complex' together with Chechnya.

The scale of accumulated troubles was revealed by three consecutive crises in mid-2004. First, an explosion in Grozny on May 9th claimed

---

[8] The trajectory of the Pankisi crisis is investigated in Jaba Devdariani, 'Georgia and Russia: The troubled road to accommodation', pp. 153-203 in Bruno Coppieters & Robert Legvold (eds), *Statehood and Security: Georgia after the Rose Revolution*. Cambridge MA: The MIT Press, 2005.

[9] Putin took a ride on a strategic bomber in August 2005 and observed the launch of cruise missiles which only increased his propensity to brag about high-precision strikes; see Aleksandr Golts, 'According to old plans', *Ezhednevny zhurnal*, (in Russian) 22 August 2005 (http://www.ej.ru/dayTheme/entry/1648/).

the life of President Akhmad Kadyrov, thus undermining a key pillar of the strategy of 'Chechenization'. Then, on June 22nd, a rebel unit conducted a night raid on Nazran, Ingushetia and managed to kill more than a hundred of policemen and soldiers without any organized resistance.[10] Finally, on 1 September, a unit of some 35-50 rebels seized more than a thousand hostages in a school in Beslan, North Ossetia and the poorly prepared assault on September 3rd resulted in more than 350 casualties.[11] The resonance of that horrible massacre was so heavy that Putin could no longer hide behind denials of the spiraling crisis in the North Caucasus.[12] In North Ossetia, the leadership of President Aleksandr Dzasokhov was deeply compromised; the weakness of federal control over Ingushetia became apparent; and the suppressed Ingush-Ossetian conflict over the Prigorodny district threatened to explode with a new force. In the emotional speech resembling Stalin's famous 'Brothers and sisters', Putin re-defined his 'counter-terrorist operation' as 'war' and hinted that the West was behind the terrorist enemy; however, the proposed measures for achieving a victory, including the direct appointment of governors and republican presidents, appeared strikingly inadequate.[13] One meaningful thing he did, nevertheless, was the appointment of Dmitry Kozak as his envoy to the Southern District with expanded authority.

---

[10] As Felgengauer pointed out, even most carefully prepared operations of this kind had high risk of failure, but the support from local population helped several groups of rebels to find their targets and then to disperse without any trace. See Pavel Felgengauer, 'Nazran: Rebels win by skill not quantity', *Novaya gazeta*, 28 June 2004 (in Russian).

[11] The independent report of Yuri Savelyev, a member of the parliamentary commission investigating the Beslan operation, has produced significant new evidence and was suppressed by the authorities; see Elena Milashina, 'People who know everything', *Novata gazeta*, 28 August 2006; Valery Panyushkin, 'The unforeseen factor', *Kommersant*, 4 September (in Russian).

[12] A thorough examination of that shocking tragedy can be found in John Dunlop, *Beslan: Russia's 9/11?* Washington DC: Jamestown Foundation, 2005.

[13] In the popular Internet journal 'Vladimir Vladimirovich', the reconstruction of that speech ended with a striking point: 'Do not you get it that we have declared this war to ourselves?'; see Maksim Kononenko, *Vladimir Vladimirovich*, Moscow: Colibri, 2005, p. 488. The anti-Western connotations are analyzed in Sergei Medvedev, '"Juicy Morsels": Putin's Beslan Address and the Construction of the New Russian Identity', *PONARS Memo* 334, Washington DC: CSIS, December 2004.

Kozak and GrOU from Cherkessk to Nalchik

Just a month into the job, Kozak had to face a sharp and unexpected crisis when an angry crowd stormed the government building in Cherkessk, the capital of Karachaevo-Cherkessia and demanded the dismissal of President Mustafa Batdyev. That relatively peaceful rebellion was triggered by a 'business conflict' involving Batdyev's son-in-law, who had performed 'hostile takeover' of a cement plant by inviting its owner to a meeting and murdering him together with six other people. Kozak managed to defuse the explosion of public anger by promising full investigation – but got a good measure of the depth of the problems with corruption, nepotism, and office abuse. He focused his efforts on reformatting the most grossly distorted structures of power seeking to prevent another eruption, which appeared quite urgent on the background of the 'orange revolution' gathering speed in Ukraine.[14]

Kozak's authority did not extend over the units and command structures of several different 'armies' deployed in the North Caucasus and engaged in various counter-terrorist activities. In order to improve, or even enforce, coordination between them, special Groups of Operational Control (Gruppa Operativnogo Upravleniya – GrOU) were created in each region of the Southern District (except Chechnya) in late 2004. They included representatives from every military, para-military and special services structure and were formally under the Interior Ministry but in fact the FSB was in charge.[15] In early 2005, these GrOU launched a series of manhunts involving hundreds of soldiers and policemen and staging assaults on suspected terrorist cells, quite often in urban quarters, with heavy arms including tanks.[16] Such indiscriminate 'special operations' sparked some protests, so in March 2005, the Federation Council approved revisions to the Law on Defense that removed any restrictions on the use of armed forces in counter-

---

[14] For a convincing risk assessment, see Georgi Derluguian, 'The coming revolutions in the North Caucasus', *PONARS Memo* 378, Washington: CSIS, December 2005.

[15] For a penetrating examination, see Andrei Soldatov & Irina Borogan, 'Rapid reform forces', *Novaya gazeta*, 5 December 2005 (in Russian).

[16] One clear account is in Aleksandr Golts, 'Tank wipes cleans all footprints', *Ezhenedelny zhurnal* (in Russian), 17 January (http://supernew.ej.ru/150/tema/goltz17/index.html).

terrorist operations. Neither 'collateral damage' nor legal issues could have prevented the enthusiastic 'warriors' from making triumphant reports to the Commander-in-Chief; receiving one of those from Interior Minister Rashid Nurgaliev, Putin reprimanded him for using confusing terms like *'jamaat'* and ordered to call terrorists by their real name.[17] That desire to simplify complex social reality translated directly into the strategy of achieving a military victory over the terrorists by exterminating their networks.

Kozak was extremely worried about that militarization of Moscow's counter-terrorist policy in the North Caucasus since the easily available evidence pointed to a further spread of *jammats* after every 'successful' operation.[18] He conducted an in-depth analysis of the crisis in Dagestan and concluded that urgent and sustained political measures were necessary in order to break the grasp on power of entrenched political clans, while the on-going escalation of military operations would inevitably lead to 'the appearance of a macro-region of social, political and economic instability'.[19] The most immediate task was to remove Magomedov from the position of power, but Putin, paying an extra-short secretive visit to Dagestan on 15 July 2005, found no signs of problems reaching a 'critical level' or any risk of a 'break-up of the republic'. Ignoring Kozak's warning about the risks of 'pushing the problems deeper inside' by applying forceful methods, Putin promised more troops and insisted that the southern borders of Dagestan should by sealed off in order to prevent the penetration of rebels towards the

---

[17] On the transformation of traditional *jamaat* and its new 'self-help' functions, see Mayrbek Vachagaev, 'Evolution of the Chechen *jamaat'*, *Chechnya Weekly*, 6 April 2005; see also Alexei Malashenko, 'Russia and Radical Islam', Carnegie Moscow Center, 6 April 2006 (www.carnegie.ru/en/pubs/media/74135.htm).

[18] For an alarmist diagnosis of the situation in the North Caucasus at that time, see Yulia Latynina, 'This is a break-down: On the systemic crisis of President Putin's regime', *Novaya gazeta*, 14 February 2005 (in Russian); my assessment was in Pavel K. Baev, 'The North Caucasus slips out of control', *Eurasia Daily Monitor*, 4 April 2005 (http://www.jamestown.org/edm/article.php?article_id=2369543).

[19] Desperate to attract Putin's attention, Kozak broke the strict Kremlin rules and leaked the report to the tabloid *Moskovsky komsomolets*; for an elaborate analysis, see Blandy, C.W., 'North Caucasus: On the brink of far-reaching destabilisation', *Caucasus Series* 05/36, Conflict Studies Research Centre, Defence Academy of the UK, 2005.

resorts of the Krasnodar kray, where 'millions of Russians are making their holidays'.[20]

That self-deceiving net assessment of the terrorist threat brought a new round of escalation of clan warfare and violent unrest in Dagestan.[21] The next major terrorist attack happened, however, against Kozak's premonition, in Nalchik, the capital of Kabardino-Balkaria, on 13 October 2005. Unlike other raids, this one involved only local residents and from the military point of view, was completely hopeless: isolated groups of 10-15 rebels attacked in broad daylight such heavily guarded targets as police precincts, OMON headquarters and FSB centers. The local GrOU was able to mobilize during the first couple of hours some 3,500 troops that hunted down most of the poorly trained 'terrorists'.[22] While the FSB and other agencies involved in the struggle against terrorism basked in the glory of their 'victory', Kozak pointed out that the attack was launched by the *jammat* 'Yarmuk' that had been reported as destroyed in early 2005. He also gathered convincing evidence about the repressions against Muslim communities that had been portrayed as 'extremist' and in fact driven to a hopeless rebellion.[23] Working together with Arsen Kanokov, the new president of Kabardino-Balkaria, Kozak was able to convince Putin that the crisis had deep roots in the resentful society and had to be addressed with political rather than military measures.

---

[20] This rather odd, if not bizarre evaluation of the situation was reported by the press but omitted from the presentation of the trip on the presidential website. As Latynina argued, 'The rebels do not infiltrate into Dagestan, they live here... To speak in the war-time Dagestan about protecting the holiday-makers in Krasnodar kray essentially means to write Dagestan off.' See Yulia Latynina, 'Boots in Dagestan', *Ezhednevny zhurnal*, (in Russian) 18 July 2005 (http://www.ej.ru/dayTheme/entry/1443/).

[21] As Markedonov argued, 'In the largest republic of the North Caucasus we face with terrorism of a higher level and quality than in the neighboring Chechnya.' See Sergei Markedonov, 'Terrorism in Dagestan will become problem no. 1', *Prognosis.ru*, (in Russian) 5 July 2005 (http://www.prognosis.ru/news/region/2005/7/5/markedonov.html).

[22] A thorough investigation of the attack can be found in Irina Borogan & Andrei Soldatov, 'Basaev left the rebels in distress', *Novaya gazeta*, 22 June 2006 (in Russian).

[23] An extensive analysis of the driving forces of the crisis in Kabardino-Balkaria, possibly informed by Kozak's staff, is in Konstantin Kazenin, 'New president and old problems: Can the attack on Nalchik happen again in 2006?', *Regnum*, 10 January 2006 (http://www.regnum.ru/news/570125.html).

Signs of an Uncertain Stabilization

Putin's new reading of the situation informed his short address to the Chechen parliament during the blitz-visit to Grozny on 12 December 2005, when he emphasized Russia's role as the 'most reliable, trustworthy, and consistent protector of the interests of the Islamic world' and argued that 'those on the other side' were driven by a 'distorted interpretation of the Koran'.[24] He even mentioned 'compromises', which marked a sharp difference from his straightforward 'go-get-them' orders earlier that year. The Year 2006 started, however, with yet another massive manhunt in the mountains of Dagestan with the use of artillery and aviation.[25] The situation showed few signs of improvement and the priorities of Russian policy were hanging in balance; quite possibly, it was the lack of success in the winter operation that strengthened Kozak's hand.

His first breakthrough achievement was the long-overdue removal of Magomedov and the approval of Mukhu Aliev as the President of Dagestan on 20 February 2006.[26] The next significant success was sacking Kabardino-Balkaria's Interior Minister Khachim Shogenov in March, which helped in discontinuing the brutal repressions against the Muslims who followed the unofficial or 'alternative' Islam and were treated collectively as terrorist suspects. Kozak followed up on that in June proposing Andrei Yarin, who had worked in his staff, as the prime minister of Kabardino-Balkaria, and in July replacing notoriously corrupt prosecutor-general in Dagestan Imam Yaraliev. Cadre reshuffling would not have achieved much of a stabilizing effect in itself but it was accompanied by a significant increase of funding from the federal budget, which the new leaders were able to distribute in a more

---

[24] My take on that rather unpolished speech is in Pavel K. Baev, 'Putin protects Islam and praises democracy in Grozny', *Eurasia Daily Monitor*, 14 December 2005 (http://www.jamestown.org/edm/article.php?article_id=2370597).
[25] See Ekaterina Rogozhnikova, 'Inefficient war', *Lenta.ru*, (in Russian) 5 January 2006 (http://lenta.ru/articles/2006/01/05/fight/). On Kozak's efforts, see Milrad Fatullaev, 'Kozak's loneliness', *Nezavisimaya gazeta*, 23 December 2005 (in Russian).
[26] A very favorable evaluation of Aliev's performance is in Yulia Latynina, 'One day of the president', *Novaya gazeta*, 10 August 2006 (in Russian).

efficient way. Through the first half of the year, the situation in the region still remained highly unstable since many trouble-spots continued to reproduce tensions.[27] For that matter, Kozak worked closely with Taimuraz Mamsurov, the new leader of North Ossetia seeking to prevent any escalation of the Ingush-Ossetian discord focused on the Prigorodny district and much aggravated by the Beslan tragedy.[28]

What made the most significant impact on the advancement of Kozak's plans and more broadly on the security situation in the North Caucasus was the gradual but steady decrease of hostilities in Chechnya. The January report of the Interior Ministry on the big reduction of terrorist attacks in Chechnya in 2005 (95 as compared with 214 in 2004) did not appear credible, particularly since the statistics on casualties showed no reduction at all.[29] Nevertheless, in the course of the year the difference with the familiar pattern of ambushes, shootouts and explosions has become increasingly apparent.[30] Many factors contributed to this de-escalation, including the 'war fatigue', but the main driving force has certainly been the consolidation of power in the hands of Ramzan Kadyrov, who has succeeded in recruiting hundreds of former rebels into his 'guard'. The Russian military have been eager to delegate the responsibility for patrolling and policing to these para-military units that are now performing key functions in enforcing order. That has made it possible to reduce the grouping of federal forces in Chechnya

---

[27] One good risk assessment is Yulia Latynina, 'The seat of tensions moves from the East Caucasus to the West', *Ezhednevny zhurnal*, 28 April 2006
(http://ej.ru/comments/entry/3673/). My assessment is in Pavel K. Baev, 'Shifting battlefields of the Chechen War', *Chechnya Weekly*, 20 April 2006
(www.jamestown.org/publications_details.php?volume_id=416&issue_id=3697&article_id=2371008).
[28] Kozak's plan for resolving that conflict developed together with the North Ossetian leadership was blocked by Ingushetia in march 2006; see Milrad Fatullaev, 'Kozak failed as peacemaker', *Nezavisimaya gazeta*, 8 August 2006 (in Russian).
[29] See Vladimir Mukhin, 'Mistakes in counting the rebels', *Nezavisimoe voennoe obozrenie*, 27 January 2006 (in Russian).
[30] That pattern is thoroughly examined in Mark Kramer, 'The Perils of Counter-Insurgency: Russia's War in Chechnya', *International Security*, vol. 29, no. 3, Winter 2004/2005, pp. 5-63.

and even disband the Regional Operational Headquarters setting instead a smaller HQs in Chechnya.[31]

The sustained decline of the terrorist threat and particularly the absence of any terrorist attacks in Moscow since mid-2004 convinced the FSB that the risk of taking prime responsibility for combating terrorism had become politically acceptable. In February 2006, a new super-structure – the National Anti-Terrorist Committee (NAC) – was created by the presidential decree under the chairmanship of Nikolai Patrushev, the head of the FSB. This seemingly illogical 'reorganization' secured for the FSB more efficient levers of control over other agencies and granted it privileged access to significant new funding. Presiding over the mostly virtual 'war' against the residual 'terror', Patrushev with few doubts claimed credit for the elimination of Shamil Basaev asserting that the explosion was not an accident but a carefully planned 'special operation' that prevented an attack aimed at derailing the G8 Strelna summit.[32]

Basaev's death, coming less than a month after the death of Abdul-Khalim Saidulaev, the formal leader of the Chechen rebels, signified a possibly crucial watershed in the campaign of violent unrest and terrorism across the North Caucasus. He personified the cause of defiant resistance but what was more significant, used his authority for connecting various terrorist cells, Islamic networks and criminal groupings. The FSB is quite aware that in the absence of such a key organizing center the capacity of isolated groups for staging a high-impact attack has diminished and so claims a larger role in directing the activities of anti-terrorist commissions and GrOU (now subordinated to them) in every republic.[33] At the same time, the overall responsibility

---

[31] Putin issued a directive on withdrawal from Chechnya of all federal forces deployed there on a temporary basis by the end of 2008, which would still leave there the 42nd Motor Rifle Division and the 46th Interior Troops Brigade; see Ivan Sukhov, 'False withdrawal', *Vremya novostei*, 10 August 2006 (in Russian).

[32] This version was elaborated in Andrei Gromov & Shamsudin Mamaev, 'The end of Basaev', *Expert*, 17 July 2006 (in Russian).

[33] Patrushev presided over the NAC meeting in Rostov-on-Don in late August and focused the attention on the high level of corruption in the law enforcement; see Sergei Kisin, 'Terrorists dispersed across the Caucasus', *Kommersant*, 26 August (in Russian).

for coordinating the activities of federal forces in Chechnya remains squarely on the Interior Ministry, which faces a hard challenge to keep the maverick Kadyrov in check.[34]

Prospects, Conditions, and Spoilers

Examining the trajectory of stabilization in the North Caucasus, the region that has for a decade and a half lived up to the reputation of 'tinderbox', is certainly a counter-intuitive analytical exercise, perhaps to the extreme.[35] It appears possible, nevertheless, to outline the broad conditions that appear necessary for sustaining this very recent trend and to identify possible spoilers. The first among them is the continuation of the political efforts organized by Dmitry Kozak towards the removal from power of the most corrupt political clans and building some new confidence in the republican leadership. His most immediate task in that is finding a suitable replacement for the completely compromised President Batdyev in Karachaevo-Cherkessiya, while further down the list is the problem of easing out of office President Kirsan Ilyumzhinov who has been ruling impoverished Kalmykia as his personal fiefdom for the last 13 years. Engaging in vicious intrigues around every replacement, Kozak needs to retain President Putin's personal trust and a direct access to the Kremlin, which inevitably becomes complicated as the problem of selecting and installing a successor looms large.

The foundation of Kozak's 'cadre management' policy is the huge volume of financial resources provided by Moscow – and in the immediate future this foundation appears solid, as the 2007 federal budget delivered to the State Duma in late August promises nice increases in transfers and subsidies. There is, however, a serious

---

[34] Nurgaliev personally supervises the work of the operational HQ in Chechnya that maintains control over all armed forces, including several Chechen battalions not subordinated to Kadyrov; see Musa Muradov, 'Rashid Nurgaliev took Chechnya under control', *Kommersant*, 22 August 2006 (in Russian).

[35] See Fiona Hill, 'Russia's Tinderbox: Conflict in the North Caucasus and Its Implication for the Future of the Russian Federation', *Occasional paper* from the Strengthening of the Democratic Institutions project, Harvard University, 1995.

problem hidden in this generosity as the inflow of federal 'petro-roubles' makes bureaucratic distribution by far the most profitable 'business' and in fact stifles entrepreneurial activity and normal economic development. Putin apparently intends to solve this problem by ordering Russia's largest companies to invest in the region but that quasi-GOSPLAN type of dirigisme will hardly improve the investment climate.[36] At the same time, Moscow has effectively withdrawn its invitation to the EU to establish a political dialogue on the problems of the North Caucasus supported by a program of European economic investments.[37]

One possible spoiler for these efforts could be the plan for merging tiny Adygeya with surrounding Krasnodar kray, which is strongly pushed by governor Aleksandr Tkachev; it is also supported by Kozak who seeks to get rid of the ineffectual President Khazret Sovmen and assumes that the Russian majority could provide a more reliable political base than the 'Cherkess Congress'.[38] Sovmen's term expires in January 2007 and his replacement with an 'outsider' who would be less hostile to the merger plan could spark a crisis that might resonate from Abkhazia to Chechnya.[39] Another and a more 'direct impact' spoiler is the situation in Ingushetia, where – even according to official statistics – the number of terrorist attacks in 2006 has doubled comparing to

---

[36] On Putin's August meeting with the 'captains of business' in Sochi about 'voluntary' investments in the North Caucasus, see Anna Nikolaeva & Tatyana Egorova, 'Business will go to the mountains', *Vedomosti*, 17 August 2006 (in Russian).

[37] One minor piece of evidence here is my experience in cooperating with SIPRI in organizing a seminar 'Transforming Conflicts in the North Caucasus' (Stockholm, 15-16 June 2006) that was supposed to bring together officials from the EU, who duly arrived, and from Russia, of which none showed up. For more systematic evidence, see Svante Cornell & S. Frederick Starr, 'The Caucasus: A Challenge for Europe', *Silk Road Paper*, Washington DC: Johns Hopkins University-SAIS, June 2006.

[38] An elaborate assessment can be found in Konstantin Kazenin, 'Union against Congress: The situation in Adygeya', *Regnum* (in Russian), 25 August 2006 (http://www.regnum.ru/news/694395.html).

[39] See on that Yulia Latynina, 'Krasnaya polyana and the Republic of Adygeya', *Ezhednevny zhurnal*, 10 April 2006 (http://www.ej.ru/dayTheme/entry/3504/); I have looked into that in Pavel K. Baev, 'Russian quasi-federalism and Georgian non-existent territorial integrity', *CACI Analyst*, 3 May 2006 (http://www.cacianalyst.org/view_article.php?articleid=4201).

2005. President Zyazikov is completely isolated in the republican political elite and relies exclusively on police and para-militaries that are hated more than feared and targeted in incessant ambushes and shootouts. Kozak's ability to control the distribution of federal funds is quite limited and he cannot touch Zyazikov who was chosen personally by Putin, while the FSB pursues the 'deterrence-by-punishment' strategy through the republican GrOU. Ingushetia appears far closer to an armed rebellion in the near future than Dagestan.[40]

A major condition for continuing stabilization in the North Caucasus is further progress in suppressing hostilities and advancing reconstruction of Chechnya. The stake on granting expanding powers in enforcing order and unlimited control over distribution of resources to Kadyrov Jr. has proven efficient in the short term but it directly undermines Moscow's plans for sustained 'normalization' of the situation in the republic. Ramzan's power rests on the armed units of *kadyrovtsy* recruited mostly from former rebels who have accepted his personal guarantees and have no trust in the federal amnesty. These gangs are far from reliable allies for the Russian troops, but Kadyrov Jr. pushes hard for the withdrawal of 'redundant' Interior forces and military units and even advocates for 'hot-pursuit' and 'search-and-destroy' operations in neighboring republics who are extremely wary of *kadyrovtsy*.[41] After the clash in Borozdinovskaya in mid-2005 and the explosion in the battalion 'Vostok' barracks in February 2006, Kadyrov Jr. has managed to normalize relations with the Chechen units that are subordinated to the Russian 42nd Division and 46th Brigade, but remains very suspicious about the operations that are conducted outside his authority.[42] It might become significant in this respect that only Alu

---

[40] See Vladimir Mukhin, 'Ingushetia becomes another Chechnya', *Nezavisimaya gazeta*, 26 June 2006 (in Russian); on the explosive potential of the Ingush-Ossetian conflict, see Oleg Kusov, 'Ossetia – Ingushetia: The main issue', *Prognosis*, 25 August 2006 (http://www.prognosis.ru/news/region/2006/8/25/kusov.html).

[41] See Vladimir Mukhin, 'Ramzan put pressure on federals', *Nezavisimaya gazeta*, 18 April 2006 (in Russian).

[42] See the interview with Sulim Yamadaev, the commander of the 'Vostok' battalion in *Kavkazsky uzel*, 21 June 2006 (http://kavkaz.memo.ru/analyticstext/analytics/id/1022301.html).

Alkhanov, the President of Chechnya, is a member of the republican operational HQs led by Deputy Interior Minister Arkady Edelev.

As Prime Minister, Kadyrov Jr. insisted on exclusive control over the disbursement of federal funding for reconstruction, which was increased five times in 2006 comparing to 2004, so that the official goal of rebuilding everything damaged by the wars by the year 2010 has become his personal PR campaign.[43] In many ways, this over-concentration of power and nascent 'personality cult' are incompatible with the Chechen traditions and the system of power balance between various clans; Kadyrov Jr. is not trusted either by groups loyal to Russia, or by disapora entrepreneurs looking for tapping into federal funds, or by former rebels. Even in Moscow he is increasingly seen as a self-assertive and uncontrollable upstart who may potentially turn to the separatist course; it still remains possible to pretend that Ramzan is a key part of the solution and not of a problem but there are hardly any serious doubts about the name of the potential spoiler.

Terrorism has during the last couple of years become an issue separate of the 'no-war' in Chechnya movement, while keeping it under control is certainly one of the main conditions for building stability in the North Caucasus. The intensity and character of terrorist attacks in this region vary and evolve, and the official data remains quite unreliable – but even a general overview of the most significant acts of terror could provide some indications about possible turns of events in the near future.[44] The attached table lists 17 attacks in the North Caucasus (outside Chechnya) that generated the most resonance, imperfect as

---

[43] The commission on rebuilding Chechnya is chaired by the First Deputy Prime Minister Dmitry Medvedev, who seeks to maintain control over key projects, for instance the reconstruction of Grozny airport; see Ivan Sukhov, 'Chechnya becomes a regular subject', *Vremya novostei*, 2 August 2006 (in Russian).

[44] According to NAC, during the last three years, 864 rebels were killed and some 3,000 arrested, while 708 terrorist attacks were prevented, including only 26 in the first half of 2006 – which presumably indicates the overall decline of terrorist activity in the North Caucasus; see Aleksei Nikolsky, 'Terror is in decline', *Vedomosti*, 30 August 2006 (in Russian).

this criteria certainly is.[45] The first impression is that surprisingly few of these attacks were directed against military assets and even those few were aimed at 'soft targets' like hospitals or barracks. Another feature that does not fit the pattern observed in the global war against terror is that the rich infrastructure of tourism – from Sochi sea beaches to ski resorts near Elbrus – was not attacked once. Putin mentioned this threat making a brief appearance in Dagestan in mid-2005 (perhaps reflecting on his own retreat in Krasnaya Polyana) but even small-scale violence against tourists has been in fact extremely rare. Yet another and even more counter-intuitive feature has been the lack of any significant attacks on the highly vulnerable energy infrastructure.[46] There were several explosions on the 'non-strategic' gas pipelines in Dagestan but overall the January 2006 blasts that left Georgia without gas and electricity for a week (No. 17) stand out as the exception that proves the general rule.

It is possible to suggest that as long as terrorism in the North Caucasus remains limited to targeting primarily local law enforcement, commercial interests and mid-level officials – it would not interrupt or adversely affect the general trend of stabilization. It would even answer the FSB interests in keeping the system of operational HQs and GrOW actively functioning as means to control the local authorities and maintain own profile. If however, the 'strategic' Tengiz-Novorossiisk pipeline or the oil terminal in Novorossiisk or Tuapse is targeted, or if a series of explosions hits some tourist hotels, the delicate balance of stabilization may be instantly upset.

One particular aspect of the terrorism/counter-terrorism interplay appears significant – but often overlooked. The issue of external funding for terrorist networks has been so grossly abused by Russian official propaganda that the rational point in it has all but disappeared. However, the death of Shamil Basaev would not close the issue

---

[45] A very useful chronicle of terrorist attacks in Russia (with a separate list for Dagestan) is maintained at *Kavkazsky uzel*
(http://kavkaz.memo.ru/newstext/chronics/id/770040.html).
[46] See my article on this, 'Reevaluation the risk of terrorist attacks against energy infrastructure in Eurasia', *China and Eurasia Forum*, May 2006, pp. 33-38.

altogether; much depends upon the unpredictable developments in various overlapping crises from Afghanistan to Gaza that both attract and generate resources available for trans-national Islamic extremism. For that matter, the demand for seasoned fighters with experience in Chechnya have quite possibly been boosted by the war in Lebanon, escalation of inter-communal strife in Iraq and Taliban's revival in Afghanistan, while the supply of funds for the Chechen cause has probably shrunk. For that matter, Russia remains fundamentally interested in the success of coalition efforts at state-building in Afghanistan and in US ability to contain the self-destructive hostilities in Iraq, while Moscow's actual stance in the global struggle with Islamic terrorism has become increasingly 'neutral'.[47]

One last condition for stability in the North Caucasus that could be briefly touched upon in this paper involves Georgia and, more specifically, its break-away provinces of South Ossetia and Abkhazia. To all intents and purposes, these quasi-states have for the last 12-15 years been a part of the North Caucasian 'insecurity complex' – and the interplay between their conflicts with Tbilisi, Russian-Georgian relations and the normalization in the North Caucasus remains strong. The forthcoming referendum on independence in South Ossetia accompanied by daily clashes around Tskhinvali might create a situation where smart policies of conflict manipulation could give way to inadequate responses and unforeseen consequences.

---

[47] This point is elaborated in Pavel K. Baev, 'Russia wrapping up its war against terror', *Eurasia Daily Monitor*, 14 August 2006 (http://www.jamestown.org/edm/article.php?article_id=2371377).

TABLE 1. MAJOR OCCASIONS OF VIOLENT CONFLICTS/INSURGENCY/TERRORISM IN THE NORTH CAUCASUS (OUTSIDE CHECHNYA)

No.	Type of event	Location	Date	Target of attack	Rebel force	Casualties	Media attention
1.	Hostage taking	Budennovsk, Stavropol krai	June 1995	Hospital	75	150	Max
2.	Hostage taking	Kizlyar-Pervomaiskoe, Dagestan	January 1996	Hospital, village	200-250	200-250	High
3.	Explosion	Kaspiisk; Dagestan	November 1996	Barracks	NA	70	Medium
4.	Explosion	Vladikavkaz, North Ossetia	March 1999	Market	NA	50-70	Medium
5.	Rebel attack	Botlikh, Dagestan	August 1999	Villages	300-500	400-500	High
6.	Explosion	Buinaksk, Dagestan	September 1999	Apartment house	NA	30-60	Medium
7.	Explosion	Volgodonsk, Rostov oblast	September 1999	Apartment house	NA	20	High
8.	Multiple explosions	Essentuki, Mineralnye vody	March 2001	Market, police station	NA	30	Medium
9.	Explosion	Kaspiisk, Dagestan	May 2002	Parade	NA	45	Medium
10.	Explosion	Mozdok, North Ossetia	June 2003	Bus	Suicide	20	Medium
11.	Explosion	Mozdok, North Ossetia	August 2003	Hospital	Suicide	50	Medium
12.	Explosion	Pyatigorsk, Krasnodar krai	September 2003	Train	NA	10	Medium
13.	Explosion	Essentuki, Krasnodar krai	December 2003	Train	Suicide	45	Medium

14.	Rebel attack	Nazran, Ingushetia	June 2004	Police stations	100	100	High
15.	Hostage taking	Beslan, North Ossetia	September 2004	School	35-50	400	Max
16.	Rebel attack	Nalchick, Kabardino-Balkaria	October 2005	Police, OMON stations	150	150-200	High
17.	Multiple explosions	North Ossetia	January 2006	Pipelines, power line	NA	None	High

The Targets of Terrorism and the Aims of Counter-Terrorism in Moscow, Chechnya and the North Caucasus

Dr. Pavel K. Baev

Introduction

This paper addresses a phenomenon that at one point threatened the very existence of the Russian state but now has shrunk to the point of political insignificance if not irrelevance. Terrorism caused a crucial turn in Russia's political trajectory in the autumn of 1999, while counter-terrorism has been one of then President Putin's trademarks and the instrument of choice for political mobilization. The instrumental role that Putin's counter-terrorist policies play in Russian society has diminished, but not disappeared, with the de facto vanishing of the terrorist threat beyond the southeastern region of the North Caucasus. It was only in February 2006 that the National Anti-Terrorist Committee (NAC) was established under the chairmanship of Nikolai Patrushev, the head of the Federal Security Service (FSB), in order to coordinate the activities of all "power structures." The new Law on Countering Terrorism was approved by the State Duma in the same month.[1] As one political commentator pointed out, "it is fashionable in Russia to affix terrorism to just about anything." (Sarafanova, 2007) This fashion has never been entirely innocent and in the electoral season of 2007/2008 it might acquire a whole new malignant dimension as it is appropriated by competing clans in the squabble of "successors" inside Putin's inner circle. Dmitry Oreshkin (2007), one of the few independent Russian political commentators,

---

[1] Concerning the FSB's interests and their expanded responsibilities through the creation of the NAC, see Soldatov (2006). My reflections on the adoption of these measures on the 50th anniversary of Nikita Khrushchev's "secret" speech at the XX Congress of the CPSU are presented in Baev (2006a); on the new anti-terrorist legislation, see Troitsky (2006)

pondered, "Apparently the national warning of a terrorist threat was indeed an exercise. But what exactly was exercised?"[2]

Before we answer this question, it is essential to take a look back at the trajectory of Russia's, "war against terror," seeking to assess the scope of the threat and to establish, to the degree possible, the rationale behind its highly uneven dynamics. That requires not only patient removal of multiple layers of official half-truths and blatant lies but also careful selection of reasonably reliable data. Only the terrorist attacks that really happened could be treated as such, since the facts supplied by the NAC on 708 prevented terrorist attacks in the last three years (including only 26 in the first half of 2006) cannot be properly analyzed (Nikolsky, 2006). Even for the high-profile attacks, the information on the number of participants and victims is also often fragmented and contradictory, to the point where only the timing and the target can be established with sufficient certainty.[3] This data provides for establishing as a point of departure for further analysis the fact of remarkably high concentration of terrorist activity in three areas: Moscow, Chechnya, and the North Caucasus, including not only the five republics (Adygea, Dagestan, Ingushetia, Kabardino-Balkaria, and Karachaevo-Cherkessia) but also three southern Russian regions (Krasnodar *krai*, Rostov *oblast*, and Stavropol *krai*). This paper will attempt to examine and compare the dynamics of terrorist attacks in these three 'fronts' seeking to provide rational explanations for timing and targeting without slipping into the abyss of conspiracy theories.

---

[2] My comment on the high terrorist alert announced by the NAC on the evening of January 16, 2007 and lifted the next day is in Baev (2007). For my earlier analysis of the instrumental use of counter-terrorism as a policy, see Baev (2004). Useful research can also be found in Stepanova (2005); Trenin & Malashenko (2004) provided a thoughtful examination of the impact of the Chechen wars on Russia's internal security.

[3] A very useful chronicle of terrorist attacks in Russia is maintained at *Kavkazsky uzel* (http://kavkaz.memo.ru/ newstext/chronics/id/770040.html); another useful list for the period between 1996 and 2004 is compiled by the BBC Russian Service (http://news.bbc.co.uk/hi/russian/russia/newsid_3621000/3621314.stm).

Moscow Leaves the Nightmare Behind

The blast in the Moscow metro on June 11, 1996 near the Tulskaya station, tragic as it was, remained an isolated incident that momentarily illuminated the fact that there was relatively little discussion of the hugely unpopular war in Chechnya. This all occurred during the bitterly contested presidential elections. However three years later it was the main issue in the narrowly failed attempt to impeach President Boris Yeltsin by the State Duma.[4] For Muscovites, the August 1999 "mini-war" in Dagestan appeared to be a local affair brought to a successful resolution. Furthermore, the small explosion in the Manezh underground mall on August 31, 1999 looked like a "normal" criminal *razborka* (sorting-out). In short, nothing prepared Moscow for the two deadly blasts that destroyed apartment houses on Guryanova and Kashirskaya streets on the nights of September 9 and 13, 1999. The city that, "does not believe in tears," was shocked and instantly ready to blame the Chechen rebels without asking for evidence.[5]

The beginning phase of the Second Chechen War did not bring any attacks of comparable magnitude. The next big shock hit Moscow on October 23, 2002, when a troop of well-armed Chechen fighters, accompanied by a dozen or so of women prepared to commit suicide-murders, captured some 850 hostages at the performance of the popular musical *Nord-Ost*.[6] The stand-off continued for some 55 hours and was resolved through an assault under the cover of poisonous gas

---

[4] On Yeltsin's efforts at minimizing the impact of the war on his campaign, see Shevtsova (1999, pp. 180-182); on the impeachment attempt, see Sakwa (2003).

[5] The blasts has never been thoroughly investigated. Allegations of an FSB conspiracy regarding these attacks are mostly associated with the exiled oligarch Boris Berezovsky and the former FSB agent Aleksandr Litvinenko, who was poisoned in November 2006, but many experts and commentators acknowledge the corroborating evidence. See, for instance, Satter (2002). As Andrei Piontkovsky (2005) argued, "There are some questions that some nations avoid asking themselves just because they subconsciously know the answers. For instance, who killed President Kennedy or who exploded the houses in Moscow *and* Volgodonsk. A clearly articulated answer could become destructive for the state and therefore we shall never hear it."

[6] This author had the pleasure and the good luck to enjoy the performance two weeks prior to the tragedy.

143

that killed up to 130 hostages. It was never convincingly established how such a large group of rebels could have arrived in Moscow and why did they not explode the thoroughly mined theater when the assault began.[7] "We have proven that Russia could not be kept on its knees," declared Putin and rewarded the "heroes," including Patrushev, absolving them of any responsibility. (Rudensky, 2002) The relatives of the victims are still trying to get to the bottom of the case, while more than a third of the Russians believe that the authorities are hiding the truth about that attack. (Berseneva, 2006; Levada Center poll, October 2006)

Putin's assertion of "victory" turned out to be entirely hollow as Moscow experienced a series of terrorist attacks again targeting the metro as well as street crowds in random places. What was particularly shocking for Muscovites was the nature of these attacks, which often consisted of suicide bombings involving young women, mostly from Chechnya.[8] Nevertheless, the city was learning to live under a permanent threat of new attacks. In the five years from September 1999 to September 2004, Moscow experienced more terrorist attacks and mourned more victims from said attacks than any other capital in the world.[9] All these attacks were associated with the war in Chechnya and they stopped abruptly after the summer of 2004 for full two years. After this lull, however, Moscow suddenly discovered terrorism of a new kind. The explosion that derailed a train from Grozny in Moscow oblast on June 12, 2005 did not make much news (there were no casualties) and the two accused attackers appeared to just be crazed

---

[7] The newspaper *Versiya* came under strong pressure from the FSB for publishing a list of questions that poked holes in the official version of events; see (2002). Boris Sokolov (2002) suggested that the terrorists never planned to detonate the explosives; the most comprehensive investigation is in Dunlop (2003).

[8] For a recent in-depth analyses of the phenomenon of suicide terrorism, see Gambetta (2005). Valery Tishkov (2004) examined the traumas of the Chechen wars; see also Panyushkin (2003).

[9] Aleksandr Cherkasov (2004) pointed out after the blast in Moscow metro a significant perceptional difference, "The same common people were in the metro as in the train in Essentuki that was exploded on December 4 – and there also more than 50 people perished. The perception, however, was different due to 'Moscow separatism' – that blast had happened out there, in the Caucasus."

nationalists ("The Accused...," 2007). The explosion in the Cherkizovsky market on August 21, 2006, however, showed that radical nationalism was indeed a serious problem, particularly against the background of the anti-Caucasian pogrom in Kondopoga, Karelia in late August as well as the "Russian march" in Moscow on November 7, 2006 under the banners, "Kondopoga – Hero-City."[10]

Leaving this new brand of terrorism outside the main scope of this analysis, we can point to several counter-intuitive features of the terrorist campaign on the Moscow "front," between its shocking opening in August 1999 and the abrupt end in August 2004. Assuming that a key goal of the rebels was to maximize the impact of every attack, it is hard to explain away the fact that not a single chemical production plant was targeted, which would have had an effect comparable with the use of a WMD. Highly vulnerable energy infrastructure was spared, and a blackout in May 2005 was caused by a technical short-circuit. The badly congested city traffic was brought to complete standstill on several occasions in 2006 when police cleared the way for the passage of some VIP motorcade, but never by explosions in tunnels or on bridges. The rebels never tried to emphasize the war in Chechnya by attacking any of the numerous military properties or academies in Moscow, many of which are not exactly impregnable. Not a single high-profile government department or state agency was targeted, nor were any buildings or monuments of high symbolic value damaged. An assassination attempt on a key figure in the state leadership was never attempted. The timing of the attacks was never chosen with the aim of spoiling an important occasion or disrupting elections. For example, the spectacular fire in the Manezh building on the night of presidential election in March 2004 was not even suspected to be, "Chechen arson." Many of the attacks obviously required careful planning and preparation but it is impossible not to see that far greater impact could have been achieved with the same amount of resources if targeting and timing were different.

---

[10] For a sharp evaluation, see Radzikhovsky (2006) as well as my short comment in Baev (2006b).

No.	Type of event	Location	Date	Target of attack	Rebel force	Casual-ties	Media attention
1.	Explosion	Tulskaya station	06/11/ 1996	Metro	NA	11	Medium
2.	Explosion	Manezhna-ya square	08/31/ 1999	Mole	NA	1	High
3.	Explosion	Guryanova street	09/09/ 1999	Apartment house	NA	109	High
4.	Explosion	Kashirskaya street	09/13/ 1999	Apartment house	NA	124	Max
5.	Explosion	Pushkins-kaya square	08/08/ 2000	Undergr. passage	NA	13	High
6.	Explosion	Belorus-skaya stat.	02/06/ 2001	Metro	NA	1	Medium
7.	Explosion	Pokryshkina street	10/19/ 2002	McDonalds restaurant	NA	1	Medium
8.	Hostage taking	Dubrovka complex	12/23-26/2003	*Nord-Ost* theater	33	130 hostages	Max
9.	Suicide bombings	Tushino stadium	07/05/ 1993	Rock concert	2	16	High
10.	Suicide bombing	Manezh-naya square	12/08/ 2003	Hotel *National*	1	6	Medium
11.	Explosion	Pavelets-kaya station	02/06/ 2004	Metro	NA	40	High
12.	Suicide bombings	Domode-dovo airport	08/24 / 2004	2 airplanes	2	90	High
13.	Suicide bombing	Rizhskaya station	08/31/ 2004	Metro	1	11	Medium
14.	Explosion	Cherkizov-sky market	08/21/ 2006	Market	4	13	Medium

Chechnya Terrorized into "Normalization"

The problem with depicting the trajectory of terrorist activities in Chechnya is that it is next to impossible to separate it from the general dynamics of insurgency as well as the deliberate suppression and distortion of information by the Russian authorities. It is clear that the phase of full-scale military offensive in the Second Chechen war, which was officially called a "counter-terrorist operation," only lasted until summer 2000 when federal forces managed to establish control over all the key villages in the mountainous region of the republic. For that matter, the desperate last stand of a company of Russian paratroopers in February 2000, which was later romanticized in two TV serials, had nothing to do with terrorism. The only proven case of "friendly fire" was one that claimed the lives of 22 OMON policemen, and as such clearly cannot be treated as terrorism. However, the ambush on May 11, 2000 near the village of Galashki, Ingushetia where 18 Russian servicemen were killed, is somewhere in the "gray area" since it happened outside Chechnya.[11]

Three specific cases of shooting down helicopters can perhaps be mentioned in this context. The first one was the suspicious destruction of a Mi-8 helicopter carrying several Russian generals over Grozny on October 17, 2001. The second one was a hit on the helicopter carrying Deputy Interior Minister Mikhail Rudchenko, Deputy Commander of Interior Troops Nikolai Goridov and several Interior Ministry officers on January 27, 2002, which was the fifth anniversary of Aslan Maskhadov's election as Chechnya's President. The third helicopter attack was the hit on the overloaded Mi-26 helicopter on August 19, 2002 that killed 127 servicemen making it the deadliest disaster in the helicopter aviation history.[12]

---

[11] For a careful examination of the February 29, 2000 battle see Cherkasov (2006); the 'friendly ambush' of the Sergiev Posad OMON is examined in Kozlov (2002); the most comprehensive analysis of the complicated pattern of war in Chechnya is in Kramer (2005).

[12] Anna Politkovskaya revealed the suspicious evidence of the October 17 missile strike and had then to flee Russia because of threats to her life; see Hearst (2002). A very useful

Several bomb explosions in 2000-2002 had all the markings of terrorist attacks, beginning with the suicide act on June 6, 2000, when two teenage girls drove a truck loaded with explosives through an OMOM checkpoint.[13]   The most significant rebel attack of this kind was the explosion of two trucks loaded with explosives in the government quarter of Grozny on December 27, 2002. The next significant attack took place on May 12, 2003 at the FSB headquarters in Znamenskoe. There were also several suicide bombings, including at least one (on May 14, 2003) targeting President Akhmad Kadyrov, a key Russian ally.

Kadyrov's assassination on May 9, 2004 stands out in the list of attacks. A powerful bomb was planted under the VIP tribune during the reconstruction of the republican stadium in Grozny and detonated during the ceremonial parade despite massive security measures.

By every account, the intensity of terrorist attacks inside Chechnya went down sharply after the assassination, while ambushes and shoot-outs continued to be rather prevalent. It was assumed that President Aslan Maskhadov ordered to expand the guerilla campaign across the North Caucasus, and his subsequent murder on March 8, 2005 marked another watershed in the decline of insurgency in Chechnya.[14] The attention of security experts was centered on Shamil Basaev who remained at large despite all the efforts of Russian security services to eliminate this, "number one enemy of the state." Rumors in the Caucasus had it that Basaev was preparing a series of attacks in July 2006, at the time of the scheduled G8 summit in St. Petersburg, with the goal to achieve an impact similar to the July 2005 London bombings that effectively derailed the Gleneagles G8 summit. In place of this planned attack, an explosion in a small village in Ingushetia on July

---

list of losses of Russian aircraft in the Second Chechen war is in Wikipedia.
(http://en.wikipedia.org/wiki/Russian_aircraft_losses_in_North_Caucasus_ since_1999).
[13] A list of suicide attacks can also be found in Wikipedia
(http://en.wikipedia.org/wiki/Chechen_suicide_attacks).
[14] For a thoughtful reflection, see Derluguian (2005).

claimed his own life, and the FSB duly portrayed it as a successful "special operation" without bothering to provide evidence.[15]

It is clear that the situation on the ground in Chechnya is far more volatile than the "return-to-normal-life" aura painted by Moscow propaganda. Indeed, it is irrefutable that only small-scale terrorist attacks are happening together with ambushes, shootouts and kidnappings; meanwhile the wave of suicide bombings has exhausted itself. Several features in this trend remain problematic even with the caveat of the protracted insurgency/terrorism campaign. It defies explanation that the rebels did not seriously disrupt any of the many elections that took place in Chechnya from October 2003 to November 2005.[16] It is also hard to understand why the rebels, who had determinedly targeted President Akhmad Kadyrov, have not perpetrated any serious assassination attempts against Ramzan Kadyrov, who has built himself a private army of *kadyrovrsy* and enforced his control over many towns and villages with extreme brutality. For that matter, it is most difficult to explain why rebels/terrorists have not interrupted the rise of the phenomenon of Ramzan Kadyrov.[17]

As the younger Kadyrov was consolidating his grasp on power, many rival clan leaders were inclined to challenge him, and Moscow also tried to strengthen President Alu Alkhanov as a counterweight to the over-confident gangster/prime minister. Kadyrov, however, never hesitated to apply force, and Alkhanov wisely opted for a ceremonial role after the shootout between his bodyguards and Kadyrov's bodyguards in Grozny in April 2006. Other competitors took their hint from the deadly blast in the barracks of the GRU-controlled battalion *Vostok* in February 2006, which was conveniently explained away as a gas canister explosion.[18] Kadyrov does not shy away from confrontations with his

---

[15] Tom de Waal (2006) wrote a sharp obituary; Latynina (2006a) made a devastating criticism of the FSB self-appraisement.

[16] Good comparative analysis of these elections can be found in Malashenko (2006a).

[17] One convincing portrait is in Matthews & Nemtsova (2006).

[18] On the shootout in Grozny, see 'Prime shooting' (2006); Anatoly Tsyganok examined the issue of controllability of the Chechen militias (2006).

neighbors either, as exemplified by his "raid" on Khasavyurt in January 2005 and further illustrated by the shootout on the border with Ingushetia in September 2006 that claimed seven casualties.(Riskin, 2006) It appeared that Kadyrov went too far in November 2006 when a group of his "guardsmen" went to Moscow and shot Movlady Baisarov, a former FSB mercenary turned political opponent, in broad daylight on Leninsky Prospekt.[19] This maverick and hugely ambitious warlord has become a serious liability for the Kremlin but the FSB cannot figure out a way to take him out since only that brutal leader appears capable of keeping Chechnya on the track to 'normalization'.

TABLE 2: MAJOR TERRORIST/INSURGENCY ATTACKS INSIDE CHECHNYA

No.	Type of event	Location	Date	Target of attack	Rebel force	Casualties	Media attention
1.	Suicide car bomb	Alkhan-Yurt	06/06/ 2000	OMON checkpoint	2	7	Low
2	Suicide bombings	Argun, Gudermes	07/02/ 2000	Checkpoints, barracks	5	40	Medium
3.	Car bomb	Grozny	10/12/ 2000	Police station	NA	15	Low
4.	Explosion	Chiri-Yurt	10/29/ 2000	Cafe	NA	14	Low
5.	Car bomb	Alkhan-Yurt	12/09/ 2000	Mosque	NA	21	Low
6.	Explosion	Gudermes	04/25/ 2001	Police station	NA	6	Low
7.	Missile attack	Grozny	10/17/ 2001	Helicopter	NA	13	Low
8.	Suicide bombing	Urus-Martan	11/29/ 2001	Military HQ	1	6	Low
9.	Missile attack	Shelkovs-kaya	01/27/ 2002	Helicopter	NA	11	Low
10.	Missile	Grozny	08/19/	Helicopter	NA	127	Medium

---

[19] Insightful appraisal is in Latynina (2006b); for my short comment, see Baev (2006c).

150

	attack		2002				
11.	Explosion	Grozny	10/10/ 2002	Police station	NA	22	Low
12.	Suicide car bombs	Grozny	12/27/ 2002	Government building	3	72	High
13.	Suicide car bomb	Znamens-koe	05/12/ 2003	FSB HQ	2	60	Medium
14.	Suicide bombing	Iliskhan-Yurt	05/14/ 2003	President Kadyrov	2	20	Low
15.	Explosion	Grozny	05/09/ 2004	President Kadyrov	NA	9	Max
16.	Rebel attack	Grozny	08/21/ 2004	Police stations	100-300	40-60	Medium
17.	Car bomb	Znamens-koe	07/19 2005	Police station	NA	15	Low
18.	Rebel attack	Roshni-chu	08/14 2005	Administ-ration	100	7	Low
19.	Explosion	Kurchaloi	02/07 2006	Barracks	NA	13	Low

The North Caucasus Edges Away from the Brink

The situation in the North Caucasus attracted much attention in 2005-2006 as this fragmented and divided 'soft-belly' of Russia experienced a rapid escalation of overlapping and mutually reinforcing crises.[20] The start of the Second Chechen war marked by the incursion into Dagestan by some 300 Chechen rebels led by Shamil Basaev. This event still seems dubious in many ways. As Trenin & Malashenko (2004, p.35) argued, much in the following military deployment, "suggests that Russian intelligence knew about the raid well in advance. Interestingly, information about the planned raid spread across the North Caucasus like wildfire." Nevertheless, the mobilization in Dagestan in response to

---

[20] See, for instance, Dunlop & Menon (2006), Blandy (2005); for my recent risk assessment, see Baev (2006d).

151

the attack not only helped Russian forces in repelling it but also created an opportunity for Moscow to isolate the war zone, thereby pushing Chechnya into a "black hole." Despite several deadly terrorist attacks at the start of the war, the North Caucasus remained generally unaffected by its early phase and the spill-over was generally contained.[21]

It was the daring night raid on Nazran, Ingushetia on June 22, 2004 by a group of 100 or so rebels that demonstrated that resistance to violent unrest was being undermined by powerful forces despite the façade of political stability in Dagestan and other republics outside of Chechnya. The Russian authorities, however, preferred to ignore the signs of destabilization and it took the horrible tragedy in Beslan School Number 1 on September 1-3, 2004 to break through this barrier of denial.[22]

Up to that time, the Kremlin focused on the growth of underground Islamic networks that provided recruits and channeled funds from abroad to homegrown terrorist cells.[23] Never mind the fact that this growth was driven by an environment of rising discontent created by the corrupt neo-patrimonial regime. This boil of discontent burst into open in Cherkessk, Karachaevo-Cherkessia in November 2004 when angry crowds occupied a government building, but the newly appointed presidential envoy to the Southern district, Dmitri Kozak, managed to defuse the crisis without bloodshed. It appeared possible, however, that an extremist attack could trigger a full-blown "color revolution" in one of the republics.[24]

Dagestan appeared to be the most vulnerable to an eruption of social unrest as the local structures of power were paralyzed by the

---

[21] Convincing analysis of that limited regional resonance at the start of the Second Chechen war is in Evangelista (2002).

[22] The report of the Russian parliamentary commission delivered in January 2007 simply rubber-stamped the official version of the events, so the most reliable source is Dunlop (2005).

[23] The impact of the Islamic factor is carefully evaluated in several works of Alexei Malashenko, see, for instance, Malashenko (2006b); my analysis of the interplay with terrorism is in Baev (2006e).

[24] For a sharp analysis of these pre-revolutionary situations, see Derluguian (2005b).

increasingly violent competition between ethno-political clans.[25] The real confrontation happened, however, in Nalchik, Kabardino-Balkaria on October 13, 2005. There was some evidence pointing to a Chechen connection, but the main reason that about 100 local men to attack several heavily guarded police stations and security HQs in broad daylight was the severe oppression of Islamic communities.[26]

Surprised by that non-heroic but undeniable "victory," the Kremlin also recognized the urgent need to strengthen its North Caucasian policy and the reconfigure its "war on terror." Kozak received an order to reshuffle the leadership in several republics. Federal subsidies for republics budgets and funding for local law enforcement were significantly increased, and "official" Islamic churches were encouraged to confront "underground" Islam. Since the beginning of 2006, these measures have brought a gradual and uncertain stabilization of the situation in the region. Even Dagestan, which in 2005 saw even more ambushes and assassinations than Chechnya, has been eliminating terrorist groups, sometimes with the use of heavy arms in residential areas.[27]

Looking back at this recent escalation of terrorist activity we can identify several features that neither fit into the picture of a localized insurgency spilling over into the immediate neighborhood nor into the scheme of radical social protest.[28] In the first case, the vulnerable rear divisions federal forces, spread over vast territory from Volgograd to Rostov-on-Don to Novorossiisk, have been targeted far less than could have been expected. In the second, it should be noted that the rich and

---

[25] Seeking to attract Putin's attention to that crisis Kozak violated Kremlin's tight secrecy rules and leaked his risk-assessment memo to the tabloid *Moskovsky komsomolets*; see Deeva (2005). Putin's express-visit to Dagestan in July 2005 did not, however, bring any changes; see Latynina (2005).

[26] On Basaev's personal involvement in launching that attack, see Borogan & Soldatov (2006).

[27] As Sergei Markedonov (2006) argued, 'In Chechnya, the struggle goes on for preserving a few "rebel islands", but in Dagestan, an Islamic mega-project is taking shape.' On the invariably successful 'special operations' involving destruction of apartment houses, see Shapovalov (2007).

[28] I pointed out to these features in Baev (2006).

soft tourist infrastructure in the region was not attacked once, which does not fit the pattern observed in the global war against terror. Putin mentioned this threat during a brief appearance in Dagestan in mid-2005, but even small-scale violence against tourists, not to mention kidnappings, has been extremely rare.[29] In both cases, it is hard to rationalize the lack of any significant attacks on the highly vulnerable energy infrastructure, such as the Tengiz-Novorossiisk and Baku-Novorossiisk pipelines and the oil terminals in Novorossiisk and Tuapce.[30] There were several explosions along some "non-strategic" gas pipelines in Dagestan, but overall the January 2006 blasts that left Georgia without gas and electricity for a week stand out as the exception that proves the general rule.

TABLE 3: MAJOR OCCASIONS OF VIOLENT
CONFLICTS/INSURGENCY/TERRORISM IN THE NORTH CAUCASUS
(OUTSIDE CHECHNYA)

No.	Type of event	Location	Date	Target of attack	Rebel force	Casualties	Media attention
1.	Hostage taking	Budennovsk, Stavropol krai	June 1995	Hospital	75	150	Max
2.	Hostage taking	Kizlyar-Pervomaiskoe, Dagestan	January 1996	Hospital, village	200-250	200-250	High
3.	Explosion	Kaspiisk; Dagestan	November 1996	Barracks	NA	70	Medium
4.	Explosion	Vladikavkaz, North Ossetia	March 1999	Market	NA	50-70	Low

[29] Putin's rather bizarre statement that the borders of Dagestan should be sealed off in order to prevent terrorist attacks against the resorts of the Krasnodar kray 'where millions of Russian are making their holidays', was omitted from the presidential webside but impressed the experts; as Latynina (2005) argued, 'The rebels do not infiltrate into Dagestan, they live here... To speak in the war-time Dagestan about protecting the holiday-makers in Krasnodar kray essentially means to write Dagestan off.'
[30] My more detailed examination of this 'safe passage' for hydrocarbons is in Baev (2006g).

5.	Rebel attack	Botlikh, Dagestan	August 1999	Villages	300-500	400-500	High
6.	Explosion	Buinaksk, Dagestan	September 1999	Apartment house	NA	30-60	Medium
7.	Explosion	Volgodonsk, Rostov oblast	September 1999	Apartment house	NA	20	High
8.	Multiple explosions	Essentuki and Mineralnye vody, Kr. krai	March 2001	Market, police station	NA	30	Medium
9.	Explosion	Kaspiisk, Dagestan	May 2002	Parade	NA	45	Medium
10.	Explosion	Mozdok, North Ossetia	June 2003	Bus	Suicide	20	Medium
11.	Explosion	Mozdok, North Ossetia	August 2003	Hospital	Suicide	50	Medium
12.	Explosion	Pyatigorsk, Krasnodar krai	September 2003	Train	NA	10	Low
13.	Explosion	Essentuki, Krasnodar krai	December 2003	Train	Suicide	45	Medium
14.	Rebel attack	Nazran, Ingushetia	June 2004	Police stations	100	100	High
15.	Hostage taking	Beslan, North Ossetia	September 2004	School	35-50	400	Max
16.	Rebel attack	Nalchick, Kabardino-Balkaria	October 2005	Police, OMON stations	150	150-200	High
17.	Multiple explosions	North Ossetia	January 2006	Pipelines, power line	NA	None	High

The Interplay between the Three "Fronts"

Even a very superficial juxtaposition of the developments in Moscow, Chechnya and the North Caucasus, as presented in Tables 1, 2, and 3, reveals that their synchronization, which would have implied some sort

155

of central organization, was in fact quite limited. The two most significant cases here were a series of explosions in September 1999 (Buinaksk-Moscow-Volgodonsk) and the chain of attacks in August-September 2004 (Moscow-Grozny-Beslan). It remains unclear, however, what the aim of such a tightly coordinated campaign would have been, since its direct outcome was the shift in public opinion in Russia in favor of the Second Chechen war. That campaign had previously been seen by the top brass as inevitable but, "hard to sell," to the Russian populace.

The one case where there was nearly perfect synchronization of attacks in all three fronts resulted in a sustained decline of terrorist/insurgent activity. This indirectly proves that the Beslan operation, to the degree that this horrible massacre could be rationalized, was a mistake. The rebels probably expected that they would catch President Putin in a perfect trap, but the actual outcome badly damaged their cause. The supposed "explosion" in Dagestan that this attack was supposed to create did not happen. It seems that the attacks were supposed to create maximum public outrage but not inflict such a huge amount of damage. Meanwhile, the amount of human and material resources used in this attack were way above what could be expected from a group of Islamic radicals or an underground network of criminal gangs.[31]

In contrast, the *Nord-Ost* hostage crisis, the May 9, 2004 explosion in Grozny that killed President Akhmad Kadyrov, and the October 2005 Nalchik episode seem more like isolated attacks, despite the fact that the number of rebels involved (in the first and the third cases) and the precision of planning (in the first and the second cases) were still considerably greater than the estimated capacity of a few small cells of extremists would be capable of. The desperate insurrection in Nalchik generally stands out in the three lists of terrorist/insurgency attacks and

---

[31] The FSB version of the 1999 Moscow bombings puts the blame on the so-called 'Karachai jamaat' allegedly led by Achimez Gochiyaev; this name – never mentioned by the leaders of the Chechen resistance – regularly comes up in the official reports on elimination of terrorist groups, for instance in Cherkessk in late December 2006; see McGregor (2006), 'Special operation…' (2006).

has more in common with the May 2005 uprising Andijan, Uzbekistan.[32]

Another feature that comes out from comparing the data in the three tables and checking it against alternative lists, is that there is very little synchronization or correlation between insurgency/terrorist attacks in Chechnya and Dagestan.[33] Despite their close proximity and the presence of a large Chechen community in Dagestan, the ambushes and explosions in this largest republic of the North Caucasus appear to be driven mostly by local factors, and their sharp escalation from early 2005 to mid-2006 did not seem to have a connection with the "ramzanization" of Chechnya.[34] Two well-prepared assassination attempts on Dagestani Minister of Interior Adilgerei Magomedtagirov in August 2006 and February 2007 show that the decline in terrorist activity in Dagestan has been relatively muted. This also shows that the difference between political and criminal motives can be quite small (Gritsenko, 2007).

On the other hand, activities in Ingushetia seem to have a very strong connection to the insurgency in Chechnya. Indeed, this connection seems so strong that the relocation of some hard-pressed Chechen rebel groups to "safe havens" in Ingushetia has turned this small republic into the epicenter of terrorist activity in the region. A series of assassination attempts that began in early 2007 shows no signs of abating and has aggravated the weakness of the political structures of Ingush President Murat Zyazikov who was installed in the job by Moscow back in May 2002.[35]

---

[32] For an illuminating comparison of these two events, see Derluguian (2005c).

[33] The separate detailed and updated list of terrorist attacks in Dagestan at *Kavkazsky uzel* is particularly useful (http://kavkaz.memo.ru/newstext/chronics/id/790621.html).

[34] On the destabilization of Dagestan, see Markedonov (2005); his more recent lengthy interview with *Druzhba Narodov* (Markedonov, 2006b) provides a good insight on the predominant orientation of the insurgency in Dagestan against the corrupt republican authorities.

[35] President Putin felt obliged to mention the assassination attempt on Ingushetia's mufti (top Islamic cleric) during his long press-conference on 1 February 2007; see Markedonov (2007); for my assessment of the terrorist interplay between Chechnya and Ingushetia, see Baev (2006).

During 2006, the spillover of instability from Chechnya to Ingushetia essentially died out, and a new "hot spot" started to shape up in the westernmost corner of the region. The plan for merging Adygea with Krasnodar kray brought tensions to the brink of violence. By the end of the year, however, when Dmitri Kozak orchestrated the replacement of Adygea's erratic President Hazret Sovmen with Aslan Thakushinov as well as the postponement of the proposed merger which had originally enflamed the situation.[36]

The ups and downs of insurgency/terrorist activity in all three "fronts" show hardly any correlation with the uneven dynamics of international terrorism. It is possible to find some symmetry between the sharp increase of suicide attacks (particularly in Moscow) in the aftermath of the Nord-Ost hostage crisis in October 2002 and the escalation of Intifada in Palestine, but there is no evidence of any direct import of the concept of training female suicide bombers. It may be also possible to argue that the decline of terrorist attacks in Russia since autumn 2004 has been caused by the concentration of al-Qaeda's efforts in Iraq and, perhaps to a lesser degree, in Afghanistan. Such reasoning, however, is pure conjecture; most experts on terrorism would disagree with Deputy Prime Minister Sergei Ivanov who asserted at the 2007 security conference in Munich, "We were fighting against international terrorism as opposed to local terrorism because there is no such thing as local terrorism in the present-day global community."[37] Untrained teenagers who attacked well-guarded police stations in Nalchik on October 13, 2005, angry men who took their revenge on brutal "law-enforcers" in Nazran on June 22, 2004, and even the members of Rasul Makasharipov's "Muslim" gang who were hunting policemen in Dagestan before being surrounded and exterminated on July 6, 2005, were all driven primarily by local agendas.

---

[36] An elaborate of this averted crisis can be found in Kazenin (2006); a useful perspective is in Latynina (2006c).

[37] My translation from 'Defense Minister on terrorism in Chechnya: The problem is solved' (2007). Ivanov's presentation was far less provocative than Putin's speech the day before, although normally he would play a 'hawk' to Putin's 'dove'; see Mayorov (2007). An excellent analysis of the local roots and agendas of terrorism is Packer (2006), see also Joes (2006).

This sustained intention to portray a protracted confrontation with home-grown rebels as a part of the global struggle against terrorism is only partially driven by the desire to stifle the international criticism of the truly barbarous methods employed for suppressing the insurgency. The other, probably more important component to this, is the justification of only limited success achieved in the wake of the use of massive military force against rebels who supposedly only number between 1200 and 1500 people according to official estimates.[38] It is the supposed "external connection" that makes it possible for the FSB and the NAC to claim a decisive success in the "counter-terrorist strike" while simultaneously warning yet once again about the high risk of new attacks which could allegedly target the Tsimlyanskaya dam or the Sosnovy Bor nuclear power plant.

While discussing major security issues with the U.S. at the 2007 Munich security conference, both Putin (2007a) and Ivanov emphasized that the Chechen problem was solved. It is not only the incessant news about ambushes and shootouts (barely registering in sterile political debates in Moscow) that cast doubt over these statements. The wars in Chechnya have made a massive impact on Russia's political transformation and Putin's system of power, which is the natural. However, there is the possibility that this has resulted in the fact that Putin's political system might need this war for performing its key functions. That makes the warnings about possible new attacks more verisimilar, particularly since the public opinion pays progressively less attention as they become part of the background of Russian political life. Chechnya still comes to Moscow, leaving a trail of bodies like Movladi Baisarov and, quite possibly, journalists Anna Politkovskaya and Paul Khlebnikov. But a far greater danger emanating from this protracted war is that the Moscow that has returned home from Chechnya has so much blood and dirt on its hands that another murder

---

[38] This figure was revised downwards only in autumn 2006. Evgeny Baryaev, the commander of the federal forces in the North Caucasus, estimated that some 700 rebels were hiding in the Chechen mountains; see Riskin (2006). A further reduction was done by Arkady Edelev, Deputy Interior Minister, who claimed that 632 rebels had taken the amnesty offer and laid arms in 2006, so that only some 450 rebels remained in Chechnya in early 2007; see Borisov (2007).

or explosion makes very little difference. That is why the accusations surrounding Aleksandr Litvinenko's murder, and Putin's association with it, are so instantly believable.[39]

The link from this poisoning in London to the Kremlin or Lubyanka square most probably will never be established beyond the reasonable doubt, and that gives Putin (2007b) sufficient ground to say, "I do not really believe in conspiracy theories and, quite frankly, I am not very worried about it. Russia's current stability allows us to look down at this from above." This confidence was apparently confirmed by a verdict against a group of terrorists who were found guilty of organizing several explosions in Moscow; the evidence, however, was not made public (Latynina, 2007). Everything seems to be under control but there is a deep shadow at the very heart of Putin's "perfect war" which society is very much unwilling to investigate. The deadly September 1999 blasts in Moscow remain unexplained, so as Ilya Milstein (2003), one of the fiercest critics of "Putinism", suggested, "Russia's history will continue to skid until Russia figures out who set the explosions in Moscow and failed to trigger the blast in Ryazan."

Conclusion

The obvious and irreducible weakness of this analysis is the absence of a working definition of terrorism, and it can be only partly justified by the reference to one of the few hard facts in the discipline of political science: the impossibility to coin a coherent and broadly acceptable definition of this fascinating and abhorrent phenomenon. Accepting the dubious proposition that you know terrorism when you see it, this author has found himself engaged in the unenviable task of fingering an elephant. The pictures illustrating this paper are expected to compensate for this methodological deficiency by providing images that speak more convincingly than academic discourse but most probably they will not survive the effort to 'upgrade' this text into an article.

---

[39] One of the most convincing journalist investigations of the murder is Barabanov & Voronov (2007).

It is rather obvious that any 'threshold' on casualties would be entirely artificial, and it is certainly arbitrary that ambushes on military or police convoys and remote-control mines or IEDs (this abbreviation for 'improvised explosive device' has entered the military vocabulary from Iraq) are not included in the analysis here, while attacks on police stations are. As far as Chechnya is concerned, the problem is not how to distinguish between guerilla attacks, targeting military and police, and terrorist attacks, targeting civilians and politicians, but how to make a comprehensive record, since terrorism is clearly one of the tactics used by the rebels. This fusion between insurgency and terrorism spills over into the North Caucasus as well, and the banditry blends into this phenomenon as well, so that it is impossible to assert with any certainty, whether the double assassination attempt on Dagestan's Minister of Interior Magomedtagirov was a manhunt organized by an 'ideological' terrorist group, or a violent competition between rival political clans, or a revenge from a gangster network.

What is certain, however, is that kidnappings and assassinations performed by *kadyrovtsy* are indistinguishable from terrorist attacks ascribed to the rebels.[40] The Kremlin might maintain that these 'death squads' are 'pro-Russian' but their only loyalty is to maverick Ramzan Kadyrov who does not ask for instructions from Moscow on methods and limits of using violent force. This 'regional dictatorship' blurs the distinction between state-organized campaigns of terror, from air attacks to *zachistki* to non-punishable rape, and terrorism as the 'last resort' tactics of the rebels. Only the 'non-governmental' terrorism is normally identified as a major security challenge in the post-post-Cold War era, but the 'special operations' favored by Putin's Kremlin deliberately transgress this distinction, so that Western commentators (Specter, 2007, p. 53) point out with apprehension that 'Litvinenko's

---

[40] In her last interview with Radio Liberty, Anna Politkovskaya characterized Kadyrov as, "a coward armed to the teeth and always surrounded by guards," and shared her wish to see him in a court which would look into every one of his long list of his crimes; see "The Last Point of Anna Politkovskaya" (2006).

murder was the first known case of nuclear terrorism perpetrated against an individual.'

The phenomenon of terrorism/insurgency/counter-terrorism/special-operations that continues to evolve in Russia defies any definition that political science might propose and evades monitoring efforts by converting facts into means of 'information warfare'. There is, nevertheless, a distinct impression (rather than a firm conclusion) emerging from this analysis that the strategy that aims to exploit simultaneously the dark fears and the short memory in the society traumatized by multiple acts of brutal terror and mesmerized by propaganda of 'victory' cannot be sustainable even in the mid-term.

The spectacular fire that raged barely a hundred meters from the Kremlin walls engulfing the historic Manezh building in the night of Putin's triumphal re-election could still turn out to be an apt metaphor for the 'normalization' perpetuated under his watch.

REFERENCES

Baev, Pavel K., "Instrumentalizing Counter-Terrorism for Regime Consolidation in Putin's Russia," *Studies in Conflict & Terrorism*, vol. 27, no. 4, July/August 2004, pp. 337-352.

Baev, Pavel K., "Khrushchev's Secret Speech and Putin's Public Praise," *Eurasia Daily Monitor*, February 27, 2006 (available at http://jamestown.org/edm/article.php? article_id=2370817).

Baev, Pavel K., "The Russian March that was not : Moscow Avoids a Holiday Pogrom," *Eurasia Daily Monitor*, 6 November 6, 2006 (available at http://jamestown.org/edm/article.php?article_id=2371616).

Baev, Pavel K., "Chechen Execution Squad Comes to Moscow," *Eurasia Daily Monitor*, November 22, 2006 (available at http://jamestown.org/edm/article.php?article_id=2371665).

Baev, Pavel K., "The Russian Military Campaign in the North Caucasus: Is Victory in Sight?", paper presented at the international conference, "The Future of the North Caucasus," Jamestown Foundation, Washington, DC, September 14, 2006 (available at http://jamestown.org/nccp-91406.php).

Baev, Pavel K., 2006e, "Contre-terrorisme et islamisation du Caucase du Nord," *Politique Etrangere*, vol. 70, no. 1, pp. 79-89.

Baev, Pavel K., 2006f, "Has Russia Achieved a Victory in its War Against Terror?", *PONARS Memo* 415, Washington: CSIS.

Baev, Pavel K., "Reevaluation the Risk of Terrorist Attacks Against Energy Infrastructure in Eurasia," *China and Eurasia Forum*, May 2006, pp. 33-38.

Baev, Pavel K., "Shifting Battlefields of the Chechen War," *Chechnya Weekly*, April 20, 2006 (available at http://www.jamestown.org/publications_ details.php?volume_id= 416&issue_id=3697&article_id=2371008).

Baev, Pavel K., "Moscow is Reminded that the 'War on Terror' is Not Over," *Eurasia Daily Monitor*, January 22, 2007 (available at http://jamestown.org/edm/article.php? article_id=2371825).

Barabanov, Ilya & Vladimir Voronov, "Who Killed Aleksandr Litvinenko - and Why," *New Times*, no. 1, 5-12 February, 2007 (available in Russian at http://www.newtimes.ru/ journal/journal_pages_001/10.html).

Berseneva, Anastasiya, "To Turn the Success into a Failure," *Novye izvestiya*, May 15, 2006 (in Russian).

Blandy, C.W., 2005, "North Caucasus: On the Brink of Far-Reaching Destabilisation," *Caucasus Series* 05/36, Conflict Studies Research Centre, Defence Academy of the UK.

Borisov, Timofei, "Basaev's Heirs are Personally Registered," interview with Deputy Interior Minister General-Colonel Arkady Edelev, *Rossiiskaya gazeta*, February 2, 2007 (in Russian).

Borogan, Irina & Andrei Soldatov, "Basaev Left the Rebels in Distress," *Novaya gazeta*, 22 June 22, 2006 (in Russian).

Cherkasov, Aleksandr, "Between the Power and the Terror," *Polit.ru*, February 7, 2004 (available in Russian at http://www.polit.ru/country/2004/02/07/terror.html).

Cherkasov, Aleksandr, "PR on the Blood of Paratroopers," *Polit.ru*, March 7, 2006 (available in Russian at http://www.polit.ru/author/2006/03/07/6_rota.html).

Deeva, Ekaterina, "How Dagestan Will be Exploded," *Moskovskii komsomolets*, July 8, 2005 (in Russian).

"Defense Minister on Terrorism in Chechnya: The Problem is solved," *Newsru*, February 11, 2007 (available in Russian at http://newsru.com/russia/11feb2007/ivanov.html).

Derluguian, Georgi, "The Last Chechen Soldier of the Russian Empire," *Izvestia*, March 10, 2005 (in Russian).

Derluguian, Georgi, 2005, "The Coming Revolutions in the North Caucasus," *PONARS Memo* 378, Washington: CSIS, December.

Derluguian, Georgi, "Nalchik as the Russian Andijan," *Izvestia*, October 18, 2005 (in Russian).

Dunlop, John B., "The October 2002 Moscow Hostage-Taking Incident," *RFE/RL Reports*, December 18, 2003 (available at http://www.rferl.org/reports/corruptionwatch/ 2003/12/42-181203.asp).

Dunlop, John, 2005, *Beslan: Russia's 9/11?*, Washington, DC: Jamestown Foundation.

Dunlop, John B. & Rajan Menon, "Chaos in the North Caucasus and Russia's Future," *Survival*, vol. 48, no. 2, Summer 2006, pp. 97-114.

Evangelista, Matthew, 2002, *The Chechen Wars: Will Russia Go the Way of the Soviet Union?*, Washington: Brookings.

Gambetta, Diego, (ed.) 2005. *Making Sense of Suicide Missions*. Oxford: OUP.

Gritsenko, Tatyana, "The Demonstrative Performance," *Vremya novostei*, 5 February 5, 2007 (in Russian).

Hearst, David, "Russia's Whistle Blower," *The Guardian*, March 16, 2002.

Joes, Anthony James, "Recapturing the Essentials of Counterinsurgency," *FPRI E-Notes*, May 30, 2006 (available at http://www.fpri.org/enotes/20060530.military.joes.counterinsurgency.html).

Kazenin, Konstantin, "Union Against Congress: The Situation in Adygeya," *Regnum* 25 August 25, 2006 (available in Russian at http://www.regnum.ru/news/694395.html).

Kozlov, Sergei, "The Secret of the Block-Post No. 53," *Nezavisimaya gazeta*, March 22, 2002 (in Russian).

165

Kramer, Mark, "The Perils of Counter-Insurgency: Russia's War in Chechnya," *International Security*, vol. 29, no. 3, Winter 2005, pp. 5-63.

Latynina, Yulia, "Boots in Dagestan," *Ezhednevny zhurnal* (in Russian), July 18, 2005 (http://www.ej.ru/dayTheme/entry/1443/).

Latynina, Yulia, "The Special Operation of the Almighty – but Not of Patrushev," *Ezhednevny zhurnal*, July 10, 2006 (available in Russian at http://www.ej.ru/dayTheme/entry/4262/).

Latynina, Yulia, "*Nemo me impuni lavessit*," *Gazeta.ru*, November 24, 2006 (available in Russian at http://gazeta.ru/column/latynina/1085365.shtml).

Latynina, Yulia, "The Seat of Tensions Moves from the East Caucasus to the West," *Ezhednevny zhurnal*, April 28, 2006(available in Russian at http://www.ej.ru/comments/ entry/3673/).

Latynina, Yulia, "The Mystery of Super-Terrorists," *Ezhednevny zhurnal*, February 9, 2007 (available in Russian at http://www.ej.ru/dayTheme/entry/6102/).

Malashenko, Aleksei, *Kak vybirali v Chechne* (How Chechnya Voted), Moscow: Carnegie Center.

Malashenko, Alexei, "Islam and Politics in Russia," *Pro et Contra*, vol. 10, no. 5-6, September-December 2006, pp. 76-94 (in Russian).

Markedonov, Sergei, "Terrorism in Dagestan Will become Problem No. 1," *Prognosis.ru*, July 5, 2005 (http://www.prognosis.ru/news/region/2005/7/5/markedonov. html).

Markedonov, Sergei, "Terrorist selection," *Polit.ru*, January 20, 2006 (available in Russia at http://www.polit.ru/author/2006/01/20/dagestan.html).

Markedonov, Sergei, 2006, "Dagestan," interview with *Druzhba narodov*, no. 1, (available in Russian at http://magazines.russ.ru/druzhba/2006/1/ma8.html).

Markedonov, Sergei, "Irony Instead of Strategy', *Polit.ru*, February 6, 2007 (available in Russian at http://www.polit.ru/author/2007/02/06/putin_kavkaz.html).

Matthews, Owen & Anna Nemtsova, "Ramzan's World: The Kremlin is Hoping a Young Strongman Can Preserve its Brutal Victory in Chechnya," *Newsweek*, September 25, 2006, pp. 28-32.

Mayorov, Aleksandr, "The Race of Successor Camouflaged as an Arms Race," *Globalrus*, February 12, 2007 (available in Russian at http://www.globalrus.ru/comments/783617/).

McGregor, Roger, "Acimez Gochiyayev: Russia's Terrorist Enigma Returns," *Chechnya Weekly*, February 1, 2007 (available at http://jamestown.org/publications_details.php?volume_id =421&issue_id=3992&article_id=2371870).

Milshtein, Ilya, "Everything has started with a big blast," *Grani.ru*, September 9, 2003 (available in Russian at http://grani.ru/Events/Terror/m.42755.html).

Nikolsky, Aleksei, "Terror in decline," *Vedomosti*, 30 August 30, 2006 (in Russian).

Oreshkin, Dmitry, "Putinism as the Munchausen's horse," *Ezhednevny zhurnal*, 24 January 24, 2007 (available in Russian at http://www.ej.ru/comments/entry/5920/).

Packer, George, "Knowing the Enemy: Can Social Scientists Redefine the 'War on Terror'?", *The New Yorker*, December 18, 2006.

Panyushkin, Valery, 2003. 'More than life', *Gazeta.ru*, 10 July (available in Russian at http://gazeta.ru/column/panushkin/159339.shtml).

Piontkovsky, Andrei, "The question not asked," *Grani.ru*, September 9, 2005 (available in Russian at http://grani.ru/opinion/piontkovsky/m.94668.html).

Putin, Vladimir V., Speech and the following discussion at the Munich security conference, February 10, 2007 (available in English at http://www.president.kremlin.ru/eng/speeches/2007/02/10/0138_type82912type82914type82917type84779_118135.shtml).

Putin, Vladimir V., Press conference with the Russian and foreign media, February 1, 2007 (available in English at http://www.president.kremlin.ru/eng/speeches/2007/02/01/1309_type82915_117609.shtml).

Radzikhovky, Leonid, "Three sources and three constituent parts," *Ezhednevny zhurnal*, November 16, 2006(available in Russian at http://www.ej.ru/comments/entry/5365/).

Riskin, Andrei, "War in the border area," *Nezavisimaya gazeta*, September 14, 2006 (in Russian).

Riskin, Andrei, "The rebels have received reinforcements," *Nezavisimaya gazeta*, 7 November 7, 2006 (in Russian).

Rudensky, Nikolai, "The victory of mass destruction," *Grani.ru*, October 28, 2002 (available in Russian at http://grani.ru/opinion/rudensky/m.13214.html).

Sakwa, Richard, 2003, "Chechnya: A Just War Fought Unjustly?" in Bruno Coppieters & Richard Sakwa (eds), *Contextualizing Secession*. Oxford: OUP, pp. 156-186.

Satter, David, "The Shadow of Ryazan," *National Review Online*, April 30, 2002 (available at http://www.hudson.org/index.cfm?fuseaction=publication_det ails&id=2089).

Sarafanova, Tatyana, "The Operation 'Central Bank – Anti-Terror,'" *Gazeta.ru*, January 29, 2007 (available in Russian at http://gazeta.ru/comments/2007/01/29_a_1308429.shtml).

Shapovalov, Aleksandr, "*Zachistki* of Residencies," *Nezavisimaya gazeta*, January 29, 2007 (in Russian).

Shevtsova, Lilia, 1999, *Yeltsin's Russia*. Washington: CEIP.

"Social-Political Situation in Russia in October 2006," 2006, Levada Center Poll (available in Russian at http://levada.ru/press/2006110202.html).

Sokolov, Boris, "Why the Nord-Ost Did Not Explode," *Grani.ru*, November 4, 2002 (available in Russian at http://grani.ru/Projects/NordOst/m.13642.html).

Soldatov, Andrei, "Minders from the Presidential Administration for Lubyanka," *Novaya gazeta*, February 20, 2006 (in Russian).

"Special Operation in Cherkessk is Completed: Achmez Goriyaev's Men are Killed," *Newsru.com*, December 25, 2006 (available in Russian at http://newsru.com/russia/ 25dec2006/kara4.html).

Specter, Michael, "Kremlin, Inc.," *The New Yorker*, January 29, 2007, pp. 50-63.

Stepanova, Ekaterina, 2005, "Russia's Approach to the Fight Against Terrorism," in Jakob Hedenskog, Vilhelm Konnander, Bertil Nygren, Ingmar Olberg & Christer Pursiainen (eds), *Russia as a Great Power: Dimensions of Security Under Putin*. London: Routledge, pp. 301-322.

"The Accused in the Explosion of the Grozny-Moscow Train Deny Guilt," *Grani.ru*, January 29, 2007 (available in Russian at http://www.grani.ru/Society/Law/m.117501.html).

"The Last Point of Anna Politkovskaya," *Novaya gazeta*, October 9, 2006 (in Russian).

Tishkov, Valery, 2004, *Life in a War-Torn Society*, Berkeley CA: University of California Press.

Trenin, Dmitri V. & Alexei V. Malashenko, 2004, *Russia's Restless Frontier: The Chechen Factor in Post-Soviet Russia*, Washington: CEIP.

Troitsky, Nikolai, "A Counter-Terrorist Operation in the State Duma," *Nezavisimaya gazeta*, February 27, 2006 (in Russian).

Tsyganok, Anatoly, "The North Caucasian Version of Anti-Terror," *Russkii zhurnal*, December 6, 2005 (available in Russian at http://russ.ru/politics/reakcii/severokavkazskij_variant_antiterrora).

Tsyganok, Anatoly, "Are the Chechen Paramilitary Units Controllable?" *Polit.ru*, December 7, 2006 (available in Russian at http://www.polit.ru/analytics/2006/12/07/armiya_chechni.html)

De Waal, Thomas, 2006, "Basaev: From Rebel to Vicious Extremist," *IWPR Caucasian Reporting Service*, 11 July (available at http://www.iwpr.net/?p=crs&s=f&o=322196 &apc_state=henicrsf0b0dd69d4b41e3718df38e196f8e8ce).

Islam in the Northern Caucasus
The Case of Dagestan

Mikhail Roschin

Islam first entered and then spread into the North Caucasus through Dagestan, which to this day remains the republic that is the most heavily influenced by Islamic teaching. Until the appearance of Islam, Avaria, the central and northern region of Dagestan, was home to the Georgian Orthodox Church, while the south was influenced by the Albanian Orthodox (Monophysite) Church.[1]

The first missionaries of Islam who arrived in the mid-seventh century in the coastal part of Dagestan were the Arabs. By the tenth century Islam had spread to southern Dagestan, and by the fifteenth to sixteenth centuries had reached its remaining regions, steadily eclipsing all other religious beliefs. Islamic clergy (ulema) took root in the Dagestani principalities and theological and legal literature based on Islamic teachings became widespread. The traditional legal forms (adat) did survive despite the Islamic influence and often underpinned the rights of the local rulers. The struggle of the population against the despotic rule of the princes (shamkhals, khans and utsmiis) often took the form of a struggle for "pure Islamic law" (Sharia).[2]

At the beginning of the nineteenth century, this struggle took a new turn with the arrival of the teachings of the Bukhara Sufi sheikh Bagauddin Nakshband (1318-1389) in Dagestan. The appearance of the Nakshband brotherhood (tarikat) coincided with the strengthening

---

[1] For more on the early Christian history of Dagestan see Takhnaeva, Patimat. The Christian Culture of Avaria in the Middle Ages within the Context of Reconstucting Political History. V-XVI centuries. Makhachkala, 2004.

[2] See Bobrovnikov, Vladimir, Dagestan," Islam in the Territories of the Former Russian Empire: An Encyclopedic Dictionary. Vol. 1, 30-31.

Russian colonial movement in the Caucasus.[3] The structural elements of the Nakshband brotherhood became a foundation for the growth of the liberation movement of the highlanders, which saw its greatest moment during the rule of imam Shamil (1834-1859), who managed to create, first in Dagestan and later in Chechnya, a Muslim state called an "immamat." In Russian historiography, this movement has been called "muridism" because in accordance with Sufi tradition the rebels called themselves "murids" [students] of their imam leaders.[4]

After the end of the war in 1861, the Russian administration of the Caucasus worked with the loyal members of the Muslim clergy, which firmly kept its role in education and justice. On the eve of the 1917 Revolution, Dagestan had over 1,700 small and 356 large mosques in addition to 766 madrasa schools that employed over 2,500 mullah-kadis.[5]

The Civil War of 1918-20 split the ranks of the Dagestani Muslims. One faction, led by sheikh Nazhmuddin Gotsinskii (the fifth imam of Dagestan), sided with the Volunteer Army of General A. Denikin, while the other faction supported the Bolsheviks, who treated Muslims with respect in the early years of Soviet rule.[6] By the latter half of the 1920's, however, Sharia courts and religious schools were closed, and the clergy (ulema) worked against the imposition of "the new lifestyle" among the highlanders, the atheistic propaganda of the Soviet state and later, the collectivization of the peasants. In the 1930's, during the course of the struggle with "anti-Soviet elements" in the republic, Islam was heavily persecuted, with many alims (men knowledgeable in Islam) being arrested and sent to the camps while mosques were closed and often destroyed.

Soviet religious policy liberalized during World War II. The Spiritual Board of Muslims of the Northern Caucasus (*Dukhovnoe upravlenie*

---

[3] See Zelkina, Anna. A Quest for God and Freedom. 2000. 100-120.
[4] See Kazem-bek, M. Muridism and Shamil. Makhachkala, 1990.
[5] According to the Committee of Religious Affairs of the republic of Dagestan.
[6] See Donogo, Khadji Murad. Nazhmuddin Gotsinskii. Socio-Political Struggles in Dagestan During the First Quarter of the Twentieth Century. Makhachkala, 2005.

musulman Severnogo Kavkaza, abbreviated as DUMSK in Russian) was created and some mosques were reopened. Headed by a mufti and located in Buinaksk (formerly known as Temir-Khan-Shura, one of the largest Dagestani religious centers), DUMSK registered religious societies (dzhamaat), appointed and removed imams in the mosques and issued official decisions (fatwas) on a variety of religious issues. The activities of the Board were completely controlled by the Soviet authorities, specifically the KGB, which often used imams as informants. Along with other Muslim boards in the USSR, DUMSK officially declared its support for the "foreign and domestic policies of the Soviet state."[7]

Dagestan played a key role within DUMSK, with most of the functioning mosques of the Northern Caucasus—27 of them by 1988—being located on Dagestani territory.[8] The high level of religious fervor amongst Dagestanis (especially in the highlands) contributed to a preservation of an informal, so-called "parallel" Islam in a variety of forms. These included the actions of Arabists and religious scholars who passed on their knowledge to the younger generations in underground madrasas, the veneration of holy sheikhs with pilgrimages to their graves, and the informal use of Sharia concepts of justice. By the 1970's a variety of religious literature started to spread in Dagestan, including the books and brochures of various Muslim fundamentalist ideologues including Hasan al-Banna, Al-Mawdudi and Yusuf al-Karadavi. In May 1989, the head of DUMSK, Mahmud Gekkiev, left his post under pressure from the Muslim community, having been accused of taking bribes, ignoring the norms of Islamic morality and cooperating with the KGB. This brought about the disintegration of DUMSK and the formation of individual Spiritual Boards in all the Northern Caucasian republics, including Dagestan.[9]

If the 1970's and 1980's saw a certain liveliness in the religious life of Dagestan, what happened in the 1990's can only be called a genuine

---

[7] Contemporary Religious Life in Russia: An Attempt at a Systematic Description. Ed. Burdo, M. and Filatova, S.B., 2005. Vol. 3. 135
[8] According to the Committee of Religious Affairs of the republic of Dagestan.
[9] Contemporary Religious Life in Russia. Vol. 3. 136.

religious renaissance. Across the entire republic, Muslim societies (dzhamaats) were reconstituted, mosques were built or repaired and madrasas, Muslim institutes and universities were opened.

In January 1990, a separate Muslim Spiritual Board was established in Dagestan, with Bagautdin Isaev, a Kumyk, elected as head and the organization moving from Buinaksk to Makhachkala in 1991. In 1990, 345 Dagestanis participated in the first mass hajj from the Soviet Union. The following year, the number of Dagestani pilgrims (khadjis) reached 900. Despite these successes, Isaev was criticized during the first general meeting of Dagestani Muslims for not being sufficiently attentive to the needs of certain communities or promoting the training of new imams. The mufti was also accused of not coordinating his activities with the Alim Union, interfering with the financial audit of the Spiritual Board and of trying to create a separate Spiritual Board for the Turkic-speaking, specifically Kumyk, population of the republic.

It is rather obvious that such sharp criticism of Isaev was engendered by the fact that the Avars (the largest and most religiously devout ethnic group in Dagestan) were unhappy with a Kumyk being in charge of the Spiritual Board and sought to control it themselves. Isaev was removed and the Alim Council chosen by the meeting's delegates elected Avar Said-Ahmad Darbishgadzhiev, the rector of the Kizilyurt Muslim University, as head mufti. To this day, the Spiritual Board has been headed and controlled by the Avars, who (in accordance to the 2002 census) make up 29.4% of Dagestan's population. In 1992 through 1994, various ethnic groups tried to challenge the authority of the Spiritual Board and create separate Kumyk, Dargin and Lak Boards.[10] These were all unsuccessful, however, and in September 1994 the Spiritual Board of the Muslims of Dagestan (abbreviated as DUMD in Russian) was officially declared to be the only rightful organization representing the interests of all Dagestani Muslims.

---

[10] Bobrovnikov. 31-32.

The majority of Dagestan's Muslims follow the traditional Sunni form of Islam as understood by the Shafii School. Sufism has been broadly embraced by the local culture and exists in Dagestan in the form of four tarıkats—Nakshbandiya, Shaziliya, Dzhazuliya (a branch of the Shaziliya brotherhood) and Kadiriya.

During the Soviet period, tarikats were prohibited and Sufi sheikhs were either suppressed by the government or operated underground. For this reason, the act of permitting one's students to teach one's own tarikat (known as iznu or idzhaza) to others was also unofficial, with few, if any, witnesses being present at the iznu (idzhaza). In the 1990's, this led to a proliferation of sheikhs as well as mutual recriminations about the impropriety of the iznu (idzhaza) and the frequent accusation that one's opponent was not actually a proper sheikh.

Today, the most influential sheikh in Dagestan is the Avar Said-effendi Chirkeevskii, who was a shepherd before becoming a sheikh. He teaches at three tarikats in Nakshbandiya, Shaziliya and Dzhazuliya. His murids (followers, students and disciples) control the Spiritual Board of Muslims of Dagestan, Muslim radio and television programs and Muslim publications. While Said-effendi's followers come from different ethnic groups, the Avars have an obvious majority.

The intermingling of the Said-effendi virda (branch of teaching) with the Spiritual Board occurred in 1996 when the head of DUMD was the former dentist Said-Magomed Abubakrov. He was an extraordinary man and a talented orator and preacher. He managed to enhance the prestige of the Spiritual Board and turn it into a power independent of the authorities. He completed the "Avarization" of the Board leadership and of the Makhachkala mosques, both of which were previously held by Kumyks. This happened at a time when the political life of Dagestan was dominated by Dargins (the head of the Governing Council of the republic was Magomed-Ali Magomedov and the mayor of Makhachkala was Said Amirov). The Avars, having led Dagestan in the second half of the twentieth century including the early 1990's, obtained control of the religious sphere of the republic as a form of compensation.

At this time Abubakrov opposed the secular leadership of the republic and demanded that Islam be made the official religion of Dagestan and also decisively confronted the fundamentalist Muslim movement in the region (referred to in the Northern Caucasus as "wahhabite"). In August of 1998, the mufti's car was destroyed by a bomb in the yard near the central mosque of Makhachkala, killing Abubakrov instantly. His killers were never found, but the republic's leadership is suspected to have played a role. As former Secretary of the Dagestani Council for Security, Mogmed Tolboev, cautiously noted, the killing of the mufti was an attempt by "internal forces in the republic" to cause a confrontation between the Sufis and the fundamentalists.[11]

In the fall of 1998, Ahmad-khadji Abullaev was elected as the new head mufti of Dagestan. His authority is not as great as that of his predecessor, making him less independent and much more obedient to the republic's leadership. DUMD is still essentially controlled by the followers of sheikh Said-effendi, but the new key figure, according to experts, is the father of the slain mufti. His name is Khasmagomed Abubakrov. DUMD is not able to control all of the communities in the republic and thus, has only relative authority. It has not been able to build a system of rigid obedience, and certain imams are completely beyond its control.

The imam of each village is elected by his community (dzhamaat) and in accordance to Muslim traditions, DUMD is unable to interfere in this process. The spiritual board tries to play the same role in the republic that the Moscow Patriarchate does in Russia but does not always manage to do so, and its relations with the secular leadership of Dagestan are contradictory at best. DUMD leaders constantly declare that Islam does not differentiate between the secular and the spiritual and they do not deny the possibility of building an "Islamic state" in Dagestan, but speak of this in a formal way, underscoring that this is currently impossible because "the people are not ready." The conflict with the "wahhabites" forces the DUMD to act cautiously and support

---

[11] "Blagovest-info," #34, 1998.

the secular authorities, all the while demanding that the rights of Muslim clergy be enlarged and that the financial aid rendered to it by the state be increased. Realistically, the Spiritual Board does not actually try as to create an "Islamic state" but rather to have Islam declared a privileged, de facto official religion in Dagestan. Concrete demands that have been made include the use of money from the republic's budget to finance the hajj to Mecca, making Friday a holiday and changing aspects of television broadcasting and the educational system. The Board consistently criticizes the leadership of Dagestan for being uncommitted to the struggle against the "wahhabites" and for extending a sort of tolerance to them.

It should be noted that Islam in Dagestan is actually quite pluralistic. Except for "wahhabism," the republic has a very powerful strain of alternative Sufi Islam unconnected to the Spiritual Board. Among the important Sufi teachers, one should note the Kumyk sheikh Muhammad-Amin Paraulkii who died in June of 1999 and nominated sheikh Muhammad-Mukhtar as his successor. The latter is also a Kumyk, and lives in the village of Kiakhulai near Makhachkala and like his former teacher, is a member of the Nakshbandiya tarikat.

A few words should be said about sheikh Tazhuddin Khasaviurtovskii (originally from the Andii village of Ashali). Tazhuddin has a great deal of authority, especially among the Ando-Tsezskii ethnic groups and has preached at three tarikats in Nakshbandiya, Shaziliya and Dzhazuliya. On July 31, 2000, I went to visit the sheikh along with his son, Ibrahim Tazhuddinov. The sheikh received us well though he was hard of hearing, blind and very ill. The sheikh's son translated my questions into the Andian language. The sheikh prayed (dua) over me, holding my hands in his own. Despite his advanced age, his hands were strong and warm, and I felt literally charged by energy afterwards.

This sheikh worked with his murids on an individual basis, with the sheikh and the murid pressing their knees into each other during prayer. Tazhuddin denied the concept of group prayer, demanding only quiet individual prayer. His followers mainly inhabit the Tsymadin, Botlikh, Akhvakhs and Khasavyurt regions. After the death

177

of sheikh Tazhuddin on September 10, 2001, sheikh Muhammed, a Dargin from the Novyi Kostek village of the Khasavyurt region succeeded him.[12]

The most famous sheikh of southern Dagestan is Sirazhuddin Tabasaranskii. He received his iznu in 1980 from the Nakshbandiya sheikh Abdulla, who had lived to be 115 and who was buried in Derbent in the late 1990's. Sirazhuddin has organized a set of madrasas across all of Tabasaran and has become a true spiritual leader of this region. He has also founded the Islamic University of Southern Dagestan, located in Derbent. On August 12-13, 2000, I was a guest of the sheikh in his home village of Khurik. A large prayer was held in his home on the 12th, during which "There is no god except Allah" was chanted repeatedly in Arabic. The prayer ritual was somewhat reminiscent of the New Age practice of rebirthing, or the kriyu technique in Hinduism (a combination meditation and breathing technique), or the written descriptions of a Khlysty (a type of Russian schismatic Christian group) prayer meeting.

Dagestan is also home to the murids of the Nakshbandiya sheikh Muhamad Nazim Kipriotskii, who lives in Lefka in Northern Cyprus and who is a the student of the Avar sheikh Abdallah Dagestani, who has lived most of his life in Syria.

Traditional Sufi Islam in Dagestan is primarily notable for its emphasis on spirituality. It is non-aggressive and the notion of "jihad" is understood to mean the believer's own desire to perfect themselves. Murids tend to treat their sheikh the same way as ordinary Orthodox believers would treat their starets. It is reasonable to suppose that the close ties binding murids and sheikhs are one basis for the Dagestanis' affection for their religious practices. It is unknown exactly what percentage of the Muslim population of Dagestan are regularly observant, but even if we were to assume that it is 20 to 30 percent of

---

[12] I was kindly given this information by the by son of the lake sheikh, Ibrahim Tazhuddinov.

the population, that would place them far above the average level of religious practice in Russia.

While the percentage of Sufi adherents is lower, it is apparently high enough to influence the formation of a particular spiritual culture typical of Dagestani Islam. As a field researcher who has worked in Dagestan over the last ten years, I have to say that except for Chechnya, this is the most religious republic in the Russian Federation. As of September 2003, the republic of Dagestan had the following officially registered institutions: 1,091 large mosques, 558 small mosques, 16 Islamic colleges and universities, 52 branch campuses of colleges, 141 madrasas and 324 mosque schools.[13] This in a republic that according to the 2002 census has a population of 2,576,000 people, 94.4% of whom are Muslim (90.1% Sunni, 4.3% Shiite) and 4.7% Orthodox.[14]

The followers of Sufi Islam in Dagestan have several hundred holy sites and tombs (ziyarat or pir) at which prayers and thanksgiving rituals are held and charity is distributed. In the 1930's, some of these were abandoned, but by the 1990's, they were once more attracting considerable veneration. The tombs contain Arab fighters from the eighth to eleventh centuries, missionaries from the tenth to sixteenth centuries, martyrs (shakhids) who died in battles with the "infidel" in the eighth to early twentieth centuries, Sufis and Muslim scholars (alims) of the thirteenth to twentieth centuries, as well as the innocently slain and the nameless sheikhs whose names and deeds are forgotten. Followers of Sufism also make pilgrimages to "holy" places of the pre-Islamic period that have been integrated into Muslim traditions such as mountains, stones, springs and trees.[15]

In my opinion, the main problem facing Muslim life in Dagestan today is the conflict between the Sufis and the fundamentalists ("wahhabites") that first appeared in the early 1990's and has still not been resolved.

---

[13] According to the Committee of Religious Affairs of the republic of Dagestan.
[14] This information was kindly provided to me by two experts on Dagestan - V. Bobrovnikov and E. Kisriev.
[15] Bobrovnikov. 31.

Any sort of discussion of Islamic fundamentalism, which first appeared in the Northern Caucasus in Dagestan, must surely go beyond the borders of this republic. Islamic fundamentalism in the Northern Caucasus is not essentially different from Islamic fundamentalism in other parts of the world. In the short term, it dates back to the second half of the 1980's, with its theoretical base coming from the classical fundamentalist works of Hasan al-Banna, Seida Kutba, Abu Al-Alia Mawdudi and their predecessors such as Ibn Teimiya, Muhammad ibn Abd al-Wahhab and others. By the mid-1990's, Dagestan became the ideological center of fundamentalism in the Northern Caucasus, while Chechnya became its testing ground.

Islamic fundamentalists in the Northern Caucasus are referred to as "wahhabites," though they do not like this term and they prefer to call themselves "proponents of salafi" (a return to origins) or proponents of "pure Islam." Fundamentalists preach an Islam based on the Koran and the Sunnah, but deny all the historical layers of traditional Sunnite practice acquired over a thousand years of its history, making it improper to refer to them as "traditionalists."[16] They are especially hostile to Sufism, which has deep roots all across the Northern Caucasus and especially in Dagestan, Chechnya and Ingushetia. According to them, the presence of a sheikh or ustaz (instructor) as a mediator between God and man contradicts a basic tenet of the Muslim faith, and they vehemently deny the possibility of pilgrimage to the "holy sites" (ziyarat) of the Sufi tradition. Fundamentalists demand a shortened form of the service for the dead and believe that the time of the four classical Sunni schools (mashab) has passed, and that today it is possible to understand the Koran and the Sunnah through one unified school.[17]

All the main teachers of North Caucasian fundamentalism come from Dagestan, but just as with all other ideological movements, there is both a moderate and a radical wing. The leader of the moderate fundamentalists was Ahmad-kadi Akhtaev (1942-1998), an Avar from

---

[16] Bobrovnikov. 32.
[17] A conversation with the imam of a Vladikavkaz mosque, July 2001.

the village of Kudali in Dagestan. In 1990, during a council of the Muslims of the USSR in Astrakhan, Akhtaev was chosen as the head of the Islamic Renaissance Party. Later, he led the moderate fundamentalist organization "Al-Islamiya." He died, most likely through poisoning, at the age of 55 on the way to his mosque in his own village. Akhtaev was in favor of the peaceful dissemination of fundamentalist ideas and saw himself as a Muslim teacher and enlightener.[18] Many of his pupils are now young imams across the whole of the Northern Caucasus, from Dagestan to Karachaevo-Cherkessia. Like his ideological comrades across the world, Akhtaev thought, "that Islam, both as an idea and a way of life, was a deliberately chosen victim of 'the new world order.'"[19] At the same time, he tried to oppose this with the non-violent preaching of his views and organized a madrasa in his home village of Kudali. Akhtaev also talked about how Islam and Orthodoxy complimented each other in Russia as a Eurasian country.

The leader of the radical wing of the fundamentalists in the Northern Caucasus is Bagauddin Kebedov (born 1945 in the village of Vedeno).[20] In 1990 along with Akhtaev he was one of the founders of the Islamic Renaissance Party, which had a clear fundamentalist bent. In 1991 he founded a madrasa in the city of Kizilyurt near Makhachkala. Kebedov turned out to be a talented preacher and his audio and videocassettes in Avar and Russian were popular not only in Dagestan, but also far beyond its borders. Unlike Akhtaev, Kebedov was apparently always enjoyed working with the public and he quickly began work on creating an organization of radical Islamic fundamentalists that he called "Dzhamaat."

During my trip to Dagestan in the summer of 1997 I had the chance to meet Kebedov and hear his sermon in the mosque in Kizilyurt. Having become the emir (head) of the "Dzhamaat" organization by this point, he explained to me that the post-Communist government of Dagestan

---

[18] "Znamia Islama," ("The Banner of Islam") #1(10), Makhachkala, 12/1998. 3.
[19] Ibid.
[20] Bobrovnikov, V. and Yarlukapov, A., "'Wahhabites' of the Northern Caucasus." Islam in the Territory of the Former Russian Empire, 1999, Vol. 2, p. 20.

is currently in the state of "shirka" (heathenism or polytheism held be equal to unbelief). The registration of the mosques or communities of the fundamentalists is unnecessary. "We are already registered by Allah," he told me. "We do not want to hold power, we want Allah to hold power. Geographical and national boundaries have no meaning for us, we work where we can. Dagestan is currently ruled from Moscow, and we do not have an Islamic society analogous to that which exists in Chechnya. We would approve a full ban on the sale of alcohol if we could, but faith (uman) and monotheism (taukid) are more important to us. In an Islamic state we would like to have the institution of mukhtasibs (morality police), and we see the habit of smoking or drug use as haram (that which is proscribed)." I asked about the possibility of an independent Dagestan and Kebedov replied that he is in favor of an Islamic state, which is key. The state of unbelief (kufr) is unacceptable for him, whether in a component part of the Russian Federation or in an independent Dagestan. These statements are sufficient to show the degree of his radical fundamentalist views. Unsurprisingly scholars refer to this approach as "political Islam."[21] During our meeting Kebedov repeatedly emphasized that Islam is a complete system for human life. As such, it must include ways for building "an Islamic society and a Muslim state."

The most successful attempt at this was undertaken by the villages of Karamakhi and Chabanmakhi of the Buinakh region of Dagestan. In 1997-1999, "Dzhamaat's" program was steadily realized. The ideology of the movement was accepted by the inhabitants, and the local Muslim community, the mosque of which was located in Karamakhi, became a small "wahhabite" republic, a bridgehead of fundamentalism in Dagestan (a sort of "independent Islamic territory"). Because of this, many young people from Dagestan and all the republics of the Northern Caucasus came there in order to seek out "pure Islam."

---

[21] See Nazih Ayubi. Political Islam. London, Routledge, 1991; and Landa, Robert Political Islam – Some Preliminary Conclusions., (Politicheskii Islam: Predvaritelnyi Itogi.) 2005.

On August 20th 1998, Sergei Stepashin, who was at the time the Russian Minister of Internal Affairs, visited Karamakhi and Chabanmakhi and made a verbal agreement with the inhabitants that they may freely live in accordance with Sharia law[22] as long as they comport themselves in a decent fashion and cooperate with the authorities of Dagestan in all other matters. Following this, the situation surrounding the two villages relaxed and their inhabitants started visiting various meetings in Makhachkala.

The community has a "Taliban" preparatory system. D.N., a graduate student in the Institute of Oriental Studies of the Russian Academy of Sciences, studied under this system in July of 1999 while living in Karamakhi, and describes it in the following way.

> It consisted of two stages. The first was the ideological preparation that included a study of the tenets of the faith, referred to as "improving the iman." This was needed since all those who take up weapons, and even those who do not take up weapons, must do everything for Allah, and any man who has other goals will be severely punished on the day of judgment.

> The second stage consisted of military training. A "brother" must know how to fight for Allah... We lived in the following way – we arose very early, at 2:30 am local time (officially the area was on Medina time, which is one hour behind the ordinary Dagestani time zone), made our ablutions, and at three we prayed. Afterwards we would study the Koran and memorize the suras (books). At six in the morning the physical training started, and we would run in the mountains for about six kilometers. As the "brothers" said "the mujahadeen is fed by his

---

[22] In everyday conversation "shariat," that is sharia, is the title given to Muslim law in the Northern Caucasus. In Muslim theology, however, sharia indicates "The Divine Law," out of which laws for Muslims actually flow.

legs"[23] and "it's hard to run in the mountains, but when we descend and attack Makhachkala, we will run like mountain gazelles." ... At the end of the course we had to take exams. Each "brother" had to memorize fifteen suras and be able to answer certain questions covered by the studies. The whole course lasted three weeks. Only after completing this course could we advance to the military training that included hand to hand combat, firing different types of weapons ranging from a pistol to a howitzer, as well as training in battle tactics suitable in mountainous terrain.[24]

This shows that religious training among the radical fundamentalists is closely linked with military training. This approach is largely explainable in terms of the concept of jihad (holy war). The concept of jihad was formulated in the Koran:

Sura 2. Al-Baqarah. (The Cows)

Verse 190. And fight in the Way of Allah those who fight you, but transgress not the limits. Truly, Allah likes not the transgressors.

Verse 191. And kill them wherever you find them, and turn them out from where they have turned you out. And Al-Fitnah is worse than killing. And fight not with
them at al-Masjid-Al-Haram (the sanctuary at Mecca) Unless they (first) fight you there. But if they attack you, then kill them. Such is the recompense of

---

[23] A mujahadeen is he who has taken up jihad, or holy war. (Author's note.) The expression is an alteration of a well-known Russian saying - "the wolf is fed by his legs." (Translator's note.)

[24] *Nezavisimaia Gazeta*, 11/18/1999. 8.

the disbelievers.[25]

In analyzing this particular passage, Vladimir Soloviev, the famous Russian philosopher and scholar of religion, has correctly noted that "despite the harsh tone of the whole invocation, it is clear that for Muhammad holy war was a religio-political measure made necessary by circumstance, and not a continuous religious principle."[26] Certain parts of this Koranic passage do allow it to be interpreted in a more radical and warlike fashion. Later, especially among the Sufis, the notion of "jihad" was spiritualized as the internal attempt to perfect oneself on the way to Allah. The notion of jihad was understood to come in four forms – the jihad of the sword, the jihad of the heart, the jihad of the tongue and the jihad of the arm,[27] and an attempt to return to the harshest possible idea of jihad had potentially dangerous consequences.

At the time of the first Chechen war, Kebedov became convinced of the necessity of a "small jihad," meaning participation in battles with the government's forces.[28] Later, while in Gudermes (Chechnya), which became home to the leaders of "Dzhamaat" at the end of 1997 after being expelled from Dagestan by the authorities (Kebedov referred to this as "the little hegira," thus invoking the "big hegira" of Muhammad), the "Manifesto of 'Dzhamaat' to the Muslims of the World" was issued on January 25th, 1998. In this document, the relations between "Dzhamaat" and the pro-Russian leadership of Dagestan was defined to be "military opposition, with all possible consequences of this fact."[29]

---

[25] al-Hilali, M.T. and Khan, M.M. Translations of the Meanings of The Noble Qur'an in English. Medina. 36-37. Al-Fitnah: polytheism, to disbelieve after one has believed in Allah, or a trial or a calamity or an affliction. The author uses a Russian translation by Soloviev (see below) for the Koranic passage.

[26] Soloviev, V.S. Muhammad: His Life and Religious Teaching. (Magomet: Ego Zhizn and Religioznoye Uchenie.) St. Petersburg, 1902. 60. The author's Russian translation of the Koranic passage is also draw from this work.

[27] Kushev, V. and Piotrovskii, M, "Jihad," Islam: A Short Dictionary, Moscow, 1983. 50.

[28] Bobrovnikov, V. and Yarlukapov, A. 21

[29] Makarov, D.V. Official and Unofficial Islam in Dagestan (Offitsialnyi i Neoffitsialnyi Islam v Dagestane). Moscow, 2000. 42.

It is true that there was some persecution of radical fundamentalists ("wahhabites") in Dagestan, but their response was always asymmetrical. Thus, in a confrontation between "wahhabites" and traditional Muslims in the village of Karamakhi on March 12-14th, 1997, the fundamentalists killed several of their opponents. On December 23rd, 1997, they attacked a Russian military unit in Buinaksk.[30] In 1997 the radicals also assailed Akhtaev, the leader of the moderate fundamentalists, accusing him of being ignorant in religious affairs, and they accused his followers of trying to frighten all opposition into silence.[31]

During the years of the first Chechen war (1994-96), the radicals formed a military wing led by a Saudi emigrant known as Khattab.[32] He was born in 1969 in Arar in the northern part of the kingdom, and headed to Afghanistan in 1987, where he trained in the camps near Dzhelalabad and fought in Dzhelalabad, Khost and in the storming of Kabul. In the 1990's, Khattab participated in the Tajik civil war on the side of the Islamic rebels. Later, however, he refused to take part in the internal battles amongst the mujahadeen in Afghanistan, viewing the conflict as a fitnah (a troubled and confused time when brother kills brother). During these years, as Khattab revealed in one of his interviews, he met Osama bin-Laden, who was not yet the head of al-Qaeda.

Later, Khattab made his way to the Dagestani village of Karamakhi and married a local girl. In 1995, he moved to Chechnya and in August of that year his armed unit became part of the Central Front of the military forces of the Chechen republic of Ichkeria, commanded by Shamil Basayev. The most famous operation of his unit was the April 1996 attack on the armored column of the 245th mechanized regiment near the village of Yarush-Mardu. Ninety-five government soldiers were killed in this attack.

---

[30] Makarov. 42.

[31] *As-Salam* #18, September 1997.

[32] It was popularly believed that Khattab was a Jordanian.

186

Following the end of the first Chechen war, Khattab organized several military training camps in Chechnya, where Dagestanis and Chechens, as well as representatives of most Muslim ethnic groups of the Russian Federation, underwent military and guerilla training. His camps were located near the village of Serzhen-yurt. In April of 2002, Khattab died while reading a poisoned letter passed to him by an FSB agent within his camp. His real name—Samir as-Suveilim—became known only after his death, since he always called himself Khattab out of respect for the second Righteous Caliph Omar ibn al-Khattab.[33]

By the start of 1999, radical fundamentalism became a major part of the political instability in both Dagestan and Chechnya, with the radicals receiving sizable financial help from international Islamic organizations. Currently, radical Islamic fundamentalism has become a revolutionary ideology that has in many ways replaced Marxism. Geidar Dzhamal, one of the most famous radical fundamentalist ideologues in Russia and one of the founders of the Islamic Renaissance Party of Russia, has noted that "Islam today functions not as a religion in the traditional secularist meaning of that term, but as an all-encompassing political ideology that seeks to defend the weak and the oppressed."[34]

In late spring of 1999, the Congress of the Peoples of Dagestan and Chechnya, an organization created by the "Dzhamaat" and a variety of other extremist groupings, declared Shamil Basayev the emir of the Liberation Army of the Northern Caucasus, and Khattab was named his second in command. Starting in late May 1999 and continuing through July of the same year, combat on the Dagestani-Chechen border occurred constantly. The radicals sought to start an invasion of Dagestan, and finally attacked in the Botlikh region, where part of the

---

[33] At the end of 2002 Khattab's older brother, Mansur as-Suveilim revealed to the media that Khattab's real name was Samir bin Salikh bin Abdalla bin Salikh bin Abdurrakhman bin Ali as-Suveilim. In the fall of 1996, after Russian troops left Chechnya after the first war Khattab received a medal for bravery and heroism from the Chechen government and received the rank of brigadier-general. *Al-Khaiat* (an international Arabic newspaper financed by Saudi Arabia), 04/29/02 and 05/01/02.

[34] *Moscow Times*, 11/16/01.

Avar population in the villages of the historic Tekhnutsal community helped the mujahadeen, allowing them to occupy a series of villages in the region. They declared this to be the Islamic Republic of Dagestan, with Sirazhuddin Ramzanov, a relative of the late Ahmad-kadi Akhtaev, named as Prime Minister.

The majority of the region's population was hostile to the invaders, with the Andian ethnic group, long an enemy of the Chechens because of conflicts over summer grazing, closing four mountain passes (including the important Kharami and Rikvani passes) to the radicals.[35] The mujahadeen were even unable to capture Botlikh, a strategic point that would open up the valley of the Andian Koisu. The majority of the local inhabitants saw the jihad coming from Chechnya as a case of Chechen aggression, and local volunteers fought alongside Russian governmental forces to contain it. The inhabitants of four Andian villages—Andi, Gagatl, Rikvani, and Ashali—held village meetings and agreed to fight against the radicals. This was due to both the Andians' adherence to traditional Sufi Islam and their total rejection of "wahhabite" ideals.[36] The women of Botlikh fed Russian soldiers the way they would feed their own children, something which was inconceivable during the first Chechen war. Having been defeated, the radicals were forced to retreat back to Chechnya, with most of the participants being Dagestani "wahhabites" and members of "Dzhamaat."

Emboldened by their success, Federal and Dagestani authorities undertook a punitive expedition against the "wahhabite republic" in the villages of Karamakhi and Chabanmakhi. The operation started on the night of the August 28-29 1999, and after a two week siege both villages were almost completely destroyed and most of their inhabitants killed, though a core group of defenders headed by Dzharulla Radzhbaddinov managed to break through and escape into the surrounding forests.[37]

---

[35] This information was kindly provided to me by prof. M.A. Aglarov who was in the Botlikh region during this time.

[36] This information was also provided by prof. M.A. Aglarov, who is an ethnic Andian.

[37] Author's field journal.

Shortly after the end of the Karamakhi operation, the villages were visited by a group from the "Memorial" human rights organization. One of them, Alexander Sokolov, wrote that the "'wahhabites' supporters within the rather affluent villages comprised around 10-20% of the population, with the rest of the inhabitants being adherents of traditional Islam. These people were defenseless before the united organization of the extremists, who were willing to use violence in order to realize their dogmatic religious vision."[38]

In my opinion, Sokolov is correct in referring to the "wahhabites," in this case the members of "Dzhamaat," as "religious schismatics." "Dzhamaat" has all the typical features of a totalitarian sect, and leaving the organization is entirely unsafe for any member brave enough to try since "Dzhamaat" keeps tight control over the unity and numbers of its members.[39]

In analyzing the actions of "Dzhamaat" in Karamakhi and Chabanmakhi, Sokolov writes that "by the summer of 1999 the 'wahhabites' came to completely control the life in these two villages. The Sharia court organized by the "wahhabites" used caning as a punishment both for the consumption of alcohol and also for participation in anti-wahhabite demonstrations in the capital of the republic. The same Sharia court, apparently on religious grounds, sentenced a man close to the leadership of "Dzhamaat" to 10 years of exile from the village as a punishment for murder."[40]

In early 1999, Basayev and Khattab invaded the Novolak region of Dagestan in order to help "Dzhamaat" in Karamakhi and Chabanmakhi. Their units rode in Kamaz trucks down the highway towards Khasavyurt and were stopped only five kilometers from the city. Had they made it into Khasavyurt, the satiation in Dagestan would have become critical, and defense trenches were already being dug around Makhachkala. In Khasavyurt, the mujahideen could have

---

[38] Sokolov, A. "What should we do if the tail wags the dog in the wrong direction?" *Express-khronika*, #39/594/25, p. 4.
[39] Author's field journal.
[40] Sokolov, p. 4.

relied on the support of the Chechen-Akkin ethnic group, which makes up more than a third of the city's population, and evidence shows that most of the invaders of the Novolak region were actually Chechens. Once again, the attempt to start a jihad in Dagestan was perceived by most locals as an aggression organized by Chechen extremists.

In theory, the idea of jihad, or gazavat, as it is traditionally called in the Northern Caucasus, is not foreign to the Dagestani consciousness. It's quite alive among the Avars, but also the Dargins, the Laks, and the Chechen-Akkins. All of the preceding five imams in the region, the most famous of whom was Shamil, were Avars. In a sense the Avars are unwilling to admit that a new imam could be a Chechen, and this was the role to which emir Shamil Basayev aspired. Basayev essentially made the idea of the immamat and the "Islamic state" unattractive and unheroic for the Dagestanis.

In September 1999, a law was passed officially prohibiting "wahhabism" on Dagestani territory, and hundreds of "wahhabites" were arrested. In the first years following the defeat of the August-September 1999, jihad the radical fundamentalist movement was seriously weakened and almost seemed to disappear. With time, however, various crises in the republic started to recur.

Corruption continued to destroy the authority of the local government. The "Death Squadrons" of the pro-Russian Chechen leader Ramzan Kadyrov started systematically terrorizing the inhabitants of the Khasavyurt region starting in 2003. All of this can probably explain the "wahhabite" movement's ability to recover from its losses and grow again. Armed bands of Islamic radicals are regularly seen near the environs of the Dagestani capital of Makhachkala today, especially in the thickets of Mount Tarki-tau that overlooks the city. This invariably leads to the question of why a crisis is once more starting to build, and why is the situation in the republic starting to be ever more tense and unpredictable?

It seems that in order to answer this question, we must remember that while remaining an administrative part of the Russian Federation,

190

Dagestan is culturally part of the Muslim world. Islam had a strong influence here even during Soviet times, and in the post-Soviet period it has at least doubled. Since Sufi Islam was traditionally part of the republic's culture, the local authorities have financially and otherwise supported the cult of Sheikh Said-effendi from the 1990's to the present day. According to many Dagestanis, the sheikh is a puppet of the Dagestani government, a puppet created with the help of the security services. Starting in the 1990s, the republic's youth have become interested in so-called "wahhabism." Young people see this as an alternative way of life, one that denies the corrupt authority of the current ruling elite of Dagestan. More and more frequently, one sees young women wearing hijab in the streets of Makhachkala and young men join the bands of radical Muslim rebels.[41] The younger generations are angered by the lack of any social or economic future in the republic and the mass corruption of the republic's leadership, believing that radical Islam ("wahhabism") is capable of changing the situation for the better. Yasin Rasulov, a graduate student of the Dagestan State University, was a very noticeable proponent of "wahhabism" in recent years. As he puts it, the "invasion of Dagestan by the 'Islamic Army of the Caucasus,' (in August-September 1999) with the goal of establishing Sharia law, the destruction of the Sharia-based Kadar enclave (the Karamakhi and Chabanmakhi area) and the current punitive actions of the authorities against the supporters of 'wahhabism' are all the continuation of the history of opposition between Russian authorities and armed Islamic rebels in the Northern Caucasus. The cooperation of the officially-loyal clergy with the authorities and with the Ministry of Internal Affairs is completely logical within the framework of this tradition, which is being continued by today's Russia."[42]

Yasin Rasulov was killed on October 12th, 2005 in Makhachkala in the course of one of the operations conducted regularly by the Dagestani

---

[41] Roshchin, M. "The 'Wahhabi' Insurgents in Dagestan," *Frontier*, #10 (Autumn), 2005, pp. 48-49.
[42] Rasulov, Yasin. "The Mirror of the Caucasus' History."
http://www.chernovik.net/article.php?paper_id=35&article_mode=

Ministry of Internal Affairs.[43]   Earlier, in July 2005, the leader of the Dagestani organization "Shariat" Rasul Makasharipov was also slain in Makhachkala, and today the military wing of the organization is headed by Rappani Khalilov.   His units make up the Dagestan Front in the unified armed resistance of the Northern Caucasus, which is headed by the president of the Chechen republic of Ichkeria Dokku Umarov. This does not mean, however, that the Dagestani "wahhabite" units are merely a branch of the Chechens, but instead we are seeing a network-type association based on common interest.

In 2005, especially in the spring and summer, the "wahhabite" rebels of Dagestan became quite active, killing policemen, blowing up trains, and even assassinating certain ministers. The assassination attempt against the Minister of Internal Affairs of Dagestan A. Magomedtagirov and the killing of the district attorney of Buinaksk B. Bitarov (which occurred on the Tolgin highway near Makhachkala on August 8th, 2006) are evidence of a well developed armed underground. The

---

[43] The role of Yasin (Makhach) Rasulov in the Dagestani "wahhabite" movement is not entirely clear. He was the most visible ideologue of "wahhabism" of the last several years, and he was noticeably better educated that his predecessors. It seems that he could have been a participant in the thoughtful intra-Muslim dialogue that is so necessary in today's Dagestan. It's uncertain how deeply involved he was in the armed resistance within the republic. There is evidence that he was killed on October 12th, 2005, though on April 11th, 2006 he was once more declared dead. It's interesting that the article in "Kommersant" about his second demise was entitled "Kontrolnaia smert ideologa "Shariata," (reoughly meaning "The corroborating death of the ideologue of "Shariat.") The article stated that "Makhach Rasulov (Yasin), one of the ideologues of the wahhabite underground of Dagestan was killed yesterday in the course of an operation in Makhachkala... As later explained by the first deputy of the head of the Ministry of Internal Affairs division in the Southern Federal Region Sergei Solodnikov, the slain man turned out the be the famous religious extremist Makhach Rasulov, who signed his articles in the local newspapers with the name Yasin. Earlier he was known as a freelance writer for the republic's weekly "Novoye delo," where he authored a column about Islam. The local Ministry of Internal Affairs representatives say that Rasulov was the emir of Makhachkal and the successor to Rasul Makasharipov. Emir Rasulov was linked to more than a dozen serious crimes, most of which were assault or terrorist acts directed towards members of the security services." The complete article may be found at:
http://www.rambler.ru/click?from=info&_URL=http%3A%2F%2Fwww.kommersant.ru
The title of the "Kommersant" article nicely underscores the potential dubiousness of the information provided. The whole issue is insufficiently clear, in my opinion, partially because it is customary to blame unsolved (so called "hanging") crimes on the dead.

question then arises—what is the future of such a movement? Can it bring down the regime currently in existence in Dagestan or become a long running destabilizing factor similar to the guerrilla movements of Latin America? While this is a difficult question to answer, it seems to me that the latter possibility is more likely. What is clear, however, is that "political Islam" is becoming more and more important in the Northern Caucasus, and it is unlikely that it can be stopped using only police measures. The tension would probably be lessened by an open dialogue among the republic's Muslim groups, and the honest admission by the republic's Spiritual Board of the fact that Dagestani Muslims hold a plurality of religious opinions.

The Struggle for Dagestan:
Reflections of a Dagestani Journalist

Abdurashid Saidov

During these complicated times even the small republic of Dagestan in southern Russia has not remained free of problems. The republic occupies the eastern part of the Northern Caucasus. An interior republic during the Soviet period, Dagestan is now one of Russia's borderlands, sharing a frontier with Azerbaijan and Georgia, and a maritime border running from Astrakhan oblast in the north to Azerbaijan in the south. The overall territory of the republic is 50,200 square kilometers, the population (according to the census of 2002) is 2,577,000, giving Dagestan an overall population density of 51.2 people per sq km. The republic is unusual in that there are at least 30 indigenous ethnic groups with their own languages living within its borders. This means that even if the most extreme separatist tendencies within the republic were realized the language of inter-ethnic communication would have to be Russian.

Of all the Muslim regions of Russia, Dagestan was the most religious yet at the same time was considered the most respectful of the traditions (adat) of the various ethnic groups that lived within its borders. And these traditions, as we all understand, do not always match religious teaching. Similarly, despite the fact that Russia converted to Christianity over a thousand years ago the contemporary Orthodox faith contains holidays and traditions derived from the polytheistic past that are not acceptable to fundamentalist Christians. The famous imam Shamil fought tooth and nail against such traditions while leading the mountaineers' struggle against tsarist Russia. As they like to say today, even Shamil could not Islamize Dagestan to the same degree that some contemporary radicals would like.

Dagestan was the most learned republic within medieval Russia. During the first half of the 19th century, when people were traded for

194

pure-bred dogs in Russia, Dagestan had numerous societies of uzdens, a word that means "free men." Elements of civil society were highly developed, much more so than in some European countries. Even during the wars in the Caucasus in the 19ᵗʰ century the Russian soldiers, burdened with serfdom and forced military service, chose the status of free men and went over to the side of the mountaineers and entered these free societies. Orthodox churches were built in the mountains of Dagestan for those who had laid down their weapons.

During the Soviet period all freedoms were destroyed. The intelligentsia and the clergy did not escape the sad fate of the rest of the country during the 1920's-40's. Lomonosov, the NKVD minister of Dagestan during the pre-war years, used to say that, "my goal is that not a single thinking person remains in Dagestan" (from the memoirs of Lev Razgon, an author who passed through all the horrors of the Stalinist camps, and the above mentioned Tarasuk was the commander of a camp where Razgon did time). By the end of the Soviet period the republic had only a few dissidents or clergymen who were willing to speak out against the regime. At the time of the dissolution of the USSR Dagestan was quite committed to the ideals of Communism, and until 1993-94 the leadership of the republic was unwilling to believe that the changes then occurring were irreversible. This attitude was clearly evident in how the hammer-and-sickle flag continued to hang above all of the governmental buildings during these years. The early 1990's, a period when Russia underwent the most painful and important reforms of its economy, was marked by the Dagestani government's quiet sabotaging of the Kremlin program. The government-run media mocked the notions of private property, civil liberties and the idea of privatization and the transition to a market economy.

It was at this time that conservative elements in the Kremlin's special services tried to split the republic along ethnic lines and foment ethnic strife, a process began during Mikhail Gorbachev's time. They used their connections with the nascent criminal groups of the time, including racketeers, scam artists, and even bandits. Besides these criminals the Kremlin also used certain retired military men as leaders of ethnic movements. The real, undeclared goals of most of these movements were anti-democratic, totalitarian, and often militaristic and destructive.

For instance, the Confederation of the Mountain Peoples of the Caucasus was created in 1990 and led by Musa Shanibov, a totally unknown professor, and a Colonel in the Russian Army, Ibrahim-Beila. It called for war against Russia and the right of all the Northern Caucasus republics to secede. Such organizations caused many problems for the democratic movements of the region. General Kakhrimanov, a political commissar of the Soviet Army, still considers himself the leader of the divided Lezgin people and periodically makes provocative statements that complicate relations with neighboring Azerbaijan and make the lives of the Lezgin living there more difficult. During the rule of Azerbaijani President Abulfaz Elchibey the leader of the People's Front of Azerbaijan came to know firsthand the full destructive, and anti-democratic effect of the Lezgin "Sadval" movement led by retired Soviet Major General Mukhidin Kakhrimanov Kakhrimanov.

During the late 1980's certain ethnic movements in Dagestan worked for a partial secession from the republic in the hope of joining the USSR (ostensibly, the RSFSR, that is the Russian Federal Soviet Republic which later became the Russian Federation). The same goals were put forth by the criminal and nationalistic regimes of South Ossetia, Abkhazia, and Transnistria. All of these were motivated by conservative agitation, with the ostensible goal of the whole affair being to show the importance of the Politburo, Communist Party, and the USSR. The idea was to show that without the Party the whole country would explode and bring grief and blood to all those who refused to cooperate with the Communists. Today life has shown that grief and blood has actually come to those who followed the lead of the reactionaries from the Kremlin.

In Dagestan, only several of the many ethnic groups that inhabit the republic have their own writing systems (based on the Cyrillic alphabet), their own radio and TV programs, their own theaters, publishing houses and the ability to study their language in school. These languages are Avar, Dargin, Kumyk, Lezgin, Tabasaran, and Tat. Russian is, of course, a mandatory and necessary language for all these ethnic groups, which they learn beginning in the first grade. The population breakdown of the republic is shown in Table 1 (see Appendix).

It should be noted that there are whole ethnic groups that speak entirely different languages that have absolutely nothing in common with Avar or Lezgin, but which are included into the Avar or Lezgin groups. See Table 2 (Appendix). For example the Bagvalins, Chamalins, Andiytsy, Godoberintsy, Botlikhtsy, Khvarshintsy and many other peoples without their own written languages make up nearly half of the 800,000 Avars that live in Dagestan. Also, there are more than 10,000 Bagvalins who live in Dagestan. There also exist extremely small groups the size of a small village that speak their own unique, unwritten language. On the eve of the recent census some of these ethnic groups attempted to identify themselves as being separate from the Avars, but many of them succumbed to influence from above. The Didoi-Tsez group, however, counted as part of the Avars until 2002 now self-identify themselves as Didoi (Tsez). The problem with providing alphabets and grammar textbooks for these poorly studied, unwritten languages is very important today, but the government does not have the will to do so.

Despite all the crude mistakes made in the field of ethnic politics during the Soviet period, the idea of "ethnic strife" is rather a fantastic one in contemporary Dagestan. It is an entirely different story when various members of the business or political elite, being part of different ethnic groups, use their leadership and finances to stir up the peace with slogans of ethnic loyalty and self-defense. In the early 1990's any threat to a government official was explained as an attack on an ethnicity's rights and demonstrations and street disorders were organized under the banner of protecting the tribe. Thus any attempt to remove a thieving Communist in the early 1990's was always greeted with protests held under such slogans as "The Avars are maligned!" and "The Kumyks are oppressed!," leading to disturbances in the squares and road closures.

197

During the same time period several ethnic armed militias were formed under the guise of "protecting the national interests" of a particular ethnicity. This is an absurd excuse, since the illnesses, problems, and hopes of all the peoples of Dagestan, as well as all the peoples of Russia, were the same during that time. These "national movement" militias controlled the nascent business in the republic and levied tithes from all of their co-nationals using the pretense of needing funds for defending the group's interests and the procurement of weapons. By 1993-95 the leaders of these groups had entered the government. Some had become members of the State Duma, some became ministers within the republic, and some managed to secure ownership of a factory, or some other piece of profitable real estate. By 1994-96 the criminals' control over the republic's economy was complete.

A new period had begun – a period of total control over the economy and the republic's supposed new leaders by those who actually hold power through the security apparatus. This meant that the obedient and totally controllable paid leaders of the mob became the titular masters of the republic, while true authority lay with the shadow leadership on the principle of, "we helped you then, you serve us now." Both sides hold enough information to compromise each other many times over, and the balance between them is not preserved on the basis of law or on the Constitution, but on the basis of making deals typical of professional criminals.

This balance was disturbed when the brothers Khachilaev, leaders of the Lak national movement, tried to move their activities into a completely legal sphere. While their murders are attributed to their criminal past, the real cause is their attempt starting in 1994-95 to play an independent role in the political and economic life of the republic. Nadyr Khachilaev became a member of the State Duma, and Magomed a deputy of the National Council of Dagestan. Nadyr is the one and only man in modern Russian history to be stripped of his legislator's immunity and accused of a dozen crimes. Having overcome all accusations he remained free, but along with his older brother was felled by the assassin's bullet.

The district attorneys, the Ministry of Internal Affairs, the FSB, the men who work in the courts all got their claws into the businesses of the republic by the mid-1990's. The legal owners of all these businesses were those men who had illegally controlled business in the early 1990's. Today any shop in Dagestan, even if it has a daily revenue of several thousand rubles (several hundred dollars) has its own "supervisor", a local beat cop who receives a portion of the profits on a monthly basis. Officials from the security services have essentially become owners of all vital objects within the republic. An interesting example is the case of a man who acquired a large business because his nephew was a district attorney, but later declared war on his own relative because of the unremitting pressure from the official.

According to Mukha Aliev, the former president of Dagestan (2006 to February 2010), the shadow economy accounts for more than 50% of business activity within the republic. While he was still the speaker of the Dagestani parliament, Mr. Aliev criticized the practice of selling the posts of district attorney and judge throughout the republic, a practice common in 2002. Aliev even had a list of prices that needed to be paid at the time. After being appointed president of Dagestan by Vladimir Putin, and after harshly condemning the tax agencies of the republic and the need to legalize the economy, Aliev has been unable to make any real changes. For example, the rate of tax collection during the first quarter of 2002 only rose 9.98%.

It is simply impossible to speak of business being conducted legally today. Therefore, it is quite reasonable to suppose that not all murders and terrorist acts directed against the security services are cases of Islamic or some other type of radicalism. They are often the work of crushed and oppressed businessmen. According to the anti-monopoly agency of Dagestan the Dagestani minister of internal affairs acts as an arbiter between contesting sides in the republic, even in cases when one of the sides is a state agency like the tax police or the anti-monopoly agency. Indeed, this sort of relationship between business and the state is not just typical of Dagestan, but is common to all of Russian business, and to all of Putin's Russia, as demonstrated by the recent events concerning Mr. Khodorkovsky and his former oil company, Yukos.

199

Locally, however, such events tend to be much more brazen. Tax inspectors complain of being unable to collect taxes from those businessmen that have patrons who are high-ranking Dagestani officials.

It would seem that with the end of Soviet rule the republic and its people have finally received economic freedom. They have the ability to make every piece of city land work and turn a profit and astonishing opportunities for private enterprise. All of this should be fueling the growth of the republic's tax revenue, but instead year after year Dagestan becomes ever more dependent on federal aid and the economy continues to stagnate. It does not take an economist long to realize the essence of what is going on – theft. When the shadow economy accounts for over 50% of the total, this is theft, pure and simple.

There is also another flowering form of theft – the misuse of governmental money. Starting with 1994, or more correctly with the operation in neighboring Chechnya, a veritable downpour of money has descended on Dagestan. "Hit the Chechens with rockets, hit their neighbors with cash!" "Federal money" became a synonym for "nobody's money." After a decade of mass misuse of funds, there hasn't been one successful, thoroughly run prosecution. One gets the feeling that the Kremlin, terrified of what happened in Chechnya, has taken the attitude of, "do anything you want, but do it as part of Russia" when dealing with Dagestan and the other republics of the region.

Today the republic is actually home to a unique phenomenon. Unlike all the other regions of the Russian Federation, Dagestan has a president who is not involved in business, not involved in criminal activity, and actually is an honest, decent man with a reputation of being a clean politician. If Mr. Abramovich does not sleep nights, he is thinking of his oil company or about soccer. If some senator or governor does have insomnia, it means he is worrying about his vodka business or his real estate. But it seems that if the president of Dagestan does have sleepless nights, it is because he is worrying about the current situation and the future of Dagestan.

The first six months of this man's administration show the true nature of contemporary Russian politics. Today Russia does not need such leaders, it only seeks to preserve that which has been created over the past fifteen years. All attempts to change anything in the republic have hit an invisible, insurmountable wall. The president has said that it is not possible to work or live like this any longer. But except for a change in the attorney general, nothing has happened. Furthermore, the attempts to remove the minister of internal affairs of the republic, a minister that many analysts and journalists believe is one of the causes of continuing terrorism in Dagestan, have been blocked by the federal authorities, and even by the President of Russia himself. Dagestan was recently visited by the Minister of Internal Affairs of the Russian Federation, Rashid Nurgaliev, who brought with him a medal and Putin's personal messages of gratitude for a job well done for the Dagestani minister. It is simply not possible to remove a minister who has received Putin's gratitude and a medal. But while he is minister, he will not change his ways of trying to enforce the law, and that means that terrorism will never disappear from the republic.

Starting in 1999, when armed conflict first came to Dagestan, the mass arrests of all who kept even the most superficial Muslim norms began. A young man who attends Friday prayers, does not drink or use drugs and who has no criminal activity to his name would be at least suspected of supporting the "Wahhabites." The release of such a man following his arrest could only be achieved if his family paid off the authorities. If no "ransom" were forthcoming, it would be simple to fabricate an indictment of illegally bearing arms or possession of ammunition. It became common at this time to plant weapons, ammunition, or drugs in the pockets or homes of the accused and to obtain confessions under torture. The torture and beatings going on in the pre-trial holding cells have been described by all the media outlets with the exception of the internal newspapers of the ministry of internal affairs and the attorney general's office. The police have become the most important threat to the safety of Dagestan's citizens.

The most popular method of counter-terrorism in Dagestan is to wreck any building that suspects may be hiding in. It is true that after Mukha

Aliev became President of Dagestan that the destruction of homes of suspected militants noticeable declined (Table 3, see Appendix), On numerous occasions Aliev declared that such a tactic was not acceptable outside of wartime. Moreover, it should be noted that multi-story city houses were also being attacked with tanks and artillery alongside any suspects believed to be hiding inside those buildings. Dozens of families have had their possessions destroyed by fire during these operations.

Even former government officials have fell victim to these operations. I recall one counter-terrorism operation in Makhachkala that ended with the death of the suspects but also the destruction of the home of 69-year-old Zubail Khiyasov, a former Dagestani deputy minister of culture and the director of a Kumyk theater. According to his family and coworkers Khiyasov was distant from radical Islam, and had even quarreled with his own daughters over their marriages to observant Muslims. He was a director of a secular, reasonably avant-garde Kumyk theater, not a church choir or a Sufi lodge. The concepts of "director of a modern theater" and "Islamic radical" are inherently incompatible. And yet ministry of internal affairs staff claimed that he screamed "Allah akbar!" while firing at them as they tried to storm the building. Most of the residents probably failed to even understand what was going on. The last scene for the aging director was his own death.

According to Russian law the bodies of terrorists are not released to their relatives for burial. This is why the body of the former Chechen President Aslan Maskhadov was never released to his family. This is despite the fact that he was the most moderate, sober, and reasonable politician that modern Chechnya has had, with the exception of Ahmed Zakaev. Maskhadov's connection to terrorism existed only in the speeches of Kremlin ideologues and prosecutors. Even his death was not the result of the professional quality of Russian intelligence services, but the dishonorable exploitation of Maskhadov's naiveté and trust – he had tried to communicate with the Russian government, he sought to peacefully end a conflict that had taken hundreds of thousands of lives. In any event, the director's body was finally released under popular protest, but the other victims of the same operation were only released

202

upon payment of $15,000. The Magomedov family lost two sons in this operation, one of whom had been released from pre-trial detention on suspicion of terrorist activity only the day before. The Magomedov's tried everything to get the bodies of their sons, but were refused. The Khiyasov family obtained his body, but the Magomedovs received nothing in return.

If we want to discuss terrorism as a result of the activity of the security services and law enforcement the case of Rasul Makasharipov, the leader of the Dagestani faction "Shariat," is most illuminating. In 1999 all video recordings show him to be a virtual shadow of Shamil Basaev, for whom he worked as an interpreter. By 2000, when the military campaign in Chechnya had gotten underway, the Kremlin announced an amnesty for all those who voluntarily turned themselves in. Rasul was one of the first to comply. Having spent several weeks in an FSB cell, he was declared innocent of especially severe crimes that would prevent him from being amnestied and was released. Shortly afterwards he was detained and questioned by men from the 6th department of the Dagestani ministry of internal affairs (the department for combating terrorism and organized crime).

This department's torture methods have shocked even men from other security services. One such torture is completely grinding down the teeth of a strapped-down victim using a file. Another – inserting a tube into the anus, threading through a piece of barbed wire, removing the tube and then pulling out the wire until the victim confesses. There is also the suspension of people by their handcuffed hands and forcing someone to sit on a bottle so that it penetrates the anus. After dealing with people like this Makasharipov chose to flee to the forests and fight against his torturers. If a man cannot find his place in civilian life, if he is constantly suspected and dishonored, then what else can he do?

When Rasul couldn't be caught, it was his relatives and men from his village that suffered. Thus Makhach Khabibov, born 1976, a father of two young children and a second cousin to Rasul was abducted along with other men from his village of Novyi Sasitli of the Khasavyurt region at the end of 2004. They were taken to Chechnya and several months later the killing of the abducted Dagestanis was presented as "yet another battle with terrorists, during which the military successfully destroyed the bandits." The slain were eventually identified by their relatives based on their clothes and other distinguishing marks. The pre-burial autopsy conducted in Chechnya where the men were still listed as "unidentified" showed that all of them had empty gastro-intestinal tracts, suggesting that they were starved by their captors.

Another second cousin, Halil, a man who is legally blind, was forced to go into hiding starting in March 2006 because weapons had been planted in his house and he was declared wanted by the authorities. People from his village say that he never left his home or his family, and even his health never allowed him to undertake any sort of criminal activity. A month later he was killed in an anti-terrorist operation near Buinaksk, which led the famous journalist Yulia Latynina to say that: "A blind terrorist can't live long."

A more recent case involved some 14-16 year old boys from a region that borders Chechnya. An unknown "benefactor" got them together for a trip to the sea, though one boy couldn't go because his grandmother kept him home to help with the household. Overseen by this "benefactor" the group was driven to the Chechen border where the leader told the boys to go ahead and that he would catch up with them in a second. They proceeded towards Chechnya, only to be met with a wall of automatic fire from Kadyrov's men. The murdered boys were then declared to be a group of Dagestanis heading towards Chechnya in order to support the guerrillas there. This supported Ramzan Kadyrov's repeated statements that Chechnya is actually at peace, and that Dagestan is the terrorist den from which all of Chechnya's troubles grow. This is not the first attempt by the current leadership in Chechnya to draw Dagestan into large-scale anti-terrorist operation. Of course many Russian generals are just itching to repeat what they did in Chechnya by bringing war to Dagestan.

The shortsighted politics of the Dagestani leadership towards those men who are willing to return to civilian life needs to be noted. In Chechnya Kadyrov can order the amnesty of any insurgent who can

204

then be taken, without being disarmed, into one of Kadyrov's bands. Things are very different in Dagestan. For three years, I had to deal with various Dagestani and federal agencies in order to arrange the return of the famous Dagestani poet Adallo, a seventy-year-old man who had been declared wanted by Interpol. I was threatened with being arrested as a terrorist sympathizer and was told that the whole undertaking was a dead end. The only condition set by the poet for his return was that he would not be held in pre-trial prison. He asked for this as he had just undergone heart surgery while in exile abroad. Adallo is a well-known songwriter and poet whose only fault lay in the fact that he knew Dudaev, Maskhadov, Yandarbiev, Basaev, and Khattab, and thus had been declared an international terrorist. Over the course of three years I appealed to numerous community leaders and members of the regional parliament. In the summer of 2004 the attorney general of the republic gave his guarantee that no repressive measures would be taken until a court had made its decision on the issue. The fact that the poet was not imprisoned was due to the positive attitude of the authorities, of the positive approach taken by the then-leader of Dagestan Magomedali Magomedov and the federal officials who agreed to accept Adallo and not hold his past against him.

The religious confrontation that ended with armed conflict in 1999 actually began in the early 1990's. Young men who questioned some of the traditions that had arisen over the past several decades appeared among the Sunni Muslims of the republic. It should be remembered that in the past the religious community was not united behind one leader or mufti, but instead followed a number of Sufi leaders (ustaz) who did not always get along with each other (almost every single Sufi leader considers only himself worthy of being called a Sufi ustaz. Therefore any followers of another Sufi leader are declared as having gone astray, a claim that a believer sees as tantamount to being declared a godless heathen). It is quite possible that these tensions were provoked and controlled by the Russian intelligence services, since a united community of believers with one leader could have been a powerful force during the late 1980's and early 1990's. Such a community could have even assumed political power, since no genuine, respected authority existed in the republic at that time. During the dissolution of the USSR and the fall of Communism there was a schism in the religious community following the appearance of "Wahhabite" enemies that completely split and confused the Sunni Muslim community in the North Caucasus.

The differences between the wahhabites and the representatives of traditional Islam were not important enough to warrant the spilling of blood. All too often they concerned secondary, even by Islamic standards, superficial attributes. "The wahhabites think that a Muslim can marry his own mother" which was one absurd accusation. An adequate and reasonable answer would be "Even it they think this possible, I will not avail myself of the opportunity!" Muslims, just like Jews, permit the marriage of cousins and similar relatives, but this does not force either religious group to do so. Uneducated members of the clergy were incredibly aggressive towards the new teachers and preachers of Islam, even though they were part of the same Dagestani Sufi school, since almost all Salafis were actually former pupils of Sufis from the republic.

By 1993 calls for physical violence against one's opponents were openly made and various villages saw fights between members of the clergy break out. In response the opposition chose to peacefully separate themselves from the traditionalists, leading to the construction of separate mosques in some settlements. But this was insufficient for the traditionalists who continued to ratchet up the social pressure and sometimes even attacked and destroyed functioning mosques under the pretence of them being "Wahhabite." The authorities, instead of pulling both sides back into a legal and orderly resolution to the conflict, sided with one side and thus supported its illegal demands.

In 1994-95 the threat of physical destruction of the activists of the religious opposition became very real, causing the leader of the Islamist opposition in Dagestan Bagaudin Kevedov (who also went by the name of Bagaudin Magomedov and hereafter is referred as Bagaudin) and his closest followers to leave the republic and seek refuge in Chechnya. The Chechens, who had dreamed of including their neighbors in the revolutionary process taking place in their republic, happily accepted

Bagaudin and other refugees in Grozny. Without committing any crimes dozens and even hundreds of Dagestanis fled their republic and sought refuge with their leader Bagaudin, and many of his followers actively participated in fighting in Chechnya during the first Russo-Chechen war (December 1994 to August 1996). It is important to remember that until the arrival of Russian forces in Chechnya Bagaudin was skeptical both about Chechen president Jokhar Dudaev and all the talk of sovereignty and independence. Unlike the "radical" Bagaudin, the traditionalists stayed in Grozny during the peaceful 1991-94 period and supported Dudaev and his regime in every conceivable way. As soon as hostilities broke out, however, the traditionalists started to help the Russian military, while Bagaudin and his followers entered the very heart of combat.

Volunteers had started to arrive among them from Muslim countries at this time, particularly the famed Saudi militant commander known as Khattab. During the interwar period (1997-99) Khattab and Bagaudin often quarreled. Specifically, when Khattab made his famous raid on Buinaksk in 1998 in which he attacked the Russian military. After this the Bagaudin sternly told Khattab that it was unacceptable to move military operations onto the territory of Dagestan. During his presence in Chechnya in 1994-99 Bagaudin did not participate in the work of local organizations and had his own political agenda, believing that any initiatives not founded on sharia law would not bring any positive results.

As a Dagestani journalist active at the time I can recall one story of my own personal meeting with Bagaudin back in 1990. One of the regional newspapers in Dagestan had published an article personally attacking Bagaudin and containing libel and lies directed at him. This was a time when the "Regarding publishing" law had come into effect in the USSR. According to this law Bagaudin could have filed suit in court and sent a rebuttal to the very same newspaper, which is what I suggested he do. In return he merely laughed. "I can only make use of a sharia court! For a Muslim to make use of any other court means to acknowledge the existence of a power other than the power of the Almighty. This is faith-breaking. Show me a sharia court, and I will appeal to it." I tried to explain myself to him; saying "Let the press learn to behave better. Let this be a lesson to them, we can win this suit, and they will stop insulting not just you, but also others! In this case, even if you do not act completely in accordance to the principles of Islam, more good than harm will come out of it." He responded by saying that "The insults of all mankind are less meaningful than the least bit of God's anger! I will remain a Muslim, and only God is our judge."

Another incident occurred in 1991 during the presidential elections in Russia. I met with Bagaudin and asked him to support the candidacy of Boris Yeltsin. He asked me "Will Yeltsin establish sharia law and an Islamic government across Russia?" And I answered that "No, but his platform is closer to the notions found in sharia – it includes a free market, the ability to leave the country freely, private ownership of land and other means of production, and much else." Nonetheless Bagaudin replied that he could vote only for someone backing sharia and Islam, since everything else belongs to Satan.

The Salafis were also opposed to the authority of former Chechen President Aslan Maskhadov who died in March 2005. The absence of funding from the Kremlin led Maskhadov to make concessions to the Islamic radicals and to lead a double game when dealing with the religious community. In the spring of 1999 Bagaudin's men were suspected of planning an assassination attempt on Maskhadov, which led to an investigation by the attorney general of the Chechen Republic of Ichkeria. It was this investigation, as it gradually moved towards arresting Bagaudin's men on assassination charges, that led to the migration of the Dagestani Salafis to the Tsumadin region of Dagestan in July 1999. The night before the military confrontation began I was told by one of the field commanders that "We have no way of going back – Maskhadov's special services will meet us. We would prefer for the Russians to meet us."

By 1999 Chechnya was becoming not only the refuge of the religious opposition, but of criminals. In order to avoid being prosecuted these men began joining Bagaudin's movement. Seeing the danger of this process certain Dagestani officials (parliamentary members and leaders of different levels of government) had contacted Bagaudin in the spring of 1999 and asked him to leave Chechnya and return to Dagestan, promising security and the cessation of persecution. Taking into account these invitations Bagaudin decided to return and came back to his home in Tsumadin region, refusing, however, to lay down his weapons. "If no one shoots at us, we will not use our weapons first," he said.

In the afternoon of the 2nd of August, however, the village of Gigatli was the site of a completely accidental, unintentional firefight. The participants were actually a group of men quite distant from Bagaudin's faction, which had settled near the village of Echeda. The group in question was led by field commander Ramzan and was located in the village of Kenkhi, near Gigatli. The two groups were almost 35 km apart, with only a difficult mountain road connecting them. By midnight on August 2nd Bagaudin's men had moved forward towards the administrative center of the Tsumadin region, while the men near Gigatli were hit by helicopter rocket strikes and forced back into Chechnya.

During the night, 2 km away from Agvali village several dozen of Bagaudin's men confronted a police checkpoint, leading to casualties on both sides. The military arrived in the region on the night of August 4th and made no attempt to negotiate a peaceful settlement. In response to my attempt to start negotiations, contact the officials in Grozny, and thus prevent wide scale bloodshed, M. Omarov, the acting military commandant of Tsumadin and deputy minister of internal affairs of Dagestan, answered harshly. "We know where, we know in what villages they are hiding. We will destroy every last one of them! There will be no negotiations!" And so the second Chechen war began.
The attempts to pursue and destroy those who had entered Dagestan ended with the attack of Basaev and Khattab, who tried to cut the military forces off from the rear. They did so by freely, without firing a shot, occupying several villages in neighboring Botlikh region and started to intimidate the authorities with their grandiose plans of attacking Makhachkala. There were actually no real attempts to leave their position near the villages of Rakhat and Ansalt. Naturally, the

military ended their pursuit of Bagaudin's small group and turned to confront Basaev and Khattab. All the branches of the military now worked in Botlikh. Following the return of Bagaudin's men to Chechnya Basaev and Khattab successfully did so as well, being passively watched by the Russian forces the entire time they retreated.

Combat in Botlikh (the site of Chechen rebel commander Shamyl Basaev's 1999 raid into Dagestan) including the use of air strikes, continued for more than a week, even though the locals knew that none of the invaders were left in the region. Basaev and his men actually watched the course of the operation on Russian television while sitting in Chechnya. "The funniest thing about all of it," I was told by men who watched these reports on television in Basaev's home in Vedeno, "was that they showed guerilla prisoners, even though we hadn't left even one heavily injured fighter in the place!" The only attempt at negotiation with Maskhadov was made by the Head of the State Council of Dagestan, Magomedali Magomedov, when they tried to discuss the situation in early September 1999. The Federal authorities, however, said that such a meeting simply cannot be. And as it may be expected "the Dagestani peoples blocked the road to Chechnya, and prevented the meeting."

The wide scale anti-terrorist operation in Chechnya began, having been intended to last "several months" according to Russian Prime Minister Putin, who also promised to normalize the situation in Dagestan in "a few weeks." As we can see the anti-terrorist occupation has not only taken far longer, but has also spread geographically. Today tension grows in Ingushetia, Kabardino-Balkaria, Dagestan, and North Ossetia. This tension negatively affects the economy of the region. Dagestan, which has a huge potential for tourism, is simply unable to develop this branch of the republic's economy. Similarly, with great possibilities for animal husbandry, no development is possible due to the lack of investment and the lack of processing facilities. Agriculture in the mountains tends to rely on manual labor, with extremely limited arable land being worked with a plow and oxen, the haying done manually, and the transport of feed being conducted by donkey or even on the shoulders of women.

The national Russian media has deliberately created the image of an unsuitable, criminal region for Dagestan, strongly reducing the development of tourism and the improvement of the investment climate. It should be noted that if one does not count the terrorist acts directed at law enforcement and various officials the level of crime in Dagestan is actually low in comparison with other regions. Felonies have declined year after year, and unlike Moscow, Petersburg, or other Russian cities there are absolutely no hate crimes motivated by ethnicity or race. One example should show the attitudes of simple Dagestanis. In April 2005 I accompanied a group from RenTV to the sites of the military clashes of the second Chechen war. Passing through the distant mountain village of Inkho, in the valley of the Andian Koisu, we were stopped by a gray-bearded old man who asked us in Avar to stop in his village for a short time and take part in the festivities celebrating the prophet Mohammad's birthday. I answered that I would be delighted, but that the men with me were Russians. This answer was actually a sort of test. To the surprise of the men with me the old man said "They too are the men of our prophet Isa, both they and us have one God, so we happily invite all to share!" This is not an exception, but the real attitude of the vast majority of Muslims in Dagestan.

The peoples of Dagestan are generally very friendly, and tend towards internationalism and religious tolerance. On the other hand, crude interference in the community that involves repression and insult leads to limitless and unpredictable resistance. That which is currently occurring in Russia – the growth of nationalism, of "Russian fascism" – which has come to victimize not only Jews, but also people from the Caucasus, has come to negatively impact the ethnic and religious equilibrium within society. Recently a tiny Dagestani baby was killed by fascist nationalists who attacked the child and its Dagestani nurse in Moscow. Using rebar they broke the child's skull and put the nurse into a two-week coma caused by a skull fracture. A similar negative effect is created by America's attempt to set up democracy in Iraq and other Muslim countries using tanks and warplanes. The United States becomes an enemy of all the world's Muslims when we see Abu Ghraib, Falluja, or occupied Baghdad. Those who saw Saddam Hussein as a

211

bloody dictator before the American invasion now tend to sympathize with him. This is the result of the policies of the current White House. It is reassuring that America does not only contain Bushes, but also the brave movie director Michael Moore, and an intelligentsia that shares his views. One would hope that America's future will be linked to exactly such men.

Returning to Dagestan's problem with terrorism, I would like to say that the spread of terrorism in the republic is heavily tied to the socio-economic conditions of the region. According to official statistics more than 200,000 people are unemployed out of a total population of 2.5 million. More than half of these are young people under thirty. There is no demand for higher education, and highly qualified specialists must take any work available in order to feed their families. In his recent speech the president of Dagestan has stated that the sources of terrorism are the "socio-economic, community-political, and spiritual and moral problems, as well as the loss of trust in government due to its corruption, injustice, crassness, and soullessness." It has been five years now, and it is time for the authorities to finally admit what the true causes of terrorism are. As a doctor I can say that the diagnosis is correct, and it remains only to treat the disease.

It does not seem necessary to explain that blood-soaked surgery in the form of a military intervention is unnecessary for treating the above-mentioned problems. On the contrary, it would be enough to rebuild the trust of the people towards their government, to destroy corruption, to improve the socio-political situation and the moral climate of the republic. None of these can be done with tanks or flamethrowers. We need to work with people, we need professionals trained in conflict resolution, we need psychologists, we need highly trained specialists in the employ of the republic's government. The official statistics from last year show that 50 officials of the highest rank within the republic do not have a college degree. If these were the 1920's or 1930's that would be understandable. But in addition to these fifty men, how many men have fake diplomas that they have simply bought? Only the truly lazy officials do not receive PhDs these days, with the older Kadyrov managing to get a PhD in the sciences, and the younger becoming an Academician, though he never attended a university!

There are no wild or backward peoples. There are only peoples that have been prevented from being enlightened and that have been driven into being wild. The once famous Dagestani poet Rasul Gamzatov wrote "Would Africa be as black, had not her path to the light been blocked?!" Ethnic groups and peoples should not have their path to the light closed off, people should be helped towards civilization, but not with tanks and bombs. What is the difference between the United States, which today establishes democracy in Iraq, and the Bolsheviks, who established Communism across one sixth of the globe with assault rifles in hand, who turned this part of the world into one giant GULAG for hundreds of millions of people?

Despite all of today's difficulties, Dagestan is rich with intellectual potential. The famous torpedo engine designer Shamil Aliev, a man whose designs are used across the world, was from highland Khunzakh. The world-famous composers Murad Kazhlaev and Shirvani Chalaev, poets, writers, scientists – one simply does not have the time to list all those personalities who are the treasures not just of today's Dagestan, but of today's Russia. Another example can be drawn from the previously unknown facts of Dagestan's Soviet period. At the beginning of the 20th century Ahmed Nabi of Godoberi, while still a beardless youth, fought against the Bolsheviks for the Gornaia Respublika ("Mountain Republic"). His contemporary Halilbeg Musayasul from Chokha was a friend of Nazhmutdin, the imam of the Gornaia Respublika. After the establishment of the Communist dictatorship in Dagestan, both were forced to flee Russia. A member of one of the ethnicities of Dagestan that lacks a written language, Nabi found himself in Prague where he graduated from the university, defended his dissertation, and finally became a department head in the university of Prague. Later, while living in Hitler's Germany he helped hundreds of thousands of people from the Caucasus who were imprisoned in concentration camps in Poland, Austria, and Germany. Halilbeg Musayasul became a world-famous painter and lived out his life in the United States, where he died in 1949. A marble impression of

213

his hand, along with a similar impression of Rakhmaninov's hand, is still preserved in the Metropolitan Museum in New York. All of this shows that the intellectual potential of the mountain peoples of Dagestan has been limitless in even the toughest times.

Today, an important investment in developing the intellectual potential of Dagestan has been made by the American philanthropist - George Soros. Thanks to his generous financial assistance a computer center was created in Dagestan's university, which provides 100 computers with internet access to the community. Over the first five years of the center's operation, 11,000 students have come to be familiar with the internet without having to pay for the access. Thanks to Soros' help the republic has received a powerful impetus in developing today's modern technologies. It would be wonderful to continue similar projects in helping schools and other children's institutions to develop civil education and acquaint the pupils with humanism and love of their fellow man. Today only 14% of all schools in the republic are up to health and fire code, and Putin's so-called national project in the realms of education and healthcare is a completely empty gesture when no material is available for education and when schools look like cattle barns.

According to official figures 15,000 children in Dagestan dropped out of school this year. This is a catastrophe, but it has not elicited due attention or involved analysis that such an issue deserves. This is the beginning of total degradation. Some of the kids in question might not see the point of continuing their education. College admission is based on bribes, and the bribes due to the professors every semester are a prequel to further bribes necessary to moving up in one's chosen profession. Thus the youth are never free of problems, even if they get through college. Admission to the police academy, for example, an institution that prepares future keepers of the law, necessitates a bribe of roughly $6,000! By Dagestani standards this is an enormous amount of money. But most of these 15,000 children left school in order to help their parents. Parents are often unable to bear the burden of maintaining their large families, so at 12 or 13 boys start to work in the fields and make their own contributions to the family budget. A certain part of those who left school, however, entered specialized religious institutions, which need to be discussed separately.

Dagestan has about 20 Islamic colleges and thousands of madrasas. This would not be a problem if the secular part of society, the ministry of education, and the appropriate committees within the government could answer society's question, "what are they studying there?" I can assure you that they are not studying the Universal Declaration of Human Rights, or international law, or modern political science. Thousands of imams, religious scholars, sharia experts, and other religious specialists are being prepared. Where will this veritable army be sent? What will this do for the economy, culture, science, diplomacy, industry, or agriculture of the republic? But the republic's leadership does not seem to care, just as it did not care about the outflow of thousands of young men to foreign Islamic institutions in the early 1990's.

It is not true that all those who graduated from Islamic institutions in Egypt, Syria, Malaysia, and Saudi Arabia in the early 1990's simply returned home with ideas of jihad or combating secular society, but since then they have all been declared "unwanted and potentially dangerous" by the official clergy. Many of these foreign graduates are progressive thinkers, rational, preach peaceful ideals, and have far deeper religious knowledge than the official clergy, who in Dagestan are often distinguished by their limited worldview and stubbornness. Tensions among the clergy often become a reason for social disturbances and schism among the faithful. Even those foreign graduates that attended secular institutions are often unwanted by society. And those unwanted in their specialties will probably seek other outlets for their knowledge and skills.

Appendix

Table 1. The ethnic composition of the population of Dagestan.

Ethnic group	Size of group (2002)	Percentage of total population
Avars	758,438	29.44%
Dargins	425,526	16.52%
Kumyks	365,804	14.20%
Lezgins	336,698	13.07%
Laks	139,732	5.42%
Russians	120,875	4.69%
Azerbaijanis	111,656	4.33%
Tabasarans	110,152	4.28%
Chechens	87,867	3.41%
Nogais	38,168	1.48%
Rutuls	24,298	0.94%
Aguls	23,314	0.90%
Tsakhur	8,168	0.32%
Armenians	5,702	0.22%

Table 2. The Avars – population numbers of the component ethnic groups.

Avars (avaral, maarulal)	814,473
Andiytsy (andii, andal, gvanal, kvannal, kuannal)	21,808
Archins (archi, archib)	89
Akhvakhtsy (akhvalal, ashvatl, ashval)	6,376
Bagulals (bagvalaly, bagvalins, bagulav, gantlialo, kvanalketsy, tlibishintsy, tlissintsy)	40
Bezhtins (kapuchins, khvanal)	6,198
Botlikhtsy	16
Ginukhtsy	531
Godoberintsy (gibdidi, ibdidi)	39
Gynzibtsy (gunzal, nakhada, khunzalis, khunzaly)	998
Didois (tsezy, tsyntintsy)	15,256
Karatintsy (kirdi)	6,052
Tindaly (idari, ideri, tindii, tindintsy)	44
Kharshiny (inkhokvarintsy, khvarshal, khvarshintsy, khuani)	128
Chamalaly (chamalins)	12

Table 3. Comparative statistics of anti-terrorist activity in Dagestan.

	January-August 2005	January-August 2006
Members of special services killed	53	22
Radicals killed	48	22
Members of special services wounded	115	29
Radicals wounded	3	0
Homes destroyed during anti-terrorist operations	12	2
Radicals and their supporters detained	54	47
Famous officials killed	7	6

The Chechen Resistance:
Yesterday, Today and Tomorrow

Mairbek Vachagaev

Introduction

Even if we ignore the earlier stages of Chechen resistance against Russian rule in the Soviet and pre-Soviet periods, we then must look to the military campaigns of 1994-96 as the start of the current stage of the Russo-Chechen war. It was during this time when the foundations of the contemporary resistance movement were formed.

Since both were former Soviet officers, Dzhokhar Dudaev, the first president of Chechnya, and Aslan Maskhadov, the commander in chief of the General Council of the Military Forces of the Chechen republic of Ichkeria, initially worked to create military structures similar to that of the USSR. Over time, however, the benefits of using guerrilla warfare against one of the largest conventional militaries in the world have been demonstrated. This approach to warfare has prevented Russia from exploiting its numerical advantage and has confused their forces by utilizing non-standard fighting techniques.

Chechens started to break with the organizational structure initially set up and supported by President Dudaev very early on in the 1994-96 campaign. This is what allowed them to successfully resist against the occupation of all of Chechnya by Russian forces, as well as to be able to act decisively throughout the course of the war. Bands of guerrillas formed in rural regions, city neighborhoods, and villages. They acted autonomously, with only nominal high-level coordination between them in 1995. Only in 1996 did Aslan Maskhadov successfully manage to start coordinating the Chechen forces, which helped to account for such victories as the capture of Grozny. The capture of the capital was a seminal event that ended this particular campaign and would have been impossible for uncoordinated groups to achieve.

In the interwar period of 1997-99 President Maskhadov once again tried to form a conventional army, but this force once again rapidly metamorphosed into guerrilla bands. This was most evident during the first real confrontation with the Russian military on Terek Ridge in autumn of 1999. This, along with Chechen Defense Minister Magomed Khanbiev's failure to form a battle-worthy conventional force proved that the army had to adapt to the prevailing conditions. This forced Maskhadov to completely change his viewpoint and radically overhaul the organizational structure of his forces. It took two years to do this during the harsh conditions of the Russian occupation, but the change was finally completed by July-August of 2001 in the Nozhai-Yurt region of Chechnya when all the important high and mid-ranking military commanders met for the first time after the abandonment of Grozny.

Leaders of the Chechen Resistance

Following the death of the charismatic Maskhadov, who had been elected in accordance with the rules of European democracy and had been confirmed as president by EU representatives, the presidency was occupied for a short time by the young and relatively unknown Abdul-Khalim Sadulaev. He was the representative of a new generation of Chechen leaders who managed not only to become the leader of the Chechen resistance, but the leader of the entire resistance in the North Caucasus. He successfully combined the roles of a young fighter and a knowledgeable theologian, and thus avoided relying upon Middle Eastern emigrants. This fortuitous combination of skills allowed him to be the first man since the death of Sheikh Mansur in 1794 to be the sole leader of the entire region, which is a region well known for rejecting most self-proclaimed leaders. Sadulaev combined youth and education, being a linguist who loved ancient philosophy and was a universally respected self-taught theologian. While Makhadov was seen by non-Chechen combatants as merely a Chechen national leader, Sadulaev was thought of as rising above his ethnic background to be the leader of all ethnicities in the region. This is a quality that is very crucial in the North Caucasus, as it contains close to a hundred different ethnic groups.

The accidental killing of Abdul-Khalim Sadulaev was a noticeable blow to both the Chechens as well as all of the North Caucasus. But this blow was small in comparison with the death of Shamil Basayev, one of the most famous leaders of the entire resistance movement. The vacancy left by Basayev was genuinely catastrophic since it was his duty to unify the variegated ethnic groups across the whole region. His status helped to coordinate regional cooperation, and his ease in mingling with other ethnicities in the region allowed the Dagestani dzhamaat "Shariat" to become his main support. It was Basayev who created the very active dzhamaat "Yarmuk" in Kabardino-Balkaria and led to the creation of the "Kataib al-Khoul" dzhamaat in North Ossetia. It was Basayev's old Nogai battalion that later on became the nucleus of the "Nogai" dzhamaat. He undertook similar efforts when working with the Ingush, the Karachai and the Adyghe. This meant that Basayev could successfully oppose Russia on territory stretching from the Black Sea to the Caspian Sea.

Dokku Umarov, the current leader of the Chechen guerrillas, has thus inherited a well-organized force capable of fighting across almost the entire North Caucasus. Even so, he probably will not be able to do much with it as he is but a pale imitation of the charismatic Maskhadov, the young warrior-theologian Sadulaev, and even the harsh but experienced warrior Basayev. He is not even considered a commanding ethnic leader in Chechnya itself, making it that much harder for him to be a leader of the entire region.

Umarov is one of those separatists who aims for independence and sees Islam as an auxiliary tool to help unite the Chechen state. For him and his many supporters in Chechnya, the religious aspect is simply part and parcel with Chechen ethnic identity. Dokku Umarov was born in 1964 in the village of Kharsenoi in the Shatoi region, of the Mulkhoi teip. He has lived in the Achkhoi-Martanovskoi region as well as Grozny, is married, and is the father of two children.[1] He is an active

---

[1] According to the "Kavkazskii Uzel" news agency (5/5/05) Umarov's 70-year old father, wife and six-month son were abducted by members of the pro-Russian Chechen security services. Two of his brothers and members of their families were similarly abducted earlier.

participant in the resistance movement and one of the few veterans of the military-political establishment still completely committed to independence.

Before the beginning of the first war in 1994, he served in the Borz special division under the command of Ruslan Gelaev. Having quarreled with Gelaev in 1996, he left the unit and commanded his own sizable unit of 200 fighters, which made him a colonel in the Chechen military.[2] Following the war he was elevated to the rank of general and actively backed Aslan Maskhadov in the presidential elections. In 1997 he was named Secretary of Defense by President Maskhadov, but afterwards he had some disagreements with Maskhadov and this position was subsequently liquidated. In 1999, shortly before the beginning of the next round of combat, he was again named to the same post. He was severely wounded during the battle for Grozny and received treatment abroad in 2000. When he returned to Chechnya in 2003, he took over the southwestern front of the Chechen military.[3]

When Maskhadov was still alive, Umarov was appointed to the post of Defense Minister, but after Maskhadov's death the new president, Sadulaev, named him Vice President and thus heir to the throne. It's unclear as to what led to this decision, though it might have been an attempt to balance the influence of the radicals and the Sufis.

Now, upon the death of Sadulaev, Dokku Umarov holds the positions of President of the Chechen republic of Ichkeria, Emir of the Governmental Committee for Defense of the Madzhlis Shura of the Caucasus, the Commander-in-Chief of the armed forces of Chechnya, and finally the Emir of the Mujahadeen of the Caucasus. Umarov is quite influential in the southwestern part of Chechnya, but he's not as popular in other regions of the republic. A follower of the Sufi Kadir tarikat and the Virdov brotherhood of sheikh Kunta-Khadzhi, he's fully

---

[2] Certain arguments with Gelaev began during the course of the battle for Goisty during the first war, and Ahmad Zakaev, Hussein Isabaev, and Khamzat Labazanov all left his unit.

[3] Replacing Isu Musaev, the former military commandant of Chechnya.

convinced that Islam in its traditional Sufi form should remain the basis of Chechen society.

Umarov has been blacklisted by Russian authorities, with their security services holding him responsible for many incidents, including: the abduction of an Interior Ministry representative, General Gennadii Shpigun, in March 1999; the separatists' attack on Ingushetia in June 2004 and on Grozny in August of that year; as well as the hostage crisis in Beslan.[4] That said, similar accusations have been leveled against many other Chechen leaders by the Russian special services.

The Social and Material Foundations

The social background of the resistance movement has changed considerably during the years of the war. At the outset it contained a broad cross-section of society, including members of the intelligentsia. After a year or so, independent partisans and Islamic adherents began to dominate the ranks and tried to actively shift the balance of power within the movement towards those with similar views. These individuals tended to be from the mountainous parts of the republic as well as those young people who sought to find the answer to their problems in religion. Many of those who supported and participated in the second campaign in 1999 have left, understanding that a repeat of the events of the first war of 1994-96 is very much unlikely to happen.

The movement is still popular among the general population, with perhaps the majority supporting it and applauding its successes. That said, the population lives in an environment where there is massive pressure from both Russian and pro-Russian special services, and thus are forced to show their "neutrality" in public. Cases of blaming the separatists for someone else's own crimes have occurred due to this atmosphere.

During the entire interwar period, those in charge of the republic, and military leaders opposed to the established leadership, prepared for

---

[4] www.gazeta.ru, "Chronicle of the day," 6/17/06, 22:26.

223

further combat. They defined the enemy as either an external aggressor to be resisted, or the local government which needed to be overthrown. Some reservists were trained during this time, though the experiences of the first war had proven that adequate manpower could be provided by simply having some Chechens move into the mountains.

The Chechen leadership and Aslan Maskhadov sought to create sufficient caches of weapons and ammunition in the mountains. With the capture of some important figures and the defection of others, many of these carefully hidden caches fell into the hands of the Russian forces. This was despite the fact that most such depots were created in a semi-secret fashion, with only Maskhadov and two or three others in each district knowing of their exact location. However, the locations of the depots created by the individual dzhamaats were known only to their commanders, and thus often remained safe.

Even all of these depots and caches would not have allowed for the separatists to survive as long as they have if it was not for the massive moral and material support provided by the general populace. Some financial help has also been provided by those businessmen who are trying to hedge their bets should the separatists come to power again, in which case they do not want to be left out in the cold. The most significant financial support for the resistance comes from those who are members of international Islamic organizations that see the Chechens as Muslim fighters in the region. But even here there are many difficulties, as Western banks have been studiously tracking their account activity.

The Ideological Underpinnings

The ideological underpinnings of the resistance movement rest on the belief in the need for independence from Russia. In the beginning, the Chechen leadership and almost all of the military commanders, excluding a few particularly odious figures among the Islamic radicals, such as Movladi Udugov, fully supported this idea. As the conflict has unfolded, however, this notion was gradually infused with Islamic ideas and terminology, mostly because the Chechens' allies in their cause

224

were gradually changing. At first, it was thought it would be possible to end the war by having the democratic European nations apply pressure to the Russian government. However, over time it was seen that the Europeans viewed the Chechens' tragedy only through the lens of their own dependence on Russian energy resources. The new resistance leader Dokku Umarov has been a steadfast supporter of the idea of independence. It is reasonable to expect that his pronouncements will focus first on the creation of the Chechen state, and only then on Islam, and only because it is the religion that is part and parcel of the Chechen ethnic identity.

The earlier tendency to lean towards European democratic ideals has been replaced by the notion of "Islamic solidarity," which has not, however, been fully accepted by the entire Chechen movement, particularly due to the "betrayal" of Chechnya by certain leaders of Muslim countries. The separatists have relied on a variety of Islamic organizations and foundations for financial help, while still making their pitch to both Western and Eastern leaders in order to support their cause. This meant that while dealing with European countries an emphasis was placed on the Chechen constitution, as it was built on Western values and ideals. This is despite the fact that it was heavily modified in 1996-1999, making it an entirely different document. Conversely, when Chechen leaders made their pitch to Middle Eastern governments, they emphasized the fact that the Chechens intended to build an Islamic state. This was made necessary by the need to find allies wherever possible, but also elicited a heavily negative response in the West. Even so, it has been necessary for the resistance to find real allies instead of relying on the mostly theoretical help from Europe.

The Dzhamaat as a Structure of the Resistance Movement

The dzhamaat is currently the most battle-tested aspect of the resistance movement, and it has representatives from all over the republic. While the dzhamaat could only be found in the foothills of the Black Mountains during the first war, the second campaign has seen its influence spread throughout Chechnya. Originally founded by Sheikh Fatkhi, while it still retains some of its individuality and autonomy, it is

225

now almost completely a part of the military forces of the resistance. The dzhamaat has certainly not been constant and homogenous, having given wholehearted cooperation to the leaders of the regime during the reign of President Sadulaev, while cooperating only in order to preserve itself from full isolation from all other possible allies during the time of the Akhmadov brothers and Arbi Baraev. In this latter case cooperation has been coerced, which is a fact that the republic's leadership has always had to keep in mind.

There is currently a danger that under the influence of old dzhamaat leaders such as Abdul-Malik Mezhidov and Usman Akhmadov, the question of rehabilitating those dzhamaat groups that had been accused of acting against the Chechen resistance leadership would be raised once more. This occurred in the summer of 1998 in Gudermes when several detachments under Sulim Yamadaev, later supported by many respected Chechen commanders, clashed with units of the Sharia Guards and the Islamic Special Forces Regiment. The rehabilitation question has been raised frequently, and at the start of the second war dzhamaat members actually demanded that Aslan Maskhadov repeal the orders outlawing the activity of the radical dzhamaat groups.

Despite this, neither Maskhadov nor Sadulaev have ever repealed the orders banishing and outlawing these groups. This refusal to make concessions suggests that the leadership thinks that it currently has the upper hand, and that a majority of public support no longer comes through the dzhamaat groups. The situation in Pankisi suggests that almost everyone wants to deal with the main resistance leader instead of the ambitious and ill-defined local dzhamaat commanders who had moved outside of Chechen territory. They often did this so as to control the delivery of aid, and thus make themselves an important factor in the resistance once again.

The demographics of the dzhamaat have also changed. The initial glut of young men who liked the uniforms, the money, and a sort of mystique that came with being opposed to those in charge have been replaced by those who know what the dzhamaat is and who it represents. It no longer represents young men who were taken with the

226

élan that these forces represented. Thus, it is now filled with those who are able to ideologically defend their ideas, obey their leaders, and are capable of overcoming Chechen traditions without any real difficulty. This is crucial, since many men were unable to abandon their loyalty to Chechen traditions and customs no matter what happened.

In a sense the relationship between the dzhamaat and the Chechen republic is yet unclear. Because of the occupation by Federal Russian forces this question is not currently relevant, but the question has been delayed by the current situation. There's a significant chance that this issue will split those who fight against Russia today. The people who will most probably foment such a schism are those who are now living outside of Chechnya, but still trying to remain politically relevant.

Chechen Dzhamaats in Russia

The form of social organization implicit in the dzhamaat is now irreversibly present in the entire Russian Federation. Moscow and other large cities have dzhamaats that unite Chechens and Ingush, as well as other North Caucasian nationalities. However, the typical dzhamaat is generally formed along narrow ethnic lines so that people who are separated from their homelands can come together in order to share their ideas and feelings. These are not terrorist organizations and are not organized in order to act against the state, but are diaspora groups that do not wish to affiliate themselves with those who officially proclaim the pro-Russian inclination of the Chechen youth. In many respects, these dzhamaats are very different, as the members are often well educated or still studying in colleges and universities. They do not accept the principles of the Kadyrov administration and often create websites that sharply condemn those who cooperate with Kadyrov and Alkhanov.

These groups are often targeted by the Russian special services, since it's assumed that they are part of those dzhamaats that are actually fighting in the North Caucasus. This inability of the Russian government to distinguish between these missionary-style dzhamaats and the radical dzhamaats that are actually part of the rebellion often promotes the feelings of alienation and bitterness that lead to their gradual association with the genuinely radical and militant dzhamaats.

It should be remembered that dzhamaats are ethnically heterogeneous. There are groups formed by Dagestanis, Tatars, Bashkirs, even ethnic Russians who have converted to Islam, which makes the dzhamaat not a purely Chechen concept. Dzhamaats that label themselves as being "Chechen" or "Tatar" generally depend on the ethnic background of the group's founder. The largest dzhamaats exist in Moscow, the Urals, the Volga region, and in Siberia, where people have experienced plenty of hostile treatment from a suspicious government. These victims of the authorities in these places seek to change the entire social structure, particularly since the government sees these dzhamaats as structures that fight Moscow's rule in Chechnya itself.

The young members of the dzhamaats have created many websites that reflect their emotions and proselytize Islam in the only form understandable to them – the Salafi school. They also condemn the followers of Sufism and the official clergy who, according to them, undermine Islam as a religion through their unislamic behavior.

Foreigners in the Resistance Movement

Too much emphasis has been placed on the presence of foreigners in the Chechen resistance movement. The Russian authorities often use this to show a link between the resistance and international terrorism. The first international volunteers appeared in Chechnya in 1995, having arrived from Tajikistan after the beginning of the first war. One of the first foreign fighters was Sheikh Fatkhi (a Chechen from Jordan) and Emir Khattab (an Arab from Saudi Arabia). The former created the first dzhamaat for non-Chechen combatants and put forth an example emulated by all other dzhamaat groups that have since sprung up in the republic. The latter became the founder of the foreign fighters' battalion within the Chechen military. Fatkhi's dzhamaat became very popular and many Chechens enlisted into it. Khattab's battalion, meanwhile, was a structure that was generally composed of non-Chechen nationals. In a training camp built next to Avtur village,

228

representatives of almost all ethnic groups of the former Soviet Union trained under the direction of instructors provided by Khattab. These instructors had entered Chechnya in 1996 and generally came from Yemen and Saudi Arabia. Here they trained their charges not only in military maneuvers, but also in the basics of Salafite Islam.

Khattab's role later shifted, and he provided financial support for his training camp and his immediate supporters. While it's often alleged that Khattab was a leader of the Salafites in Chechnya, he always indicated that his job was purely military, and that he did not deal with politics or religion. It would have been impossible to acquire funding from across the whole world without some ideological base, but President Maskhadov recognized Emir Khattab's neutrality in 1998 after the Sufi-Salafi conflict. In fact, Khattab and his comrades were among the few foreigners not ejected from the republic on the president's orders.[5]

By the start of the second military campaign, foreign fighters composed only a small portion of the total military strength of the resistance. Many left in 2000, believing that staying was tantamount to suicide. Many romantically-inclined younger men who had come to help the Chechens were stopped at the Russian border and the long wait necessary to sneak across the border disappointed them, which led them to leave Georgia or Azerbaijan having never set foot in Chechnya. While websites worldwide called for aid to the Chechen mujahadeen, this was often simply PR with no real substance to it. After 2001 most foreigners became middlemen who connected the Chechen combatants with those who would be able to finance their actions from abroad.

Is There an Al-Qaeda Connection?

The events of September 11th, 2001 in New York City and Washington, DC was a genuine holiday for the Russian military leadership, since it

---

[5] July 14-15 saw a large-scale confrontation between the Chechen leadership's forces under Sulim Yamadaev and the Sharia Guards of Abdul-Malik Medzhidov and the Islamic Special Forces Regiment of Arbi Baraev.

saw this disaster as cause for a change in Washington's position regarding Chechnya. In order to clarify the situation for the Americans, serious efforts were made to link the Chechen movement to Osama bin-Laden. Thus, Russian special service forces would conveniently find disks showing how Chechen fighters had studied flying, or would find cassettes in Arabic making light of the American tragedy.

The Chechen leadership was completely unaware of al-Qaeda's existence, and tried to understand what sort of organization it actually was. Aslan Maskhadov officially demanded a clarification from his press secretary, since neither he, nor most of the Chechen fighters knew anything about this organization before the whole world learned of it in September 2001.

The American operation in Afghanistan, where the Russian leadership also hinted of a Chechen connection, did not yield positive results for the Russian government, since no Chechens were killed or captured. Journalist Andrei Babitskii from Radio Free Europe/radio Liberty and Sofi Shikhab from *Le Monde* also searched for any traces of Chechen involvement, and concluded that it was pure propaganda.

Since then, there has not been even a single shred of evidence demonstrating any cooperation between al-Qaeda and the Chechen resistance, even through foreign intermediaries. Al-Qaeda never saw Chechnya as a front line of struggle the Muslim world, never saw the Chechens as allies, and never even sought to infiltrate the republic. Iraq, Palestine, and certainly Afghanistan were much more important to al-Qaeda's interests. It's significant that the deaths of presidents Maskhadov and Sadulaev, and even that of such a pan-Islamic figure as Shamil Basayev, did not elicit a single word of condolence from al-Qaeda representatives. Such total silence is probably the best indicator of the lack of any meaningful connection between the Chechen resistance movement and this terrorist organization.

The Media of the Chechen Resistance Movement

The most widely available and most popular media outlets for the resistance are internet publications. The most important of these are "Chechenpress" (Ahmad Zakaev) and "Daymohk" (the administration of the president of the Chechen Republic of Ichkeria), with the latter essentially being the main website of the Chechen president, and originally created as a counterpoint to "Chechenpress," which operated as an anti-presidential site during Maskhadov's time. There are also websites of a totally different nature, including those of social organizations that support the uprising or even personal sites advocating the principle of Chechen independence. These include "Caucasuslive" (a journalistic collaboration between Ahmad Sardali and Khazman Umarov) and "Chechentimes" (Zakhar Abukhanov).

There are several dozen individually run youth websites on which young men and women living outside Chechnya try to express their views on the events occurring in their homeland and show their support for those fighting for Chechen freedom. These sites are geared towards a young audience and feature music, chat rooms, and so forth. Websites geared towards intellectuals calling for Chechen independence are far and few between, with the largest being www.chechen.org (Mairbek Vatchagaev), which focuses on scholarly materials written on Chechnya and the Chechen people, as well as www.zhaina.com, which features Chechen literature.

There are also Islamic-themed sites that also advocate independence, generally providing materials about the ideological underpinnings of jihad and the need for an Islamic state. These include www.alqoqaz.net (Chechen jihad, in Arabic) and "Kavkazcenter" (Movladi Udugov), with the latter claiming to be a pan-Islamic publication that devotes a great deal of space to news from Afghanistan, Iraq, Lebanon, and Palestine. Newspapers like *Ichkeria*, *Chechentimes* and others have disappeared, including those that had been published up to 2003. With the arrest of couriers in Chechnya this form of media has had to be abandoned. They have largely been replaced by the internet publications mentioned above, despite their lack of professionalism. They often feature music clips and scenes of violence right next to each other. This is probably because many of them are created by young people who not only show their solidarity with the cause of independence, but also embrace that which generally attracts contemporary youth – music, bulletin boards, and chat rooms.

The Political Wing of the Resistance

The number of politicians in the Chechen resistance movement is relatively small, and there are very few well-known names, with the palette of viewpoints being rather limited. There are a few different camps, the first being the "traditionalists," or those who want to build a state on democratic principles, which may be slightly modified in order to take account of ethnic traditions. The chief members of this cadre include Ahmad Zakaev, Umar Khanbiev, Apti Bisultanov, Said-Hasan Abumuslimov, Selim Bishaev as well as other parliamentarians. There is also a second, "radical" wing that envisions the future state as being founded solely on Islamic principles as seen by the Salafi school.

The existence of these two camps has long been suspected, but in the past they felt it was unwise to publicize this division during the heat of war. The fissure came to light when Movladi Udugov, one of the original proponents of the "radical" approach, published an article entitled "A Mujahadeen's Thoughts" on his website "Kavkazcenter" and argued for a strictly Islamic approach to state-building. The argument was presented as if it was the view shared by the majority of Chechens, which led to Ahmad Zakaev putting forth a counter-argument. Without directly criticizing Udugov, he noted that the Chechen people have other paths open to them, and that such a crucial decision needs to be made by the entire Chechen nation.

This discussion of post-war possibilities ended the taboo against criticizing the Chechen leadership, with Chechen media outlets dividing into either the pro-Udugov and pro-Zakaev camps. The radical wing has generally been much more aggressive in its arguments concerning post-war Chechen society, and has framed all traditionalist initiatives as potential capitulation before the Russian government.

232

They have frequently called for the top leaders to clarify their positions on important issues, and have often backed their arguments with the Koran and other Islamic scholarship, making successful counter-arguments difficult to make.

All of this means that a coherent and unified political wing of the Chechen resistance has not yet been formed, with no one stepping forward to lead the political wing. The two competing parties, have not yet settled their differences, which is painfully apparent. It's notable that Ahmad Zakaev is a very important counterweight to the Islamists, and has tried to unify all those who share his point of view. However, many who oppose Zakaev, regardless of their true political or religious beliefs, have generally affiliated themselves with those demanding an Islamic state in post-war Chechnya. Thus, there is no single force that can act as the unifying political component of the resistance movement. Furthermore, there is a sense that political unity is often surpassed by the notion that "the man with the rifle will decide," meaning that the destiny of post-war Chechnya is being put off until the end of conflict with Russia.

The Chechen Resistance Movement after the Death of Shamil Basayev

The death of this critical figure of the resistance has naturally created a certain amount of disorientation. Shamil Basayev acted as the coordinator of all the armies of the Northern Caucasus. His authority was unquestioned, especially in the two bands that were initially part of his own units – the Nogai battalion and the Ingush dzhamaat. Following the 2001 flight of Mahomed Kebedov (often known as Muhammad Kizilurtovskii, the spiritual leader of all Dagestani Salafites) to Istanbul, Basayev became the virtual military leader of the Dagestani dzhamaat. While never completely controlled by Shamil Basayev, this dzhamaat, named "Shariat," was in close contact with him both while it was quartered in Chechnya in 1999-2000, and even later after it had moved back to Dagestan.

Basayev and several of his comrades from Kabardino-Balkaria formed the "Yarmuk" dzhamaat there. Though originally considered a primarily Balkar group, it was actually mostly composed of Kabardins. This showed Basayev's skill in organizing a dzhamaat in what was ostensibly the most stable and pro-Russian republic of the North Caucasus; a place where many Russians came to vacation. The fact that both Kabardins and Balkars are particularly non-observant Muslims made this a low-risk area for the Russian government, making the whole task even harder for Basayev

Another never fully-completed goal was the organization of a dzhamaat in Karachaevo-Cherkessia. This was made difficult by the fact that even though the republic was home to one of the oldest dzhamaat groups in the USSR, the dzhamaat had shifted over time from political to missionary activity. Furthermore, its leader and founder of the local branch of the Islamic Renaissance Party, Magomed Bedzhiev, had left for Moscow and had lost touch with his followers. It was only with the start of the second Chechen war that the dzhamaat once more entered the debate over the role of Islam in the republic. Building upon this, it was possible to find those who had already fought in Chechnya (there were only a few who had done this, but several of these had passed through Khattab's training camps) and thus further reconstruct the dzhamaat. It is still impossible to say how complete the process is by this point, though it's certain that seeds have been planted that will eventually grow into a new problem for the Russian authorities.

Thus the Nogai, Ingush, Dagestani, Kabardino-Balkar, and quite possibly the Karachaevo-Cherkess dzhamaats form one overarching structure that has been designed specifically in order to maximize the damage to Russia's interests in the region. The goal of the Chechens, including Dokku Umarov, is to build on Shamil Basayev's legacy by ensuring that these groups retain a unified front against the Russian troops in the area.

Plans for Expanding the Armed Resistance Further into Russia

Basayev's strategy encompassed the whole region, and he was probably the creator of the so-called Caucasus Front that was officially created by President Sadulaev after Maskhadov's death on May 5th, 2005. The Caucasus Front is part of the Armed Forces of the Chechen Republic of Ichkeria and is commanded by Emir Abu-Muslim. It was comprised of divisions from these following regions: Adygea, Ingushetia, Kabardino-Balkaria, Karachaycvo-Cherkessia, Krasnodar Stavropol (which moved them out of the Western Front), and the reconstituted North Ossetian sector.

The dzhamaats were also included into the Caucasian Front, with the "Shariat" group becoming part of the Dagestani Front. Two months later, in August 2005 "Chechenpress" reported that field commanders had agreed to, "create a unified intelligence and counter-intelligence organization of the Caucasian Front using the appropriate structures of the Chechen Republic of Ichkeria." Thus, it is possible to see that Chechen political structures are gradually becoming regional structures, which provides a successful example of a pan-ethnic, pan-republican entity that the Russian government has long been unable to create in the Northern Caucasus.

But even this seemed insufficient for Basayev, and shortly after his death Dokku Umarov used this concept in the creation of two new fronts – the Ural Front and the Volga Front.[6] Does the Chechen leadership actually have the ability to create two new fronts deep inside Russian territory? It's still impossible to say. First of all, one should remember that the idea of the Caucasus Front was also initially greeted with great skepticism. Secondly, although the idea does have its propaganda purposes, a real, if weak, basis might exist for the successful implementation of these fronts. These regions do have social dzhamaats, which that can be changed very quickly, as Kabardino-Balkaria and Karachaevo-Cherkessia show. The fronts have in areas of Russia that are outside what is normally considered the central region,

---

[6] "Chechenpress," 07/09/06.

and with large minority populations, including the independently-minded Tatars and Bashkirs. While it's unlikely that the Tatars are ready to demand their independence, something of which the Kremlin is well aware, that has still not stopped the creation of regional divisions for counter-extremism and anti-separatism activity, headed by FSB director Patrushev, in all these republics. The Chechens are effectively becoming a force that can be the foundation for striking serious blows against Russia in the most unexpected places and regions.

Russia Admits that it is Fighting Professionals

FSB director Patrushev has recently declared that one federal and several dozen regional operations headquarters will be created across Russia in establishing a National Anti-Terrorist Committee. In light of President Putin's recent statements about peace and tranquility, the security chief's actions suggest that Moscow is very concerned about the threats posed by its discontented citizens. The creation of these headquarters will require the unified action of numerous branches of the government, including the armed forces. This also readily hints at the concerns of Russian politicians.[7] The fact that this is not a regional, but a countrywide effort suggests instability, even if it is not blatant separatist activity, exists or has the potential to exist in other regions.

In Chechnya itself, Russia's Interior Minister Rashid Nurgaliev has stated than the Regional Operations Headquarters of the Northern Caucasus will be reorganized, with a separate branch established in each North Caucasian republic.[8] This is ostensibly being done in order to assure a faster response time to local disturbances by the separatists. In reality, little has actually changed, since he then explained that he would be heading the Chechen headquarters himself. Essentially, despite the new approach, the top men in the Russian security services are still watching Chechnya. This was merely a rotation of those in charge.

---

[7] *Novosti*, 05/15/06.
[8] *Kommersant*, #154 (#3485), 08/22/06.

This interaction between the various branches of the security services has always been interesting for both academics and journalists. All operations are conducted in secret, meaning that other services learn of them much later, oftentimes from the media. The various arms of the government are often at odds with each other. The Ministry of Internal Affairs does not care for the military, everyone dislikes the FSB, the GRU is always at odds with the FSB despite their similar duties, the military fears and dislikes Kadyrov's men, who in turn fail to hide their loathing for the military. With such an arrangement it's clear that Moscow is periodically forced to rotate those in charge. The Attorney General has long ceased being an organ of justice in Chechnya, and instead works to conceal numerous crimes against humanity. The courts have shown how politicized they are by finding people who have confessed to killing peaceful Chechens innocent.

"The south of Russia has seen a growing wave of especially despicable crimes. Thousands of criminals evade justice," declared Yurii Chaika, the Attorney General of the Russian Federation at an inter-ministry meeting concerning security in the Southern Federal District on Friday. He stated that, "terrorism, kidnapping, and associated crimes are the most severe problem." According to Chaika these crimes are, "the most serious factor that leads to instability in Dagestan, Ingushetia, and Chechnya. Terrorist acts on the Makhachkala-Buinaksk road show that our enemy is both strong and very dangerous. Every tenth crime in southern Russia is linked to illegal weapons."[9] Finally, the head of the Ministry of Internal Affairs of Ingushetia has admitted that 170 guerrillas were eliminated there, thus proving that the Ingush dzhamaat has between 100 and 200 members.[10]

Islam as a Part of the Kremlin's Pressure on the Region's Inhabitants

Moscow is once more attempting to tightly control the spread of Islamic ideology in the problematic Northern Caucasus. Events in Chechnya and the spread of armed conflict across the whole area

---

[9] "Interfax-Yug," 08/25/06
[10] "Interfax-Yug," 08/31/06. Beslan Khamhoev press-conference in Nasran.

confront the Russian government with the same problems that were present during the Soviet period. This means that the state seeks to subjugate all of the structures of Muslim society and isolate, as far as possible, the Muslims of the Russian Federation from all foreign contacts. The Russian government sees the activities of various Islamic foundations and humanitarian organizations as being contrary to Russia's well-being.

The muftis of the Northern Caucasus, represented by the Coordinating Center for Muslims of the Northern Caucasus (its head, serving his second term, is the mufti of Karachaevo-Cherkessia and Stavropolskii Krai, Ismail-khadji Berdiev) raised the question of Islamic education in the region during a meeting with Dmitrii Kozak, the Presidential Representative in the Southern Federal District.[11] It was expected that the Russian government would make concessions to the official Muslim religious leaders in exchange for their loyalty to the Kremlin's Caucasus policy. These expectations seem to have been accurate. Recent events in the Northern Caucasus (particularly the Chechen wars of 1994-1996 and 1999-2006) have forced the Kremlin to try different approaches to solving the problems posed by Islam. This specifically means trying to place all the religious leaders (imams, mullahs, theologians, etc.) under strict control. The wars in Chechnya have shown that Moscow has lost ground in this effort compared to the Soviet period, when the only Islamic institute in the whole country was in Tashkent, the only madrasah was located in Bukhara, the only religious council was in Ufa, and the almost complete lack of mosques made it easy for the KGB to track those who refused to embrace atheism.

With the fall of the USSR, the post-Soviet countries were quickly filled with Islamic missionaries from the Middle East and Turkey, many of whom tried to influence political events in Muslim-heavy regions of the Russian Federation. Starting in the 1990's and up to 2000, for example, the Ministry of Justice of the Russian Federation officially registered and permitted unfettered activity for a variety of Islamic foundations and organizations. These organizations included a branch of the

---

[11] "Interfax," 7/13/06

238

League of the Islamic World, a regional bureau of the World Muslim Youth Assembly, the Russian foundation "Ibrahim ben Abd al-Aziz al-Ibrahim" (based in Saudi Arabia), a branch of the humanitarian organization "International Humanitarian Call" (from the UAE), a branch of the scientific society "A Commission for the Study of Scientific Signs in the Koran and the Sunnah," and a branch of the humanitarian organization "Islamic Relief."[12] According to other sources, Al-Haramein, a Saudi foundation, and IHH, a Turkish organization were also active in the region. Not only were all of these groups officially registered and accredited in Moscow, but several of them had regional offices across the Northern Caucasus in cities such as Mahachkala, Nalchik and Maikop.[13]

Since none of these entities managed to be reaccredited by the Russian Ministry of Justice in subsequent years, numerous educational institutions ceased to operate. After official governmental inquiries, steps were taken to eliminate the following: The International Dagestani-Turkish College and its branches, the Karachaevo-Cherkessia Turkish Lyceum, the Islamic Institute of Kabardino-Balkaria, an Arabic language school in Ingushetia, the Al-Fatkh madrasah in Udmurtia, and the Rasul Akram college in Moscow, among others.[14] All Islamic institutions in Chechnya were also shut down. Overall, the Northern Caucasus was home to more than two dozen Islamic institutes, up to 200 madrasahs, and numerous maktabas (Koranic study schools), which were available at almost every mosque.[15]

Recent statements made by Kozak are interesting for several reasons. First of all, the creation of a new regional university was mentioned, which was later modified by the muftis to the creation of two

---

[12] Dobaev, I.P., Nemchina, V.I. The New Terrorism Across the World and in Southern Russia: Its Essence, Evolution, and Ways of Countering It. Rostov-on-the-Don. 2005.

[13] www.polit.ru, 10/24/04. Malashenko, A. "Global Islam."

[14] Institute of Religion and Politics. 5.5. Measures for the prevention of terrorism in southern Russia.

[15] Malashenko, A. Islamic Guideposts. (Islamskii Orientiry) Ch.3. "Islamic self-identification."

universities, since the population of the Northern Caucasus is split between two schools – the Shafii and the Hanafi. Chechnya, Ingushetia and Dagestan are all aligned with the former, while the Muslims of North Ossetia, Kabardino-Balkaria, Karachaevo-Cherkessia and Adygea are partisans of the latter.[16]

The necessity of creating religious institutions of higher learning isn't new. This has been the case for 15 years. The 1990's saw a boom of in the building and repair of mosques. While the Union of Religious Affairs indicated that in 1985 there were only 47 mosques in the region (27 in Dagestan, 12 in Checheno-Ingushetia, 8 in Kabardino-Balkaria), by 2000 Dagestan alone had 1,585, while Ingushetia had 200, Chechnya had 400 (in 1999), Kabardino-Balkaria had 96, and Karachaevo-Cherkessia had 91 (both in 1997). Meanwhile, the first mosque was opened in Cherkess in 1999. During this time, Northern Caucasian society was simply unable to provide a sufficient number of qualified religious personnel to provide leadership for these new institutions. In order to correct this deficit energetic young men were sent to study Islamic philosophy in the Middle East.[17]

A second important point made by Kozak during his meeting with the muftis was that a university was necessary in order to limit influence from overseas. As he put it, "it's necessary to study pure Islam, so that young people will not need to go to a place to learn it somewhere on the side."[18] This suggests that this university would be created in order to counteract the influence of the Islamic centers of the Middle East, thus pushing those wishing to learn Islamic teachings into an institution where the control of the Russian state could be so strong as to reduce the quality of the education offered.

From 1996 to 1998 up to 1,500 Dagestanis studied abroad.[19] In 1998 hundreds of students from Kabardino-Balkaria and Karachaevo-

---

[16] www.grozny-inform.ru, 7/15/06.
[17] Bobrovnikov, Vladimir. "An Islamic Renaissance" in the Russian Caucasus: A Few Lessons, The Foundation for Strategic Culture. 12/28/05.
[18] Interfax-Religion, 7/14/2006.
[19] According to the Board of Religious Affairs of Dagestan.

Cherkessia also studied abroad (with Karachai and Balkar students generally choosing Turkey because of the favorable conditions extended by its religious colleges to Turkic-speaking students), and thousands of Chechens were studying in the Middle East, Pakistan and Malaysia. Before opening this university, Kozak noted, it is necessary to, "first determine the educational program of these colleges, and only then discuss the creation of such colleges."[20] This suggests that the state would have a voice in what is taught, who is taught, and how the teaching is done in such an Islamic university.

According to the deputy mufti of Chechnya, Magomed-Sharip Dadaev, the republic currently has eighteen functioning madrasahs, three of which were opened this past August. One of them is in Duba-Yurt (the foothills), another is located in Veduchi (the highlands), and the third is in Naur (beyond the Terek),[21] which demonstrates the spreading influence of Islamic training across the whole republic, including those regions earlier thought to be cool towards Islam.

Finally, there is the question of actually reestablishing the office of unified head mufti of the Northern Caucasus through the institution of the Coordinating Center for Muslims of the Northern Caucasus. Though the Center has been located in Moscow since its inception in 1998, there has been talk of moving it to Mineralnyi Vody, in Stavropolskii Krai. This is not an accidental choice since the city is centrally located within the Caucasus region and is thus geographically very convenient. That said, this site would be a serious concession by the Muslims of the North-East (Ingushetia, Chechnya, Dagestan), who had hoped to once more make Dagestan the center of Islam in the region, just as it had been during the Soviet period.

There is also the matter of whether this organization should be in existence at all, which is a question raised by the muftis of Ingushetia, Chechnya and Dagestan following the resignation of Ingush mufti Mahomed-khadji Albogachiev as president of the Center. Having lost

---

[20] www.grozny-inform.ru, 7/14/06.
[21] "Caucasustimes," 8/24/06.

241

the presidency and also the location of the organization's headquarters they might question the need for the existence Center, and thus use the office of unified head mufti instead.

In fact the collapse of the former Spiritual Board of the Muslims of the Northern Caucasus occurred in 1989 precisely because it lost the support of Dagestan and Chechnya. The former head mufti, Mahmud-khadji Gekkiev, a Balkar, was physically ejected from the headquarters of
the Board and was accused of being a Hanafi (from the northwest), and thus unable to represent the northeastern Shafii Dagestan, Chechnya and Ingushetia.

While today's Russian authorities may be able to repeat the actions of the Soviet government, it's possible that the results will end up being the same as those seen in the 1980's and 1990's.

"Chechen" has Become Synonymous with "Enemy" for the Typical Russian

Moscow has learned its lessons from the first military campaign during which Chechnya's neighbors actively aided it, and this time it has taken pains to neutralize the Dagestanis, Ingush, and Kabardins.

The campaign of Muslim bands in Dagestan in 1999 was characterized by the Russian government as an attack by the Chechens on Dagestan, even though the first forces to attack were from the Dagestani dzhamaat led by Bagaudin Kizilurtovskii. The whole campaign actually raised many questions, but provided very few answers (Shermatova, Sonabar, "The Islamic Factors in the Hands of the Political Elites.")[22]

In Ingushetia, the Russian authorities had to contend with the position of former president Ruslan Aushev, who had long blocked the spread of all anti-Chechen attitudes promoted by Moscow.[23] Kabardino-Balkaria

---

[22] Islam in the Post-Soviet Space, Moscow Carnegie Center, Moscow, 2001.
[23] "Echo Moskvy" radio broadcast, 9/15/05.

242

also saw endless rumors of how Chechen refugees were filling up the resorts of the republic, thus promoting unfriendly relations and contributing to mass street fights that took place between Chechen and Kabardin youth.

The mechanism of violence was so well-established that the creation and operation of concentration camps in Chernokozovo, Tolstoi-yurt, Grozny, and Urus-Martan was presented as an effective measure by the authorities up until 2002. Shootings took place in humanitarian zones. There were police operations in which old men, women, and children were killed (as in Aldy, 02/05/00 and Kotyr-yurt and Alkhan-yurt).[24] Torture was used in Chernokozovo that seemed to harken back to the conquest of the Chechens in the 18th and 19th centuries.[25]

Russian authorities in Chechnya have a groupthink mentality that portrays every Chechen as an enemy. In fact, the chief Russian army commander in Chechnya, General Shamanov, declared that even an unborn child in this region is a potential terrorist. This all points to evidence of an ingrained illness of Russian society. It's hard to imagine how President Putin could try to act as the equal of the leaders of the developed nations in the G 8 given this attitude.

The image of the Chechen as an enemy is so strong that even propaganda to the contrary undertaken by Vladislav Surkov, one of the most influential members of Putin's administration, is unlikely to bear much fruit. Every month people can see movies in which the Chechen is shown as the enemy of the Russian state, which leads to the assumption that Chechens are inherently harmful to their interests. Chechens doing business in Russia always provoke inquiries from the security services, making it necessary for almost all businessmen to hire people of Slavic background to be the public face of their enterprises.

---

[24] Velikhov, Leonid. "Itogi," 04/15/00.
[25] "Welcome to Hell: Arbitrary Detention, Torture, and Extortion in Chechnya." Human Rights Watch, Oct. 2000.

This is not just the case in Russia. Even the French Foreign Ministry has officially prohibited Chechens from entering the country. It seems only a matter of time until other European states follow suit.

Yet while Russian propaganda has tried to push its own version of the events that are taking place in Chechnya, it has not been really successful in this endeavor. Most seem to have the general opinion that the Chechens are generally victims of a vicious crime, and not members of a global terrorist organization.

The Role of the Chechen Diaspora in Western Political Life

Today, the Chechen diaspora has a growing role in the establishment of a larger Chechen society and nation. According to unofficial figures, there are 100,000 Chechens living in Europe, more than 20,000 in Turkey, the Middle East, Azerbaijan, and Georgia, 100,000 in Kazakhstan, and 200,000-300,000 in Russia proper. While in 1999-2000 Chechens were still trying to adjust to their new life in their new countries, but by 2003 they started to create social and political groups in order to promote their issue and to deliberate on the situation in Chechnya.

Almost all countries have officially registered ethnic societies, and many have established cultural centers for these ethnic groups. There are further attempts to create a pan-European organization which will be the voice of the whole of the western Chechnya diaspora (see for instance, the work done by Ramzan Ampukaev). There are even attempts to create an international organization that would unite those people who want to openly oppose Russia's policy in Chechnya (these are being led by A. Sardali, Khamzan Umarov). On the other hand, there are those in the diaspora who are ready to be seen as the political wing of a larger resistance movement. These include Ahmad Zakaev in the UK, Apti Bisultanov in Germany, Selim Bishaev in France, Hussein Iskhanov in Austria and others.

With time, the influence of the diaspora will undoubtedly grow as people add a European education and newfound political skills to their high commitment to the Chechen cause. The diaspora will seek out its place in the grand scheme of things at the end of the Chechen war and will want a role in establishing a stable society in Chechnya after the war is won.

Political elites who are courting Chechen sympathies find it very important to show that they are supported by the largest possible number of Chechens. To so this, they oftentimes use the outdated World Chechen Congress (headed by Deni Taps, the leader of the St. Petersburg diaspora, and Magomed Shishani, an American professor). This was most recently used in an attempt to arrange talks between Chechnya and Russia (represented by various NGOs from Russia on one side and Ahmad Zakaev and Ruslan Khasbulatov from the Chechen side). When the Chechen party tried to ask for support from the Congress, it went into session in Denmark in autumn of 2002.[26]

Pro-Russian authorities in Chechnya are also trying to elicit the support of the Congress for a meeting in October 2006 by having it say that it accepts the influence and power of Ramzan Kadyrov, thus legitimizing his leadership. Of course only those people that will not raise their voice in opposition will be invited, so it's hard to view this proposed meeting as a genuine global event that seeks to probe the true opinion of the diaspora as opposed to just seeking the coronation of Kadyrov.

"Chechenizing" the Conflict?

Since 2002 Russian authorities have understood that they will have to be heavily involved in Chechnya for the foreseeable future, and have therefore tried to "Chechenize" the conflict. That is, they are seeking to pit Chechen separatists against those Chechens who want to remain a part of the Russian Federation. Thus, they would be able to frame the Russo-Chechen conflict in a totally different light. In its recent public statements, the Russian government has stated more and more frequently that Moscow wants to be an honest broker between the warring Chechen factions.

---

[26] BBC Radio, 10/28/02.

245

The criticism of the Russian press' coverage of the conflict and of the NGOs has forced Moscow to shift its burden to what is generally called the "pro-Russian forces".   Thus, police operations became the responsibility of the pro-Russian Chechen Ministry of the Interior, and later everything else was handed off to Ramzan Kadyrov, whose recent actions have fully eclipsed the past crimes.   The prison in Tsentoroi is still considered the bleakest place in Chechnya, even more so than the widely known wartime concentration camp Chernokozovo.   Chechen police and Chechen soldiers form the "North" and "South" battalions (later renamed "East" and "West") organize attacks on the Chechen rebels with more and more frequency, thus seeming to reaffirm Moscow's position about the intra-Chechen nature of the conflict.

The leadership of the resistance movement categorically rejects this view, believing that they are fighting only against the Russians and the Russian government, including those Chechens who have sided with Russia.   Such men are seen as being bereft of an ethnic pride and, just like the Tatars, Osettians, Kabardins and other ethnic groups that might come to fight against the Chechens, do so only because Russian government troops, have called   them "Russian" regardless of their geographical or ethnic background.

The Cultivation of Individual Personalities by Moscow

As Chechen reporter Zaindi Choltaev says, "Chechen folklore has many stories that lionize individual heroes, but none of them hold up because these heroes are wealthy, affluent, or hold the reigns of power." This, unfortunately, is exactly what is happening in Chechnya today. Chechens have always made heroes of those brave men that have had the best character.   Ramzan Kadyrov lives in a palace and leads a lifestyle unavailable to the vast majority of Chechens.   It seems impossible that Ramzan Kadyrov could be an epic, heroic figure.[27] The establishment of a genuine cult of personality is virtually impossible in Chechen society. What we see today is derived from the support that

---

[27] Radio Freedom, 08/25/06.

President Puttin grants Kadyrov, while many others wait and hold their peace.

Television, newspapers and magazines must devote 30-50% of their coverage to the positive events occurring in Chechnya. People are, however, willing to say that in its current state, the republic needs a firm, totalitarian ruler in order to prevent chaos. After so many bloody years and the persistent fear of death many just want to relax. Even the constant disappearances and arrests without trial tend to be placed on the back burner, while more attention is focused on the rebuilding of Gudermes, Argun, and Grozny. Although people want to see positive stories, they are not ignorant of what is going on with regards to freedom and human rights.

The population does think positively of the insurgents, and distributes vidoes and audio cassettes of their exploits. During an independent survey conducted by "Kavkaztimes" when asked, "Who would you like to see as the president of Chechnya?," people put Abdul-Khalim Sadulaev in second place, far ahead of Alkhanov or Putin.[28] Keep in mind that this survey was conducted in an atmosphere where government pressure is prevalent. When asked the question, "Who is responsible for the abductions in Chechnya?," approximately 50% of the respondents mentioned the Russian or pro-Russian security services.

Annual Amnesties

It's possible to say with a great deal of certainty that the numerous amnesties declared by the Russian authorities are pure propaganda. It's difficult to discuss the results of these amnesties, when after all of these years most of those who "surrendered" were persons who did not actually fight, but often played a political role in the interwar period.

Even the FSB has been forced to admit that most of those who surrender themselves were those insurgents who did not genuinely

---

[28] "Kavkaztimes," 06/12/06.

affect the situation in the Northern Caucasus. "Those who have surrendered up to this day have generally been participants of the first Chechen campaign, and we do not even have a file on most of them."[29]

The pro-Russian media frequently writes that there are only a few dozen insurgents left in the mountains, but the Secretary of the Chechen Security Council, one of Alu Alkhanov's men who provides information as a counterweight to Ramzan Kadyrov, states that 400 Chechens are on the FSB insurgency list. That is, 400 Chechens are definitely known to be on that list, and it is unclear how many more are on that list.[30] In order to somehow bolster this failure to stop the insurgency, the Russian government tends to blame foreign involvement.[31]

Each year the authorities try to apprehend at least one well-known name, and this year they have settled for the "surrender" of Ahmad Umarov, the brother of the resistance leader. It was well known that he, along with his father and nephew, was abducted last year and was considered missing until he turned up in Ramzan Kadyrov's office. Dokku Umarov's brother had not fought in either of the Chechen wars. His only crime was that he is a close relative, and thus could be used to open up channels of communication with the Chechen rebels. As with his father, Ahmed, Ramzan Kadyrov needs important names, but with Sadulaev and Basaev recently killed he is content to settle merely for a large count of 400-500 men who surrender and thus declare the, "utter and final annihilation of the Chechen rebels," just as Moscow wants.

The Moscow-Dzhokhar Negotiation Process

The changing situation allows for many different possibilities in the negotiations with the guerrillas. Though considered the official victors, Moscow knows that things are far worse than they appear, and the now

---

[29] *Novosti*, 08/17/06
[30] "Interfax," 08/31/06, German Bok.
[31] "Cacasustimes," Sergei Bogomolov has declared the FSB has determined that foreign intelligence services and organizations have interfered with the amnesty process in the Northern Caucasus.

larger regional (not merely Chechen) conflict can only be stopped via negotiations with the leaders of the resistance, instead of relying on the so-called pro-Russian forces in Chechnya. Such negotiations would require the existence of men capable of speaking for the warring factions. This could be almost anyone including one of the many individuals that represent the resistance in the West.

The negotiation process is very much a closed one and different possibilities for the process are being discussed, with various trusted Kremlin insiders acting as middle men. While the details are not being disclosed, various declarations and statements by Chechen politicians show that attempts at making the situation more transparent are underway, and that potential concessions are being discussed with the opposing side.

The potential negotiators suitable to the Chechens include those figures already well known to them, but also able to make headway with Moscow. These include Arkadii Volskii, one of the main negotiators during the first war and Dmitrii Kozak, who arranged for something reminiscent of negotiations in the Sheremetyevo airport in Moscow between Ahmad Zakaev and Viktor Kazantsev in 2001. Evgenii Primakov is another possibility, since it's well known that in 2002 he had proposed his own plan for normalizing the Chechen situation and accused the Russian generals of not being ready to begin the negotiating process in 2001-02. There is, however, the possibility that Moscow will believe that it can successfully suppress the separatist movements in the region, and will thus ignore Chechen attempts to negotiate, which can only lead to a protracted struggle in Northern Caucasus. It's hard to imagine that the Russian government will be able to emerge as a clear-cut winner in this case.

The West and the United States have taken a wait-and-attitude towards the conflict and are trying to see exactly what Russia will do. Criticism of Russia's policies in Chechnya has mostly evaporated, though it has been replaced by an actual presence in the region, which allows these sides to see just how much the Northern Caucasian situation impacts their strategic interests in Georgia and Azerbaijan.

249

It's obvious that the West is unwilling to act as the middleman in any negotiations, since unlike Kosovo, the Chechen situation seems perfectly clear for Western politicians. Having accepted the propaganda of the Russian military machine they believe that Chechnya has fallen into factional strife. This is completely untrue, and only the decisive actions of Chechen guerrillas re-focus the attention of the world on the need to start negotiations between Moscow and Dzhokhar.

Russia's Policies of Pressuring Chechen Politicians in the West

Russia cannot allow members of the Chechen resistance to lead an active political life. This is a case of the old Soviet syndrome in which any opposition figure is considered to be an enemy of the state. Now, as in earlier years, any declarations or meetings of Chechen politicians in the West are painfully received by the Russian elite, including President Vladimir Putin, who demands the extradition of political refugees at every turn.

The Russian government has not been above tweaking the facts, something clearly shown by the Zakaev court case in London and the Ilias Ahmadov case in America. In order to get the next Chechen politician the Russian government is willing to spend significant sums of money. For example, in order to change British public opinion regarding Ahmad Zakaev, the Russian pro-Presidential youth organization set up protests in front of the British embassy in Moscow, and even demonstrations in London itself. Multiple interviews with the press were conducted, all demonstrating Moscow's attempt to blacken the reputation of the Chechen politicians and show them to be Islamic terrorists and nothing more.

The Russian Ministry of International Affairs makes protests at the level of its ambassadors, thus trying to force governments to refrain from receiving separatist politicians. By declaring certain persons "wanted by Interpol," the Russian government seeks to curtail the movement of many Chechen politicians, but this is futile, since all countries with well formed Chechen diasporas (including the US) already have men able to make decisions on their own in their corner of the world.

Another form of pressure is the pressure applied to those relatives of Chechen politicians that still reside in the republic, demanding the cessation of political activity in order to avoid the arrest of family members on trumped-up charges.

Moscow is afraid of the Chechen immigrants, but the hundred thousand strong Chechen diaspora is today a well organized community that is knowledgeable about human rights and the laws of democratic governance, and is capable of demanding and exercising its rights. This is a well-educated diaspora, and it will be difficult, even impossible, to demand blind obedience from it. And if we remember that every Chechen refugee has a large family at home, a family that helps and supports him in every way, including the financially and legally, then the Russian government will have to deal with completely different Chechens. These are Chechens whose values aren't just supported by their historical grievances, but are also strengthened by contemporary Western values.

Sufism and Salafism

From the very beginning, Moscow's pawn Ahmed Kadyrov had tried to present the events in Chechnya as the conflict between the Chechens' traditional Sufi form of Islam with the newly arrived Salafi members of the Islamic Renaissance Party. It is thoroughly improper to simplify the situation in this manner, especially since doing so is very convenient for Moscow and Chechnya's pro-Russian leadership.

Even if there was a confrontation, there was never a question of what party would prevail. The followers of Salafi were so few in number they were unable to take the reigns of power. Even though Aslan Maskhadov gave several governmental posts to the Salafis in 1997, it was not necessary, though it did give the Islamist party an entryway into Chechnya.

251

The radicals entered the dzhamaats and accepted the leadership of the president of the Chechen Republic of Ichkeria. This meant that they agreed to temporarily suspend any and all religious conflicts. The Sufis felt that the Salafites would attempt to destroy their chosen form of Islam and never truly trusted the Salafis. Thus, Ahmed Kadyrov's propaganda fell on willing ears and helped to enflame the Sufi-Salafi confrontation. Everywhere he went, Kadyrov spoke of how the Salafites were to blame for everything, and how peace would come to Chechnya with their extermination. Ramzan Kadyrov later followed his father's example to the point where government posts have been assigned on the basis of belonging to particular Sufi brotherhoods.

This question is actually completely irrelevant to contemporary Chechen society. For instance, Shamil Basayev was a member of the brotherhood of Ali Mitaev (Kadirite tarikat), even though he led combat groups from dzhamaats generally considered to be Salafite. Amongst the dzhamaats themselves the Ingush dzhamaat can not be considered Salafite since most of its members are followers of Kunta-khadji Kishiev (Kadirite tarikat), making it difficult, and entirely unnecessary, to draw the line between Salafi and Sufi combatants.

"Chechen Peacekeeping Forces?"

Following the recent crisis in Lebanon the question of international peacekeeping forces, including Russian forces, has been raised. With the Kremlin's partial blessing, the possibility of sending ethnic Chechens as peacekeepers has been discussed, with the general public being generally in favor of this idea.

Ramzan Kadyrov sees this as a great opportunity for sending a contingent made up of troops of his enemies Sulim Yamadaev and Magomed Kakiev (the battalions "East" and "West," formed partially in opposition to Kadyrov himself), while also showing that he and the Chechens can be relied upon in such a complicated and delicate situation. This has the additional side effect of muting all Western criticism of Russia's actions in Chechnya. Chechens fighting under the

Russian flag in an Arabic country will be seen as also having defeated "terrorism" in Chechnya itself, which will be a huge victory for Putin.

Arab countries will find it difficult to criticize the pro-Russian Chechens (and thus Moscow), since they are helping their Muslim brothers in Lebanon, thus laying the ground for a change in perception in the Middle East of the Chechen situation. Such a victory for Russian propaganda risks ending the flow of financial aid from those independent sources that acted in the belief that the Russian government is oppressing the Chechen people. Even if Chechen troops are not sent to Lebanon, the very fact that such a possibility can be discussed hints at Russia's success with its policies in Chechnya.

Conclusion

The events in the region are unfolding in accordance to the guerrillas' plans. The Russian military and security services are unable to staunch the spreading conflagration in the Caucasus.

"The terrorist den in Chechnya has been destroyed, but the situation in the Northern Caucasus has not improved," Nokolai Patrushev, the head of the National Anti-Terrorist Committee declared at a meeting in Rostov-on-the-Don.

> "Terrorist acts are now taking place more frequently in Ingushetia and Northern Ossetia, where the populaces are arming themselves. Opposing the growth of crime in these and other regions of the Southern Federal District is made difficult because of corruption, predominantly among the security services."[32]

It's been noted that the crime rate, especially serious crime, has essentially doubled in certain regions, with 78 terrorist acts taking place in the first seven months of 2006 alone.

---

[32] *Kommersant*, #158 (#3489), 08/26/06.

Well-organized and active military formations are the reality of the day, not only in Chechnya, but in the Northern Caucasus as a whole. This reality cannot be solved through bombs. Once Moscow understands this it will realize that it is better to use the authority and influence of international organizations, which will help to avoid the threat of national dissolution.

In the near future it seems that no radical changes will occur, neither in Chechnya, nor in the whole of the Northern Caucasus. Dokku Umarov will not alter the current layout since he participated in the planning for the Caucasus Front. Umarov's relative political inexperience, however, will probably make him emphasize military operations.

In his most recent interview Umarov stated that he will no longer negotiate with Moscow. However, now that he is the number one man in the resistance he will have to change this attitude. In addition, in an interview given after the death of Shamil Basayev, Umarov accused the West of having betrayed the interests of the Chechen people in favor of its own economic interests. It's strange that there was no criticism of the countries of the Muslim East, since unlike the West they do not even criticize Russia for violating human rights. Apparently Umarov, like his predecessors, hopes to find his allies there, despite never having received even verbal support from that region.

Dokku Umarov will most likely be more like Maskhadov than Sadulaev, and he will have to rely on such figures as Ahmad Zakaev and Usman Firzauli in order to help him achieve his goals. He'll have to work hard to be able to move from the role of local politician to that of a leader of all the North Caucasus dzhamaats. This will require actions that will allow him to inherit this leadership, including the oaths of fealty necessary for one taking Sadulaev's position. These will need to come from the Dagestani, Ingush, Kabardino-Balkar, Karachai as well as Nogai dzhamaats.

On the whole, the political maturity of the Chechen resistance movement no longer relies on just one man. The disappearances of such leaders as Maskhadov and Sadulaev are obvious losses, but they do not alter the set of principles on which the resistance operates. The Russian government faces a growing problem in that it is not sure who to deal with. New names tell them nothing, and they keep blaming everything on foreign involvement, which is minimal, if not totally absent. Thus, a change in the leadership of the resistance will not significantly alter the actions or goals of the overall movement. Furthermore, it still allows them to prepare for military actions, even if the exact date of their execution remains unknown.

Military Jammats in the North Caucasus:
A Continuing Threat

Dr. Andrew McGregor

"The creation of a Caliphate in Russia is only the first part of their plan."
-- Russian Federation President Vladimir Putin, November 11, 2002

Introduction

The last few years have seen a concerted effort by the pro-independence Chechen leadership to consolidate scattered Islamic resistance movements across the North Caucasus. These locally based jammats (Islamic communities) champion a Salafist approach to Islam, a regional moral revival, and a steadfast opposition to Russian 'colonialism'. In many ways these groups are Islamic inheritors of an earlier (and largely secular) pan-Caucasian movement. The late Chechen warlord Shamil Basayev spent years developing ties to the independent jammats in order to bring them under Chechen command in a united North Caucasian front against Russian Federation rule. Basayev's death on July 9, 2006, was a major setback to the expansion of the Chechen struggle to the rest of the North Caucasus, though it does not appear to have had much impact on the level of militant activity in the region so far.

The growth of the jammats as locally based centers of Islamist resistance raises a number of questions. How has the military jammat evolved from its communal roots? How does it reconcile its Salafist ideology with basic pan-Caucasian sentiments? Most importantly, do the military jammats constitute a serious threat to the integrity of the

256

Russian Federation? Some of the answers can be found through an examination of the origins of the military jammats, their connection to the pan-Caucasus movement, and their role in the expansion of the Chechen/ Russian war through the North Caucasus and even into Russia itself.

Pan-Caucasus Movements

Though the Muslim North Caucasus is divided into scores of ethnic groups and as many languages, there have been significant attempts to unify these groups in the past, most significantly Imam Shamil's Islamic state of 1834-59 and the short-lived Mountain Republic of 1918. Soviet rule was designed to divide and weaken the region's Muslims, but the collapse of the communist state allowed a revival of the pan-Caucasus movement.

The Confederation of the Mountain Peoples of the North Caucasus (KGNK) was formed in 1990 by a group of writers and academics, including its leader, Musa Shanib (a Kabardin, aka Yuri Shanibov) and the Chechen poet Zelimkhan Yandarbiyev. The Confederation had no representation from Dagestan and nor real constituency; the delegates were all self-appointed representatives of their peoples but did not include representation from Dagestan. In a move to be more inclusive, the organization changed its name to the Confederation of the Peoples of the North Caucasus (KNK) in October 1992.

It would be war that would galvanize the movement, with the KGNK declaring war on Georgia in support of the Abkhazian separatist movement in August 1992. A volunteer force of several thousand fighters was assembled. This 'volunteer peace-keeping battalion of the Mountain Confederation' was composed mostly of Cherkess, Kabardins, Adigheans and Chechens. The Chechen 'Abkhazian Battalion' was the largest single volunteer unit and included the late Ruslan Gelayev and Shamil Basayev, both of whom would go on to become major warlords in Chechnya. The volunteers, with covert training and equipment from the intelligence services of the Russian Federation, played an important role in helping the Abkhazians defeat a

257

ramshackle Georgian paramilitary force. The involvement of the GRU (Russian Military Intelligence) in organizing and equipping KNK fighters led to persistent rumours that Shamil Basayev was, and remained, a GRU officer until his death. (see the recent remarks of Chechen parliamentary speaker Dukvakha Abdurakhmanov; *Agentstvo Natsionalnykh Novostei*, August 22, 2006) KNK leader Musa Shanib (a Kabardin, aka Yuri Shanibov) came under suspicion from Russian authorities for suspected separatist activities and was arrested in September 1992. Shanib escaped, or was possibly released, a short time later following a public outcry over his detention.

The fall of the Abkhazian capital of Sukhumi to Abkhazian and KNK fighters in October 1993 marked the peak of the KNK's strength and influence. The collapse of North Caucasian solidarity began with disputes over unfulfilled promises made to the KNK fighters over compensation for their efforts. With the outbreak of war in Chechnya in 1994 the Kremlin began to regard the KNK as a threat to the unity of the Federation. Moscow had no desire to see a North Caucasian legion joining the Chechen separatists, but support for the Chechen cause from the other North Caucasus republics actually proved to be weak. A rift formed between Chechen leaders who felt their defense of Abkhazia had entitled them to similar support from their fellow Muslims in their independence struggle.

Confederation fighters were not especially welcome in largely secular Abkhazia, particularly those considered Islamists. Because of different forms of worship practiced throughout the North Caucasus, Islam ultimately proved to be a divisive influence in the volunteer battalions. Discipline was poor among the opportunists who followed the first wave of idealists to Abkhazia. It was mainly the sheer disorganization of the inexperienced Georgian paramilitaries that ensured their defeat in 1993. Nevertheless, it was the links established here that Basayev would call on to create his 'Islamic Peacekeeping Army' in 1999. By then many of the volunteers had picked up another two years of combat experience in the Russian/Chechen war of 1994-6. Shari'a law was introduced as a form of military discipline in the volunteer battalions; Islam added a religious motivation in fighting against the Georgian

Christians as well as a means of unifying the disparate assembly of Mountain fighters.

When war between Chechnya and Russia broke out again in 1999 the KNK backed the Chechens, but were unable to offer anything more than moral support. Many members of the movement feared Chechen domination. Shanib's Chechen successor as leader of the KNK, Yusup Soslambekov, was assassinated in Moscow in July 2000 (Soslambekov was a Chechen parliamentarian and early supporter of Chechnya's first president, Dzhokar Dudayev).

With Russian forces on the attack in Chechnya, leading KNK member Zelimkhan Yandarbiyev maintained that "all the Moslem countries should participate in the Chechen jihad, providing it with both military and humanitarian support." (Al-Jazira TV, July 6, 2000) By 2002 Yandarbiyev had abandoned the Pan-Caucasus ideology for more specific aspirations; "Our aim is Chechnya as an independent Islamic state." (Zerkalo [Baku], September 24, 2002) After leaving the KNK, Yandarbiyev's assessment of the group was critical; "At the time of the Georgian-Abkhazian conflict the Confederation was ruled by (Yusup) Soslambekov, (Musa) Shanibov, and other people, who worked under the direct supervision of the Russian special services...We all know that unfortunately the Russian special services directed this organization from the very beginning" (*Georgian Times*, January 28, 2003) After briefly serving as Dudayev's successor as president of Chechnya, Yandarbiyev was assassinated by Russian agents in Qatar in 2004 where he had been involved in fund-raising for the Islamist element of the Chechen resistance.

Both the Pan-Caucasus and the Islamist movements in the North Caucasus have always had to contend with nationalist movements that reinforce ethnic divisions rather than promote unity. Such divisions are unsurprising in a region experiencing mass deportations under Soviet rule and the subsequent re-assignment of land belonging to deported groups. The irredentist flavor of many of these national movements inevitably brings them into conflict with their neighbors. In Dagestan alone there is a broad range of nationalist groups, such as the Lak 'Kazi-

Kumukh' or 'Tsubars', the Lezgin 'Sadval', the Dargin 'Tsadesh', the Nogay 'Birlik', the Kumyk 'Tenglit', the Avar 'Union of Avar Jammat', etc.

Dagestani Origins of the Military Jammats

A jammat is simply a communal organization designed to enable the pursuit of an Islamic lifestyle. They are found in many parts of the world and most are entirely peaceful organizations. In Dagestan, the formation of mountain jammats with economic and political functions followed closely on the Islamization of the region.

The Dagestani jammats of the 18th and 19th centuries were largely self-sufficient and were typically based on a single ethnic group. The jammats gradually took a role as protectors of community land against incursions from neighboring jammats or other ethnic groups. In this way they developed a limited defensive military role. In times of extreme crisis the jammats could create alliances against a common threat.

The model for the modern North Caucasus military jammat is found in Dagestan's 1990s 'Muslim Jammat', led by its Amir, Bagauddin Magomedov (aka Bagauddin Kebedov, an ethnic Khvarshin). Membership of the jammat was mostly, but not exclusively, from the Dargin ethnic group. With at least thirty major ethnic groups and languages, ethnic tensions are never far from the surface in Dagestan. Peace and stability are ensured by a complicated political structure that reserves certain political offices for specific ethnic groups (much like Lebanon religiously-based system). Unfortunately the same system promotes stagnation, corruption and an almost complete reliance on federal subsidies.

The Muslim Jammat had two military leaders, Saudi jihadist Ibn al-Khattab (Samir Ibn-Salih Ibn 'Abdallah al-Suwaylim) and Jarulla Rajbaddinov of Karamakh, the latter a self-styled 'Brigadier General' in command of the jammat's 'Islamic Guard'. Al-Khattab, a veteran jihadist with experience in Tajikistan and the 1994-96 Russian/Chechen war, married locally but was often away in Chechnya, where he ran guerrilla-training camps in the interval between wars. The camps were attended by militants from across the North Caucasus.

Jammat leader Bagauddin was one of the Dagestani leaders of the Islamic Revival Party (IRP), an early Islamist movement initiated in the late 1980s as the Soviet Union began to show signs of dissolution. In the early 1990s IRP demonstrations led by Bagauddin's mentor, Abbas Kebedov, succeeded in driving Mufti Mahmud Gekkiyev from office (the Mufti was viewed as an agent of the old Soviet regime). By 1997 Bagauddin was leader of the newly formed Islamic Jammat of Dagestan, a Salafist community dedicated to creating shari'a-ruled enclaves free of federal authority.

Bagauddin once declared, "For us, geographic and state borders have no significance; we work and act in those places where it is possible for us to do so." (Mikhail I Roshchin, "Dagestan and the War Next Door", Institute for the Study of Conflict, Ideology and Policy, *Perspective* 11(1), September-October 2000) The Muslim Jammat believed Dagestan's government to be in a state of *shirk* (paganism). They strongly opposed the traditional Sufi lodges, believing that they violated the Salafists' core doctrine of *tawhid* (monotheism) through the veneration of saints and pilgrimages to the tombs of holy men.

The Salafists, who soon became known as 'Wahhabis' (pejoratively in Russian), centred their jammat in the Buinaksk region of Dagestan. Previously obscure villages such as Karamakhi and Chabanmakhi became Salafist strongholds that attracted the presence of young Islamists from across Dagestan and further points in the North Caucasus. The presence of the veteran jihadist Ibn al-Khattab gave the jammat a military dimension, with al-Khattab providing training to would-be mujahideen for what seemed an inevitable conflict with the Russian state. Volunteers received basic Islamic instruction that had to be mastered before the candidate could begin military training. A library was available, featuring works by Islamic reformers such as Indian/Pakistani Abu Ala Maududi, Egyptian Muslim Brothers Hassan al-Banna and Sayyid Qutb, and Magomed Tagaev.

A Dagestani Avar, Tagaev authored two influential Russian-language works calling for armed rebellion against Russian "occupation: <u>Our Struggle, or the Imam's Army of Insurrection</u> (Kiev, 1996), and <u>Jihad, or How to Become Immortal</u> (Baku, 1999). These works found great favor with the Salafist Islamists of Dagestan, who saw to their distribution throughout their communities. In 1999 Tagaev served as Minister of Information in the short-lived (and self-appointed) 'Islamic Government of Dagestan'. Tagaev was eventually extradited from Azerbaijan in April 2004, and sentenced to 10 years in a hard-labor camp for his part in the Salafist uprising. (Interfax, April 10, 2004)

The murder of the *mufti* of Dagestan, Sa'id Muhammad-Haji Abubakarov, by a radio-controlled mine in August 1998 was a turning point for the Salafist movement in Dagestan, which was immediately blamed for the assassination. The charge was never proven, and there were many other suspects, including Avar leader Gadji Makhachev, and fellow high ranking clerics. Even the then president Magomed Magomedov was accused of the murder in rallies organized by Khasavyurt mayor Saigidpasha Umakhanov in 2004. (IWPR, August 19, 2004)

Mufti Abubakarov was a critical opponent of the Salafists (referred to, pejoratively, as 'Wahhabis'):

> "Their teaching is constructed on quicksand. They deny what our grandfathers and ancestors believed. Can we defile the graves of our ancestors simply because Wahhabis consider that there should not be gravestones in the cemeteries? In disputes they appeal to the authority of Imam Shamil, who created the Caucasus imamate, and Islamic state. Well, this is true, but Imam Shamil cited holy men, many of whom were sheikhs of Sufi orders and religious leaders. It is against them that the Wahhabis are arguing by affirming that the true Muslim does not need mentors since between him and Allah there

should be no intermediaries." (*Moskovskie Novosti*, 25 August 1998)

As a political foundation for his activities, Basayev formed the Congress of the Peoples of Chechnya and Dagestan (co-chairmen Movladi Ugadov and Magomed Tagaev – Kommersant, Ag 5, 05), supported by the 'Islamic Peacekeeping Brigade' under the command of al-Khattab.

Following Russian attempts in 1999 to suppress the semi-autonomous 'Wahhabite' enclave, Chechen warlor Shamil Basayev his Arab ally Ibn al-Khattab attacked northwest Dagestan with a mixed force variously referred to as the 'Islamic Peacekeeping Army' or the North Caucasus Liberation Army. The attacks failed in part because Dagestanis were accustomed to *ghazawat* (holy war) leaders or Imams coming from the Avar ethnic group. While the insurrection attracted numbers of Avar youths, neither Basayev nor al-Khattab fulfilled this basic condition for leadership. Certainly neither even pretended to possess any real religious leadership, admitting that they were warriors who had spent months trying to determine the Islamic authority for their incursion into Dagestan.

The over-ambitious declaration of the Islamic Republic of Dagestan met with steadfast opposition from most of Daghstan's Muslims, who were not prepared to abandon their carefully balanced system of local government (which did indeed help preserve peace between the republic's many ethnic groups) and the much-needed subsidies provided by the central government of the Russian Federation in favor of a Salafist-led Islamic state. Basayev's attacks initially focused on the Botlikh Rayon of Dagestan, where the Andi population organized their own Sufi-based jammats to oppose the Islamists.

The jihadists' subsequent penetration of the Novolaksky Rayon did not fare any better. The failure of the Dagestani population to join a popular uprising against Russian rule seems to have taken Basayev by surprise. Bagauddin Magomedev, Lak politician Nadir Kachilayev and Ibn al-Khattab had all assured Basayev that the Dagestanis were only waiting for a signal to join a general rebellion. In fact the Salafists' verbal and sometimes physical assaults on the dominant Sufist brand of Islam and its followers in Dagestan had made the Islamists extremely unpopular. Bagauddin's movement made conciliatory moves towards the traditional Sufi community in 1998 as the Salafists refocused on replacing state control with Islamic government, but it was too little, too late. A bitter rift ensued between Basayev and Bagauddin after the failure of the invasion, though Basayev's differences with al-Khattab proved only temporary. While he was still mufti of Chechnya, the late Akhmad Kadyrov saw Russian hands behind the Salafist revival in Dagestan, "The Kremlin deliberately fostered 'Wahhabism' in the Caucasus, in order to divide Muslims and unleash yet another war – a religious war – there." (Jamestown Foundation *Prism*, August 7, 1998)

The Islamic Basis of the Jammats

The Islamic nature of the military jammats is unquestionable. Much of their effort is taken up with verbal or even physical assaults on the 'hypocritical' local leaders of 'official Islam'. The spiritual boards responsible for Islamic activities in the Russian Federation were notorious in the Soviet era for including large numbers of KGB or GRU agents and informers. Suspicions linger to this day, and the spiritual boards are often regarded as being far too close to the regimes they serve. In August 2004 the 'Mujahideen of Dagestan' declared that "the position of the so-called 'clerical department of Dagestan' is anti-Islamic. This is a structural organization of Russian secret services, working for Moscow, against their fellow people and against Muslims. Its main mission is to provoke strife and discord among the nations of the Caucasus." (Kavkaz Center, August 14, 2004) A statement from the Shari'a Jammat, for example, warned the Dagestani "spiritual board" (the administrative structure for official Islam) ,"to either shut their mouths or we would shut them for them and then bury them." (Kavkaz Center, August 3, 2006)

The political opening brought on by the collapse of the Soviet Union allowed religious students the first opportunity in decades to study at Islamic schools in Egypt and Saudi Arabia. The severe and ostensibly authentic version of Islam encountered by Caucasian religious students in Saudi Arabia and other Gulf states contrasted with the rich traditions of Caucasian Sufist Islam, which soon came under fire from the Salafists for its numerous innovations (*shirk*) based on local customs rather than 'authentic' Islam.

The Jammats are mainly Salafist, although there are occasional efforts to incorporate Sufist Muslims into the communities. Bagauddin Magomedov's Salafist jammat made the mistake of constantly attacking the Sufi tariqats, creating much needless opposition within Dagestan. The current jammats tend to be more inclusive. Much of the appeal of Salafism is economically based in the Caucasus. The austerity of Salafism and its opposition to the extravagant and often ruinous ceremonies accompanying local occasions like funerals and marriages had an immediate appeal following the economic collapse of the 1990s.

The military jammats have made a point of broadening their ethnic base, rather than incorporating members of only a single ethnic type. The Kabardino-Balkarian Republic's (KBR) Yarmuk Jammat, for instance, has issued statements rejecting its depiction as 'a monoethnic [Balkar] organization', emphasizing the membership and even leadership roles of Kabardins in the jammat. (Utro.ru, February 4, 2003) The North Caucasus Sufi lodges tend to have a more homogenous ethnic base than the Salafist jammats, which are open to a broader membership. Islam in the jammats tends to focus on the principle of tawhid (the unity of God) without the intercession of shaykhs or saints.

An important element of any Islamic insurgency is whether participation is individually obligatory (*fard 'ayn*) for all Muslims, as opposed to a community obligation (*fard kifayah*), i.e., one that is met by the participation of traditional armed forces belonging to a Muslim state. Modern Islamist ideologues such as the Egyptian Muslim Brother Sayyid Qutb and the Palestinian founder of al-Qaeda 'Abdullah' Azzam took a hard line on interpreting this question, with Azzam going so far as to insist that jihad is *fard 'ayn* (mandatory) until every piece of land that was once under Muslim rule is retaken.

265

With reference to the situation in their republic, the KBR's Yarmuk Jammat cited the three conditions under which jihad becomes *fard 'ayn* under the Hanafite school of Islamic law followed in the northwest Caucasus:

1) At the moment of invasion our nations wer Muslim and were attacked by infidels (Kafirs);

2) Our lands were Muslim and were invaded by Kafirs;

3) Shari'ah was the ruling law, the Law of Almighty Allah, and it was abolished by the invaders

Dagestan's Shari'ah Jammat has likewise insisted on the compulsory nature of resistance to Russian rule ,"Jihad in the Caucasus is obligatory so long as the infidels continue to occupy an acre of Muslim land. It is obligatory to all, including men and women. During the time of the Imam Shamil, when there were not enough troops, the women took up arms to defend their villages, as happened in the battle of Akhulgo." (this was the site in Dagestan of an 80 day Russian siege in 1839) (Kavkaz Centre, August 3, 2006)

Dagestan's Shari'a Jammat has suggested a change in the motivation in the young men who seek to join the mujahideen in the last decade ,"Whereas before in the camps of Khattab near Serzhen-Yurt [1997-98], some people came out of curiosity and the desire to acquire Islamic knowledge, today young people dream of becoming martyrs on God's path. And that means the time has come - the time of a Jihad and the victory of Islam." (Kavkaz Center, August 8, 2006) The jammat also notes that the new generation of Muslims has the advantage of not having been indoctrinated in the Soviet *'jahiliya'* (state of ignorance), thus leaving their minds open to the message of Islam.

Immediately following the Basayev/Khattab incursion into Dagestan, many of the other North Caucasus republics began a campaign to root out and destroy all traces of 'Wahhabism' in the region. Although the term 'Wahhabi' applies to followers of a specific Saudi Arabian Islamic reform movement founded in the 18th century, in the Russian context it covers a broad and often convenient spectrum of religious/political beliefs, at times applying to everyone from hard-core Salafist gunmen to those who simply attend the mosque on a regular basis. Though the number of Islamist militants in the northwest Caucasus was still extremely small in 1999-2000, rumors of an impending Islamist/'Wahhabist' coup were promoted by local authorities. According to Khazretali Berdov, head of the Nalchik city administration:

> Wahhabism in our republic [KBR] is by no means a horrifying myth. The Wahhabites work according to a well established plan: first, they infiltrate existing religious organizations, then they spark off confrontation between traditional Muslims and extremist factions. Finally they start shouting and screaming about the suppression of Islam in the Caucasus. (CRS no. 58, November 17, 2000)

Many jammat members were arrested and brought to trial on all types of charges relating to armed insurrection and attempted overthrow of the state. The unfamiliarity of both state prosecutors and media with the jammat structure at the time is reflected in the numerous references to 'the terrorist organization called Jammat'.

In a post-communist world of corruption and criminality the jammats assumed a communal security role that at times came into conflict with the police. The arbitrary brutality and torture allegedly practiced by state police in the Muslim republics gave the jammats a new purpose – revenge. Most of the jammats' so-called 'military operations' across the North Caucasus are in fact part of a ruthless, no-quarter battle between police and those with experience of police violence. An example is the case of Gadzhi Abidov, his brother Shamil, and Sharaputdin Labazanov, who were tried for the murder of police Major Tagir Abdullayev in 2005. According to their testimony they committed the murder in revenge for torture inflicted by Major Abdullayev three months earlier. (*Moscow Times*, March 15, 2005).

Despite the militant nature of the new 'military jammats', leadership still tended to be drawn from Imams and local religious authorities. In the Stavropol region two Imams were convicted of organizing, "a gun-toting Wahhabi gan'" that killed five policemen in 2002 before the group was broken up. (ITAR-TASS, October 27, 2004) Here again, Basayev used connections established in 1999 to help raise the "Nogai Battalion" under the leadership of three brothers who had accompanied Basayev on his invasion of Dagestan, Ulubey, Kambiy and Takhir Yelgushiyev. Takhir was killed in 2002 and Ulubey was killed while allegedly planning a major operation under Basayev's direction in Kizlyar in August 2004. (*Vremye Novostei*, August 2, 2004)

Shamil Basayev: Organizing the Resistance

Though the Basayev/Khattab invasion of Dagestan will be remembered as a stunning miscalculation that played into the hands of the "hawks" in the Kremlin, the connections Basayev made with the militant volunteers of the "Islamic Peacekeeping Army" would later serve as the basis for Chechen attempts to broaden their war against Russia by creating new fronts across the northern Caucasus. The fierce fighting against the Russian Army separated the wheat from the chaff in the Islamist rebellion. Bagauddin, Siraj al-Din Ramazanov (Prime Minister of the "Islamic State of Dagestan") and Nadir Kachiliyev proved to be fighting a word of words, but the men who stood firm with Basayev formed strong bonds that could be called upon in the future.

The late president of Chechnya, Shaykh Abdul-Halim Sadulayev, described the North Caucasus expansion of the Chechen war as part of a plan intended to extend until 2010. (*Chechnya Weekly*, July 6 2006) The scheme was adopted at the 2002 Majlis al-Shura meeting during the presidency of the late Aslan Maskhadov. As both a military veteran and a religious leader (though his authority in this area was challenged by his enemies), Shaykh Abdul-Halim seemed to Basayev and others an ideal candidate for the role of Imam of the North Caucasus. Following

268

in the tradition of Shaykh Mansur and Imam Shamil, Sadulayev would lead the region's Muslims in a general uprising against infidel rule (at least in theory), and Basayev was quick to arrange an oath-taking of personal loyalty to Sadulayev by the leaders of the various Caucasian jammats. Sadulayev claimed the existence of jammats composed of ethnic Russians in the Russian republic that had pledged their loyalty to him as Amir of the Majlis al-Shura. (*Chechnya Weekly*, July 6 2006) The Shaykh also announced the creation of a new 'Caucasian Front' incorporating

Ingushetia, Ossetia, Stavropol, the KBR, the Karachaevo-Cherkessian Republic (KCR), Adyghei and Krasnoyarsk before the entire program crashed to a halt with Sadulayev's death at the hands of federal forces in June 2006.

Surviving Basayev's Death

Though the Chechen resistance may be reluctant to admit it, Basayev's death was a major blow to creation of the "Caucasian Front". The defiant reaction of Dokku Umarov (current ChRI president) to Basayev's death was to announce the creation of two new sectors in the larger "Caucasus Front". The statement creating a Ural Front and a Volga Front amounted to declaring an expansion of the war to the Russian republic. The Volga Front was placed under the command of Amir Jundulla, while the Ural Front is led by Amir Assadulla, a former member of the "Ingush Mujahideen" and a leading participant in the 2004 raid on Nazran.

Should a negotiated settlement be reached at some point between the representatives of the Chechen Republic of Ichkeria and the Russian Federation it is difficult to see how the jammats would fit into such an agreement. Would the orphaned Jammats revert to independent activities under local leadership or would they gradually dissolve under the weight of Russian security forces freed from deployment in Chechnya? (see Mayrbek Vachagaev, *Chechnya Weekly*, August 3, 2006) The recent and controversial "Manifesto for Peace in Chechnya" presented by ChRI Foreign Minister Akhmed Zakayev after the death of Shamil Basayev made no mention of the jammats. In an August 2006 statement meant to refute the damage caused to the Jammat movement by Basayev's death and to establish the continuing viability of their organization, the "Military Command of the Ingush Center of the Caucasian Front" presented a lengthy list of military operations carried out since Basayev's death on July 10, 2006. (Kavkaz Center, August 29, 2006)

The growth of the locally based military Jammats has been concurrent with the declining importance of the foreign mujahideen led by Jordanian Abu Hafs. The Arab jihadists have found more accommodating territory (in a cultural, linguistic and even climatic sense) for the pursuit of their struggle in Iraq, part of a general abandonment of the Chechen cause in the Arab world. Abu Hafs al-Urdani has commanded the international mujahideen since the death of Saudi Amir Abu al-Walid ('Abd al-Aziz al-Ghamidi) in April 2004. Though precise numbers are hard to come by, at this point foreign jihadis are not likely to amount to more than a few score members, with Turks probably as well represented as Arabs.

A Moral Revolution

The Jammats routinely assail the corruption and lax moral standards of the region's rulers. The trade in narcotics, the existence of prostitution, the use of alcohol and a general moral decay are all laid at the door of the official power structures. The Yarmuk Jammat detailed their objections to conditions in the KBR in their August 2004 founding statement:

> We are fighting against tyrants and bloodsuckers, who put the interests of their mafia clans above the interest of their nations. We are fighting against those who get fat at the expense of the impoverished and intimidated people of Kabardino-Balkaria, whom they brought down to their knees...These mere apologies for rulers, who sold themselves to the invaders, have made drug addiction, prostitution,

270

poverty, crime, depravity, drunkenness and unemployment prosper in our Republic. It is their corrupt policies that undressed our daughters and our sisters and brought them to lechery and permissiveness…On their orders Muslims of Kabardino-Balkaria get kidnapped and tortured. On their orders our mosques are getting closed down. (Kavkaz Center, August 24, 2004)

Bagauddin Magomedov favored the creation of a force of moral police (*muhtabisin*) to enforce the observance of shari'ah law in daily life. (Statement of July 1997, quoted in; Mikhail I Roshchin, "Dagestan and the War Next Door", Institute for the Study of Conflict, Ideology and Policy, *Perspective* 11(1), September-October 2000) A rmed Salafists created their own system of law enforcement in northwest Dagestan in 1997-98, driving criminal elements and drug dealers from their villages.

The Nalchik Narcotics Control Department raid in December 2004 is the outstanding example of the use of arms by the jammats to correct immoral conduct. The department as a group was accused of running the local illegal drug trade and in the ruthless attack no attempt was made to ascertain the individual responsibility of those police present for these alleged crimes. Some consolation for was offered by a leading KBR mujahid for honest police officers who fell in mujahideen assaults:

We know that among government officials there are many people who did not join the law enforcement bodies and other state government structures to rob the people. They work in good faith, combat crime, the drug business and corruption. There are many Muslims among them, who observe religious requirements fully or partially. If these types of people suffer from our actions this will happen only because we do not know them and cannot distinguish them from atheists and corrupt people. If they suffer by mistake, they will be recompensed for this on Judgment Day, and if they get killed, they will become

271

martyrs, if they are true believers… (Kavkaz Center, March 25, 2005)

Operations of the Military Jammats: Dagestan

Considering the origin of the military jammats, it should be unsurprising that Dagestan is today the home of the most active of all these organizations. For some years now Makhachkala has been a virtual battleground. In Dagestan the rebels are less likely to be found in the mountains than in the cities, with the urban warfare of assassinations, bombings and gunfights replacing the tactics of a mobile guerrilla force. The fighters have even renamed Makhachkala 'Shamilkala', after the great 19th century Dagestani Imam and rebel leader.

Support for the jammats is far from universal. Many in Dagestan regard Russian rule as the only thing that prevents the region from exploding into a multi-sided civil war. While corruption is endemic in Dagestan, like the other North Caucasus republics, ethnic imbalance in access to the proceeds of corruption generally tends to be more provocative than Islamic or separatist motivations in sparking opposition to the government.

Like its counterparts in the North Caucasus, Dagestan's Shari'a Jammat has concerns that go far beyond religious revival. The group points out the poor educational level of the Dagestani leadership, their proclivity for corruption, and the prevalence of nepotism. The republic's leaders are characterized as ,"intellectually and morally backward riff-raff," and an ,"unmanageable rabble or ignoramuses and half-wits." (Kavkaz Center, July 31, 2006) The difficulty of progressing through the clan-based power structure has persuaded many educated young Dagestanis to leave the republic, an issue the jammat also addressed in a response to government claims that the rebel Muslims lacked the intellectual abilities and administrative skills to form a government;

Among the Muslims there are many educated people and brothers who are honest and care about God's

272

religion. They include doctors, engineers, teachers, psychologists, managers and builders, economists and businessmen. By mobilizing the intellectual potential of Muslim youth, we shall be able to effectively run the economy and the state. The brothers who are today studying in higher educational establishments, and not just Islamic ones, will be involved in building an Islamic state. (Kavkaz Centre, July 31, 2006)

The Shari'a Jammat has also taken a strong position against the activities of the Spiritual Board of Muslims in Dagestan (SBMD), an Avar dominated directorate headed by Sa'id Effendi of Chirkey (Avars are the largest ethnic group in Dagestan). The SBMD is responsible for the operation of the republic's officially registered mosques, and vehemently opposes the existence of all unauthorized expressions of Islamic faith. The Board has been responsible for a number of seemingly provocative decisions, such as the May 2004 ban on the distribution of Russian translations of the Koran (despite Dagestan's historic ties to Arab Islam, few in the republic can now read the Koran in its original Arabic). (Caucasian Knot, May 24, 2004) The Shari'a Jammat has warned that those involved in replacing the Imams of Dagestani mosques on political grounds will face 'severe punishments'.

Much of the insurgent acitivity in Dagestan appears to be directed by Lak guerrilla leader Rappani Khalilov, a dangerous and experienced field commander, tightly integrated to the Chechen forces, and a former close ally of Shamil Basayev. Khalilov is Amir of the Dagestani Front of the ChRI Armed Forces and is alleged to control the activities of the Dagestani jammats, though this is difficult to confirm. Khalilov appears to spend much of his time in eastern Chechnya (a group of his men was spotted there recently – Interfax, September 7, 2006). A veteran of the Russian army, Khalilov was a brother-in-law of Arab mujahideen leader al-Khattab and participated in the 1999 attack on Dagestan. After a period in Chechnya Khalilov took the fight back to Dagestan in March 2001, launching a wave of attacks. (Gazeta.Ru, May

21, 2003) Khalilov was blamed for the May 9, 2002 bombing of a military parade in Kaspiisk that killed 45 and wounded 170.

Rasul Makasharipov was the first leader of the Shari'a Jammat and the former leader of *Dzhennet* (*Jenet* – Arabic: "paradise"), a militant group that evolved into the Shari'a Jammat. Like Khalilov, Makasharipov's relationship with Basayev went back to the 1999 Dagestan incursion, when Makasharipov served as Basayev's Avar interpreter. He surrendered to Dagestani authorities in 2000, but was released in an amnesty a year later. Within a year he was assembling his own organization, finding willing recruits from young Dagestanis who had suffered at the hands of the police. According to one of his followers, "Makasharipov spoke about the necessity to stop persecution and humiliation of Muslims in Dagestan. He said this could be done by killing policemen." (*Moscow Times*, March 15, 2005) Good to his word, Makasharipov launched a vicious three year campaign of retribution against police officials. Operating mainly in the Makhachkala region, Shari'a hit squads have killed dozens of high-ranking police officers and investigators while fighting to the death when cornered. Hand-grenades, bombs, mines and small arms are the weapons of the jammat's campaign against the police.

The FSB reported the death of Makasharipov in a tank attack on a home in Makhachkala, January 15, 2005, although the jammat commander surfaced four days later to refute these claims. Makasharipov was finally killed in a gunfight in Makhachkala on July 6, 2005. There are reports that after Makasharipov's death the Shari'a Jammat splintered into several smaller groups, though assassinations and bombings continued at the same pace. Gadzhi Melikov took over as Amir of the Makhachkala-based group that continues to use the name 'Shari'a Jammat' until his own death in a spectacular firefight in the Dagestani capital on August 26, 2006.

The military jammats of the Caucasus are often divided into Special Operations Group at an operational level. Among the subdivisions of the Shari'a Jammat are the Abuldzhabar Special Operations Group, the Asadulla Special Operations Group and the Mahdi Special Operations

Group. The Riyadus al-Salikhin Special Operations Group (Shamil Basayev's "suicide squad") has also been reported as carrying out assassinations and other attacks on police. (Kavkaz Centre, August 21, 2006)

A leaflet entitled "Address to the Police of Dagestan" and signed by "The Mujahideen of Dagestan" appeals directly to the often poorly paid policemen of the republic:

> We, the Mujahideen of Dagestan, are once again addressing the policemen of Dagestan, who still possess sound judgment. For a miserable sop from your oppressors, you are risking your own lives. We are calling you to quit this job and to not stand between us and the unlawful authorities of Dagestan, which are in power today...Your rulers want to retain their power over you at any cost. They are sacrificing your lives and putting you under our bullets... [The leaflet finishes with a distinctly Salafist invocation] Return to the religion of monotheism, pure from all admixtures of polytheism and all sorts of innovation. (Kavkaz Center, August 11, 2004)

Despite the ferocity of the battle between Islamists and police in Dagestan, it should not be interpreted as a sign of an incipient general uprising. The mujahideen of the Shari'a jammat and the guerrilla band of Rappani Khalilov have not yet managed to rouse more than a tiny portion of the republic's population to their cause.

Another active jammat in Dagestan is the Khasavyurt Jammat, formerly under Amir Islam Batsiyev until his capture in 2005. (Interfax, February 7, 2005) His successors, the Amirs Vagit Khasbulatov and Shamil Taimaskhanov, were killed October 2, 2005 in a wild shootout near Kizilyurt. (*Kommersant*, October 3, 2005) Chechen militants belonging to the Gudermes Jammat have also been operating in the Khasavyurt region, according to Dagestani police. (Itar-Tass, February 22, 2005)

Though there are many signs that Dagestan's military jammats often receive information from collaborators within the security structure, constant pressure from the police may have led the jammats to split up into autonomous three-man cells, an effective means of resisting police infiltration or interrogation. (*Nezavisimaya Gazeta*, May 17, 2005) Dagestani president Mukhu Aliyev has alleged in the past that "traitors" in the government were working closely with 'the terrorists'. (NTVru.com, May 13, 2002)

Operations of the Military Jammats: Ingushetia

The "Ingush Jammat" may have its origins in the battle for the entrance to Chechnya's Argun Gorge (known as the 'Wolf's Gates') in 2000. Here a group of Ingush volunteers mounted a stubborn defense against the overwhelming force presented by Russian arms. According to Chechen sources, only seven fighters survived, each of whom became a leading member of the Ingush Jammat. (*Chechenpress*, June 23, 2004)

The Ingush Jammat had a prominent role in the rebel raid on the Ingushetian city of Nazran in June 2004. According to pro-Russian Chechen president Alu Alkhanov (a former police general) Basayev's Ingush deputy, Magomet Yevloyev (AKA 'Magas'), led the Nazran operation. Yevloyev was raised in Grozny and was a sub-commander under Basayev in the second Russian/Chechen war before Basayev assigned him to use family and clan ties to begin raising armed units in Ingushetia. (Interfax, June 28, 2004) Ilyas Gorchkanov, the Amir of the Ingush Jammat, was killed in the October 2005 raid on Nalchik.

Aside from the participation of nearly 100 Ingush insurgents in the Chechen-led raid on Nazran, the Ingushetian rebellion is primarily one of ambushes and assassinations, largely against police and Interior Ministry units. Despite belonging to the same Vainakh ethnic group as the Chechens, rebellion in Ingushetia was slow to build, due to a prevailing atmosphere of loyalty to the Russian Federation. Political interference and growing severity on the part of state security forces in an apparent pre-emptive campaign against Islamist separatists eventually began to turn Ingushetia into one of the most active centers of resistance to federal rule. ChRI Foreign Minister Ahmad Zakayev described the situation in Ingushetia prior to the assault on Nazran:

> It can be stated with certainty that the war in Ingushetia began already at the moment when the Kremlin forced President [Ruslan] Aushev to retire and installed its humble protégé [Murat] Zyazikov in his place, a Chekist cadre. From that time on, Ingushetia became a zone of the bloody trade of the Russian death squads. Murders, hostage-taking, terror against the Chechen refugees and complete lawlessness became a daily reality in Ingushetia...Finally, the indignation of the people reached a critical mass and took the form of a direct, armed riot. (Chechenpress, June 22, 2004)

Zyazikov, who has been the target of several assassination attempts since taking over the presidency, offered his own take on the Nazran raid:

> This inhuman action was aimed not only against the Ingush people, but also against tens of thousands of Chechen refugees living in Ingushetia. Its objective was to destabilize the republic, expand the theater of military operations, and spread fear among the civilian population...The republic's residents can be confident that any barbarous actions will be rebuffed in a resolute manner.(Interfax, June 22, 2004)

In their July 24, 2004 declaration of a jihad to establish an Islamic state, the Military Council Majlis al-Shura of Ingushetia presented an optimistic assessment of Islamist aims in a deteriorating Russian Federation:

> Weakness in domestic and foreign policies, a collapsing economy, desertion in the army, failure of reforms, administrative anarchy, lack of security,

drug trafficking, AIDS, elimination of social morals compared to the strengthening of the Mujahideen and orderliness in the organization of combat operations speaks about changes and the future victory coming soon. False ideologies are collapsing; nations all around the world (including Russia) are focusing their eyes on Islam as the only source of true justice, law and safety from tyranny, abomination and ignorance. (Kavkaz Center, July 10, 2004)

Retribution by the police for the murder of their comrades in the Nazran raid began immediately. According to the Ingush Interior Ministry, 170 of the raiders have been eliminated. (Ingformburo, September 1, 2006) Ingush journalist Yakub Khadziyev has noted the pernicious influence of the North Caucasus custom of blood feud on the struggle between insurgents and police:

The members of illegal armed formations who are still at large are also not waiting for the security officers to come after them or for a bullet from someone settling a blood feud, but are waging a real struggle with the republic's law-enforcement bodies. No-one knows how many years this struggle will go on for. The relatives of the dead and the detained from both sides are virtually taking part in a bloody feud of retribution against one another. (Ingushetiya.ru, August 25, 2006)

In a similar fashion to some of the other North Caucasus republics, the conflict in Ingushetia has degenerated into a brutal contest between police and insurgents. The homes of policemen have been burned to the ground and security operatives of all types are constantly subject to assassination by gunmen. Ruthless interrogations of detainees too frequently provide the insurgency with new recruits after their release.

Also active in Ingushetia is the Khalif Jammat, whose leader Alikhan Merjoev, (responsible for the Ingush sector of the Caucasian Front) was

278

killed by FSB (Federal Security Service; former KGB) agents in Karabulak in October 2005.

Operations of the Military Jammats: Kabardino-Balkaria

The first major Islamic jammat in the KBR was the Kabardino-Balkar Jammat, led by Imam Musa Mukozhev and Anzor Astemirov. Mukozhev studied Islam in the Arab world and developed a large following in the KBR. The K-B Jammat avoided militancy, devoting itself to the study of Islam and promoting freedom of worship. After Basayev's disastrous terrorist operation in Beslan in September, 2004, the jammat came under pressure to dissolve from the police. Accused of participation in the December 2004 raid on the Federal Drug Control Service in Nalchik, Astemirov threw in his lot with Basayev. Both Mukozhev and Astemirov were close
associates of Ruslan Nakhushev, the head of the Islamic Studies Institue in Nalchik. Nakhusev disappeared after reporting to FSB headquarters in connection with the Nalchik raid. He was charged in absentia a week later with terrorist activity.

The KBR's Yarmuk Jammat was founded by Muslim Atayev (AKA Amir Se'ifulla), a Balkar veteran of the Pankisi Gorge training camps in Georgia. Atayev led a group of 20-30 KBR volunteers in the Ruslan Gelayev-led field force that crossed back into the North Caucasus republics in the autumn of 2002. After fighting in Ingushetia, Atayev led the KBR guerrillas back into their home republic, creating the 'Kabardino-Balkarian Islamic Jammat "Yarmuk" in August 2004 as a local independent militant operational group. The jammat's founding statement cited government closure of mosques and interference in Islamic practices as core reasons for their embrace of jihad. (Kavkaz Center, August 31, 2004)

The KBR police (who are mostly Kabardins) took the threat seriously. The head of the religious extremism unit (a frequent target of the fighters) suggested, "Yarmuk presents a real threat to the security of the people of the republic. Members of this jammat are experienced fighters who have undergone special technical and psychological preparation in order to carry out subversive activities." (CRS no.255, September 29, 2004) Basayev was nearly killed in the KBR town of Baksan on an organizing tour when his presence was detected in a house. The building was assaulted and a policeman killed before a wounded rebel blew himself up with a grenade, enabling Basayev and his companions to escape in the chaos. In December 2004, the jammat struck the Federal Drug Control Service in Nalchik, shooting several narcotics officers it described as 'drug dealers' and seizing a large quantity of arms. The jammat stated that the officers had been killed according to Sharia' law, which prescribes the death penalty for dealing in narcotics. (Kavkaz Center, December 14, 2004) Amir Atayev and several comrades were killed not long after in a spectacular January 2005 urban gun-battle after being cornered by police in a Nalchik apartment building.

Anzor Astemirov was the successor to Atayev as chief of the Yarmuk Jammat. Astemirov was the director of the Institue for the Study of Islam and a student of Dagestani Salafist preacher Ahmad-Kadi Akhtaev, who was poisoned in 1998.

The sudden appearance of hundreds of armed gunmen on the streets of the KBR capital of Nalchik on a quiet morning in October 2005 took the republic and the Kremlin by surprise. Throughout the city bands of insurgents attacked police stations, government offices and the local FSB headquarters. The raid was planned by Basayev and directed by Yarmuk leader Astemirov. Surprisingly the insurgents were Balkar and Kabardin in nearly equal numbers, demonstrating that political/religious repression combined with clan politics was capable of bringing armed rebels into the street.

Although the jammat developed in the Balkar villages of the mountains, their statements avoid any hint of Balkar nationalism in favor of appeal for ethnic unity amongst Muslims. A January 2005 statement mentions the 19th century colonization and subsequent expulsion of much of the population of, "Kabarda, Balkaria, Karachai, Cherkessia and Adygea", reminding these groups of a common experience and common grievance. (Kavkaz Center, January 21, 2005)

280

The Yarmuk Jammat remains active; a fierce gun battle between armed members of the jammat and federal security forces was reported in a forested area just outside of Nalchik following the discovery of a rebel base on August 12. (Interfax, ITAR-TASS, August 12, 2006) The jammat is now part of the Kabardino-Balkar sector of the Caucasus Front. (Chechenpress.org, October 17, 2005)

Operations of the Military Jammats: Karachaevo-Cherkessia

According to the reports of the security forces, the leading group of Salafist militants operating in the Karachaevo-Cherkessian Republic (KCR) is the Karachai Jammat, also known as 'Muslim Association No. 3'. The group is allegedly led by Achimez Gochiyayev, a self-described 'patsy' in the 1999 apartment building bombings in Moscow and a fugitive from federal authorities ever since. Gochiyayev was accused of working with Salafist Imam Ramzan Burlakov to create Islamic jammats in the KCR during 1996-99, a period Gochiyayev claims he spent in Moscow doing business. (*Moscow News*, June 23, 2002) Despite occasional messages from Gochiyayev in which he denies having anything to do with the North Caucasus insurgency, Russian security forces maintain that Gochiyayev is an elusive terrorist mastermind responsible for a series of bombings and terrorist attacks in Moscow as well as the Caucasus.

Dozens of jammat members in the northwest Caucasus were prosecuted behind closed doors in 2002 in relation to a series of car bombings and an alleged plot to overthrow the KCR and KBR governments in the summer of 2001. Although even security officials questioned the likelihood of a small number of lightly armed militants mounting a successful coup, the roundup was proclaimed a triumph for 'anti-Wahhabist' counter-terrorism efforts. The alleged ringleaders were Khyzyr Salpagarov and the brothers Aslan and Ruslan Bekkaev. (Isvestia.ru, May 12, 2002) Salpagarov was an Imam and Amir of the KCR's Ust-Djeguta Jammat. His eventual testimony described a wide plot engineered by Shamil Basayev, al-Khattab and Ruslan Gelayev. Salpagarov was alleged to have attended one of al-Khattab's training

281

camps in Chechnya in 1998 before returning to the KCR to initiate jihad operations. (*Moscow News*, June 23, 2002)

The Imam was convicted and sentenced to 19 years and confiscation of property for 'preparing an armed uprising'. The details of the conspiracy did not seem to concern the KCR president, General Vladimir Semenov (a Karachai):

> When I heard how the whole country is being told about an attempted coup d'état in Karachai-Cherkessia, I did not know whether to laugh or cry. What coup, what nursery of Wahhabism? We were among the first in Russia to ban religious and political extremism. I can't say that we have absolutely no Wahhabis, but the population has a single view on this, they reject it. (CRS no.152, October 24, 2002)

Islamic insurgency in the KCR is usually associated with the Turkic Karachai people. The Hizb al-Tawhid Jammat is almost exclusively Karachai. In 2002 its Amir, Dagir Bejiev, described the importance of Salafist preacher Ramzan Burlakov bringing Karachais to jihad; 'Today over a thousand of the best sons of the Karachai Nation are participating ias much as it is within their capabilities in the process of the revival of Islam, at their home as well as across the entire Caucasus. Ramzan was the initiator of this revival'. (Radio Kavkaz, July 17, 2002) Burlakov is reported to have led 150 Karachai mujahideen to Chechnya in the early days of the second Russian/Chechen war, where he was killed in combat.

The KCR Interior Minstry estimates there are at least 200 radical Islamists in the republic prepared to take arms against the government. Insurgents tend to travel freely between the KCR and the neighboring KBR.

Operations of the Military Jammats: North Ossetia

Despite the continuing violence in North Ossetia (much of which carries undertones of Ossetian-Ingush ethnic rivalry and disputes over land), the local FSB directorate has denied the very existence of an 'Ossetian Jammat'. (*Caucasus Times*, August 4, 2006) Responsibility for assassinations and attacks on police in North Ossetia is regularly attributed by Chechen websites to a local group known as the Kataib al-Khoul Jammat and its 'Sunzha' Special Operations Group.

A statement from the Kataib al-Khoul Jammat taking claim for the destruction of a Russian armoured personnel carrier (APC) described the type of local knowledge and access to inside information that enables the jammats to operate; "The Mujahideen of the Kataib al-Khoul Jamaat know all the dislocation areas, stationary and mobile posts as well as all the secrets used by Russians and traitors in the border area between Ossetia and Ingushetia and the routes of military convoys... We have flight charts of the aviation deployed in Ossetia, we know all the airfields of military airplanes and helicopters. Allah willing, already this year Ossetia will cease being a safe airspace for (the Russians)". (Kavkaz Centre, September 7, 2006)

Conclusion

Abdul-Halim Sadulayev observed that the North Caucasus jammats shared with the Chechens "one common goal - liberation from colonial slavery and achieving freedom and independence. Like the Chechen people, all the peoples around us have risen up and want freedom and independence." (*Chechnya Weekly*, July 6 2006)

Some jammats are now describing themselves as regional units of the Caucasus Front, using names such as 'Mujahideen of the Caucasian Front of the CRI Armed Forces', suggesting a greater integration with the Chechen command. Regardless of conditions in the North Caucasus republics, the jammats and associated militant groups enjoy the active support of only a minority of the population. Many Muslims have made clear that the militants do not speak in their name. Despite the Islamic basis of the Jammats, their activities and membership are still subject to ethnic, territorial and economic considerations. The Sufi *tariqats* still hold the allegiance of most North Caucasus Muslims, even in Dagestan.

In the last year the jammats have not displayed any ability to mount coordinated attacks that would test the response abilities of federal armed forces. This is no doubt due to difficulties in communication between armed groups justifiably wary of electronic communications. Basayev's great talent was his ability to travel throughout the North Caucasus, organizing the resistance, planning attacks, and providing a link to the ChRI military command. The warlord used sympathizers in the security services and exploited the corruption that prevailed in government structures to enable his safe passage through checkpoints, though he was constantly in danger of exposure.

Pro-Russian Chechen President Alu Alkhanov recently estimated that there are only 500 guerrillas still operating in the North Caucasus. (Interfax-AVN, August 3, 2006) Indeed, Ramzan Kadyrov has proclaimed that 2006 "is the last year of bandits in Chechnya". (Interfax, July 31, 2006) The Jammats typically claim that their ranks are increasing to the point where many would-be mujahideen have to be turned away. FSB chief Patrushev seemed to confirm this possibility when he stated that rebel attacks in Ingushetia and North Ossetia during the period January to July 2006 had increased by 50% over the same period last year.

Federal and Republic authorities have had great hopes for the amnesty announced for political militants this summer. Chechen Deputy Prime Minister Adam Demilkhanov recently claimed that only 50 mujahideen and 30 foreign-born 'mercenaries' were still active in the republic. (Interfax, August 29, 2006) According to FSB director Nikolai Patrushev, 224 insurgents have answered the call to surrender since the amnesty program was put into place on July 1, 2006. (Ekho Movsky, September 5, 2006) The amnesty campaign has been extended until the end of September 2006. Efforts are being made to tie the amnesty to job

284

creation programs, without which the ex-mujahideen might once more 'go to the forest'.

Besides creating new fronts for jammat activity in the Caucasus, the Chechen armed forces have signaled that they are prepared to operate beyond the traditional Russian boundaries of the conflict prescribed by Maskhadov and Basayev. On June 8 the State Defense Council of the Majlis al-Shura council announced that it had given operative powers to President Dokku Umarov to authorize Chechen operations abroad to eliminate those sentenced to death by the Shari'ah courts for participation in what the council refers to as the 'genocide of the Chechen people'. The task was assigned to the Chechen Special Services under the direction of the ChRI Department of Special Operations.

While the military jammats remain a virtually impenetrable and highly flexible source of instability in the North Caucasus, they by no means represent a legitimate challenge to the Russian armed forces. Attacks on police occur on a regular basis, but there has been no major raid or insurgent campaign since last year's events in Nalchik. Losses in police ranks are easily replaced in a region with dramatically high levels of unemployment, like the North Caucasus. The real question is whether a war against the police constitutes a revolution? The jammats have not been able to relieve pressure on the Chechen mujahideen , as was intended by the creation of new fronts, nor are they any closer to achieving their aim of an Islamic state in the North Caucasus, despite their embrace of pan-Caucasianism.

The Rise and Fall of Arab Fighters in Chechnya

Murad Batal Al-Shishani

Introduction

Arab volunteers who follow the Salafi-Jihadi philosophy have played a major role in the dynamics of the Russo-Chechen conflict since they started pouring into Chechnya in February 1995. They became a force to be reckoned with from 1997 to 2000 after the conclusion of the first war. Through allying with powerful forces in Chechnya, the Salafi-Jihadists tried to exert their ideology on the Chechen community and politics. This, in turn, prompted the second Russian invasion of Chechnya when Chechen hard-line nationalists invaded Dagestan to support three villages that proclaimed the establishment of an Islamic state in 1999.

Despite this important role of Salafi-Jihadism in Chechnya, the study of this phenomenon raises many methodical problems, the first of these being defining the movement itself. The media has used the term Wahhabis for the Arab fighters in Chechnya. This term is not accurate since these Arab fighters are Salafi Muslims who are also Jihadis seeking to achieve their political goals through violent means. Therefore they are different from traditional Salafis who refuse to oppose political leaders and use violent means. Wahhabis adhere to an ideology that dates back to the eighteenth century when Sheikh Mohammad Bin Abdul Wahhab promoted religious reforms in the Arab Peninsula and ended up allying with the al-Saud family, the ruling dynasty in Saudi Arabia today. The alliance with al-Saud has blurred the line between politics and religion.

It should be noted that in Russia the term Wahhabi is given to many Muslim political opponents. In Russia and the other former Soviet republics, religious figures acting outside "Official Islam" or outside the normal governmental channels are labeled Wahhabis.[1] The reason why the Russian government labeled Chechen fighters Wahhabis is rooted in Russian stereotypes towards Chechens. Russian authorities throughout the centuries, from the tsars to the Communists, and even the current regime, have arrogantly described Chechens as "barbarians," "thugs," "enemies of the people," "fanatics" and "gangsters." Wahhabism is just the latest and most potent pejorative label they have at their discretion to use for Chechens. When used in the context of Russian Orientalism, Wahhabism is synonymous to persecution, expansionism and primitiveness.[2]

Since the resumption of fighting between Chechens and Russian forces in 1999, the Russian government claims it is on a counter-terrorism campaign against groups of "gangsters" and "mercenaries," which makes it difficult to differentiate between the facts and propaganda concerning the phenomenon of foreign fighters in Chechnya. This is particularly true in the case of Arab fighters. The Russian government has labeled these Arab fighters as "terrorists" as well. The Russian government has used this Arab involvement to paint the Chechen resistance with the broad brush of terrorism. As such, it is necessary to discern between the roles of the Chechen resistance and the Arab fighters.

Secondly, there is a need to find actual facts in the face of Russian propaganda. Since 1989 Russian forces had repeatedly claimed that the real name of Khattab, the prominent leader and trainer of Chechen resistance fighters, was Habib Abdul Rahman, a Jordanian, until it was proven that he was actually the Saudi national Samer Swailim. At the same time, Russian intelligence sources described Khattab's predecessor, Abu al-Walid al-Ghamidi, as the current leader of Arab fighters in Chechnya, Abu al-Hafs al-Urdini as the Arab fighters' mufti and Abu Omar al-Saif and Abu Zaid al-Kuwaiti as money distributors,

---

[1] See: Moshe Gammer, "The Road Not Taken: Dagestan and Chechen Independence," *Central Asian Survey*, Vol. 24, NO.2 / June 2005, P.P 97 – 108.
[2] Turki Ali al-Rebi'o, *al-Khallfih al-tarikhyah llda'wa al-Wahabiya fi Manthor al-Istshraq al-Rossi*, (The Historical Background of Wahhabism from the Perspective of Russian Orientalism), *al-Ijtihad*, Issues 47-48, Summer-Fall 2000, Beirut, p.p. 237-247.

so as to be able to tie them with al-Qaeda. If this were true, there would be more than one group of Arab fighters operating in Chechnya. These same sources have repeatedly published many incorrect names of Arab fighters in Chechnya, which makes it that much more difficult for the researcher to find the correct facts on this phenomenon aside from Russian propaganda.

The purpose of this paper is to study and to understand this phenomenon and its effect on the Russo-Chechen conflict, Chechen society and the Chechen secessionist campaign. This paper will attempt to shine light on the identity and ideology of Arab fighters in Chechnya. It will also discuss the commotion these fighters have caused in the Northern Caucasus and in Chechnya. This paper will try to understand the facts that brought this phenomenon to Chechnya, as well as what helped eliminate it at a later stage. This paper will then conclude by highlighting different perspectives on the future of Chechnya.

Definition: Who are They and What do They Want?

Infrastructure:

Foreign fighters, Arabs in particular, who are between the ages of 20 and 40, are divided into three different categories:

1) *The professionals:* they have had previous war experience in places like Afghanistan, Bosnia and Tajikistan. These are the majority of Arab fighters in Chechnya.

2) *Young volunteers:* they are inexperienced youths who decided to volunteer in Chechnya after being recruited by Jihadi propaganda through means like cassettes and CD's. They have

not previously participated in any fighting and Chechnya is their first radical Jihadi experience.[3]

3) _Young Chechens:_ they are from Turkey or Chechnya, and are motivated by nationalism more than religion. These youths are mostly inexperienced, and even though some of them joined the Salafi-Jihadi movement in Chechnya, they are excluded from our analysis.[4]

In analyzing the ethnic background of Arab fighters in Chechnya, we notice that they are 59% Saudis, 14% Yemenis, 10% Egyptians, 6% Kuwaitis and 11% from other countries (see fig. 1).[5] It's worth noticing that this distribution of nationalities is in proportion with second generation Salafi-Jihadis, which is also dominated by Saudis.[6] Egyptians, who dominated the movement in the first generation, are no longer the chief ethnic group. Saudis are dominating the third generation as well because the war in Iraq has increased the number of mujahideen from Morocco, Sham countries (Syria, Jordan, Palestine, Lebanon and Iraq), and Western Muslims.[7]

---

[3] Brain Glyn Williams, "The 'Chechens Arabs': An Introduction to the Real al-Qaeda Terrorists from Chechnya," _Terrorism Monitor_, (Jamestown Foundation, Washington, DC) Vol. 2, Issue 1, 15 January, 2004.

[4] The Russian government surprisingly alleged many times that these two countries played a major role in "supporting terrorism" in Chechnya, some Western scholars, also, quoted that, See :Lorenzo Vidino, How Chechnya Became a Breeding ground for terror? _Middle East Quarterly_, Summer 2005. Also, see: Paul Murphy, The Wolves of Islam: Russia and the Faces of Chechen Terror, Potomac Books, 2006, p.144. For further details on Turkish volunteers in Chechnya, see: Brain Glyn Williams & Feyza Altindan, Turkish Volunteers in Chechnya, _Terrorism Monitor_, Vol. 3, Issue 7, 7 April 2005.

[5] These figures created by the author by analyzing 51 biographies of Arab volunteers in Chechnya.

[6] Brain Glyn Williams, the "Chechens Arabs"..., Op. Cit. also: A'del al-Tarefi, _Ajyal al-Mujahdeen fi al-Dakhel wal Kharj_ (The Mujahdeen's Generations Inside and Outside), _al-Watan Saudi Newspaper_, 21 January 2004.

[7] See: Murad Batal al-Shishani, Abu Mus'ab al-Suri and the Third Generation of Salafi-Jihadists ,_Terrorism Monitor_, Vol. 3, Issue 16, 11 August, 2005, also: The Salafi-Jihadist Movement in Iraq: Recruitment Methods and Arab Volunteers, _Terrorism Monitor_, Vol. 3, Issue 23, 2 December 2005.

The Arab fighters in Chechnya came to Grozny with different levels of experience in fighting abroad. They came from places such as Tajikistan, Bosnia (where in most cases Afghanistan was their last battlefield experience prior to Chechnya) and Arab countries. We notice that 51% participated in the Afghan war, 11.7% began their experience in Bosnia and Tajikistan, while 13.7% of them are participating in Jihad for the first time in Chechnya. The Jihadi background is unknown for 23.6% of the Arab fighters in Chechnya. The second generation of experienced Salafi-Jihadis in Chechnya formed their own ideological and strategic perspective of Chechnya that we will look at later in the study.

Leadership:

The leadership of Arab fighters is both military and ideological. On the military level, this paper will look at Khattab,[8] Abu al-Walid al-Ghamidi[9] and the current leader, Abu Hafs al-Urdini.[10] On the

---

[8] Khattab is *nom de guerre* of Same Saleh Swilim, born in 1969; in the north city of A'r'ar; went to Afghanistan in his early years when he was 17 years old. Khattab moved to Tajikistan to assist Islamic opposition in their struggle against the government in 1992 before he moved to Chechnya in 1995. Russian intelligence assassinated him with poisoned letter in April 2004.

[9] Abu Al-Walid (1970-2004) is the *nom de guerre* of "Abd Al-Aziz Bin Ali Bin Said Al Said Al-Ghamdi", originally from the al-Hall, in "Bljishri governorate" located in the southern of Saudi Arabia. He had been trained in his early jihadi years in *Maktb Al Khadamat* (bureau of Services), which created by Abdullah Azzam in early 1980s. abu al-Walid then joined Khattab in fighting in Bosnia, Tajikistan, and Chechnya. See: Murad Batal al-Shishani, The Killing of Abu al-Walid and the Russian Policy in Chechnya, *Central Asia-Caucasus Analyst*, Wednesday / May 05, 2004.

[10] There is no accurate information on Abu Hafs. The sole source of information is the material published by Russian newspapers, which mostly originate from Russian Intelligence. Abu Hafs was born in Jordan, is 40 years old and holds Saudi nationality; he participated in the fighting in Tajikistan alongside Khattab and Abu al-Walid in the early 1990s, and accompanied them to Chechnya between 1995-1996, where he served as military trainer in Khattab's camp near Sergen-Urt and married a Chechen woman. Abu Hafs assumed the role of al-Qaeda's representative in Georgia in 2002, where he went by the name "Amjad." Other resources said that his real name is "Yusuf Amerat". See: Abu Hafs and the Future of Arab Fighters in Chechnya, *Terrorism Monitor*, Volume 3 Issue 7 (April 07, 2005).

ideological level, there are Abu Omar al-Saif[11] and Abu Zaid al-Kuwaiti.[12]

The core military leadership gained its experience in the days of the holy war in Afghanistan against the Soviet Union. Khattab, al-Ghamidi and al-Urdini were all born in the late-1960s, came from conservative religious backgrounds and left their homes to go to war at an early age. The military leadership of Arab fighters in Chechnya had a clear hierarchical chain of command. They corresponded with each other over leadership issues through e-mail, as Abu al-Walid al-Ghamidi did after Khattab was killed. This also happened when al-Ghamidi was killed and Abu-Hafs took over. They sent e-mails to Jihadis and other outside supporters explaining how their predecessor died. Jihadis also promoted a charismatic image of their leaders as experienced, selfless,

---

[11] Mohammad Bin Abdullah al-Saif al-Jaber al-Buaynayn al-Tamimi is from the Bani Tamim tribes that are widespread in the Arabian Peninsula. His tribe is originally from Jubail North East Saud Arabia. He was born in Qassim and has been killed at the age of 37. Abu Omar al-Saif's participated in *Jihad* in Afghanistan in 1986, and joined Abdullah Azzam then returned to Saudi Arabia after the Russian army's withdrawal and the civil war broke in Afghanistan. Al-Saif completed his university education in the College of *Shari'a* at Imam Muhammad Bin Saud Islamic University. Abu Omar al-Saif went back to Chechnya in "1996 with his Saudi wife; two-year-old firstborn son; and two-month-old daughter, Asmaa, at the time." In Chechnya, he was responsible for the Islamic courts and became an ideologue for Arab fighters there. He has had married a Chechen woman. He had three children with his Saudi wife, the youngest a six-year-old boy he had in Chechnya when his wife was staying with him before she went back to Saudi Arabia in 1999 with her three children. See: Abu Omar al-Saif: His Life and After His Death, *Chechnya Weekly*, Volume 7, Issue 3 (January 19, 2006)

[12] Or Abu Omar Al-Kuwaiti, his real name Ahmad Nasser Eid Abdullah Al-Fajri Al-Azimi, who was an actor in children programs until he became religious and worked as an *Imam* in Safwan Bin Omayah Mosque in Kuwait, the capital. His services where terminated "for breaking the Ministry of Awaqaf's regulations regarding collecting donations from mosque goers and he was expelled from his work." Some resources indicate that following that incident he moved to Afghanistan in 1998, trained in the al-Farouk camp during the American raids on Afghanistan in 1998, and then went to Chechnya in October 1999. other resources said that he went away to Chechnya, without stopping in Afghanistan. In Chechnya, Al-Azimi got married and had two boys, Omar and Abdullah. The grandfather is demanding that they be returned to Kuwait, as they are Kuwaitis. See: Is the Salfi-Jihadist Way Still an Obstacle to Russia in Chechnya? *Central Asian-Caucasus Analyst*, Wednesday/May 18, 2005.

benevolent, loyal to the cause, and invincible. This propaganda helped to recruit fighters in Chechnya later on.

The ideologues generally have a different religious background. Abu Omar, for instance, holds a B.A degree in Islamic Shari'a from Imam Mohammad Bin Saud Islamic University. He was a disciple of the renowned Saudi Sheikh Muhammad Saleh al-Othimeen. Later, Abu Omar became the spiritual leader of the Arab fighters and the head of Islamic courts after the end of the first war in 1996.[13] Also, Abu Zaid al-Kuwaiti's experience as an imam made him an ideological leader for the Arab fighters in Chechnya. He even wrote biographies of the fighters in Chechnya. Al-Saif and al-Azmi were from the same ideological background. One of al-Azimi's brothers quoted al-Azimi as saying, "Arab fighters [in Chechnya] rely on one of Sheikh Muhammad Bin Othimeen's disciples for religious decrees (Fatwas). He explained to us how a Jihad should be conducted according to Islamic law (Shari'a), which stipulates that Jihad is directed against only Russian soldiers and not civilians."[14] Obviously that quote refers to Abu Omar al-Saif.

We notice that the military and ideological leadership tried to integrate into the Chechen populace by marrying Chechen women. Abu Omar al-Saif, al-Azimi and Abu Hafs are married to Chechen women and have had children. Abu Hafs has married twice. His second wife is the widow of the military commander Abu Jafar al-Yamani who was killed in Chechnya in 2001.[15]

The Ideology:

The Salafi-Jihadi ideology is a synthesis of the conservative Salafi ideas that are based on the literal interpretation of religious texts supporting the establishment of the historic first Islamic society and the Jihadi ideas that believe that violence is the main tool, if not the only tool, by which it will be possible to establish a Salafi Islamic state. This ideology

---

[13] For further details on al-Saif see author's essay: Portrait of a Chechen Mujahid Leader, *Terrorism Monitor*, Vol. 2, Issue 8, 23 April 2004.

[14] Al-Rai'a al-A'am, (Kuwait) 23 February 2005.

[15] Al-Rai'a al-A'am, (Kuwait) 23 February 2005

thrived in Afghanistan and became a recognized ideology mainly expressed today by al-Qaeda.

The perspective of the Arab fighters of Chechnya, as Salafi-Jihadis, did not deviate from this core belief. They called for the Islamization of political rhetoric and the eventual establishment of a Shari'a state and Imamate in Chechnya.[16] Later, they endeavored to make Chechnya a launching pad and a safe heaven for Jihadis who have ties to the Middle East. The intention to apply Shari'a law and to establish an Islamic state through force was very obvious when the Shari'a courts were set up after the first war in 1999. The implementation of Shari'a law is the biggest goal for Salafi-Jihadis. In response to a question at a meeting for Chechen fighters on June 18, 2003, Abu Omar al-Saif made the implementation of Shari'a law and the renewal of the Chechen constitution in accordance with Shari'a a priority.[17] Therefore, Arab fighters were more concerned with the establishment of an Islamic state than helping Chechnya escape Russian oppression.

This highlights the role of battle for these Arab fighters as the main method, if not the only method, of political transformation. Ahmad al-Azmi or Abu Omar/Abu Zaid al-Kuwaiti has promoted five critical points to support this thesis: 1) the mujahideen look weak when they engage in peaceful resistance; 2) the mujahideen are strong because NATO and the United States are joining forces to fight them; 3) avoiding the loss of good and virtuous mujahideen in battle is contradictory with true faith; 4) it is wrong to fear "methodological change" in the battlefield because the right methodology is already with the fighters in the battlefield;[18] lastly, al-Azmi also proclaims that 5) if monotheism isn't achieved with Jihad it becomes tradition and not

---

[16] Moshe Gammer, Between Mecca and Moscow: Islam and Political Islam in Chechnya and Daghestan, *Middle Eastern Studies*, Vol. 41, No.6, November 2005, P.837.

[17] www.qoqaz.com, Acssed October 2003.

[18] Ahmad Al-Azimi, "*Fadl Al-Jihad wal Mujahideen wal rad ala al-Muthabbitin*" (The benefit of *Jihad and Mujahideen* and a response to demoralizing attempts), www.qoqaz.com. Accessed in December 2003.

religion, which goes to the heart of the Salafi-Jihadi goal of establishing an Islamic state using violent means.[19]

Concerning al-Azmi's thoughts on Chechnya being a safe heaven and its geopolitical significance towards the Middle East, we can also look at other Salafi-Jihadi perspectives of Chechnya from two prominent Salafi-Jihadi ideologues. These would be Ayman al-Zawahiri,[20] the number two man in al-Qaeda, and Abu Mus'ab al-Suri, who is believed to be in a Pakistani prison.[21] These two have spoken about the importance of seeking a safe heaven and a launching pad for their continuous and widespread global battle and the importance of Eurasia as such a springboard into the Middle East, the heart of the Islamic world. Al-Zawahiri describes Eurasia as, "the real battlefield, a theatre of huge operations and Islam's base of operations."[22] Abu Mus'ab al-Suri corroborates al-Zawahiri's quote adding that Islamic cadres must stand side by side with Jihadi movements in Central Asia and later carry on the battle into the Middle East.[23]

According to al-Zawahiri, Eurasia is essential in helping to set up an "Islamic Jihadi Belt."[24] He envisions the Chechen and Afghan wars as the "buckle" and "tongue" of the belt that could be formed without involving too many due to the special circumstances of these regions. Al-Zawahiri thinks that the success of the Chechen experience, which will bring in thousands of Jihadis from all corners of the Islamic world, will form a Jihadi hub close to the oil-rich Caspian Sea, separated from Afghanistan by only the neutral state Turkmenistan. This proposed "Islamic Belt" will then connect southern Russia to Pakistan and the mujahideen in Kashmir in the east, as well as connecting them with Iran and Turkey, both sympathetic to Central Asian Muslims, in the

---

[19] Ibid.

[20] Ayman al-Zawahri, "Fursan Tahta Rayat An-Nabi" (Knights Under the Prophet's Banner), published as a series in the London-based Arabic newspaper *Al-Sharq Al-Awsat*, December, 2001.

[21] Abu-Mus'ab al-Sori, "Al-Muslimoun fi Wasat Asia wa Ma'rakat Al-Islam Almukbila" (Muslims in Central Asia and Islam's Next Battle), downloaded from the internet.

[22] Al-Zawahri, Op. Cit.

[23] Al-Sori, Op. Cit.

[24] Al-Zawahri, Op. Cit.

south and west. This will then work to dismantle pro-American Russia, which is why Americans will not intervene to stop Russian atrocities in Chechnya.[25]

Abu Mus'ab al-Suri's perspective is not much different than al-Zawahiri's even though he believes there are also signs of the Jihadi movement in Uzbekistan. He envisions the belt of control for the mujahideen stretching from Bangladesh through Northern India, Kashmir, Pakistan, Afghanistan and all the way to Central Asia with Muslims in Turkmenistan as well as the Caucasus and Ural Mountains forming a huge geographical corridor of safe havens for an active Jihadi movement.

The Environment From Which the Arab Fighters Emerged (1991-1997):

Arab fighters found a receptive environment in Chechnya at the beginning of its independence movement, even though Chechens are adherents of two Sufi orders, the al-Naqshabandiya and al-Qadiriya, which played a major role in preserving Chechen national identity in Russia. They were simply seeking to resurrect their national and religious identity at the beginning of the nineties, just like other minorities that had been oppressed for years in the Soviet Union. To that end, they started to break away from the oppressive Russian and Soviet yoke. This movement away from Russia was exacerbated by an accompanying structural transformation in Chechen society when Russian Slavs began to emigrate from the Muslim territories of the Soviet Union.[26] As the nationalist fervor increased, 99.7% of Chechens felt that their mother tongue should be allowed to be their official language. This was the highest percentage of native populace who felt this way in Russia, followed by 91.2% of Dagestanis who felt the same way.[27] Similarly, ethnic Russian emigration from Chechnya was the

---

[25] Ibid.

[26] Alexandre Bennigsen, "Islam in Retrospect", *Central Asian Survey*, Vol.8, No.1, 1989, p. 90.

[27] Henze, "The Demography of the Caucasus According to 1989 Soviet Census Data", *Central Asian Survey*, Vol.14, No.2, 1991, p. 156-169.

highest, with 11.8% of the populace emigrating outside the region, followed by 11.2% of the populace of Dagestan also emigrating. During Soviet times, Russian presence in non-Slavic areas was the highest in Chechnya and Dagestan.

Russian emigration from Chechnya emptied Chechen cities because ethnic Russians had largely dwelled in urban areas. Chechens from the countryside, who were strong adherents of Sufism, started to move into these newly vacant urban areas, causing an agricultural crisis in Chechnya. Chechnya's proportion of urban population became the highest in the northern Caucasus.[28] It was these citizens who formed the nucleus of the new social structure that generated many new questions that needed answering. This elite generally favored the creation of an Islamic realm rather than remain part of Russia, as it considered itself part of the Islamic center, which contributed to attracting Islamic ideas in governance, economics and society.[29] This is contrary to Sufi rural ideals that concentrate on more passive forms of resistance and identity preservation.[30]

This change of ideals was accompanied by high rates of unemployment and frustration that led to a protest movement. The Soviet Union ensured that Soviet Russia had the highest industrial production (70% of total industrial production in the Soviet Union) and depended on Muslim territories for raw materials for this industry. This cultivation of raw materials made Chechnya the poorest and most underdeveloped area in Russia and even among the poorest and most underdeveloped areas in the Soviet Union.

In the 1980s, 200,000 people were unemployed in Chechnya, despite the fact that the Soviet Union still insisted that unemployment was

---

[28] Larisa Ruban, "Growing Instability in the North Caucasus: A Major Threat to Russian Regional Security", www.ourworld.comuserve.com.

[29] Tamara Siertseva, "Cultural Transformation and Change of Identity in the Northern Caucasus", *Religion, State & Society*, Vol. 24, No. 2/3, 1996, p.p. 39-40.

[30] Anna Matveeva, "The Islamist Challenge in Post Soviet Eurasia", in Lena Johnson & Murad Esenov (eds.), Political Islam and Conflicts in Russia and Central Asia, The Swedish Institute of international Affairs, Conference Papers (24), 1999, p. 37.

nonexistent. To make matters worse, Chechens were treated as second-class citizens during the Soviet era and were generally not allowed to participate in higher education or assume high-ranking positions in the government.[31] This encouraged the Chechen elite to change their attitudes towards Arab-Islamic groups, consequently spreading Middle Eastern Islamic ideas among students who subsequently started pouring into the Middle East for education.

Scholarships where granted to Chechens by Islamic centers founded in the area, such as King Fahd University in Ingushetia as well as others. Reports indicated that 1,500 Dagestani students were studying in the Middle East. Also, pilgrimage-seekers increased during this time. This included 12,700 registered Dagestani pilgrims at the beginning of the nineties.[32] This paved the way for the existence of political Islamic movements in the North Caucasus similar to the "Political Islam" which existed in the Middle East, such as the al-Nahda Foundation that opposed Sufism because it is incapable of presenting a political method for these transformations. The leaders of these Islamic movements were Islam Khalimov, Movladi Udogov, Adam Deniev and others.[33]

Also, concurrent to this new Islamic trend was the establishment of al-Jammat al-Islamiya by a Chechen Islamist living in Jordan named Fathi Mohammad Habib (Abu Sayaf).[34] Abu Sayaf became the major

---

[31] Carlotta Gall & Thomas De Waal, Chechnya: Calamity in the Caucasus, New York University Press, 1998, p.p. 79-80.

[32] Gammer, Op. Cit, P.835., also: Vladimir Bobrovinkov, "Al-Azhar and Shari'a Courts in Twentieth Century Caucasus", Middle Eastern Studies, Vol. 37, No. 4, October 2001, p.p. 13-14.

[33] Mayrbek Vachagaev, "Evolution of the Chechen Jammat", Chechnya Weekly, Vol. 6, Issue 14, 6 April 2005. also author's book: Murad Batal al-Shishani, Islamic Movement in Chechnya and Russo-Chechen Conflict (1991-2000), al-Quds Center for Political Studies, Amman, 2001 (In Arabic), p.p. 19-22.

[34] born in Jordan in 1941, was schooled in Amman then traveled to Germany to study electronic engineering and continued his study in the United States before he left to Afghanistan to participate in "Jihad" in early 1980s. He did not participate in actual combat because of heart problems evidenced by surgery in Aman in 1958 - but assisted through Al-Ithad Al-Islami (Islamic Unification), a movement led by Afghani leader Abd Rab El-Raswl Sayaf. After the collapse of the Soviet Union he went to Chechnya and using his knowledge of Chechen language and customs began Da'awa (calling for Islam), and

motivator for Arab fighters to come to Chechnya. The environment was ripe for Chechnya to receive these Arab fighters due to the drive towards a more fundamentally Middle Eastern application of Islam in Chechnya. At the same time, Sufi movements became active in mobilizing the masses for an independent state in the face of increasing opposition to Russian rule and corruption in the republic.

It was during this time that the first Chechen president, General Dzhokhar Dudaev, emerged as the leader of the independence movement in 1993. Although he had been depending on elite Soviets and open economic policies since he came to power in Chechnya in 1991, Dudaev was redirecting the republic towards as more Islamist philosophy. He promised Ali Izzat Bigovich that he would supply Bosnia with money and weapons. He also visited Saudi Arabia, Jordan and Libya.[35] While visiting Iraq, Dudaev indicated his shift toward the Qadiris and began to ally with them. He also visited Sheikh Abdul Qadir Jilani's Mausoleum, who was the founder of the al-Qadiriya order.[36] Dudaev then appointed Zelimkhan Yandarbaev as vice president, who was closer to the Qadiris than political Islam at that time, and had started the independence movement.[37] It was during this time that the Naqshabandis began to oppose him.[38]

By turning to a more fundamentally Islamic circle and allying with Qadirya, Dudaev overcame his initial political crisis, which, in turn, led directly to Russian military intervention and the start of Russo-Chechen war in 1994, which would continue until 1997. Dudaev was killed in this first war, but the Chechen army won the war and forced Russia to withdraw after the arrival and participation of Arab fighters.

---

established a religious educational institute. He also helped in sending students to study in Arab countries. Fathi was dead by 21st of August 1997 in Chechnya.

[35] Gall & Waal, Op. Cit, p.p. 109-110.

[36] Al-I'raq Newspaper, 23 November 1993, p.1.

[37] Gall & Wall, Op. Cit. p.p. 32-33.

[38] Mayrbek Vachagaev, "The Role of the Sufism in Chechen Resistance", Chechnya Weekly, Vol. 6, Issue 16, 20 April 200, also, al-Shishani, Op. Cit. p.p. 150-156.

Arab Fighters Turn into a Major Force

Despite the fact that Arab fighters played a role in the war and participated in liberating Grozny, which earned them respect from the Chechens,[39] the first war from 1994 to 1996 was primarily characterized as a nationalist uprising, with Islam merely playing a subsidiary mobilizing role.[40] Indeed, Arab fighters only had a marginal role in the outcome of this war. It was only in the aftermath of the victory and by securing de facto independence that the notion of an Islamic state started to gain traction as a plausible outcome of the war.[41] This is when Arab fighters started playing a major role in Chechnya.

The war with Russia destroyed everyday institutions in all of Chechnya and ruined 80% of the Chechen economy, which resulted in high rates of unemployment and economic depression. This consequently paved the way for external influences in Chechen politics and gave rise to the Arab fighters' Salafi-Jihadi ideology, which attracted frustrated young men. These men were frustrated since the results of the brutal war with Russia only seemed to be unemployment and economic deprivation.

In the first war, the leader of the independence movement, Dzhokhar Dudaev distributed funds to field commanders to secure his command and control over the situation. However, with Dudaev's death by a Russian guided missile in 1996, Zailamkhan Yanderbaev assumed the presidency and announced that Chechnya would be an Islamic state with Shari'a courts, causing charity organizations and individuals from the Middle East, particularly from the Gulf states, who favored Salafi-Jihadis to become active in Chechnya.

---

[39] Willhelmseh Julie, "When Separatists Became Islamists: The Case of Chechnya", Farsvrest Farsknings Institute (FFI/RAPORT), Norwegian Defense Research Establishment, 2 February, 2004.

[40] Lorenzo Vidino, "The Arab Foreign Fighters in Chechnya and the Sacralization of the Chechen Conflict", al-Nakhlah, the Fletcher School Online Journal for Issues Related to Southwest and Islamic Civilization, Spring, 2006, p.2.

[41] Paul Tumelty, the Rise and Fall of Foreign Fighters in Chechnya, Terrorism Monitor, Vol. 4, Issue 2, 26 January, 2006.

Even though some of these organizations began operations very early on in Chechnya, their activities peaked with the arrival of Arab fighters and their leader Khattab.[42] These organizations included the al-Haramain Institution, the International Forum for Muslim Youth relief organization and BIF, which opened a factory for Islamic women's clothing to support Chechen women.[43] These organizations and the Arab fighters that streamed into Chechnya at this time played big role in Chechnya in the face of Russia's reneging of its promises and agreements. This was particularly the case with Russia's promises to help rebuild Chechnya in the Khasiv-Yurt Agreement of 1996, which former Russian president Boris Yeltsin declared had put an end to the ongoing 400-year conflict.[44] These infringements were perceived as Russian tactics that sought to undermine the first democratically elected secular nationalist President of Chechnya, Aslan Maskhadov, who was opposed to the radical Islamists and nationalists.[45]

These charity organizations, which were shutdown by Russia in 1999, supported the creation of a Chechnya based on Islamic law and helped to fund the training camps setup by Khattab. They aimed to disseminate the Salafi-Jihadi ideology, or what they called "correct"

---

[42] Julie, Op. Cit.

[43] *USA* vs. BENEVOLENCE INTERNATIONAL FOUNDATION, INC., and ENAAM M. ARNAOUT , Case No. 02 CR 414, UNITED STATES DISTRICT COURT FOR THE NORTHERN DISTRICT OF ILLINOIS EASTERN DIVISION.

[44] Julie, Op. Cit., also: Svante E. Cornell, "The War against Terrorism and the Conflict in Chechnya: A Case for Distinction" , in Fletcher Forum of World Affairs , vol. 27 no. 2, Fall 2003, p. 171. Irina Mukhina found that "kidnap business" in Chechnya making income higher than Russian [supposedly] re-construction Chechnya fund. Mukhina concludes in her study that Chechens are not fighting for independence but it's for terrorism; that she found that attacks conducted by Chechens out side Chechnya in peace time higher than in war time. Mukhina problematically did not study the targets of that attacks; also she did not compeer the attacks with the entire operations of Chechen resistance to measure the differences n Chechnya between terrorists and independents especially Chechnya experienced different fighting groups in the years of wars, see: Irina Mukhina, Islamic Terrorism and Question of National Liberation: or Problems of Contemporary Chechen Terrorism, Studies in Conflict & Terrorism, 28, 2005.

[45] Miriam Lanskoy, "Dagestan and Chechnya: The Wahhabi challenge to the State", *SAIS Review*, 22, 2002:2, summer-fall, pp. 167-192.

Islam, as opposed to what they called the historically "infidelized" sect, Sufi Islam, which was the traditional Muslim sect of Chechnya.

In a book written by Fahd al-E'ssyemi, a whole chapter was devoted to a report by a visiting delegation from the World Assembly of Muslim Youths to Chechnya. The report announced the opening of an office for the forum in Chechnya under the name "Youth Committee for the Islamic Republics and Russia," so that they could disseminate the true Islamic aqeeda (faith) and teach the youth the proper religion.[46] When talking about Chechnya, the report concentrates on a religious mission as well as missionaries' requirements. It states that each missionary would need about $100 per month in Chechnya owing to the fact that Chechens are ignorant Sufis.[47] The funds offered by this organization attracted Chechen youth to the Salafi-Jihadi ideology as they could drastically ameliorate their horrible economic condition. Arab fighters, with their Chechen supporters, began to try to implement their ideology through religious courts and training camps and to attract more Arab fighters from the Middle East so as to turn Chechnya into a Jihadi center as Ayman al-Zawahiri had hoped.

Religious Courts:

In accordance with Salafi-Jihadi ideology and the Arab fighters' perspective of religious rule, in 1996 Chechen Vice President Zailamkhan Yanderbaev declared Chechnya to be an Islamic state, which led to the establishment of a religious court system. Thirty religious courts were set up, five of which were located in Grozny.[48] These courts handled cases of marriage, divorce, consumption of alcohol and the implementation of an Islamic code of punishment. The courts' verdicts were final with no right to appeal.[49] As much as these courts were a substitute for Russian laws and a symbol of

---

[46] Fahd al-E'ssyemi, Ma'sat Ikhwanan fi al-Shishani, (Our Brothers Tragedy in Chechnya), the World Assembly Of Muslim Youths, Riyadh, without date, p. 148.
[47] Ibid, p. 150.
[48] Nida'ul Islam Magazine, December 1997.
[49] Vladimir Borovinkov, "Mythologizing Shari'a Courts in Post-Soviet North Caucasus", *ISIM Newsletter*, 5/2000, p.25.

independence,[50] they were also a political weapon used by Islamists to affect internal matters in Chechnya. They also represented a further move towards the Arab-Islamic circle. The code of punishment was taken from the 1983 Sudanese criminal code. Ironically, that code of law was created according to the Maliki doctrine of Islam, even though all Chechens were adherents of the al-Shafiai doctrine.[51] The head of the religious courts was the Saudi Abu Omar al-Saif. He relied on Jordanian Chechens to employ Arabic speaking judges who were not qualified for the job.[52]

Abu Omar al-Saif clearly denoted his inclination towards the Arab world in these remarks:

> When religious courts were set up in Chechnya, we referred difficult cases to Sheikh Muhammad Saleh al-Othimeen. We found him to be very responsive, interactive and serious in aiding us. He consistently answered our questions without complaint. He even gave us his private phone number so that we could call him at any time.[53]

Chechnya: The Pivotal Jihadi Launching Pad

In between the two wars, an alliance was established between the Arab fighters and Chechen field commander Shamil Basayev who made Khattab his brother, which has a deep meaning in Chechen tribal society. This alliance was supported financially by Khattab and was protected by Basayev. However, the alliance was provisional since both parties had different ideas concerning the ultimate unification of the northern Caucasus. It was the formation of this alliance that

---

[50] See: Chechnya's Chop-Chop Justice, Economist, 1997.
[51] Borovinkov, al-Azhar and Shri'a..., Op. Cit. p. 20.
[52] See: Venora Bennett, Crying Wolf: the Return of War to Chechnya, Picador, London, 1998, p. 515.
[53] Mohammad Bin Abdullah Al-Seif, "Al-Jihad Al-Shishani Fi Hayat Al-Sheikh Ibn Otheimeen, (the Chechen Jihad in Ibn Otheimeen's life), Al-Bayan, London, Issue 160, Vol. 15, March 2001, p.p.65-66.

encouraged the Salafi-Jihadi forces in Chechnya to invade neighboring Dagestan in September 1999 so they could support a few small Dagestani villages that had declared the implementation of Shari'a law. That invasion gave Russia the pretext it needed to start what it called a "war on terrorism," which was characterized as a religious war, as opposed to the first war, which had been framed in a nationalist context.

Julie Willhelmsch presented an important research paper on the alliance between Islamists and nationalists in Chechnya. She studied why certain Chechen leaders, including Shamil Basayev, Zailamkhan Yanderbaev, Movladi Udogov, Salman Raduev, Arbi and Mosvar Barayev adopted such a radical Islamist position. She found that the main reason for their position was so they could solicit funds from Khattab and confront Aslan Maskhadov with this ideology so that they could turn Chechnya towards the Middle Eastern or Arab circle.[54]

Svante Cornell explains the adoption of radical Islamic philosophy in Chechnya by ascribing it to Chechens' disappointment that western nations failed to support their own concept of self-determination and democracy in Chechnya compared to how they supported Bosnia's plight in the Balkans.[55] Furthermore, in the period between the two wars, the Salafi-Jihadis' perspective of the area shifted to a position that supported the unification of the North Caucasus. To that end, they attracted unemployed Chechens to their training camps, which they set up in Chechnya, particularly in Urs-Martan. There are some estimates that between 1,600 and 2,000 warriors from Dagestan, as well as other regions in the North Caucasus, and even from Central Asia trained in these camps. There were many other ethnic groups there as well.[56] At the same time, the Salafi-Jihadis started a recruitment campaign in the broader Islamic world. DVDs entitled "Russian Hell" were to be found everywhere in these regions.

---

[54] Julie, Op. Cit.
[55] Cornell, Op. Cit, p. 174.
[56] Julie, Op. Cit.

A'del al-Tarifi, a Saudi writer, described the situation in Chechnya prior to the eruption of the second war in 1999 as follows: "Georgia, the mujahideen outlet, witnessed a huge wave of Saudi and Arab fighters heading to participate in the war in Chechnya thanks to the intense propaganda campaign by Khattab and other Jihadi sites on the internet."[57] Sure enough, the number of Arab fighters in Chechnya increased substantially in that period. Around 45% of the Arab fighters being discussed in this paper entered Chechnya in the period between the two wars or slightly before the start of the second war. Comparatively, 29.5% entered during the first war. The timeframe when the other 25.5% of these Arab fighters entered Chechnya is unknown (see fig.2). This demonstrates the increased importance Salafi-Jihadism found in Chechnya during this time. These fighters and their leaders even went so far as to consider Chechnya the pivotal launching pad of Jihad. They therefore vigorously recruited fighters and secured funds for the Chechen war in Islamic countries with the help of the Jihadi propaganda videotapes.

When discussing fundraisers in Chechnya, we can look to the biography of Saudi Salafi-Jihadist Yousef al-Ayyri, who was killed by Saudi forces in 2003:

> Sheikh Yousef sponsored fundraisers for the Chechen mujahideen. He collected large amounts of money for them. He had many disappointing encounters with religious scholars. I remember one such encounter with Sheikh Salman al-Odah when Khattab said that in Dagestan, 'with one million dollars I can fight and resist the Russians until winter's end.' Sheikh Yousif asked one of the wealthier men there, who had agreed to give him 8 million riyals, whether Sheikh Salman intended to give him a receipt or call on him. But Sheikh Salman

---

[57] al-Tarifi, Op. Cit.

refused because he did not believe in the Chechen cause.[58]

The journal Al-Battar, the second largest Saudi Salafi-Jihadist publication, reported that Khalid al-Sbiet, an active Saudi Jihadist, who was killed by Saudi forces,[59] and who had participated in the Russo-Chechen war was also active in fundraising. Also, the Yemeni activist Mahmoud Hamdi al-Ahdal, the number two man in the Salafi-Jihadi movement in Yemen, who is currently being tried for many crimes in Yemen, established the Caucasian Charity Organization in Yemen. In his trial, the Yemeni attorney general stated that al-Ahdal had collected money for the mujahideen in Chechnya and gave the funds to Khattab's representative without specifying the amount or place where the money was collected.[60]

The website "Azzam Publication" produced a FAQ about Chechnya for those who wanted to volunteer in the war. Even though the site indicated that Chechnya did not need volunteers since the roads were closed until March or April (2000 or 2001), it instructed potential volunteers to go to Afghanistan to train, or to contact locals who previously participated in Jihad. This demonstrates the importance of representatives like al-Ayyri, al-Ahdal and others in recruiting and fundraising operations.

Videotapes of the Chechen war spread all over the Islamic world and served as one of the major methods of recruitment. Two Arab fighters who participated in the war, Ayyub al-Toyjri and Abdulrahman al-Salib (Abu Yaser al-Nashmi), attributed their desire to participate in it to these videotapes.

When looking at two of these videotapes entitled "intssarat al-a'eed" (Aeed Victories) and "Russian Hell 3," Mohammad Abdulaziz pointed to the two purposes of the tapes: propaganda and recruitment. These

---

[58] Al-Ayyri's biography, *Sawt al-Jihad*, Sha'ban 1424, Issue 1, p. 19.
[59] Yahia al-Ghamdi, Allah Aknbar: Gholbat al-Roos, (Allah is Great: Russia Defeated), *Al Battar Journal*, Rajb, Issue 18, p. 20.
[60] *Al-Sharq al-Awsat*, 14 March 2006.

tapes refute Russian claims concerning the Chechen war. According to Abdulaziz's analysis, there is proselytizing on the videotapes that promotes the recruitment of mujahideen by portraying Chechnya as a place where men can give up their luxurious lives for the sake of religious unity in this foreign land. The tapes then depict some confrontations with the Russian war machine, and demonstrate the destruction of a Russian armored vehicle as a reiteration of the power of Islamic faith over the Russian military. Furthermore, the tapes show the mujahideen, outside the war zone, comfortably chanting and praying, and generally depicting the first Islamic society without corruption. In the end, these videotapes depict smiling martyred fighters amidst the background sounds of enthusiastic chanting. They call this part "the eternal journey."[61] This is the enormous effort that goes into making Jihad desirable for Muslims.

Thus, the second Russo-Chechen war was provoked, in part, by the burgeoning alliance between Arab fighters and radical Chechens. This was then exploited by the Russian government, which justified the savage war in Chechnya by calling it a war on terrorism despite the fact that Russian policy had isolated the legitimate and moderate Chechen president who had ignored the increasing activities of Islamic groups in the area.

The second Russian war in Chechnya in 1999 changed Russian policy in the region. Ex-intelligence officer Vladimir Putin came to power promising to restore Russia's superpower status and promising to fight Islamic fundamentalism in Russia. The Chechen independence movement became synonymous with international terrorism, particularly after September 11. Russia was able to affect world opinion through a policy of diverting reporters covering the war away from the human rights violations being committed in Chechnya. A pro-Russian government was installed in Chechnya. This government was headed by the former Mufti of Chechnya who had fought against the Russians

---

[61] Muhmmad Abdul Aziz, al-Jihad Kfi'el Mr'i: al-A'qeeda w al-Harb fi Aflam al-Shishan, (Jihad as Watching Act: Faith and War in Chechnya Films), *Islam Online*, 2 August 2004.

in the first war and switched sides, partly due to the increasing influence of Salafi-Jihadis in Chechnya.

As mentioned above, whereas the first war was considered to be a nationalist struggle, the second war was characterized and exploited as a religious war by Russian propaganda. The role of Arab fighters was manifested in female suicide operations. Chechen females, covered in black dresses, participated in hostage crises in Nord-ost, in Dabrovka-Moscow in 2002 and in the Beslan School incident in September 2004. In the face of all contrary evidence, Moscow tried, through the pro-Russian Chechen government, to show that conditions were normalizing in Chechnya by endorsing a new constitution in the republic. This was despite the numerous reports of human rights violations leaking from Chechnya. Furthermore, contrary to Russia's desires, Ramzan Kadyrov, the son of an assassinated Chechen leader, became the actual strongman of the republic while Alu Alkhanov remained the nominal president. Nonetheless, the killing of Chechen resistance figures by Russian forces and the fall of the Arab fighters were inevitable.

The Fall of the Arab Fighters (2001-2006)

The ascent of the Arab fighters in Chechnya carried the seeds of their demise as well. The attempts to Islamize the Chechen state prior to the second war deepened the divisions in Chechen society. In addition to that, the brutal Russian tactics in the second war and the attacks of September 11, 2001 played a role in accelerating the decline of this phenomenon in Chechnya. The demise of the Arab fighters' role in Chechnya was ultimately the result of the following causes: the division in society; cessation of funding for Islamic groups; Russia's liquidation of Chechen military leaders; and the differences in the agendas of the Arab fighters and of the leaders of the independence movement.

1.   The Division in Society

In accordance with the call for purifying society, the Salafi-Jihadist movement in Chechnya strove to impose its ideology through an

307

Islamic court system. This court system imposed an Islamic dress code for women, prohibited alcohol and enforced Islamic punishments. Sufis saw this as an attempt to impose strict and foreign patterns of Islam. This was especially true as the Salafis tried to impose an Islamic dress code in a society that had a strong tradition of a looser style of dress. [62] This made the Salafi-Jihadist movement seem alien compared to the socially tolerant Sufi Islam that Chechens practiced. As a result, the great esteem Arabs used to enjoy in Chechnya declined. [63] They used to enjoy such high regard that some folk tales maintained that Chechens were of Arab origin.

As the opposition between Sufis and Salafi-Jihadists increased, the situation came to a head when it reached armed conflict in 1998. Salafis have always harbored a deep animosity for Sufis. For the first time in decades Sufis, especially followers of the Qadiri way, began to support Russia. The most significant shift came when the former mufti, Ahmad Kadyrov switched to the Russian side and headed the pro-Russian government that Moscow installed in Grozny after the beginning of the war of 1999.

The success of the allies who participate in a war depends mainly on the acceptance of the locals who shelter those people, particularly in tribal communities. But the Salafi-Jihadist ideology was not conducive to the traditions of Chechnya; and consequently the role of Arab fighters in Chechnya receded.

2. Cutting off Funding

A major problem faced by Arab fighters in Chechnya was the lack of funding as a result of decreased funding and support, especially from the Gulf countries. Since the attacks of September 11, 2001 and the increase in terrorist attacks in Gulf countries, particularly Saudi Arabia, the international community had declared war on the funding channels

---

[62] Vakhit Akaev, Religious–Political Conflict in the Chechen Republic of Ichkeria, in Jonson & Esenov (eds.), Op. Cit, p. 48, also: Muried Atkin, the Rhetoric of Islam Phobia, *Central Asia and the Caucasus Journal of Social and Political Studies*, 2000, www.ca-c.org
[63] Bennett, Op. Cit, p. 448.

of radical Islamic groups. The lack of funds posed a threat to the activities of Arab fighters in Chechnya and Salafi-Jihadist ideology for two major reasons: 1) It threatened the movement's ability to continue fighting, and 2) those funds were the legitimizing factor behind the movement's presence in Chechnya. Consequently, without these funds in hand, the Arab fighters' alliance with Chechen fighters was severely damaged.

A letter by Abu Omar al-Saif, the movement's ideologue in Chechnya, entitled *"Risalah Lel Olama'a wa Tollab al-Ilm, wa at-Tojar, Wa Kafat al-Moslimeen"*[64] (A Letter to Scholars, Students, Merchants and all Muslims) gives evidence to the crisis that the lack of funding provoked, and goes on to describe Russia's alliance with Hindus and apostates against Islam. In the letter, Omar al-Saif says that financial aid has decreased to an unprecedented level since the onset of the [second] war and attributes the problem to the pressure exerted by "crusaders." In 2003, al-Saif put a recording on qoqaz.com instructing the Islamists committing acts of violence in Saudi Arabia to direct their fight against Americans and not the Saudi government. [65] In this context, Abu Zaid al-Kuwaiti (Ahmad al-Azimi) published another letter a month later on qoqaz.com entitled *"Fadl al-Jihad wal Mujahideen wal rad ala al-Muthabbitin"* (The Benefit of Jihad and Mujahideen and a Response to Attempts to Demoralize Us). [66] In this letter he repeated much of what al-Saif said, particularly with regard to instructing Islamists to direct attacks at U.S. forces in Iraq instead of local governments in the Gulf.

On October 27, 2003, Abu al-Walid al-Ghamidi, the commander of Arab fighters in Chechnya, published a letter on qoqaz.com to all Muslims wishing them well during the holy month of Ramadan and

---

[64] Abu Omar Al-Saif, "Risalah Lel Olama'a wa Tollab al-Ilm, wa at-Tojar, Wa Kafat al-Moslimeen" (A Letter to Scholars, Students, Merchants and all Muslims), www.qoqaz.com.

[65] The recording available on this link http://www.qoqaz.com/ab.rm, "Ra'i Al-Sheikh Abu-Omar Lel Mujahideen Fi As-Sau'diyah" (Sheikh Abu-Omar's Opinion to the Mujahideen in Saudi).

[66] Ahmad Al-Azimi, "Fadl Al-Jihad wal Mujahideen wal rad ala al-Muthabbitin" (The Benefit of Jihad and Mujahideen and a Response to Demoralizing Attempts), www.qoqaz.com. Accessed in December 2003.

calling on them to donate funds to mujahideen and refugees, thereby defying the policy of diverting funds. [67] With the increase in acts of violence, Gulf governments imposed restrictions on the activities of donors. The largest funding channels for Arab fighters in Chechnya were in Gulf countries. Therefore, those letters and their calls for avoiding clashes with local authorities were indicative of the crisis Arab fighters were facing in Chechnya and the threat that the lack of funds posed to the legitimacy of their presence there, which eventually led to their fall. It should be noted here that the cessation of funds harmed some humanitarian organizations that did not support the fighters, but strived to alleviate the suffering in Chechnya.

3. Assassinations and Closed Borders

Since the onset of the second Russian war in Chechnya, Russia has closed all Chechnya's borders. Therefore Arab fighters who wanted to go to Chechnya were stopped on the Georgian border. A review of the biographies of a number of Salafi-Jihadists in different regions indicates that they were not able to enter Chechnya, thus depriving Arab fighters from the chance to increase their numbers in Chechnya. In spite of Russia's tightened grip on the borders of Chechnya, Russia tried to give the impression that the number of Arab and other foreign fighters was the largest component of the Chechen resistance. In the aftermath of the attacks of September 11, 2001, this prompted the Russian government to paint the moderate forces in Chechnya with the heavy brush of terrorism, which increased their isolation.

Russia also adopted a policy of assassination in dealing with the leaders of the Chechen independence movement. When the Russian government handed over the Chechen operations to the Federal Security Service, the Kremlin's top official in Chechnya at the time, Sergei Yastrzhembsky, declared that, "stability in Chechnya will not be restored unless the leadership of the Chechen army is liquidated," and

---

[67] Qosat Estshhad Al Qaed Khattab, [The Story of Leader Khattab's Murder], October 27, 2003, www.qoqaz.com.

310

that, "special security forces, Ministry of Interior forces and the Russian army need to liquidate Chechen leaders."[68]

These assassinations began with Arbi Barayev. Salman Raduyev then died in prison under mysterious circumstances. Zelimkhan Yandarbiyev was assassinated at the hands of the Russian intelligence in the Qatari capital of Doha. This has obviously culminated in the recent assassination of Shamil Basayev. Even moderates such as Aslan Maskhadov and Adbul-Halim Saidullayev were not immune to that policy.

The assassinations of Salafi-Jihadist leaders began with Khattab, who was killed by a poisoned letter, followed by Abu al-Walid al-Ghamidi, Abu Zaid al-Kuwaiti and Abu Omar al-Saif. They were the targets of secret operations. Assassinating these leaders created a huge gap in the chain of command. Prior to Abu al-Walid al-Ghamidi, who succeeded Khattab, there were Abu Bakr Aqida, Ashraf al-Shantili (an Egyptian), Hakim al-Madani, Yaqoub "Jam'an" al-Ghamidi and then Abu Jaffar al-Yamani. These men were all killed in combat, and their deaths all created a problem in command.

While assassinations are generally considered an unacceptable method of resolving political conflicts, Russia succeeded in weakening the Salafi-Jihadist movement by eliminating the leadership that was a major element in the structure of the Arab fighters. They played an instrumental role and had a vast amount of combat experience. Meanwhile, this policy had a negative impact on the Chechen leaders. Since the assassination of Dzhokhar Dudayev in 1996, Chechen resistance has increased in intensity with every subsequent assassination. That resistance, both moderate and radical, received two heavy blows with the assassinations of Maskhadov and Basayev respectively.

---

[68] AFP, January, 2001.

4. Differences in the Agenda of Arab Fighters and the Independence Movement

One of the major factors in the decline of the Arab fighters in Chechnya and the Salafi-Jihadist movement is that their agenda was different from the Chechen independence movement, which merely focused on getting rid of Russian rule. The Salafi-Jihadist agenda had a wider scope, including the United States, Israel, India and others.[69] In addition, the Chechen independence movement called for a secular state, while Salafi-Jihadists called for a religious state.

The independent Chechen Ministry of Affairs, headed at the time by Ilyas Ahmadov, had written about these disparities, especially after the attacks of September 11 and Russia's attempts to label its war in Chechnya as a war against terrorism. According the Ministry of Affairs, there are four major differences between the Chechens' struggle for independence and international terrorism: 1) The struggle in Chechnya has deep historical roots, unlike modern international terrorism's targeting the West; 2) Chechens are fighting for an independent state while international terrorism is a non-state actor; 3) Chechen resistance is based on a national struggle while international terrorism is not; and 4) Chechen resistance is involved in a defensive war unlike terrorism. [70]

Conclusion

We can thus conclude that there are substantive reasons for the weakening presence of Arab fighters in Chechnya. Their presence is no longer legitimate given the lack of logistic support and the fact that they are no longer welcome by the Chechens. Most importantly, the difference between the agenda of the Arab fighters and that of the Chechen independence movement is the final "nail in the coffin" for the Arab fighters' role in Chechnya.

---

[69] See, Brain Glyn Williams, the "Chechens Arabs"…, Op. Cit.

[70] Peace Plan Prepared by the Chechen Foreign Affairs Minister, Ilyas Akhmadov: "The Russian-Chechen Tragedy: The Way to Peace and Democracy: Conditional Independence Under an International Administration", February 2003, p.p.20-21.

As a result, Jihadists started looking for a new battleground. Iraq naturally emerged as the most appropriate place. The Arab fighters' literature in Chechnya discussed Iraq and advised Jihadists on how to manage their fight against the American occupation by promoting guerilla warfare and instructed readers on political and military command. This literature thus created a sectarian approach for solving the Iraqi crisis, as indicated by Abu Omar al-Saif's writings. [71] There are two main indicators that Arab fighters are searching for a new front: 1) the names of some of those returning from Chechnya are popping up in other theatres of the Jihadi struggle, such as Tora Bora or Saudi Arabia; [72] 2) studies indicate that the funds that previously went to Chechnya are now going to Iraq. [73]

In the same context, some Russian sources indicate that there are Chechen fighters in Iraq. However, this argument has been refuted, [74] since it is not logical that Chechen nationals would leave their own war-torn country to fight another war in Iraq alongside people with whom they have such fundamental differences in opinion. [75]

It becomes evident that the independence movement has been labeled as terrorism since the attacks of September 11, 2001 because of the presence of Arab fighters in Chechnya. While they have had a certain influence in the present phase of Chechnya's struggle for independence, their role was limited in the Chechen independence movement as well as the overall Russo-Chechen conflict. However, Russia was keen on magnifying that role in order to gain international support, especially from the West, which was willing to accept any war against radical Islam. Therefore, Russia isolated the moderate national movement represented by President Aslan Maskhadov, who was ready to negotiate and who, in the ceasefire he declared at the beginning of February 2005 for all Chechen resistance factions, proved the extent of his influence

---

[71] Al-Shishani, Portrait of a Chechen Mujahid Leader, Op. Cit.

[72] Tumelty, Op. Cit.

[73] Julie, Op. Cit.

[74] Are there Chechens in Iraq, *Chechnya Weekly*, Vol.4, Issue 26 (July 17, 2003).

[75] See: On the Chechens in Iraq See: Murad Batal Al-Shishani, Chechens in Iraq: What the 'Experts' Do not Know, *Arab News* (Saudi Arabia), 1, February, 2006.

and control over the Chechen resistance. [76] But Russia insisted on comparing him with Osama bin Laden, refused to negotiate with him, and finally assassinated him, thereby opening the way for the radical movement, headed by Basayev, to assume control over the resistance. But his assassination raises even more questions about the future of the Chechen resistance and the effect that the phenomenon of Arab fighters left on the ideological level.

At present, power in Chechnya is based on a Sufi alliance with Russia, especially the Qadiri order. Just as Sufi religious thought dominated the political scene at the beginning of the independence movement in the early 1990s, it has made a comeback with its support of Russia.[77] On the other hand, even though the role of Salafi-Jihadists has declined, the influence of the Jammat al-Islamiya, with its socio-military structure and tribal loyalty, has increased in the past 20 years. The Jamaa Islamia has affiliate organizations in neighboring regions in the North Caucasus, such as the Shari'a Jamaat in Dagestan and the Yarmouk in Kabardino-Balkaria, which embody an ideology of resistance against Russia in the North Caucasus.[78] Additionally, there is Doku Umarov,[79] the Chechen field commander and successor to Abdul-Halim Saidullayev, who was close to the ideology of the Jamaa Islamia and who promised to continue the fight after Basayev's death.

Based on this, we can say that even if the Chechen resistance is weak at the moment, there are several factors that could lead to its resurgence. First of all, studies indicate that there is an increase in resistance operations in neighboring regions in the North Caucasus, especially in Nalchik.[80] This means that there is more support of the ideology of the Jamaa, which benefited from the calls for unity from the Arab fighters.

---

[76] Murad Batal al-Shishani, Maskhadov's Cease-Fire and the Situation in Chechnya, *Central Asia-Caucasus Analyst*, Wednesday / February 09, 2005 .

[77] C.J Chivers, Revival of Sufi Ritual in Chechnya, *The New York Times*, 24 May 2006.

[78] Andrew McGregor, Islam, Jamaats and Implications for the North Caucasus - Part 1, *Terrorism Monitor*, Vol. 4, Issue 11 (June 2, 2006).

[79] Vidino, "The Arab Foreign Fighters in Chechnya and the Sacralization of the Chechen Conflict", Op. Cit, p.7.

[80] Murad Batal al-Shishani, From Grozny to Nalchik: Is The North Caucasus Heading back to the Nineteenth Century?, *Central Asia-Caucasus Analyst*, October 19, 2005.

Secondly, while it is true that Sufis have become pro-Russian, it is connected with their desire to demonstrate their rejection of Wahhabism. However, this does not obviate their historical enmity toward Russia; and had there been another leader other than the mufti, Ahmad Kadyrov, they would not have changed sides. Moreover, a new generation of angry Sufis is maturing;[81] and the fact that Ramzan Kadyrov is linked with many cases of corruption and criminal activity in Chechnya, means that Doku Umarov and other Sufis will possibly revive the resistance in Sufi ranks, especially the Sufism in Chechnya that is characterized by tribal allegiances now that the Wahhabi threat has disappeared because there are no Arab fighters left in Chechnya.

---

[81]Vachagaev, the Role of the Sufism in Chechen Resistance, Op. Cit.

Figure 1

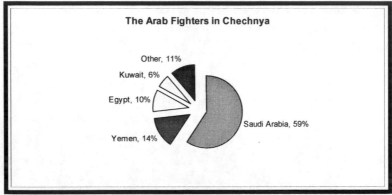

Source: the figures compiled by author from source mentioned in note 5 of the footnotes.

Figure 2

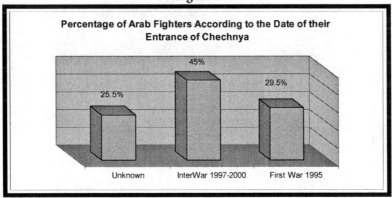

An Inside Look at Karachaevo-Cherkessia

Fatima Tlisova

Introduction

The Karachaevo-Cherkessia autonomous oblast was first created in 1923. It was then transformed into a republic in 1993. The territory of the republic represents 0.08% of the total landmass of the Russian Federation. Its capital, Cherkess, is about 2,000 kilometers from Moscow.

Karachaevo-Cherkessia is located on the western slopes of the Greater Caucasus mountain range. Within Russia, it borders Stavropolskii Krai, Krasnodarskii Krai, and Kabardino-Balkaria. To the south, it shares an international border with Georgia, including the disputed region of Abkhazia.

The republic is rich in natural resources, with large deposits of gold, silver, copper, wolfram, marble, and numerous mineral springs. The southern part of the republic, known as the Elbrus region, is a potential tourist area that has many slopes suitable for downhill skiing, vast areas of pristine forests, alpine meadows, and clean waterways. Unfortunately, the infrastructure of the area is rather underdeveloped, thus making tourist development difficult.

Despite the ample natural resources of Karachaevo-Cherkessia, the economy is in bad shape and according to the Russian magazine *Expert* has been in a recession for many years. The decline in economic output there is actually the largest such decline in all of the Northern Caucasus. The investment climate is both unattractive and risky due to political

317

instability, the absence of any sort of benefits or guarantees for investors, and the poorly developed infrastructure of the republic.

The weak economy has generated a high rate of unemployment. An almanac on the socio-economic conditions of the Northern Caucasus notes that Karachaevo-Cherkessia has a higher rate of unemployment than any other region of the Russian Federation besides Ingushetia and Chechnya. Although the official rate is stated as 1.5% of the working age population, the real level is closer to 15%. Similarly, the average per capita monthly income in the republic is 440 rubles (about $15), and ranks 85th out of the whole country. Once again, only Dagestan and Ingushetia have lower recorded income levels in the Northern Caucasus.

The best way of illustrating these income levels is to describe the life of an average village. Most of the money in each household is spent on basic foodstuffs and everyday household goods. These are sold on credit in little shops, with the buyer's name being added to a special notebook along with a list of all monthly purchases. When wages are paid, the debts are settled, even though this generally uses up the entire salary. During the next month the family once more lives on credit, and the process then repeats itself. Clothes, for instance, are purchased only in the most extreme cases, such as when a child has grown and can no longer wear his old clothing.

As of July 2006 the poverty line of the republic was thought to be at 413 rubles, which is four times lower than the national average. The income of the political and business elites in the region is thought to be at an all-time high of several thousand times larger than that of the general populace. As economic inequality has increased, the mistrust and dislike towards the ruling elite has risen proportionally.

Sociological polls conducted in 2005 by Dr. Erizheva have shown that 97% of the population live in discomfort, with 59% consistently irritated or tense, 31% fearful or worried and 7% feeling spiteful. Only 3% are satisfied with their lives. The same poll showed that 73% of the population is willing to protest publicly, with 27% willing to bear arms against the authorities. These results may seem skewed, but the facts on the ground suggest that they are correct. The situation in Karachaevo-Cherkessia changes rapidly and unpredictably. For example, in the one year interval between October 2004 and October 2005 various groups seized the republic's main government building three times over. During the second of these three incidents the rebels held the republic's "White House" for a total of three days, but no leader or group emerged to take advantage of this situation and thus promote the idea of revolution. The Kremlin referred to this spontaneous outburst of hostility as a provocation planned by Western intelligence services.

The crisis affecting the local government's ability to interact with the general public is most extreme in the case of law enforcement. A good example of this was the heavily publicized meeting of the republic's Minister of Internal Affairs, Nikolai Osiak, with the populace of three regions in Karachaevo-Cherkessia in order to address their concerns over the work of the police. This meeting was heavily publicized by the republic's media, but out of more than 40,000 people that lived in the regions in question, only six came to actually speak with the minister.

Osiak's predecessor, Aleksandr Obukhov (who was fired in early 2006), has said in one of his interviews that the high level of corruption and pervasive nepotism made it impossible to expect any level of professionalism from the police. The distrust isn't just a local phenomenon – Moscow has never appointed a member of one of the republic's ethnic groups to the top position within the republic's Ministry of Internal Affairs.

The killing of local police and federal security agents is yet another way to gauge the population's attitudes towards the government. Sixty members of various security and law enforcement agencies have been killed since 2000, with 16 having been shot since January 2005. This includes FSB officers as well as various officers of special units stationed within the republic. The vast majority of these attacks occur in Karachaevsk and the Karachaevskii region. This is the part of the republic closest to Georgia. Despite a very heavy security presence it is barely controlled by the authorities.

319

In July of 2006 the Russian Minister of Defense Sergei Ivanov has declared that two mountain brigades will be created by the Ministry and stationed in Karachaevo-Cherkessia and Dagestan by the end of the year. This will be part of the federal "National Borders" program that aims to create an effective international border stretching from the Black Sea to the Caspian. Russia will have thus corrected a problem that has existed since the disintegration of the USSR. The removal of two "heavy" military bases from Georgia will coincide with the creation of two "light" brigades for Karachaevo-Cherkessia and Dagestan. "The border needs to be sealed," Ivanov has said. He also noted that the equipment of each member of these brigades would cost 125,000 rubles (excluding weapons). "This is an expensive operation," the minister noted, "but we can afford it, and money has been set aside in the budget for this purpose."

The reaction in the border regions of Dagestan was immediate – a new wave of protests broke out and the locals interfered with the construction of the base. In Karachaevo-Cherkessia the inhabitants of Kobu-Bashi village held a protest in front of the republic's Peoples' Council building in Cherkess. People were enraged by the plan to build a tank training ground near their settlement. They were initially provoked by the plan to shift the Russian bases from Georgia to the republic's territory.

In fact the base in question, along with the tank training ground, is already under construction in the Zelenchuk region of Karachaevo-Cherkessia. The area picked for the training grounds by the military is a piece of municipal land in the northern part of Kobu-Bashi, with training exercises planned every March and September. The main source of income for the villagers in this region is raising individual cattle, a pursuit that will become impossible if the community's grazing and haying grounds become a training area for the military. In addition, the military's proposal would also strip away all of the village's sources of drinkable water.

According Nikolai Khaianka, the head of the "Storozh" municipal union, a map has been created that shows almost the entire village

320

given over to the training grounds. "Essentially, the question has become whether there will be a village or a training area here," he says. "This small valley already contains a firing range belonging to the Cherkess border guards located some distance from the village, which already makes life very hard for the villagers. Grenade launcher training already causes all the windows in the village to shake. If a training grounds is located directly next to the settlement it's easy to imagine what would happen when tank guns are fired."

The allegations of the villagers have been contradicted by members of the republic's government. Dzanibek Suyunov, the deputy head of the government, said during his speech in the People's Council that the government's studies show that, "no special danger is presented to the village by its close proximity to tank training grounds." This caused a number of critical responses from the deputies of the Council, with Hasan Khubiev, the head of the budget committee, responding that, "the condition of the houses in the village is such that one howitzer salvo will simply destroy them."

The strengthening of the Georgian border is a potentially destabilizing factor in Ingushetia as well, since almost all access to the Dzheirakh region will be lost. This region contains ancient towers and tombs, which are considered to be the historical and cultural roots of the Ingush, that mark the homeland of the G'alagaev people. Beginning in June this region may only be visited by those holding a special permit issued by FSB border guards.

An information ban prevents one from getting an accurate picture of what goes on in Karachaevo-Cherkessia. This past winter, for example, the republic's government warned of the heightened risk of terrorist acts, leading to a month-long closure of all schools, kindergartens, colleges and trade schools. All ambulatory patients were discharged from hospitals and spare beds were made available in case mass casualties ensued. It is known that police crackdowns occur regularly and torture is widely practiced, making most young men in the republic extremely wary of the authorities.

There was one well-known recent episode. In February 2006 mass detentions of young Muslims occurred in the city of Karachaevsk. Among those detained was one Albert Bogatyrev, an imam of a suburban mosque and a favorite of the people who considered him a holy man. On the day of his arrest two searches of Bogatyrev's home were conducted within a half hour of each other. Nothing was discovered in the initial search, but the second turned up a Kalashnikov assault rifle and two grenades. The imam's mother, Asiyat Uzdenova filed a complaint with the district attorney of Karachaevsk claiming that the weapons were planted. After three days of being kept in the courthouse jail the imam was placed in a mental hospital in the nearby village of Kubran and was diagnosed with schizophrenia.

Despite regular purges, there are those among the special services who are Islamic sympathizers. In March 2006 police lieutenant Safar Laipanov was detained in Karachaevsk having been accused of being part of the "wahhabite underground." It was said that the authorities had proof that he trained in Khattab's camps and was linked to the murders of police and FSB officers in Karachaevsk in the winter of 2005. This was the first official admission that a series of murders of men from the services had actually taken place. These facts have not been mentioned again, but it's not easy to forget the reality of the situation.

The Different Ethnic Groups

This rather uneasy republic contains only 0.3% of Russia's overall population. It is home to roughly 440,000 people, 117,000 of whom live in the capital city of Cherkess (2002 Russian census). The demographic situation is unstable, with the population declining and the child mortality rate rising, while more people emigrate from the republic rather than immigrate to it.

Except for Dagestan, Karachaevo-Cherkessia has the most complex ethnic makeup of any republic in the Northern Caucasus. There are five major ethnic groups in the republic. These are the Russians (40% of the population), the Karachai (36%), the Circassians or Cherkess

322

(9.7%), the Abazins (6.6%), and the Nogais (3.1%). In the past several years, the ethnic balance of power has shifted in favor of the Karachai. This is the most important factor influencing the current political situation in the republic.

Russians

The Russians in question are ethnic Russians that live in Cherkess as well as the Cossacks who live in the rural areas of the western parts of the republic. This group is not itself politically influential. It is amorphous but tends to be used as a tool in the power struggles of the various ethnic elites. During any election the supposed loyalty of the Russians in the republic is thought of as an ace in the hole during negotiations with the Kremlin. This is why various ethnic elites maintain their own Russian social organizations. These include "Rus," "Ia - Rusich," "Kazachka," etc.

In the last year, the Cossacks have tried to strengthen their hand by creating a regiment made up of recruits from local ethnic groups under the excuse that this would be a rebirth of the "Dikaia Divizia" ("Wild Division") which was famous in the Northern Caucasus during tsarist times. [1]

"The Council of the Atamans[2] and the Great Council of the Terek Cossack Host decided that they have the right to form an Abazin regiment, which foreshadows a special Circassian regiment that was once part of the Wild Division," the sotnik[3] of Psyzh, Kambiz Evgamukov, said. "In making this decision, the Council of the Atamans has underscored that the special Circassian and Kabardin regiments of the Wild Division, founded by the Grand Prince Michael, were faithful

---

[1] A "Host" (or "Army") is the technical term for a regional Cossack community (the Don Host, Kuban Host, etc.) regardless of how militarized or effective it actually is. (Translator's note here and below.)

[2] An "ataman" is the highest rank of officer and official among the Cossacks

[3] "Sotnik," literally "centurion," commander of a hundred men. Mid-ranking Cossack officer and official.

to the last to Nicholas II and have never swore an oath of fealty to anyone else."

The Terek Cossack Regiment is the most multi-ethnic out of the eleven Cossack regiments of the Russian Federation. Along with the Abazins it includes the Alan (Ossetian) region commanded by Marat Kazaev, and has individual members that are Armenians, Greeks, and Kabardins. Thus the Kabardin Yuri Psheunetov, who commanded the Georgivskii division until recently, has become part of the Elder's Council of the division since his retirement. The command of the Terek Host has received a request from Ingushetia to authorize the formation of Cossack units made up of Ingush.

Karachai

The Karachai (who call themselves the "K'rachailyla") are the largest indigenous Turkic ethnic group in the region, and are related to the Balkars that live in Kabardino-Balkaria. Karachaevo-Cherkessia is home to 85% of all of Russia's Karachai. They are mostly mountain dwellers who are traditionally Muslim, and live in three regions in the south of the republic.

Along with other North Caucasian ethnic groups the Karachai were deported to Central Asia in the 1940's. Having returned in 1957 they were able to take a leading role within the republic. For 28 years the head of the republic has been a Karachai. Karachais hold all the chief posts in the republic's government and 53 out of 72 votes within its parliament. By 2003 all of the largest industries of the republic, which were once owned by Russians, had been taken over by Karachais. The Karachais also have close political ties with the neighboring Balkars.

The Karachai national movement has undergone some serious changes in the early 21st century. In the 1990's the people seemed united in their political goals and showed themselves to be active and inclined towards separatism. However, today the Karachai do not have a single ethnic leader and are split into warring clans. The older leaders, romantic idealists who cared nothing for money, were separatists like Boris

Batchaev who dreamed of a free Karachai-Balkaria. They offered unlimited support to Dzhokhar Dudaev, but have since left the political stage.

Two important figures currently compete for influence among the Karachai: Mustafa Batdyev and Islam Burlakov. Batdyev is the current president of the republic, one of the wealthiest men of the Northern Caucasus, and a friend of such men as Anatoly Chubais and Yegor Gaidar. He comes from the poorest of the clans, however, and his authority does not come cheaply.

Burlakov, his opponent during the presidential elections and the head of the High Court of the republic is supported by the Karachai elite because he comes from a respected family. He is able to use his position to periodically show his superiority over Batdyev. For instance the struggle over the mayor's race in Cherkess was taken to court by Burlakov's pawn. His side was granted victory by one of Burlakov's protégés. Thus, the chief justice was able to remove one of the president's men as mayor. The mayoral elections in the second largest city of the republic, Karachaevsk, also had to be decided in court. This election pitted presidential supporter Safar Salpagarov against a close friend of the chief justice, the parliamentary deputy Islam Krymshamkhalov. The case has been in court for several months now and has led to several public demonstrations by supporters of the two candidates.

Burlakov's media resources include the locally popular *Vesti Gor* newspaper, and the recently acquired *Kavkaz* insert for the national *Moskovskii Komsomolets* newspaper. Mustafa Batdyev controls all of the governmental media including the local branch of the "Rossia" TV network, his own television company which rents airtime from the national TNT TV network, as well as the daily governmental newspapers published in the five main languages of the republic's inhabitants. It should be noted that the republic does not have any independent media outlets.

In any event, this political duel between Batdyev and Burlakov has essentially become essentially moot after President Putin's decision to appoint, rather than elect, governors. That said, the competition for dominance within the Karachai community as well as influence in the local government and the republic's economy continues unabated.

The Islamic factor in Karachaevo-Cherkessia is most strongly felt among the Karachai. The first lists of "wahhabites" were compiled by the Russian security services in Karachaevo-Cherkessia and it was here that the first "extremist" dzhamaat was organized. This dzhamaat was called "Muslim Society Number Three," and was created in the village Uchkeken by imam Bidzhi-Ulu (with the legal name of Muhammad Bidzhiev), who was one of the founders of the Islamic Renaissance Party in the USSR. At the same time an old pool hall in Karachaevsk was converted into a mosque belonging to the Mezhdid Society headed by Achemez Gochiyaev.

In August 2001, the then-minister of internal affairs of the republic declared that, "the wahhabites have created a net of dzhamaats in all of the settlements of the republic where there are training camps in the mountains staffed by Arab instructors." He also indicated that up to 8,000 inhabitants of the republic were ready to take up arms. These statements preceded several terrorist acts in Russian cities, acts that were blamed on Achemez Gochiyaev and his Karachai dzhamaat. This led to repressions that affected all Muslims under 30. The Karachai dzhamaat still exists and still undertakes certain operations – such as the individual killings of federal officials – but is no longer the small army that it was previously.

Certain data shows that the current head of the Karachai dzhamaat is an ethnic Balkar. The organization has its own internet website where declarations, details of operations undertaken by the dzhamaat, and pictures of shahids are posted.[4] Roughly a hundred photographs and biographies of men from Karachaevo-Cherkessia who had fought in the

---

[4] Literally, a "martyr for the faith." In contemporary Russia the word has the vernacular meaning of "suicide bomber."

republic and in Chechnya are available. A separate section is devoted to the events in Nalchik and includes the portraits of those men killed while participating in the attack.

Circassians

The Circassians, or Cherkess, are related to the Adyghe and the Kabardins and share the same self-given name – "Adyghe." "Cherkess" is also a widely known name of this ethnic group. They belong to the Caucasus language family, and their history contains tragic and heroic moments during the longstanding struggle with Russia for their independence.

In the 18th century Cherkessia held wide-ranging territories between the Black and the Caspian Seas and the Circassians were the largest ethnic group in the Northern Caucasus. In the 19th century, the Circassians did not participate in imam Shamil's war with Russia, but had their own resistance movement that outlasted Shamil's by five years and kept the northwestern part of the region free from Russian influence.

After their war with the Russian Empire the Circassians lost about 90% of their population, with several tribes being completely annihilated, and many more emigrating to the Ottoman Empire. The total number of Circassians living in the three republics of Kabardino-Balkaria, Karachaevo-Cherkessia and Adygea today is about a million. Roughly another six million Circassians live in Turkey, across the Middle East, in the U.S. and in other countries. The Circassians seek to unite and obtain their own state, with Circassian national organizations working for the return of the emigrants' descendants to their historical homeland.

The Circassian national movement has numerous issues to deal with. For many years the Circassians in Karachaevo-Cherkessia played the same role as the Russians, even though they had their own elite. Since the death of Yuri Kalmykov, the most influential Circassian leader and former Minister of Justice of the Russian Federation (who resigned in protest during the first campaign in Chechnya), the Circassians have become merely another electorate pool that the central government controls.

The Circassians have been a tool for elites set on pressuring the Kremlin for their own ends. In the early 1990's the Karachai and the Circassians agreed to divide the republic and secede from Russia as two independent states. The date of this secession had even been agreed upon. The Kremlin, however, came up with its own solution to this problem. In order to distract people from the idea of separatism a scenario of "national oppression" was played out, with the Circassians portrayed as the oppressed minority, and the Karachais as their torturers. Even today the older members of the Circassian national movement keep trying to recycle this setup to argue for a separation from Karachaevsk and a union with Stavropolskii or Krasnodarskii Krai.

The older leaders do not, however, have much influence among the younger generations of Circassians. It has become fashionable for the younger generations to know the history and culture of their people and to speak their own language. Younger people see the anti-Karachai attitudes as part of Russia's divide and conquer policy in the region. They have different ideals and idolize different leaders, even going so far as to write heroic songs and creating videos about them. They then share these productions via cell phones and the internet as much as possible.

Limiting the access to contemporary information technology and higher education is one part of Moscow's discriminatory policy towards the peoples of the Northern Caucasus. The impending loss of national conscience is the consequence, most likely desired by the Russian authorities, of the general education programs available in the schools. These schools only teach local languages three hours a week (the same amount as English). This level is even considered to be advanced study, compared with Russian, which is taught for twelve hours a week. This is combined with a negative and demeaning portrayal of the local languages. To this day the children of the Northern Caucasus learn the history of the Russian state in a way that does not reflect the true

328

history in this region. Textbooks almost completely ignore the history of the Caucasus and of the ethnic groups of the region, since Moscow finds it useless, not to mention potentially damaging, to tell the truth about its involvement there.

The facts about the availability of modern technologies speak for themselves. There are only 1,000 computers available for the 56,000 students attending classes in this region. Access to the internet is unavailable not only in schools, but also in whole swaths of the republic. The three internet cafes that exist in Chekess belong to the same official provider, Yugtelecom. The majority of Yugtelecom's shares are owned by the state. In April 2004 the FSB withdrew the licenses issued to all other telecommunication providers. This was also the case in Nalchik.

The October events in Nalchik, which were largely organized and implemented by Kabardins (Circassians), were a litmus test that showed the true status of the Northern Caucasus. The probability that the sort of events that transpired in Nalchik will spread to other Circassian territories is small, if for no other reason than the fact that Islam is far less of a social factor in Adygea or Karachaevo-Cherkessia than it is in Kabardino-Balkaria.

If ethnic separatists and Islamists come together, however, they will be a powerful force with strong internal and external support. A growth in separatist attitudes could make the Circassian peoples the strongest danger to Russian rule yet in the Northern Caucasus. Moscow understands this and is paying attention. One example of this is the order concerning, "The celebration of the 450th anniversary of the voluntary union of Adygei, Karachaevo-Cherkessia, and Kabardino-Balkaria with Russia," signed by President Putin in October 2005. This "holiday" will receive billions of rubles worth of subsidies from Moscow, which will essentially bribe the already loyal elites of the region.

This distortion of history is a PR campaign comparable only with the mass voluntary "surrenders" of guerrillas in Chechnya. Every week

329

Ramzan Kadyrov declares that, "the armed bands across Chechnya have been destroyed," and that, "the remaining 15-20 bandits will soon be destroyed as well." This is followed by a story played up by the Russian media about a new party of guerrillas surrendering, making one wonder how "the remaining 15" can keep surrendering in the hundreds over and over again. Similarly, the 450th anniversary of the voluntary union celebrates a union so "voluntary" that 90% of the indigenous peoples were eliminated in order to make this union a reality.

Two more ethnic groups of the republic do need to be discussed, since they have a noticeable influence on the republic's politics and actively participate in the processes affecting the region despite their relatively small numbers.

Abazins

The Abazins are one of the world's disappearing ethnic groups. According to the recent census there are only about 30,000 Abazins left, and almost all of them live in Karachaevo-Cherkessia. The Abazins, along with the Circassians and the Abkhaz form the Abkhaz-Adyg subgroup of the Caucasian language family, with Abkhaz and Abazin being essentially different dialects. The Abazins are considered the most warlike group of the Adyghe family.

During the last seven years, the main goal of the Abazins was the creation of one unified Abazin municipal region that would unite Abazin villages spread throughout the republic. This, according to the Abazin leaders, would help to preserve their disappearing ethnic group. During these years the Abazin movement was headed Muhamed Kilba, an Abkhaz hero and comrade of Shamil Basayev during the Georgian-Abkhaz war. After Kilba entered the business world his role was assumed by the parliamentarian Ualii Evgamukov, who proposed the whole plan of creating the Abazin region in the republic's parliament.

In September 2005 the Abazins picketed the main governmental building of the republic in Cherkess for more than a week and accused the authorities of ignoring their rights. The protest ended with

330

storming the building, with Abazins blockading the parliamentarians within the main conference hall and demanding an immediate resolution of the question of the Abazin region.

Following the intervention of Dmitrii Kozak, the presidential representative in the Southern Federal District, the question was settled in Moscow, with the Kremlin ordering the republic's leadership to create an Abazin region immediately. Fradkov signed the official order creating the Abazin region in August 2006. Within the republic itself, however, the map of the new region is still top secret, since the question of territories and borders may elicit a negative response of all those affected. The disputed territories in the Ust-Dzhegutin region of the republic might be a source of conflict between the Abazins and the Karachai. If the authorities have left these lands to the Karachai, it's possible that the Abazins anger will take particularly active forms. The inhabitants of Abazin villages openly speak of fighting to preserve their homeland.

The Nogais

The Nogais are a Mongolic ethnic group that is somewhat close to the Turkic-speaking Karachai. Nogais live in compact settlements within two regions of Karachaevo-Cherkessia, and also in neighboring Dagestan and Stavropolskii Krai.

The Nogai battalion is respected by the Chechen rebels. The village of Kangly on the Karachaevo-Cherkessia border with Stavropolskii Krai is the site of harsh and frequent police actions. This spring the mujahadeen of one of the Nogai villages fought with units of the Stavropol spetznas commandos and of the Ministry of Defense after being blockaded in a residential building.
The national movement of the Nogais is nominally led by Magomed Sanglibaev, a former Communist functionary. However, the real leader is Amin Urakchiev, the intelligent and ambitious leader of the republic's anti-monopoly service. While remaining in the shadows he has managed to sustain the Nogais as a cohesive force and set forth the goal of creating a Nogai region in Karachaevo-Cherkessia. The

demands of the Nogais have become particularly relevant after the Abazins achieved the creation of their own autonomous region, even if its only on paper. This question elicits much passion among the Cherkess leaders of the Adyg-Khabl region, which stands to lose much of its territory if the Nogai region is established.

Conclusion

All of the above clearly shows that none of the ethnic groups within Karachaevo-Cherkessia feel comfortable or satisfied with their status within the republic. Those political and ethic leaders shaped by Soviet life are more interested in serving the Kremlin than in representing the interests of their own people, leading to a loss of authority and control over the actual flow of events. They have not, however, been replaced by strong new leaders, leaving the national movements leaderless and torn by factional strife. Due to the large number of troops in the region the dzhamaats are unable to openly function, conduct propaganda, or recruit new members. They do conduct occasional attacks on members of the security services. The population at large is apathetic and deprived of basic social services. The Kremlin itself is apathetic in its policies towards Karachaevo-Cherkessia and prefers to let the security services take care of the peace and well-being of the locals.

Kabardino-Balkharia:

Sleeping Beauty and the Awakening of the Circassian Heartland

Fatima Tlisova

Introduction

In comparison with the many problems that have flared up across the Northern Caucasus during the last decade, Kabardino-Balkaria has long remained the most peaceful, stable, and loyal republic in the region. Because of this enduring stability the late Shamil Basayev once dubbed the republic "sleeping beauty." And it is with the waking of Kabardino-Balkaria that a Rubicon has been crossed and it is now truly possible to talk about the spread of hostilities to the North-Western Caucasus and also of the participation of the most numerous local ethnic group – the Circassians (Adyg, Kabardins) in the anti-Russian resistance movement. This paper is an attempt to analyze the causes for "sleeping beauty's" awakening and a detailed chronology and description of the Nalchik uprising in October 2005.

Geographical Factors & Governmental Structures

The Republic of Kabardino-Balkaria (abbreviated as KBR in Russian) is a federated republic and component part of the Russian Federation. The republic is governed by the president and the parliament. Parliamentary members are elected to five year terms by direct, universal vote and may be reelected an unlimited number of times. Until 2005 the president was elected directly, but after the legislative changes made by Vladimir Putin, he is appointed by the President of the Russian Federation and confirmed by the local parliament and serves five year terms. The president has the power to dismiss the parliament, but the parliament may impeach the president.

The republic has a territory of 1,247,000 square kilometers. In the south, Kabardino-Balkaria borders Georgia, in the east – Ingushetia and North Osetia, and in the west – Stravropolskii krai and Karachaevo-Cherkessia. The population is close to a million people.

Due to comparably advantageous socio-economic conditions the republic was long held to be the most stable of all the regions in the south of the Russian Federation even though it had a high unemployment rate and backlog of payments to the federal budget. This stability is mostly due to the positive image of the republic and its large recreational and tourist facilities in the Elbrus region and in the capital of Nalchik. Nalchik, with a population of 400,000, has a reputation for being the most beautiful and one of the largest cities in the Northern Caucasus. There is a stable business climate and well-developed business infrastructure. The most successful businesses in Kabardino-Balkaria are construction, oil, banking, and tourism. The major Moscow-Baku highway and railroad pass through the republic. Kabardino-Balkaria has its own regional airport and number of locally based airplanes and there are direct and regular flights to Turkey, the United Arab Emirates, and many cities across Russia.

The republic has ample reserves of fossil fuels, including oil and natural gas. Extraction is still in its infancy and the investment climate is fairly bleak. Risk factors include the uncertain military situation, the high level of corruption in the local government and regulatory institutions, the high participation of government officials in business, and poor regulation.

Ethnic Composition

According to the census of 2002 there are 498,702 Kabardins, 226,620 Russians, and 104,951 Balkars residing in the republic. Due to their overwhelming numbers the Kabardins traditionally occupy leading positions in all aspects of social and political life. They are a member of

334

the Circassian (Adyg) ethnic group and are closely related in language and culture to the Circassians of Karachaevo-Cherkessia and the Adygs of Adygeia. Along with other Circassian peoples many Kabardins were deported to the Ottoman Empire during the 19th century after the end of the Great Caucasus War with the Russian Empire. Due to the existing equilibrium within the republic the Kabardins hold top political posts, including the presidency, key ministries, and leading positions in the enforcement and financial organs of the government.

The Balkars are the second largest native ethnic group in the republic. The Turkic-speaking Balkars are related to the Karachais in neighboring Karachaevo-Cherkessia. They were deported to Central Asia by order of Joseph Stalin in the 1940's, allowed to return to the Caucasus by Nikita Khrushchev, and finally rehabilitated by Boris Yeltsin. Despite their small numbers, the Balkars are the main players in the republic's permanent inter-ethnic contest, a contest that often grows into open confrontation. The Balkars live predominantly in the highland areas of the republic – the Elbrus, Chegem, and Cherek districts. These areas, however, contain the most economically vital objects of the republic – the Cherkess Hydroelectric Plant, the Tyrnyauskii Gornoobogatitelnii Kombinat (TGOK) mining facility, and the skiing resorts in the vicinity of Mount Elbrus. The Balkars traditionally occupy the secondary and tertiary positions within the republic's government and hold governmental posts such as speaker of the parliament and vice-prime minister.

Within Kabardino-Balkaria Russians are an ethnic minority that has neither any real political influence nor functions as an effective buffer in inter-ethnic conflicts. In this respect they are very different from their neighbors in Karachaevo-Cherkessia, where the Russian population has a notable role in politics and the society at large. Russians traditionally hold the post of prime minister and also lead the security and police agencies of the republic's government.

It is important to note that the security components of the republic's government are fully under the control of the Russian Federal government. Thus the leaders of the local branches of the Ministry of

335

Internal Affairs, the FSB, the Tax Police and other federal agencies are not subordinate to the republic's government, but answer directly to Moscow. This structure demonstrates the purely formal nature and unreality of the so-called civil society and representative government within the republic, though this pattern is fairly common in all republics of the Northern Caucasus.

The Kabardin nationalist movement saw its heyday in the early 1990's. In September and October of 1992 the powerful and influential organizations "Adyge Khase" and "The Kabardin Peoples' Congress," led by Professor Yuri Shanibov declared that they intended to succeed from Russia and form an independent sate. These demands found widespread support among the general populace, demonstrations in Nalchik reached a fever pitch, and the whole republic was on the brink of war. The situation was resolved by the efforts of president Valeri Kokov. Shanibov was abducted and arrested, demonstrations were dispersed by the police and army divisions, and the leaders of the "Congress" were subjected to unceasing persecution. In this way Kokov, a Kabardin, quickly and brutally ended the aspirations of the Kabardin nationalist and separatist movement, earning himself a reputation of an internationalist and a loyal government official in the Kremlin's eyes.

Following the destruction of the "Congress," the "Adyge Khase" movement came to the attention of the authorities. The offices of the organization suffered a pogrom at the hands of the police, its archives were burned, its leaders beaten, and the organization finally disbanded. As a replacement for the old "Adyge Khase," which originally functioned as an informal national parliament, a new organization with the same name was created in 2002. The goals of this new entity are completely different and if its current declarations are to be believed, come down to propagandizing the idea of Circassian love and gratitude to the Russian state. On the whole, today's Kabardin civic groups and organizations are disunited, unfree, and thoroughly controlled by the state. Their influence in Kabardin society is fairly low.

Interethnic conflicts within the republic do not have a particularly long history, but are almost predictable in their regularity. The foundation for the confrontation between the two titular ethnic groups of the republic (the constitution of Kabardino-Balkaria defines the Kabardins and Balkars as the titular and thus republic-forming ethnic groups) was laid during the 1940's deportation. The Balkars were removed to the last man, while the Kabardins were allowed to remain in their homeland. This inequality and injustice strongly changed the Kabardin-Balkar relationship when the latter returned from Central Asia. Balkars remain unsatisfied with the rehabilitation process, including the payment of compensations by the Federal government and the restitution of lost lands.

That said, it needs to be remembered that all restitution moneys were publicly transferred by Valeri Kokov into the keeping of Balkar national organizations and the president forbade any ethnic Kabardin officials from have anything to do with their disbursement. Kokov explained this wise step by saying "This money could be a point of contention, even if it's given to those who deserve it. And if Kabardins participate in the process, this could lead to conflict between our peoples." Kokov was correct, most of the money was misspent and the compensations that actually reached ordinary Balkars were tiny. The absence of Kabardins from the distribution process did not forestall Balkar anger, however. Currently the main cause of contetnion is territorial – whereas before the deportation the Balkars controlled four districts of the republic, after the deportation they had only three, with the territory of the Khulamobezengii district having been divided between its neighbors.

The first mention of the persecution of the Balkars occurred in the early 1990's, during the so-called "sovereignty parade" in the Russian Federation. Nalchik was overwhelmed by demonstrations and an appealing and ambitious Balkar leader entered the political stage – retired Soviet General and head of the former Transcaucasus military district, Sufian Beppaev. Extremely charismatic, possessed of a military man's bearing and thunderous voice, Beppaev became president Kokov's number one enemy and brought together thousands of protesters in Nalchik's central square. The General's main demands were the return of all Balkar territories as they existed before 1942, the withdrawal of these territories from Kabardino-Balkaria and a union with Karachai (which would in turn withdraw from Karachaevo-Cherkessia) into a new component part of the Russian Federation.

In writing about the events of 1994-96 in the republic the Russian press frequently noted the parallels between two Generals – the Chechen leader Dzhokhar Dudaev and his Balkar counterpart. The respected journal "Profile" put the headline "Conflict in Kabardino-Balkaria – will Beppaev be another Dudaev?" on its front page.[1]   In another instance the local newspaper "Gazeta Yuga" opened its report on the situation with a quote from General Beppaev – "I have started forming a Balkar army."[2] In a national congress of Balkars held in Nalchik a State Council of Balkaria was created, and Sufian Beppaev was elected its leader.   The congress declared that the Balkars were leaving Kabardino-Balkaria and requested that the Kremlin temporarily establish direct presidential control over the new republic.

Despite his ambitions, Beppaev never demanded anything other than a new republic within the Russian Federation.   The call for "an independent, free Balkaria" was put forth by Rasul Dzhappuev, the creator of the separatist wing of the Balkar national movement. This grouping had as many followers as Beppaev's, but was far harder to control.

Once again president Kokov managed to keep Kabardino-Balkaria from passing out of Russia's control.   Diplomacy, instead of repressions, came into play this time. Following extended negotiations General Beppaev agreed to take the position of human rights envoy for the President of Kabardino-Balkaria, and thus be responsible for the disbursement of Federal restitution funds to the Balkar people (the results of which were mentioned above).   Beppaev's defection to Kokov's camp was seen as high treason by most Balkars and deprived

---

[1] *Profile*, #18, 1996.
[2] *Gazeta yuga*, #21, 1996.

the general of his high standing, thus splitting the Balkar camp into two independent and mutually hostile factions.

The most recent flare-up in Kabardino-Balkar relations occurred in 2004-2005 during the discussions surrounding the new "borders of municipalities" law, since the Balkars saw this as a new attempt to deprive them of their lands. The new law introduced the notion of "intermunicipal" lands and allocated control of such areas to the republic's government, rather than the nearby municipalities. "Intermunicipal" lands were all those areas located between towns and villages and were previously used by the local residents for grazing and agriculture. Despite the fact that the new laws were enforced all across the republic, only the Balkars voiced their objections and saw the new policies as directed against their rights and freedoms.

In May 2005 Artur Zakoev, a widely respected forty-year-old leader of the Balkar people, was murdered in Nalchik. Zakoev, a father of five children and a mayor of one the city's suburbs, was gunned down on the porch of his own house. All remaining Balkar leaders, including Beppaev, condemned the death as an act of political assassination, and demonstrations once more shook the republic.

In late May 2005 a national Balkar gathering in honor of Zakoev was held in Nalchik. The police refused to let people from the suburbs into the city and the governmental buildings in the center of town were surrounded by a triple cordon of officers. The authorities seriously expected wide-scale social unrest and demonstrations were forcefully dispersed. This led to unceasing protests in the predominantly Balkar districts in the Elbrus region and a group of Balkar women declared a hunger strike. This, too, led to police repressions, with all transport to the Baksansk valley where the districts in question were located being cut off. Journalists were not permitted to enter the area and the movement of goods was curtailed. Despite theses measures, Balkar protests continued during the entirety of the summer of 2005.

The end of this wave of social discontent came with the change in political leadership that followed the death of Valeri Kokov. Arsen

339

Kanokov, an ethnic Kabardin, was appointed the new president of the republic. The Balkars saw this as yet another blow to their ethnic interests and the situation might have led to another burst of Balkar protest activity, but the unexpected rebellion of "Youth-Muslims" in Nalchik essentially put an end to all ethnically-based conflicts in the republic. Today the republic has almost zero real ethnically-based conflicts. Competition over assets in the tourist industry is still present among the ethnic elites, but the ethnic factor is exploited for the sole purpose of exerting political pressure or advancing the business interests of small groups of well connected individuals.

The major economic issue is the distribution of property in the tourist zones near Mount Elbrus where Balkars compose the majority of the population. Before 2005 land allotments in the area were distributed by the local authorities. This led to a situation where most land accessible to the tens of thousands of climbers and skiers heading to Mount Elbrus, the tallest mountain in Europe, were covered with tiny, low class hotels offering inferior service. The local people who owned these hotels tried to make the maximum amount of money with the smallest possible investment. The new president, a major businessman, has become a danger to these small operators since Kanokov has decided to make improvements to the area and to do so by attracting capital from Moscow and abroad. This became the reason for the conflict of interests between the Balkar elite and the team of the new president. Kanokov managed to shift the negotiations with the hotel owners in the Trans-Elbrus area, which were initially of nationalist nature, to the business mode. However, taking into account the local mentality, it is still difficult to predict the outcome of this standoff. Nonetheless, it is quite clear that the potential for conflict in this particular case is not sufficient to cause major inter-ethnic tensions. That said, it is quite clear that the potential for conflict connected with this issue if far from being serious enough to cause major inter-ethnic problems.

As mentioned above, the Balkar ethnic movement is currently divided into two independent wings. The "Alan" organization is still headed by Sufian Beppaev, has a quality office in downtown Nalchik, and has a cordial relationship with the authorities. Currently "Alan" is merely a loyal PR organ of the rulers of the republic. Following his acceptance of a government position and the scandal surrounding the distribution of Federal funds Beppaev's influence has rapidly declined. In 2005-2006 the General harshly condemned the policies of the security services towards the republic's youth and in April 2006 he was the victim of an unsuccessful assassination attempt and suffered severe injuries.

The other grouping, "Balkaria," is headed by Rasul Dzhappuev and has long endured pressure from the security services, including indictments for extremist activity. Interference from the services and courts tended to end in rather insignificant punishments, however, and today "Balkaria" has also become a much more compliant organization. The notion of seceding from the Russian Federation has been dropped and "Balkaria" is only a threat to the peace of mind of the local authorities with its numerous letters alleging the persecution of the Balkar people within the republic.

The contents of the last letter sent by "Balkaria" to the Kremlin in the fall of 2006 suggest that the organization is now working with the FSB. The letter in question makes a point of bringing to light a "world-wide Circassian conspiracy" aimed at destroying Russia and creating a "Greater Circassia." Balkar analysts are fond of describing the numerous "Circassian ambassadors" ensconced within many world governments and the existence of a "Circassian lobby" within the Kremlin itself. The nature of this information makes it fairly easy to determine what organization provided these materials to the writers in "Balkaria."

It should be clear from all of the above that by the beginning of the 21st century Kabardino-Balkaria does not have a single civic organization or social institution that is capable of seriously influencing society at large. A sort of vacuum has descended upon the republic and only religion has been able to successfully fill this gap. Following 70 years of Communist rule a renaissance of Islam has been able to provide the spiritual nourishment that so many people had been hungering for and thousands of young people aged 14 to 40 have made the mosque a normal part of their lives.

Religious Structures

In July 2004 the Kabardino-Balkaria committee on religious affairs published data about the religious communities officially registered within the republic. It was indicated that around 160 organizations have been registered, with most of them representing Muslim, Christian, or Jewish communities. The committee underscored that all religious organizations showed tolerance towards representatives of other religions. At the same time, the report hinted that certain conflicts exist among the Muslims of the republic, saying that "not all Muslim communities of the republic have chosen to participate in the Muslim Spiritual Board and that those who refused to recognize the authority of the official Islamic leaders and formed separate groups were refused official registration by the republic's ministry of culture."

While veiled, this is an important admission of the real conflict between the official and unofficial Muslim clergy in the republic. With the authorities thoroughly backing the established clergymen, this conflict has led to the creation of a branching web of youth groups that are united by a single religious idea. These groups are numerous and well organized, making them a concern for the authorities and thus the target of numerous official repressions. This movement has generally been called the "Young Muslims" ("Mladomusulmane") by most experts (using a term coined after the Young Turks movement in Ottoman Turkey) and originated as a moderate opposition to the official clergy among the younger believers. Later on, the "Young-Muslims" was transformed into first a spiritual, and later a political opposition to the rulers of the republic. In this case "opposition" does not indicate an affiliation with any specific movement or leader. The leaders of the jammat have rejected all attempts at an alliance undertaken by the republic's various opposition groups. The jammat is an independent and powerful political force that has recently transformed itself into a military jammat and declared Kabardino-Balkaria a part of the Caucasus Front.

342

Islam

According to most scholars of Islam within the Russian Federation the Muslims of Kabardino-Balkaria belong to the traditional Hanafi school of Islam. Professor Alexei Malashenko of the Carnegie Center in Moscow visited Nalchik in 2002 and spoke with the leaders of Muslim youth groups in the republic. In his book *Islamskii Orientiry Severnogo Kavkaza* (The Islamic Guideposts of the Northern Caucasus) which was written a year after his visit he refers to these men as Hanafi believers.[3] This opinion of a famous Russian scholar is a sharp contrast to the governmental and Spiritual Board opinions that label the "youth-Muslim" jammats of Kabardino-Balkaria as "wahhabite and extremist."

Both locals and outside observers generally see the origin of the schism among the Muslims of Kabardino-Balkaria in the scandalous disappearance of the funds collected for the construction of a municipal mosque in Nalchik, in 1993. The money was collected throughout the republic, with the effort being accompanied by numerous fundraising events and the wide-scale participation of the press. Donations were deposited in the bank account of the head mufti of Kabardino-Balkaria (the official Muslim leader and head of the Muslim Spiritual Board of the republic) Shafig Pshikhachev. The account was opened in the "Nart" bank, where Pshikhachev's sister held the post of head accountant. Soon after the fundraising ended it came to light that the money had simply disappeared, leading to a massive scandal that was widely covered by the local and national press. Mufti Pshikhachev couldn't provide any meaningful explanation of the situation or the disappearance of the money. Commenting on the situation in an interview with the "Portal Kredo" internet news agency in November 2005 Pshikhachev stated that "Yes, the donations were deposited in the bank. But in this we, let's be honest, made a mistake. For five years we tried to come to some decision about the architectural plans and then resolve the question of land. All of this went on until August 1998, when the default hit the country. "Nart" simply ceased to exist, with

---

[3] Alexei Malashenko, *Islamskii Orientiry Severnogo Kavkaza (The Islamic Guideposts of the Northern Caucasus), date?*

some help, one should add, from the then-administration of the republic."

Despite the money's disappearance, the republic's government took no legal or investigative measures against the mufti. The trust and respect felt by the ordinary believers disappeared completely and Shafig Pshikhachev left the republic for Moscow where he now holds the post of executive director of the "International Islamic Mission" organization. The post of head mufti was taken over by Shafig's nephew Anas Pshikhachev, a graduate of the Islamic University in Libya.

Looking back on what followed, it is clear that the disagreements between the "Young Muslims" and the Muslim Spiritual Board ran much deeper than simply the conflict over one leader's misallocation of funds, consequently the replacement of the head mufti could do little to pacify the situation. The charges leveled by the opposition organizations were quite harsh and the "Young-Muslims" were increasingly unwilling to compromise. What, then, were the differences that so split the co-religionists of Kabardino-Balkaria? In order to answer this question, it is necessary to analyze the views of both sides.

The Muslim Spiritual Board

As of today, what exactly are the roles of Muslim Spiritual Boards (Dukhovnoe Upravlenie Musulman, DUM) in the republics of the Northern Caucasus? The DUMs are unified religious governing bodies for the Muslims in the region. The DUM has local appointees (imams) in every village and town and it regulates all religious laws and ceremonies for Muslims, including the way in which births, weddings, funerals, and the division of property are carried out. Most of the Board's imams are retired former Communist functionaries that have neither a theological education, nor any knowledge of Arabic. The whole organization is entirely loyal to the government and the security services.

344

The Muslim Spiritual Boards of the Northern Caucasus are overseen by the Muslim Coordinating Center of the Northern Caucasus (Koordinatsionnyi Tsentr Musulman Severnogo Kavkaza), an organization created in 1999. The history of the Center is an interesting one. The Russian Council of Muftis was called together twice by the Kremlin, with the central authorities insisting that a clear definition of the term "wahhabism" be officially created. It was thought that should the Council of Muftis accept the threat posed by wahhabism, it would be easier to openly combat the phenomenon. For example, the muftis from Tatarstan and the Volga region refused to agree to the definition of "wahhabism" as "religious extremism," while the North Caucasus muftis were willing to accept this formulation. This led to a major schism in the Russian Council of Muftis and the creation of the Muslim Coordinating Center of the Northern Caucasus, which officially accepted all of the Kremlin's definitions during its first meeting. The Center unites the Spiritual Boards of Dagestan, Chechnya, Ingushetia, North Osetia, Kabardino-Balkaria, Karachaevo-Cherkessia, Stavropol province, Adygeia and Krasnodar province.

Ismail Berdiev, a Karachai from the village of Uchkeken in the south of Karachaevo-Cherkessia has been the head of the Center since 2003 and was re-elected to the post in 2006. The jammat from Karachaevo-Cherkessia has frequently called Berdiev a traitor and the mufti has avoided several assassination attempts. Even though the head mufti has never even been wounded in these attacks, seven DUM clergymen were killed in Karachaevo-Cherkessia between 2004 and 2006. These include Abubekir Kerbizhev, Berdiev's deputy and imam of the Kislovodsk mosque. Kerbizhev had cursed members of the jammat from his pulpit, labeling them wahhabites and extremists and calling on all Muslims to fight against them. The imam was slain at the entrance to his house the very next day.

The murder of official Muslim leaders regularly occurs in Ingushetia and it is probable that the phenomenon will continue to spread across the North Caucasus. In 2006 Anzor Astemirov, the military emir of Kabardino-Balkaria, used his address on the "Kavkaz-center" website to declare that "the traitors from amongst the imams will be warned and given time to correct their behavior. If they do not heed the warnings, they will be destroyed."

The Coordinating Center works in advancing the Kremlin's policies in the region. Representatives of the organization generally accompany Russia's President during his visits to the Arab countries or Turkey, and until the late Ahmad Kadyrov became the president of Chechnya he was a permanent fixture of such delegations. During these visits the representatives of the Center strive to enhance Vladimir Putin's positive image.

Ismail Berdiev's recent open letter to Vladimir Putin is quite interesting and deserves to be reproduced in full. The author argues for a change in the Russian Constitution and an additional presidential term for Putin. The letter was published in regional and national newspapers on May 8th, 2007.

> The elections of the President, the leader of the Russian state, are near. During the last seven years we have all witnessed Russia's transformation – the maturation of the political system, resurgent economy, and growing influence in foreign affairs. Finally, we have all once more started to feel that we are citizens of a Great Country.
>
> There are many possible reasons for this miracle, but as a theologian, I will not emphasize political or economic conditions and even consider such a point of view mistaken. Blessed is the state that has a just ruler. Justice, righteousness, and the desire to fulfill the Almighty's commandments make a ruler pleasing to Allah, who gifts society with His mercy and makes it rich and prosperous.
>
> I'm sure that Russia has found such a ruler in you over the past seven years. Millions of believers, Muslim and Christian, have seen that the return of the country towards its spiritual roots is not the result of some political manipulation, but the result of one man's will. A man who is undoubtedly deeply religious

346

and one who seeks to use power for the benefit of those millions of people that elected him, rather than for personal enrichment.

In the March of next year Russian citizens will need to elect a new President. Who will replace you? Will he have the same firm hands with which to hold the President's power? Will he have the same enlightened mind with which the affairs of a Great Sate may be understood? And most importantly, will he have the same pure heart, a heart directed toward the Almighty? A heart that can withstand those great temptations that Iblis (in Islam Iblis is the name given to the devil) sends to those in power? These are questions often asked by simple believers.

I'm sure that the question of succession is not just a question asked by the Muslims of the Northern Caucasus, whom I represent in writing this letter, but by all Russian citizens. I do not wish to ask you to violate the law. Quite the opposite – today is the day to fulfill the law and let the one source of the true power in the country – the people – speak. It is time to have a referendum about amending the Constitution in order to allow the President to serve a third term.

The people believe in you, love you, and thus will surely never lie to you and thus show what the proper decision is during this crucial time.

Praying for you,
Ismail Berdiev,
Russian citizen, director of the board of the Muslim Coordinating Center of the Northern Caucasus.

Even overlooking the sycophantic tone of the letter, the reasons for a sharply negative response to this missive among the Muslims of the Northern Caucasus are quite clear. The attitudes expressed in the letter

347

can not be the foundation for overcoming the divisions between the official clergy and the jammats.

Much like the Russian security services, the Spiritual Boards use the terms "wahhabite" and "religious extremist" when referring to their younger opponents. Specifically, when speaking at a briefing in the ministry of internal affairs of Kabardino-Balkaria on April 27th, 2007 Anas Pshikhachev noted three important goals for the DUM of the republic:

1) Coordination with the government, the police, and the special services,
2) Combating religious extremism and "wahhabism,"
3) Maintaining a close relationship with representatives of other "traditional religions."

In so doing, the head mufti repeated the goals set by his predecessor Shafig Pshikhachev five years earlier in a similar briefing in May 2002. The stable relationship between the Spiritual Board and the police is quite clear.[4]

The Kabardino-Balkar Jammat

Who, then, opposes the DUM? Who are the "Youth-Muslims"? The youth jammats of Kabardino-Balkaria are a web of small groups, some of which number five members, while others a hundred to a hundred and fifty. Groups are generally formed on a geographic and residential basis. Each group has a leader – an emir. Members of the same group tend to be very close, they not only pray together, but also support and assist each other in everyday life. Local jammats are component parts of larger ones, including neighborhood and municipal groups, with all jammats coming together to be part of the one jammat of Kabardino-Balkaria. The republic's jammat is led by an elected emir, a man of undisputed authority and high reputation. The jammat has governing

---

[4]*Gazeta yuga*, February 20, 2002.

institutions, including a court, a high council (shura), educational societies, as well as manufacturing and retail businesses.

This structure was created in Kabardino-Balkaria with record speed between the mid-1990's and 2003. According to Professor Irina Babich, member of the Russian Academy of Sciences and specialist on the Islamic society of Kabardino-Balkaria, the Kabardino-Balkar jammat had almost 10,000 members in 2005. "You could raise 10,000 young men today to fight the government in Kabardino-Balkaria," she said in an interview with internet news agency "Kavkazskii Uzel" on May 27th, 2006.

This massive structure was formed by a small group of young men with undeniable talents in leadership and organization. The leaders of the movement are highly educated, having received both college educations in Russia and religious educations in the Islamic universities of Saudi Arabia, Jordan and Egypt. Some of them fought in the First or Second Chechen Campaigns and many have participated in Circassian national movements. Specific individuals will be discussed below.

As an example of the disagreements between the official clergy and the younger believers, it's instructive to list the accusations leveled at DUM by Musa Mukozhev, the emir (leader) of the Kabardino-Balkar jammat, in an interview with the "REGNUM" news agency in the fall of 2004:

1) Members of DUM work with the security services and thus assist in the repressions against the younger people. The imams secretly create lists of those young Muslims that regularly attend mosques and then pass them to security personnel, where the lists are used to make arrests, fabricate indictments, as well choose victims to torture and demean.

2) The members of DUM are both ignorant and greedy. Imams do not know the foundations of Islam and do not understand the holy books. The emir illustrated this ignorance with the curious story of how in one village the

349

local imam made the funerary prayers over a dead man using an Arabic geography book that he believed to be a Koran. In addition they charge people for making certain mandatory prayers and follow traditions both atypical of Islam and expensive for the average believer. According to the local traditions that are supported by the imams, the family of a dead man must spend around 60,000 rubles on the funeral and the wake, with such expenses sometimes reaching 200,000. Most people in Kabardino-Balkaria are unable to earn that much money in the course of a decade.

These disagreements between the DUM and the jammat of the younger believers have become a gaping chasm following the repressions of the "Young-Muslims" by the security apparatus and the subsequent approval of these actions by the official clergymen who showed their solidarity with the "struggle with wahhabism and religious extremism."

The Leadership of the Kabardino-Balkar Jammat

Musa Mukozhev, 40, a man who has since the late 1990's became one of the most important leaders in the republic's political arena. Mukozhev has a great deal of authority among the younger believers and was elected emir of the Kabardino-Balkar jammat when it was originally formed.

In 1990 he finished a course of Islamic Studies at the DUM in Nalchik and then the Islamic Institute of Kabardino-Balkaria and interned in Jordan. Starting in 1994 Mukozhev was the director of the Islamic Center of the Kabardino-Balkar DUM. In 1997 he was appointed as imam and preacher to the village of Volnyi Aul (one of Nalchik's suburbs), where his Friday prayers were so popular with younger believers that the mosque was too small to hold those who came to listen. Hundreds of Muslims traveled to Volnyi Aul not only from across the republic, but even from across the whole region. Predictably, this level of popularity became a concern to the Russian authorities and the mosque was raided repeatedly, with some believers being arrested, often using violent means, during prayer. The mosque was finally

350

closed by the republic's police in 2004. In 1998 Musa Mukozhev was elected emir (leader) of the Muslim community (jammat) of Kabardino-Balkaria and ever since that day he has been a staunch opponent of the official clergy and the DUM.

The Attorney General's office of the Russian Federation has accused Mukozhev of participating in a series of terrorist acts in the cities Piatigorsk, Mineralnyi Vody and the republic of Karachaevo-Cherkessia. "File #91169, regarding Mukozhev, Artur (Musa) in connection with accusations pertaining to the commission of the terrorist act in the city of Piatigorsk, on December 8th, 2000, and in the cities of Mineralnyi Vody, Esentuki, and the village of Adygee-Khabl in Karachaevo-Cherkessia on March 24th, 2001" has been made inactive based on article 208, part 2 the RSFSR Criminal Code – "lack of proof of commission or relation to the commission of the abovementioned crimes." The security services of Kabardino-Balkaria suspect Mukozhev of being connected to various Chechen field commanders and of providing them with aid, as well as popularizing "wahhabist" ideas among the republic's youth. That said, no accusations or indictments have led a conviction in court so far.

Despite the constant arrests and persecution, there is reason to suspect that the authorities see Mukozhev as comparably a moderate and a man that is open to dialogue. The head of the anti-religious extremism unit of the UBOP (Organized Crime Division) of the republic noted in a briefing at the republic's ministry of internal affairs on September 21st, 2004 that "those Muslims from Mukozhev's jammat that have not broken the law, but oppose the official clergy, should not be lumped together with bandits. It's time to open up dialogue and unite against the real bandits."

In a September 2004 interview given to the "REGNUM" news agency Mukozhev stated that his jammat unites around 40 Muslim groupings in Kabardino-Balkaria, and the overall number of his follower's totals around 10,000, a figure later confirmed by professor Irina Babich (see above).

Unlike his associate Astemirov, Mukozhev managed to stay on the right side of the law for much longer. In all of his press releases the emir showed himself a staunch opponent of war in Kabardino-Balkaria, and in 2004-2005 he frequently declared that it was with great difficulty that he was keeping his jammats from undertaking armed vengeance for the repressions undertaken by the government and the security services.

It is still unclear what role Mukozhev played in planning the October 13th attacks in Nalchik, since he never accepted responsibility for any part of the attacks. Following the attacks the emir was completely silent until September 2006, leading to a multitude of theories and assumptions. For example, in May 2005 the Kabardino-Balkar division of the FSB started spreading information about a schism in the jammat leadership, even claiming that Astemirov had killed Mukozhev. The author of this paper can testify that these allegations of murder were a propagandist trick, since in early summer 2005 Mukozhev, already in hiding, met with me for an interview. The emir continued to insist that he is an opponent of war in Kabardino-Balkaria, but noted that the question is being actively discussed and that with the passage of time he has less and less arguments in favor of a peaceful resolution. The conspiratorial nature of our meeting suggested that a decision about undertaking military action had already been taken.

Anzor Astemirov, 31, referred to as "Sayfullah" – "The sword of Allah" in military dispatches. A Kabardin prince by birth, with the Astemirov family holding one of the highest ranks in Kabardin nobility, Anzor received a religious education in Riyadh, Saudi Arabia and fought in both of the Chechen Wars. Following his return to Nalchik, he has worked as a journalist.

Astemirov is Mukozhev's deputy and close friend. Along with the emir Anzor was arrested by the Attorney General's office in 2001 in connection with the terrorist acts in the cities of Piatigorsk, Mineralnyi Vody, Esentuki, and the village of Adygee-Khabl. Both of the accused spend two months in the "Belyi Lebed" ("White Swan") jail in Piatigorsk, a place widely known across the Northern Caucasus.

The investigation of the Mukozhev-Astemirov affair was conducted by **Igor Tkachev**, the senior investigator for especially important matters in the Northern Caucasus Office of the Attorney General's office of the Russian Federation. Tkachev had previously investigated the participation of journalist **Andrei Babitskii** in illegal armed bands, the "plot to overthrow the government in Karachaevo-Cherkessia and Kabardino-Balkaria," and the situation surrounding the "Russian Taliban" – the former prisoners of Guantanamo Bay.

In a number of articles, and over the course of several years, the opposition-minded "Novaia Gazeta" has related much about Igor Tkachev's activities. Articles provided numerous eyewitness accounts of unparalleled torture used by Tkachev's investigators, as well as tales of extortion of large bribes intended to either free the imprisoned or lighten their fate. Journalists relate how Tkachev is given the most doubtful cases, cases with a predetermined outcome, and instructed to fabricate the evidence necessary to make these a success. Many of his cases also have strong political overtones.[5]

This suggests that the "Mukozhev-Astemirov case" should have been yet another great success in the Attorney General's struggle against terrorism. Unexpectedly the investigation was terminated based on article 208, part 2 the RSFSR Criminal Code – "a lack of proof of commission or relation to the commission of the abovementioned crimes." Following his release, Astemirov became one of the founders of the Institute for Islamic Studies in Nalchik and held the post of assistant director of research before he disappeared into the guerilla underground. In October 2005 Anzor was appointed commander of the Kabardino-Balkar sector of the Caucasus Front and he is known to specialize in the planning of large military operations.

Anzor Astemirov took responsibility for organizing the attack on an office of the Narcotics Police in Nalchik in December 2004. As a result of the raid four officers of the Narcotics Police were killed and

---

[5] For example see: *Novaia gazeta*," #40, 2004; #88, 2002; #71, 2006; #26, 2003; #10, 2000.

Astemirov's men managed to capture the entirety of the office's arsenal, including 275 firearms, as well as large numbers of grenades and ammunition. The attackers took no casualties. The Russian government has named this attack one of the most daring in the entirety of the Northern Caucasus and the event is still under investigation by the Attorney General's office. Part of the captured weapons were later found in a cache in Ingushetia, while another part was used in Astemirov's next large scale attack – the October 13th, 2005 events in Nalchik.

Rasul Kudaev, 33, has a reputation as a scholar among the Muslims of the Northern Caucasus, and his achievements are such that he bears the title of sheikh. It should be noted that there are actually two different men known as "Rasul Kudaev" in Kabardino-Balkaria. One of them is a former prisoner of Guantanamo Bay and is currently incarcerated in Nalchik under suspicion of leading one of the groups involved in the events of October 2005. This particular Kudaev is not one of the leaders of the Kabardino-Balkar jammat and the information below concerns the other Kudaev, who holds one of the most important positions in the jammat organization.

Rasul Kudaev was educated in a madras and then in an Islamic Institute, both of which were opened by the DUM in Nalchik in 1992. Following the DUM's recommendation he entered and completed the Institute of Arabic Language and then the Department of Islamic Sciences in Riyadh, Saudi Arabia. In 2000 he graduated from the most prestigious Saudi university – the Mohammad ibn Saud Islamic University – with a degree in sharia law.

In 2002-2002 Kudaev taught the Islamic sciences in the Arabic Academy in Moscow, where he was also a graduate student of Financial and Banking sciences. After returning home to Nalchik he lectured on Islamic law, as well as leading prayers and preaching in different mosques of the republic during 2002-2004. Due to his education Kudaev held the eminent position of judge within the Kabardino-Balkar jammat. His authority was so high that not only jammat members, but other residents of Kabardino-Balkaria (including members of the government) and the people from the whole of the Northern Caucasus, appealed to him when in need of conflict resolution.

In the summer of 2004 Rasul Kudaev left Russia following the insistent pleas of his friends from the jammat. His life was in danger and he was continuously persecuted by the Russian security services. Though Kudaev has not returned to Nalchik since that time, the Russian intelligence services believe that he has maintained his ties with the jammat. In the spring of 2006 two mujahadeen were killed in a Nalchik suburb during a gun battle with the police. Their belonging included CDs with personal correspondence intended for the leaders of the jammat. Audio recordings on the discs justified the necessity of jihad in Kabardino-Balkaria and the voice of the preacher has been identified as that of Rasul Kudaev. That said, Kudaev's status remains uncertain – his name periodically appears and then disappears from the lists of wanted men. According to sources within the Russian intelligence services Kudaev's file is currently being worked on.

Ruslan Nakhushev, 49, is an Arabist, has completed the KGB Academy of the Soviet Union with honors and then went on to complete the Andropov Academy of Foreign Intelligence. As a matter of personal choice Nakhushev retired from the service with the rank of major. Following his retirement he headed the Kabardino-Balkar department of General Lebed's Peacekeeping Mission in the Northern Caucasus. Nakhushev searched out and rescued people from imprisonment in Chechnya. Alone, and without any bodyguards, he would travel to the camps of the abductors and negotiate with them. In 2001 he came into close contact with the leaders of the Kabardino-Balkar jammat and helped them resolve certain legal problems, the release of Mukozhev and Astemirov from jail in Piatigorsk being accomplished with Nakhushev's help.

Mukozhev and Astemirov were Nakhushev's deputies in the Institute of Islamic Studies that he had founded. His role in the jammat is interpreted in different ways, with many Russian media outlets suggesting that his participation was part of his mission as a secret

355

agent of the FSB. His purported goal was to prevent the jammat from becoming militarized. According to a different theory, Nakhushev was actually a member of the jammat and in the 2000's held the post of deputy emir in charge of legal questions and relations with official government structures. A number of news outlets controlled by the intelligence services have also published articles about the "betrayal" perpetrated by a former KGB officer who came to side with the insurgents ("Severnyi Kavkaz" newspaper, Russian government publication "Rossiiskaia gazeta.")

During the repressions against the jammat Ruslan Nakhushev regularly spoke out in favor of the "Young-Muslims." In an interview with the Russian "REGNUM" news agency in September 2005 he noted the following problems in Kabardino-Balkaria:

1)   The massive violation of the rights of local Muslims by the security services,

2)   The essentially anti-Islamic extremist bias of the local government,

3)   The widespread ignorance of the younger Muslims,

4)   Discrimination on the basis of religion at work, in education, in society, and even the family,

5)   Massive unemployment and low standard of living.

Following the October attacks the prosecutor's office of Kabardino-Balkaria accused Nakhushev of terrorism, inciting terrorism, and of aiding and abetting terrorists. The local FSB division demanded that money laundering and financial support for the jammat also be included in the list of charges, but the prosecutor's office did not find the evidence compelling. Following his first interrogation at the FSB Nakhushev vanished without a trace on November 4th, 2005.

The Kabardino-Balkar ministry of internal affairs and FSB believe that Nakhushev is alive and on the run, being listed as wanted among other organizers of the Nalchik attacks. Russian human rights organizations believe that he was probably killed by the Russian special services. Be that as it may, Nakhushev's earlier analysis proved correct, and the situation in the republic has continued to heat up.

The Socio-Economic Collapse in the Republic and the Increasing Influence of the Ministry of Internal Affairs.

Valeri Kokov first became the leader of Kabardino-Balkaria in 1985 as the local Communist party secretary, but was then elected to the presidency in 1992 and remained at the post until his death in September 2005. In the early 1990's Kokov was already a high-ranking member of the Federation Council, a member of the State Council and had a huge influence in the highest political circles. The Kremlin considered Kokov's approach to ruling Kabardino-Balkaria – a personal authoritarianism bordering on a dictatorship – a particularly favorable one for a republic being torn asunder by internal conflicts and contradictions.

Human rights organizations and the opposition accused Valeri Kokov of massive corruption, the sale of offices, theft of governmental funds, and the impoverishment of the republic. In the last years of Kokov's rule, when the president was sick with cancer and often absent from his post, the republic descended into a morass of problems and conflicts. The debts of the republic to the Federal budget reached 2.9 billion rubles, a sum larger than twice its annual budget. An equivalent amount of money was owed as back pay to government employees within the republic, with doctors, teachers, and officials missing pay for two or three months in a row as late as 2005, when the problem of government salaries was solved across the rest of Russia in 2003.

The massive debts of the republic's government to the energy companies led to limitations in everyday life for the general population, with heat, electricity, and water being disconnected on a regular basis. From 2003-2005 the government of the republic did not have a finance minister, since none of the local officials agreed to accept the prestigious post out of fear of being blamed for the ongoing monstrous theft of governmental funds. At the same time, the capital of Nalchik acquired new suburbs filled with luxurious mansions owned by government officials. Social discontent and inequality were reaching critical levels.

During the same period of time the security branches of the government came to play an increasingly prominent role, with the republic's ministry of internal affairs making especially noticeable gains in power and standing. The staff of the republic's police grew to levels unheard of in the region – 15,000 men. Policemen interfered in all aspects of social life and came to control both businesses and the criminal world. The relationship between the security services and the populace came to be that of mutual hatred, with the common people being financially dependent on the policemen. On September 18th, 2001 the republic's "Gazeta Yuga" newspaper published a list of 362 crimes committed by ministry of internal affairs staffers during that year. A large percentage of the crimes listed are particularly severe and include murders, rapes, armed robbery, extortion, and instances of going beyond the line of duty.

Khachim Shogenov, a general, minister of internal affairs of Kabardino-Balkaria from 1992 to 2006, an ethnic Kabardin, a powerful and rather sinister figure in the life of the republic. Paid an official salary of less than a thousand dollars a month, Shogenov is considered one of the republic's unofficial dollar millionaires. His family owns a hotel near Mt. Elbrus, a horse track in Nalchik, as well as a number of mansions in Nalchik and apartments in Moscow. All of this property was acquired during the General's tenure as head of the republic's police ministry. Shogenov himself lives in a mansion in Chegem, one of Nalchik's suburbs. The home stands on five hectares of land and includes its own lake, and has numerous servants, as well as a stable with a dozen purebred Arabian racing horses. ("Gazeta Yuga," 2/23/2006)

This feudal minister has introduced medieval working methods into his agency. It was Shogenov's leadership that first brought mass arrests,

358

torture, and deliberate humiliation to the republic. Secret lists of "wahhabites" were compiled, and came to include 422 residents of the republic. By the early 2000's the police became an evil feared more than any other by the populace.

In this environment of domination by the security services, a declaration made in Moscow in 2001 destroyed Valeri Kokov's multi-year efforts to maintain the image of a stable and peaceful republic for Kabardino-Balkaria. Vladimir Ustinov, then the Attorney General of the Russian Federation, declared that a plot aiming to overthrow the governments in Kabardino-Balkaria and Karachaevo-Cherkessia and create an Islamic state had been uncovered.

This declaration was made shortly before Vladimir Putin's trip to the republic in September 2001. According to the Attorney General, Chechen field commander Ruslan Gelaev's fighters were going to cross the Caucasus mountains into Karachaevo-Cherkessia and Kabardino-Balkaria from the Pankisi gorge in Georgia. Once there, they would be met by locals ready and armed for an uprising. These statements were roundly criticized in the Russian press as either unfounded or at least wildly exaggerated. Despite the criticism, many residents of the supposedly unstable republics were arrested, even though in the end only four went to court and were sentenced.

Two months after Ustinov's announcement, the Kabardino-Balkar ministry of internal affairs confirmed the existence of locals that were in contact with Chechen guerillas. Fuad Shurumov, head of the Kabardino-Balkar UPOB (Organized Crime Division), noted during a November 2001 briefing that there were locals waiting for Gelaev's group, but that "no specific persons or addresses were discovered."

Black Lists, Raids & Special Operations

Starting in 2002 reports of events in Kabardino-Balkaria start to remind one of the military activity in Chechnya, even though the republic was still officially considered peaceful. In 2001 alone, one district near Mt. Elbrus and the Georgian border saw six special operations, all of them pitting the security services against either individual fighters or groups of mujahadeen.

In March 2002 Valeri Kokov declared in a briefing at the ministry of internal affairs that lists have been made of those extremists that "want to scratch beautiful Kabardino-Balkaria. But we will never allow anyone to do so. Each of the 400 men in question is under constant observation and the security services are prepared to take any measures necessary, including physical destruction, towards these men."

In 2002-2003 the authorities undertook a massive counterstrike against the "religious extremists" in the republic. Mosques were closed, unfounded arrests made, and rumors of torture and humiliation during interrogations started to spread.

In 2003, in the town of Baksan, twenty kilometers west of Nalchik, spetsnaz troopers battled a group of unknown enemies concealed in a private home. The ministry of internal affairs reported that Shamil Basayev was in the house, but Basayev managed to escape unharmed from the town, accompanied by his wife and bodyguards, despite the fact that governmental forces surround the town and control the airspace overhead. One of the rank and file that participated in the operation anonymously revealed that with the fall of darkness all governmental forces were recalled by order of a high-ranking official from one of the security agencies.6

Soon afterward 170 members of the Kabardino-Balkar jammat were simultaneously detained, beaten, and humiliated. A group of the men had their beards shaven with broken glass, another had crosses shaved into their heads, some had vodka poured into their months. All of these violent humiliations were detailed in reports sent to all levels of the government – starting with the local prosecutor's office and going all the way up to the President of Russia. In the reports local Muslims asked for the policemen and FSB officers responsible for these offences

---

6 *Gazeta yuga*, August 29, 2003.

against their victims' religion to be punished. All of the reports were ignored.

In April 2004 the first mass abduction in the republic occurred in the southern town of Tyrnyauze. Nine locals disappeared from a bus that is later found abandoned on a curb and with obvious traces of gunfire. The missing are located two days later, tossed out of cars on the sides of roads across North Osetia and Stavropol province. According to the victims they were abducted by Russian security men, tortured with knives and needs, special electronic devices, and electroshock. The questioners wanted to find out of president Valeri Kokov was tied to the Chechen separatists or the local Islamists.

By this time military confrontations with groups of the mujahadeen became common occurence in the republic. In July 2003 a police patrol in Tyrnyauze was attacked and a policeman seriously wounded. At the same time UPOP releases information about the seizure of the books "Nizam mudzhakhida" (about methods of conducting jihad) and the textbook "Special agent training according to the GRU spetsnaz method" from members of the local jammats.

In October 2003 a police sergeant was killed in a shootout in one of Nalchik's suburbs. During the same month, eight mujahadeen were killed in the course of an operation in Elbrusski district. According to the ministry of internal affairs they were members of the "Yarmuk" group and consisted of locals that had once fought under the command of the Chechen Ruslan Gelaev. Muslim Ataev, a man from a local Balkar village, is named leader of the band.

In the summer of 2004 the authorities ordered all mosques in Nalchik and its suburbs simultaneously closed. Members of the jammat continued to gather together and pray in the streets in front of the closed mosques.

In August 2004 an eight hour battle took place near the summer house of minister Shogenov. Two policemen and two insurgents were killed, with the attack also being attributed to Ataev's group.

361

In September of the same year Rasul Tsakoev, a close friend of Ataev, is abducted by the security services from the Nalchik suburb of Khasania. Three days later Tsakoev is tossed out in a junkyard showing obvious signs of being tortured. Before his death the man relates that he was tortured and that his assailants demanded that he sign a confession detailing the way he provided Chechen militants with cellular phones and food. Tsakoev's death led to massive demonstrations in Nalchik, in the aftermath of which the prime-minister of the republic, the head of the ministry of internal affairs, and the chief prosecutor of the republic met with jammat leader Musa Mukozhev in the government building in Nalchik. During the meeting Mukozhev demanded an end to the repressions and a reopening of the mosques. The representatives of the government demanded that the jammat stop interfering in politics and join the official Muslim Spiritual Board. The first and only attempt to negotiate made by the authorities during the entire conflict ended in failure.

Soon after, at the end of September 2004, the "Kavkaz-center" website announces that "Everyone should be aware that, as of today, by the mercy of Allah, the Kabardino-Balkar military jammat "Yarmuk" has been formed. Divisions of "Yarmuk" are quartered across the republic and are working towards meeting those military goals set before them by the demands of jihad."

On December 14th, 2004 the abovementioned attack on the Narcotics Police occurred. The daring nature and meticulous planning of the whole operation led Russian authorities to declare that Kabardino-Balkaria was home to a serious resistance movement, with Muslim Ataev's group being the organizing force behind the recent raid.

A week after this attack minister Khachim Shogenov declared that a special division for counterterrorism will be formed within the republic's ministry of internal affairs and staffed with 300 officers. At the same time, the numbers of the elite SWAT-style SOBR and OMON units in the republic are doubled.

2005 brought with it the largest demonstrative security operation undertaken in any peaceful republic in the Northern Caucasus region. In January a massive "demonstrative-training" operation aimed at destroying Muslim Ataev, the leader of "Yarmuk," was held in the northern suburbs of Nalchik. An undertaking of this size, bringing together divisions of the ministry of internal affairs, the FSB, and the military is the first such operation to be held outside Chechnya, and is conducted within a residential part of the city. Armor (tanks, BMP and BTR armored transports), GRU spetsnaz, aviation, OMON and SOBR troopers, and a regiment of line army troops – a total of over 3,000 personnel – participate in an operation directed against four women, three men, and an eight year old baby. Preparations for the assault took two full days during which time the residents of three five-story, 100-aparment homes were left outside in minus twenty seven degrees Celsius (-27C) weather without warm clothes or food. The actual assault took six hours and concluded with the "destruction of seven members of "Yarmuk," along with their leader Muslim Ataev," as the situation was summarized at a press-conference by General Arkadi Edelev, head of the Antiterrorist Center of the Northern Caucasus. In reality three families were first blockaded in their apartments and then destroyed without being given a chance to surrender. One of them was the family of Muslim Ataev, and included his infant daughter, whose body was then later secretly removed from the apartment. The charge of child murder is denied by the authorities despite eyewitness accounts and the burial site of the girl is still unknown to her relatives.

Subsequently similar "training" operations run in a maximally realistic way, with the inclusion of real victims, were also conducted in other republics of the North Caucasus region.

The anti-Ataev operation raised new questions for the security apparatus – the weapons recovered from the apartment of the slain did not match those earlier stolen from the office of the Narcotics Police. This cast doubt on the investigators' sole theory that Ataev was responsible for the previous attack.

Concurrently with the growth of the police ministry's power in 2005, the repressions against Muslims became increasingly widespread. Two instances need to be especially mentioned, since during later interrogations all the participants of the October affair in Nalchik pointed to them as the events that pushed them onto the path of armed resistance.

First, in the spring of 2005, nine female students of Nalchik State University are arrested when they stayed in a lecture hall after the end of class in order to jointly read the Koran. The girls are detained for ten hours and are humiliated with interrogations and searches. The university leadership does not attempt to defend its students and even warns them that they will be expelled if they are ever arrested again, despite the fact that all of the girls are honor students. The Muslim Spiritual Board of the republic also does nothing to support the young women and Shafig Pshikhachev, the former head mufti of the republic, declares that "the whole incident with the girls may have never actually happened" in a statement to the "Portal Kredo" website.7

The second incident is the beating of pregnant Elena Gasieva, a resident of Nalchik, in the summer of 2005. The young woman left her house in order to buy bread, but was arrested by a police officer. Detained at his office, the woman was subjected to repeated blows to the kidneys and ordered to sign a blank piece of paper. Following the beating Gasieva had to be taken to the hospital where the doctors barely managed to save her child.

It's fairly clear why these two incidents were particularly infuriating to the "Young Muslims" of the republic. Across the entirety of the Caucasus, and especially in Kabardino-Balkaria, the worldview of the locals has been formed by centuries of traditions that see violence towards women as unforgivable. Throughout 2005 combat between the security services and the rebels became constant and regular. Both sides suffered dozens of casualties. Large weapons caches were discovered in Nalchik's suburbs, and in the town of Chegem two

---

7 Portal Kredo, August 19, 2005.

guerillas blew themselves up while trying to construct a bomb. A bomb-making laboratory was later discovered in the basement of their house.

In February 2005 two of Mukozhev's and Astemirov's deputies were abducted. After a week of searching, their relatives located them in the "Belyi Lebed" jail in Piatigorsk, showing signs of being tortured. Based on their interrogations the blame for the Narcotics Police raid was shifted the Anzor Astemirov and 13 other members of the jammat, with all of the men being declared wanted by the police.

The "Kavkaz-center" website published the latest declarations of the Kabardino-Balkar jammat. "Yarmuk" warned of upcoming military operations and requested that the civilian population avoid the offices of the security services in order to avoid becoming victims. Members of the security apparatus were advised to quit while they had the chance and thus save their lives.

The October 2005 Attack on Nalchik

On October 13th, 2005 small groups of guerillas simultaneously attacked 18 sites in Nalchik that belonged to the security, police, and intelligence services. Russian President Putin ordered the blockade of the city in order to prevent reinforcements from other republics from entering the area. At the same time all communications, including telephone and cellular communications, as well as radio signals were jammed. These measures disrupted the rebels' communications and seriously affected the outcome of the whole affair.

The events of the 13th and 14th were described with great detail by the press worldwide and even whole studies of those days are fairly common. It's worth remembering that as a result of the gun battles in the city 35 members of various security services, 12 civilians, and 37 insurgents were killed. Subsequently the number of dead insurgents more than doubled. Most of the attackers had no military experience and were insufficiently well armed. Less than 200 men participated in the attacks, 99% of whom were residents of the republic. The slain included one Osetian, four Balkars, one Ingush, and one Russian, with the rest being Kabardins. The socio-economic background of the attackers was more heterogeneous than their ethnic background, with doctors, lawyers, teachers, businessmen, and the sons of wealthy and respected families being found among the dead. The local jammats represented in the attack originated in various districts of the republic. Almost all members of the Zolskii jammat (from the town of Zalukokuazhe in western Kabardino-Balkaria, 10 km from Piatigorsk) were either killed or tortured to death, while the jammats of Nartan, Terek, Chegem, Shalushka, Kenzhe, Nalchik and Moscow suffered serious losses.

Observers noted that there were no wounded guerillas, with witnesses relating that even the lightly wounded were finished off since orders had been given to take no one alive. In accordance with the instructions of the Russian President the bodies of the slain were not removed from the streets until the morning of the 16th. Nalchik's residents spent several days in a state of shock and children recognized their own dead relatives and teachers in the streets. Later this barbaric treatment of the bodies of the slain was confirmed with photographs and video. The dead were never buried and their bodies were never returned to their relatives.

A period of the harshest repressions followed immediately after the 13th. Waves of mass arrests and raids rolled across Kabardino-Balkaria. There were rumors of people dying during interrogation and the creation of new black lists, with these now including even the names of children. Lists of ostensibly unreliable children were compiled by the schools and minors were questioned by the members of the security services in the offices of school directors, with parents being neither informed nor allowed to be present.[8]

The existence of new lists was confirmed by the new head of UBOP, Arsen Tishkov. During a July 2006 briefing in the ministry of internal affairs of the republic he noted that new lists of Islamic radicals have

---

[8]*http: www.regnum.ru* (Russian) March 2, 2006.

been compiled, this time including 5,000, rather than 422, residents of the republic. The jails of the republic currently hold 90 persons awaiting trial for the Nalchik affair, each of them having been charged with five criminal offenses including terrorism, attempted overthrow of the government, and participation in an illegal armed group.

The rebellion in Nalchik was defeated and the jammat bore irreparable loses, a fact made abundantly clear by the relative peacefulness of the republic over the last year and a half. On an ideological level, however, Russia suffered a crushing defeat comparable to the defeat in Beslan. Just as the loyal Osetians realized that their loyalty did not save their children from being murdered en masse, so did many Circassians realize that war had come to their homes and that regardless of how they saw Russia, Russia saw no reason to treat them with any real care.

One indicator of the times and of public opinion is observed rise in resignations of security personnel. Many such instances were linked to family pressure, since relatives often asked "Why hold down a job that can cost you your life?" But there were quite a few individuals who left the service in a deliberate refusal to serve a government that would force them to kill their ethnic brothers. The recent growth in Circassian separatism is an unequivocal result of the October 13th attacks.

What do we currently know about the Kabardino-Balkar jammat?

Official information and the declarations of the jammat's leaders are curiously similar in this case, no matter how atypical such similarity may be for a propaganda war.

"Intelligence shows that the surviving leaders and members of the criminal gangs have not given up on criminal activity and under the guise of "jihad" are currently preparing new terrorist acts directed against the civilian population," said minister Khachim Shogenov in January 2006. "There is evidence that they have ample financial resources. Well known international terrorists have claimed responsibility for the Nalchik attacks, but this is only one part of a well-financed attempt to destabilize the situation in the south of the Russian Federation and the country as a whole."

Soon after he made these statements, Shogenov was relieved of his duties as minister of internal affairs. This was seen as a major victory for Arsen Kanokov, the new, forty nine year old, president of the republic. While the two men never liked each other on a personal level, there was also a serious struggle over power between them. Having become well entrenched during the previous president's tenure, Shogenov saw himself as boss of the whole republic despite the appearance of the new president and even refused to attend governmental meetings when invited by Kanokov.

Shogenov's dismissal has made it easier for the new president to find solutions to the Balkar problem. The Balkars thought Shogenov a nationalist and a driving force behind many of the government raids conducted in their territory and have now become more open to dialogue. Kanokov finally had the chance to work with the Balkars using the "softer methods" that he has claimed to favor. The president also earned a "plus" in the eyes of the jammat, since he fired their worst enemy. On the other hand, Shogenov's dismissal has not changed the overall situation in the region – the confrontation between Russia's armed forces and the insurgents remains unaltered. .

During a March 2007 briefing in Rostov-on-the-Don the head of the Operational Headquarters in Chechnya and deputy Minister of Internal Affairs of the Russian Federation General-colonel (three star General) Arkadi Edelev confirmed this point by saying that "Chechnya is no longer the leading unstable factor in the Northern Caucasus. We are more concerned about Ingushetia, Dagestan, and Kabardino-Balkaria. There are two well prepared and deeply concealed terrorist groups active here – the Astemirov and Mukozhev gang and also Salpagarov's group (Salpagarov is one of the emirs of the Karachaevo-Cherkess jammat).

There is a good reason for mentioning Salpagarov in the same sentence as the leaders of the Kabardino-Balkar jammat. Sources in the

368

resistance camp indicate that the Kabardino-Balkar jammat has close ties with the Karachaevo-Cherkess jammat, as well as the "Kutaib-al-Houl" ("Brigades of might") jammat from North Osetia. It's possible that these connections deepened following the Nalchik incident, since there is information that when the Nalchik attacks were being planned the Kabardino-Balkar jammat attempted to contact the jammats in Karachaevo-Cherkessia and Adygeia in order to organize simultaneous attacks in all three republics, though this plan did not succeed.

Even before October 2005, however, the ties with Ingushetia were much closer. Ilyas Gorchkhanov, one of Shamil Basayev's close associates and a leader of the Ingush front, spent a long time hiding in Kabardino-Balkaria. Before coming into close association with the Kabardino-Balkar jammat Gorchkhanov was already wanted for being a part of Khattab's unit and later as an organizer of the attack on Nazran in the summer of 2004. Ilyas Gorchkhanov played an important role in planning the Nalchik attacks and participated in them personally. His unit was given one of the crucial targets – the local FSB office – and it was there that Gorchkhanov was killed during the ensuing firefight. It's possible that with Gorchkhanov's death the connection with the Ingush jammat has been lost, but no definite information on the subject is currently available.

Anzor Astemirov noted in his recent statements (available on www.kavkaz.center.com, www.camagat.com, and www.kabardeyonline.org) that the numbers of the jammat's members increase everyday. He has also said that all social groups within Kabardino-Balkaria, including government officials and security personnel, are helping the mujahadeen. According to the emir the jammat has currently chosen to fight a guerrilla war combined with precision strikes, especially those aimed at terminating especially odious members of Russia's governing and security organizations.

On September 23rd, 2006, almost a year after the Nalchik attacks, emir Mukozhev broke his long silence. "Kavkaz-center" has published Mukozhev's statement entitled "Having entered into jihad we have found true freedom." This particular statement is crucial for understanding the current state of the Kabardino-Balkar jammat. A number of fundamental points need to be noted:

1) An admission that the older tactic of a "peaceful coexistence between the government and the jammat was a mistake." "We couldn't ignore that the war in Chechnya, so near to us, is continuing and try to pretend that we have no connection to the mujahadeen there. When our jammat was formed we tried to find a "golden mean" and combine a call for peace with jihad. In reality this was not a golden mean, but an attempt to combine two contradictory things – peace and war."

2) The dissolution of the jammat and formation of Muslim communities into battle groups. "Today the Kabardino-Balkar jammat does not exist in the same form that it did previously. By decision of the shura (council) the emirs of all local jammats are freed from their duties and military commanders will be appointed in their place."

3) A call to armed resistance. "If today I meet a man who wonders whether he should go to mosque or to commit jihad, the first thing I tell him is – you must fight."

4) Mukozhev's statement also contains an admission of participating in the Chechen War. "The emirs of the Kabardino-Balkar jammat have long participated in the war against the kafirs (unbelievers), secured supplies for the mujahadeen, transported weapons, cared for the wounded, and directly participated in military operations."

The last point in interesting because this is Mukozhev's first admission regarding participation in the Chechen hostilities, whereas before only Astemirov was known to be a participant.

On the whole the statements made by Mukozhev and Astemirov allow certain conclusions to be drawn about the current state of the Kabardino-Balkar jammat. They can be summarized as follows:

1) A schism occurred in the jammat when the decision to begin military operations was taken. As a result, some of the organization's members stopped obeying their emirs.

2) Autonomous military units have been created in Kabardino-Balkaria, each with its own commander.

3) The commanders of these groups are still in contact with each other and important decisions are made by means of a council (shura).

4) These military jammats have ties to other resistance groups across the region and consider themselves to be part of the Caucasus Front.

5) The jammat receives support from different socio-economic groups, including individuals in the local government and security services.

Both Mukozhev and Astemirov are wanted by the Russian Federal government and international law enforcement agencies. Despite the large rewards offered for both men and the serious efforts made by the Russian security services since December 2004, neither man has been found. This fact confirms the broad-based support that the resistance movement has in Kabardino-Balkaria and the North Caucasus as a whole.

The Republic of Adygea: An Overview

Andrei Smirnov

The Geography and People of the Republic of Adygea

Territory and population

The autonomous republic of Adygea is situated in southern Russia on northern foothills of the Caucasus mountain range. The republic is encompassed by Krasnodar krai, a region in the North Caucasus populated largely with ethnic Russians.

The area of Adygea is 7,800 square km (3,000 miles). According to the 2005 Russian Census the population of the region is 444,000, 52.6% of which is considered urban. The population density is 58.5 people per square km.

Maykop and Adygeisk are the two main cities in the republic. Furthermore, there are seven municipal districts (Koshekhabl, Teuchezh, Maykop, Giaginsk, Krasnogvardeysk, Takhtamukay, Shovgenovsk), five townships, 43 rural settlements, and 225 villages (2006 data). Maykop, with a population of 190,000 is the capital of Adygea. The population of Adygeisk, a city built to facilitate the resettlement of some Adygea auls (villages) flooded during the construction of the Krasnodar water reservoir, is 13,000.[1]

Over 80 ethnic groups live in the republic, but three make up the vast majority of the population. Approximately 64.5% of the populace are ethnic Russians (283,000 according to 2002 data), 24.2% are Adygeis, and 3.4% are Armenians.[2]

---

[1] www.adygheya.ru, the official site of the Adygea republic
[2] Ibid.

The distribution of Russians and Adygeis in Adygea is as follows: Russians prevail in the central part of the region - in the capital Maykop and in the Maykop and Giaginsk districts. The Adygeis prevail in the west, east, and northeast of the republic. The Teuchezh and Shovgenovsk districts and the city of Adygeisk consist almost entirely of Adygeis (Regnum).

Adygea is divided into a northern plain located in the Kuban Lowland, foothills that extend from Maykop to Kamennomostsky, and a mountainous region located south of Kamennomostsky on the slopes of the Greater Caucasian range. The peaks of Shepsi, Oshten, Fisht, Chugush, and Pseashkho range from 2,000 to 3,238 meters (6,561 to 10,623 feet) and stretch from south to east in the mountainous part of Adygea.[3] Chugush Mountain is the highest point in the republic (3,238 m or 10,623 feet).

Migration

The Soviet government pursued the same policy in Adygea as in other regions populated with enthnic minorities. The government set up large industrial enterprises and brought ethnic Russians from other parts of the country to work there. Thus, the proportion of ethnic Russians was artificially increased in many republics which had been previously populated by other ethnic minorities.

This process also took place in Adygea, but there were some small differences. In addition to Russians coming in from outside the republic, the industrial area of Krasnodar krai was also included in Adygea. Thus, in 1936, Maykop, which then had practically no indigenous population became the capital of Adygea. In 1962, Maykop district, which was almost totally comprised of ethnic Russians, was included in the republic. Even today, non-Russians make up no more than 20% of the populace in this region of Adygea. This process radically changed the ethnic composition of the region. In 1922, when

---

[3] *Russian Civilization*, Internet magazine, www.rustrana.ru

Adygea was established as an autonomous oblast, The Adygeis were in the majority. Yet , less than 20 years later at the start of World War II, there were far more Russians than Adygeis. It should be noted, however, that this strong numerical predominance of the alien population, was compounded by the heavy emigration of Adygeis in the Northwest Caucasus in the 19th century due to a mass deportation following the end of the Caucasian Wars at that time.

The collapse of the USSR in 1991 created a second influx of people settling in Adygea as people from regions which were undergoing conflict both in Russia and in the former Soviet Union moved to the republic. These refugees came from Abkhazia, Azerbaijan, Armenia, and Chechnya. The migrants also included retired military servicemen and pensioners from Russian regions to the north. Under Russian law, retired inhabitants of the extreme northern territories of the country were entitled to a permit to live in any southern area of Russia. Adygea, and especially Maykop, have attracted and are continuing to attract Russian pensioners due to the availability of cheap housing. Moreover, the influx of a great number of retirees, particularly former Russian military officers, became a serious factor in the political life of Adygea.

The quickly increasing Armenian diaspora also deserves a special mention. Armenians began to inhabit the Black Sea area, including the present territory of Adygea, immediately after the 19th century deportation of the Adygei. At the same time, in the 1860s-1870s, the Russian government expelled Circassians (Adygeis) to Turkey. The settlement of Armenians in Adygea continued during Soviet times and was especially strong during the post-Soviet period. The Armenians now have a strong presence in Adygea and even prompted the authorities open a direct flight from Maykop to Yerevan (incidentally the only flight scheduled in the Maykop airport). Armenians are the third-largest ethnic group in Adygea and are actively settling throughout Adygea, including the mountainous region of Adygea which had previously been inhabited almost solely by the Adygeis.

An Adygei group arrived in Adygea from Kosovo in 1998. They were descendants of those who had left the Caucasus late in the 19th century and settled in the Ottoman Empire, which then included Kosovo. The

374

immigration of the Adygeis from Kosovo (a total of 156 families) was not quite a success; they encountered serious difficulties in the republic, including unemployment. After that no serious attempt was made by the Adygeis in other countries to return to their historical homeland. There are currently only about a thousand repatriates living in Adygea and their numbers are increasing quite modestly.

Those who now leave Adygea usually leave for Ukraine. In fact, the emigrants to Ukraine are 33% of the total number that have left the republic for the last 15 years. Indeed, Adygea is the only republic in the North Caucasus where the total loss of population exceeds the birth rate. As is the case with Russians, whose population growth is also stagnating, a large Adygei family is rare today.

Lines of Communication

On a map Adygea looks like an island inside Krasnodar Krai. The isolation of the region from the outside world can be felt in reality. It is not easy to get to the republic despite, by Russian standards, a good network of roads, railways and an airport. The only direct flight from the old airport in Maykop is to Yerevany. To reach the republic by air from Moscow or abroad, you need first to fly to Krasnodar, the capital of Krasnodar krai. Then you can go to Maykop from Krasnodar by bus or take a taxi. There is no direct rail line connecting Krasnodar to Maykop, the capital of Adygea. One needs to go by train first to the city of Belorechensk in Krasnodar krai, and then by car or a fixed-route taxi to Maykop 25 km (15.5 miles) from the Belorechensk railway station.

Adygea also has no direct access to the sea. The nearest seaport of Tuapse is located in Krasnodar krai on the Black Sea coast 150 km (93.2 miles) away from Maykop. The two main arteries of Krasnodar krai, the roads to the ports of Novorossiysk and Tuapse and to resorts on the Black Sea coast, cross Adygea, and as such play a part in the politics of modern Adygea.

The republic's administration repeatedly made attempts to open a world-class airport in Maykop to make transportation to the outside world accessible. The construction of a motorway from Maykop through the southern part of Adygea, Lagonaki Plateau, and the Greater Caucasus Range, to Sochi is also constantly discussed. The road is designed to enhance the tourist capabilities of Greater Sochi and Adygea as well as the whole Black Sea region by considerably increasing the number of skiers visiting the republic, as well as upgrading the infrastructure of Adygea to Sochi's level in Krasnodar krai, which is the most popular Russian resort on the Black Sea. However, the Adygea-Sochi road construction plan still only remains on paper, most likely for political reasons as much as economics. These political reasons will be explained in greater detail below.

Natural and Water Resources

Most of Adygea lies in the valley of the Kuban and Laba Rivers. The Kuban River is a major navigable river in the Caucasus. The republic also has many mountain rivers such as the Belaya, Laba, Pshish, Psekups, Kisha, Dakh, Sakhray, Khodz, Fars and many others. They originate in glaciers and the permanent layer of snow that is on top of the mountain peaks.

Wild fruit forests, chestnut and nut plants that grow in this region are very valuable. The wild fruit forests of Adygea are a unique natural phenomenon. They take up an area of over 15,000 hectares (36,000 acres). The presence of wild fruit trees and wood gardens is due to ancient Adygeis who cultivated wood gardens for hundreds of years. The wild fruit forests that we see now are only the remains of the famous "Circassian gardens" that fell into decay after the mass deportation of most Adygeis to Turkey at the end of the 19th century.

The water resources of the republic are widely used in farming. Adygea has built the Shapsug, Shendzhiy and Krasnodar water reservoirs, with the Krasnodar reservoir being the largest in the North Caucasus. It is 46 km (28.5 miles) long and 8 to 12 km (5 to 7.5 miles) wide, with an average depth of 7 m (23 feet). The construction of the reservoir in the early 1960s had serious environmental consequences and caused enormous economic damage to the republic. It is worth noting that the increasing economic use of rivers in Adygea and the creation of

376

reservoirs has led to the deterioration of the environmental situation, especially to the fish population. At the same time, the mountainous region is an area that has all prerequisites to become a popular health resort.

Mineral Resources

The Republic of Adygea has many mineral resources, including thermal and mineral underground water, building materials, gold, mercury, lead, and zinc. Oil and gas reserves are particularly important in this region.

Adygea has a great variety of minerals and sources of building materials, including brick and haydite clay, sand, gravel, and ornamental stone. Today there are seven known deposits of brick clay and loam (five of which are currently in use, while the remaining two are in reserve), five deposits of sand-gravel materials (only one is used), and two deposits of gypsum building plaster (one of them - Shuntukskoye - is operated by Russkie Samotsvety plant). The republic also has large reserves of rubble.

There are several deposits of mortar sand in the Teuchezh district, which can be used in the glass-making industry. Two deposits of high-quality limestone were recently discovered in Adygea. There are also promising deposits of natural facing materials, but they have not been properly explored yet. They include the unique Verkhnekurdzhipskoye deposit of decorative facing stones which is the only one of its kind in the North Caucasus. There are areas used for the production of fertilizers. The estimated reserves of phosphorites were estimated at 180,000 tons. Deposits of molybdenum, tungsten, barite, polymetals (lead, zinc, and copper), rare-earth metals, silver, and gold are quite common in the mountainous part of Adygea. However, the local Geological Service has not conducted a detailed assessment of these deposits.

Both the foothills and the plain of Adygea have oil and gas deposits. Oil reserves were estimated to be 171,000 tons as of January 1, 1992 (only 3,000 tons of which are produced each year). The Republic of Adygea

377

also has natural gas fields. The fields under development include the Maykop field (which is practically depleted), the Koshekhabelskoye field (which originally had 10.2 billion m³ or 360.2 billion cu. feet, of which only about eight percent has been harvested) and a part of the Nekrasovskoye gas condensate field. Exploration is underway in the Severo-Kuzhorskoye field (with an estimated 1.6 billion m3 or 56.6 billion cu. feet), prospects were discovered in the Vostochno-Kuzhorskoye field (2 billion m3 or 70.63 billion cu. feet) and Vostochno-Giaganskoye field (4.4 billion m3 or 158.4 billion cu. feet). Expected gas reserves in these field total 20 billion m3 (706.3 billion cu. feet). The Nekrasovskoye field is at the final development stage.

Land Resources

Adygea has significant areas of fertile soil that can yield good grain harvests, industrial crops, or vegetables. In addition, the soil is favorable for cultivating high-quality forests. But the construction of the Krasnodar water reservoir in the 1960's has led to a sharp deterioration of soil quality in the northeastern portion of the republic. The crops cultivated in the areas adjoining the water reservoir are barely suitable for food because of their toxicity.

The Economy of the Republic

The basic economic sector of Adygea is agriculture and related industries such as food processing, consumer goods, and wood working. The republic has also a number of machine-tool factories and small plants which produce building materials.

The republic, along with Chechnya and Azerbaijan, used to be a major supplier of petroleum for the whole Soviet Union prior to World War II. In 1940 up to 87% of Soviet oil was produced in the North Caucasus. Adygea has also yielded 70 billion cubic meters (2,472 billion cubic feet) of gas, 4 million tons (29 million barrels) of condensate, and over 100,000 tons (730,000 barrels) of oil for the last 50 years.[4] But the known oil and gas reserves in the fields that had supplies this energy have practically been depleted. According to Yugnedra, a government agency that surveys mineral reserves in the Southern Federal District, the older oil fields in Adygea are almost 99 percent depleted.[5] The decision to explore and begin new fields of production has been delayed. Consequently, Adygea has long been purchasing oil and gas from other regions in Russia, as well as coal from Ukraine.

Since the collapse of the Soviet Union in 1991, the economy of Adygea has remained in a sate of permanent crisis. The republic has completely failed to adapt to the global economic changes in post-Soviet Russia. The economic crisis was particularly acute in the 1990s. There was a permanent decline in production between 1991 and 2002 in all industries. Neither privatization of business in the republic nor creation of private farms brought about a breakthrough in the economy or any great improvement in living standards. The industrial recession continued in Adygea all through the 1990s and early 2000s. The collapse of the Soviet system of economic management broke off established economic ties between factories and reduced the supply of raw materials. Business became difficult because of the unsettled situation with the system of payments to each other by industrial and commercial enterprises. The slump was also caused by a drop in demand for products made in Adygea.

In the past two years, this general trend began to change. Since Khasret Sovmen was elected president of Adygea on January 13, 2002 and due to general improvement Russia's economy, some economic growth has become noticeable in the region but nevertheless no significant economic progress has been made.

Redivision of property began in Adygea between 2002 and 2004. This was due to the chaotic bankruptcy procedure which the result of poorly written laws. Control was particularly contentious over the machine-

---

[4] *Sovetskaya Adygea,* August 31, 2002
[5] *Yuzny Reporter,* September 6, 2005

tool, consumer goods, and textile sectors that represent the core of Adygea's industry. This included the Maykoppromsvyaz plant, the Zarem gearbox factory, the Maykop Distillary, a large cannery in Yablonovsky township, and the Giagin Sugar Mill. As in other regions of Russia, privatization schemes often involved artificial bankruptcy, which allowed businesses to be bought at low prices. The profits from these purchases were then concealed, hence allowing the buyer(s) to avoid paying taxes.

Two hundred and fifty businesses went bankrupt in the republic from 2002 through 2004. However, since that time, only 20 of them have become solvent again.[6] Early in 2004, the republic's parliament decided to appeal to Tatyana I. Trefilova, Director of the Federal Service for Insolvency and Financial Rehabilitation of Russia; and to Vladimir Yakovlev, Chairman of the Supreme Arbitration Tribunal of Russia, and V.V. Kuznetsov, Chairman of the Supreme Qualification Commission of Judges. The parliament asked if it might be possible to replace the management of their local bodies in Adygea. It is indicative that Adygea's President, Khasret Sovmen, participated in the session of the parliament as well as the appeal to the federal authorities. The indicated that the new president of Adygea had come into a sharp conflict with the clan of his predecessor, Aslan Djarimov. Sovmen counted on Moscow's support in his struggle with the local clan. After all, this hindered the Republic's economic development. At the same time, the local parliament deputies, who mostly belonged to Djarimov's clan, hoped that officials from Moscow would take their side and support their attempt to retain their property.

The property dispute stabilized somewhat later as tax collection rates increased, but many major factories of Adygea continue to have severe economic difficulties and have not been able to operate on a regular basis. This is exemplified by the Giagin Sugar Mill which has had to operate intermittently.

---

[6] *Severny kavkaz*, February 25, 2004

The true living standards of the populace of Adygea are not clear either. Officially, its living standards is one of the lowest in the Southern Federal District, but real incomes of enterprises and the growth in salaries and income of the population may differ from official statistics. For example, farmers in northwestern Adygea, which is crossed by the road from Krasnodar to the Black Sea, make a good portion of their living from roadside trade, which is not accounted for very well. And many inhabitants in these regions work in Krasnodar Krai where wages are much higher than in the republic.

In any case, industrial development, attracting investment (particularly in agriculture) and improving living standards are urgent needs for the republic. At the same time, the shadow economy is on the rise in Adygea. Its numbers are not included in official statistics and, of course, taxes are not collected from it. It is particularly rampant in commerce in the region, and even is widespread in major companies and state-owned enterprises. The concealment of profits leads in turn to concealment of real wages. At present 49 entities in Adygea officially have wages in arrears (mostly farms), but judging by the fact that there are no strikes or protest rallies in the region it can be concluded that wages are paid under the table after all. In January through August 2003, the then Prime Minister of Adygea, Gennady Mikichura, managed to suddenly transform the republic so that it declared the highest wage level in the Southern Federal District without applying any fiscal methods to the employers who concealed real wages of their employees. What leverage Mikichura used against company managers is not known but when he left the wage arrears and low wage levels began to creep in again. Currently, more than 2,000 employers in Adygea officially pay wages at a level below the cost of living.[7]

The current crisis in relations between Adygea and the Kremlin means that it is critical for the republican administration to legalize wages to demonstrate the economic robustness of the region. The trouble is that the current economic situation in Adygea is greatly affected by politics. The economic problems of Adygea gave the Russian authorities the

---

[7] *Regnum*, June 17, 2006

pretext to initiate the process of merging Adygea with Krasnodar krai, which has led to growing discontent among the Adygei. The official reason given for this is that having Adygea immersed in the better economic environment of the krai will bring about an economic recovery in Adygea too. To counter this proposal, Adygea's leaders offered their solution to the problem, which would keep Adygea independent from Krasnodar krai. Adygeis count on foreign investment from the Adygei Diaspora abroad. But this has encountered strong opposition from the Russian leadership. At the same time, subsidies from the federal government are very unstable and are often late.

Despite these problems private investors continue to come to the region. Many companies in Adygea are currently controlled by investment groups based in Moscow or St. Petersburg, with money from the Adygei diaspora still trickling in despite great obstacles. The percentage of repatriates in middle management in Adygea is not large (at most 10%) but will probably grow with time. Repatriate Adygeis already own the most popular restaurants and cafes in Maykop. Repatriates also own several private fixed-route minibuses in the capital and some small businesses like a bag factory in Maykop district.

Apart from the economic blockade by the Russian government, the development of Adygea's economy is hindered by problems characteristic of the Russian economy in general such as clans, corruption, and the inefficient administration of the government in Adygea. This is particularly true of the agricultural sector, where just like in many other Russian regions, there is an acute problem of embezzlement from the government budget.

Subjected to increasing pressure from the Kremlin, Adygea's leadership has made vigorous attempts recently to improve their management system and control over allocated funds.

Historical Background of Adygea
Emergence of the Adygei-Circassians in the Northern Caucasus: Pre-Russia

The name that the indigenous people of this region give to themselves is Adygeis. They are better known in the world as Circassians (from the Mongol word cherkesud). The present generation of Adygeis living in Russia is the remnant of a formerly large nation that used to live in a region of the North Caucasus that extended from the Black Sea into present-day Chechnya. In Russia today, the Adygeis live in three republics (Adygea, Kabardino-Balkariyya, and Karachai-Cherkessia) and in two districts of Krasnodar krai.

The Adygeis' ancestors are thought to be tribes of Meots, Sindys, Acheis, Zikhis, Kasoges, and Kerketys who had lived in the Northwest Caucasus and in the Black Sea coast of the Caucasus since the first millennium, BC.

The Adygeis were already considered a nation unto themselves in the 10th century. Their language belongs to the Northwest Caucasian (Abkhaz-Adygei) group of the Caucasian languages. For millennia, the Adygei have been in close contact with tribes of Asia Minor such as the Greeks, Cimmerians, Scythians, and Sarmatians. The Adygeis settled at that time mainly in the northwest foothills and plains of the lower reaches the Kuban River and in the eastern coast of the Black Sea from the mouth of the Don River to Abkhazia.

The Mongol invasion changed the map of the eastern and central North Caucasus. In 1238-1239, the Mongols seized the Ciscaucasian plains. The Golden Horde established its state here in the early 1240's, with its southern borders extending to the Crimea and foothills of the Caucasus. It was during this time that some Adygeis (Kabardians) migrated eastward to the Central Ciscaucasia (now Kabardino-Balkaria), which in turn led to the schism of the common Adygei language into the western Adyghei (Adygei) and eastern Adyghei (Kabardian) dialects that later became the basis for modern Adygei and Kabardian languages.

In the 17th century, some Adygeis separated from the Kabardians, migrated westward once again, and settled in the upper reaches of the Kuban River. This was the so-called "Besleney tribe" who live nowadays

383

in Karachai-Cherkessia. A second group migrated from Kabarda and joined them at the turn of the 19th century. As a result, the original Adygeis split into three distinct nationalities: the Adygeis, the Kabardians, and the Circassians. In the end, all of these Adygei groups had their own territory in addition to common language and spiritual and material culture.

In the 12th and 13th centuries, Adygei slaves were often exported to markets in the Middle East, particularly in Egypt where they were purchased by sultans to be security guards for the Mamluks. The influx of slaves enabled one of the Adygeis - Al-Malik as-Zakhir Barkuk al-Cercesi - to seize power in Egypt and to establish the Circassian dynasty of Mamluks that ruled Egypt and Syria from 1382 until 1517.

The Adygeis became Christians during the rule of the Byzantine Empire, but Christianity declined at the end of the 15th century immediately after Byzantium disappeared from the political map.

Islam began to penetrate Circassia (Adygea) after the conquest of Byzantium by the Ottomans and the establishment in the Crimea of the Crimean Tatar Khanate, which was a vassal to the Turkish (Ottoman) empire. The Turks and Crimean Tatars initially tried to conquer the Adygeis in an effort to impose Islam on them. But they changed tactics when they encountered strong military resistance from the Circassians. Ottoman missionaries and merchants were later sent to Circassia and as a result of their efforts Sunni Islam took root among the Adygeis starting in the late 16th century.

The acceptance of Islam by the Adygeis accelerated their gradual orientation towards Turkey. It was also accelerated by tighter economic relations, including marine trade between the Turks and Ubykhs, an Adygei tribe that lived along the Black Sea coast. Adygei historian Samir Khotko wrote in his History of Circassia that,

> "there were two reasons for the success of Islam in Circassia: first, the increasing imperial designs of Russia, which created resistance in Circassia; and

secondly, intense propaganda from the Ottoman Empire, which had evolved into a political, military, and economic partner of Circassia by the beginning of the 17th century after several major military failures there at the turn of the 16th century."[8]

In the 18th century, the Adygeis occupied the area from the mouth of Kuban River along the Black Sea coast to the Psou River and along the northern slope of the Caucasus Mountains up to Ossetia. As late as the first half of the 19th century they occupied territory stretching from the Black Sea Coast to the North Caucasus. As Imperial Russia began its southward advance, the Adygeis' territory dwindled to 180,000 km² (69,480 miles) by the 1830s.[9]

Adygeis and Russia: The Caucasian War in the 19th Century

The current political situation in Adygea cannot be understood without a thorough analysis of the history of relations between the Adygeis and Russia. When talking to Adygeis, it is evident that the Caucasian War, which ended 150 years ago, is still fresh in their collective memories.

The Adygeis' ancestors first encountered the Russians' ancestors in the 10th century. In 944, after the Khazar Khanate (a powerful state in the southern part of modern-day Russia) was defeated by Kiev's Prince Svyatoslav, the city of Tamatarkha became part of Russia and was re-christened Tmutarakan. The Tmutarakan Principality incorporated Eastern Crimea and the Taman Peninsula in what is now Krasnodar krai. The population of the principality included Slavs, Adygeis, Greeks, and Alanians among others. As soon as the nomad Kipchaks (Polovts), hostile to Russia, cut Tmutarakan off from Russia, the Slavs of the northeastern Caucasus eventually mixed with the Adygeis. After this, Russians and Adygeis had no further contact for another 600 years. This ended when Ivan the Terrible and the Kabardine prince

---

[8] Khotko, Samir, <u>History of Circassia</u>, St. Petersburg Press, 2001.
[9] Trakho, Ramazan, <u>The Circassians</u>, Munikh Press, 1953.

Temruk formed a strategic alliance against Turkey and the Crimean Khanate in 1557. This alliance was strengthened by the marriage between Ivan the Terrible and Temruk's daughter, a Circassian by the name of Goshevnai, (she was later christened and renamed Maria). From this point forward, there was constant contact between ethnic Russians and Adegeis, which has continued to this day.

The 18th century saw a new stage in Russian-Adygei relations. The former friends and allies became open enemies and armed opponents. This was due to Russian imperial policy in the North Caucasus. It took from the reign of Catherine the Great to the reign of Alexander II, almost a whole century, to completely subjugate the region. It was at this time that Russia forced many Adygei to emigrate to the Ottoman Empire.

The erection of a fortress in Mozdok in 1763 triggered direct warfare against the Adygeis. During the second half of the 19th century there were a lot of pitched battles between Adygeis and Russian troops. The Adygeis and yje Chechens, living in the eastern North Caucasus, attacked the Russian fortresses of Stavropol, Azov and others. In reponse, the Russian command reinforced these fortresses and built new fortifications along the Caucasus. The Western Adygeis relied upon protection from Turkey, which had several fortresses along the Black Sea coast, the strongest of which was the fortress at Anapa. However, Turkey's presence was not sufficient enough to alter the overall military balance in the region.

When war broke out between Russia and Turkey in 1787, the Kabardines (the eastern Adygeis) supported Turkey. In June 1790, the Turkish commander, Batal-Pasha, the governor of Anapa and Sundjuk (known as Novorossiysk today), crossed the Kuban River, but on September 28 he was defeated and taken prisoner, ending any chances for the Kabardines to ally with him.

It was at this time that the Adygeis, together with the Chechens, created a united Caucasian front. Al Mansur, a Chechen sheik, played an important role in this strategy from 1785-91. Under Mansur's leadership Islam spread across most of the North Caucasus. It was Mansur who came up with the idea to unite the nations of the North Caucasus and launch jihad against Russia. In addition to his military activities in Chechnya, Mansur also fought in 1788 in Maly Kabarda and defeated the Russians. During the Russo-Turkey war Mansur offered his assistance to the Pasha on Anapa.

Meanwhile Count Gudovitch, the commander of the whole Caucasus line, set his heart on capturing Anapa, which had become a political center in the struggle against Russia. Although the Pasha was willing to surrender Anapa, Mansur fought to continue the struggle. Nevertheless, the fortress was captured on May 1791 and Mansur was taken prisoner.

Turkey ended up losing the war, and a peace treaty was signed with Russia on December 29, 1791. After this, the situation in Kabarda, Western Circassia and the rest of the North Caucasus went tragically downhill. Russia continued to erect new and stronger fortifications along the line as more and more Cossacks settled in the region. Cossacks became a special caste of free men used by the Russian government to protect the borders of the country. The Western wing of the Caucasus Line was protected by Cossacks who settled on the Taman peninsula in 1792. It was at this time that they launched a campaign to conquer Western Adygea.

Gradually the circle around them Adygea began to shrink. New fortresses were erected along the Black Sea coast, while northwestern Circassia became increasingly isolated from the rest of the Caucasus.

In the early 19th century, when Georgia became a part of Russia, Prince Tsitsianov, the chief commander of the Caucasus front, launched an attack at Kabarda which resulted in gradual subjugation of the Kabardines to the Russian State. Meanwhile the Adygeis of the Black Sea continued to escalate their resistance.

As V. Gatsuk, a Ukranian student of the Caucasus has noted, "the resistance of the Circassians was as stubborn as that of the Dagestani resistance and inflicted a lot of casualties among the Russian invaders on the right flank of the Caucasus front."[10]

The casualty rate of the Russian army while fighting against the Adygeis was due in large part to the guerrilla methods used by the Circassians. In this respect it is interesting to quote the words of Edmund Spencer, a English traveler who visited the region at this time, who wrote in his <u>A Journey to Circassia</u>, The Adygeis,

> "are so crafty and cunning that it is hard to outwit them: no enemy will be able to predict their moves for they seem to appear from underground; now they are at one place, then at another, and they can creep in the grass like a snake and all of a sudden surprise a sentry standing at the fortress gate; in word, every tree, crig or bush can serve as a hiding place."[11]

The warfare that Russia led against the Western Circassia flared up anew in the 1830's as soon as Turkey recognized Russia's claim to that country, which was specifically recognized in The Russo-Turkey Peace Treaty, signed at Adrianopolis on September 14, 1829. From that point on, no foreign nations could dispute Russia's control of Circassia. According to that treaty, Turkey conceded Russia's claims to the northwestern Caucasus. The year 1830 saw the start of regular military operations in the Caucasus led by General Paskevitch. For the next eight years practically all of the Czar's army was directed against the Adygeis. Offensives were mounted both on land and sea. The Czar's troops marched across the whole forest belt as well as the mountains around Gelenjik and Anapa, leaving the ruins of burned villages and smoking forests behind them.[12]

Even after this, the Adygeis would not surrender and took every opportunity to strike back. In reponse to the pressure coming from

---

[10] Ibid.
[11] Spencer, Edmund, <u>A Journey to Circassia</u>, Adamant Media Corporation, 2001
[12] Trakho, Ramazan, <u>The Circassians</u>, Munikh Press, 1953.

Russia, the Adygean tribes attempted to unite. In 1830 they called a convention and declared a confederation the tribes for the purpose of uniting in their struggle aginst Russia. This act resulted in an escalation of aggression where neither side was willing to surrender. The Adygeis attacked Russian fortresses and destroyed Russian armies when they dared invade their homeland. Despite the huge losses, the Russian leadership would not give up. James Cameron who visited the Russian forts along the Black Sea shore wrote that, "the world has never witnessed a greater scale of human death."

Every attempt at negotiations between the Russian government and the Adygei tribal chiefs failed. The Adygeis demanded that the Russians withdraw while the generals demanded complete submission and recognition of the Russian emperor. The only concession that the Russian government was ready to grant was profitable trade relations between the Adygeis and Russian government. This policy was supported in the early 19th century during the reign of the Russian emperor Alexander I. Among the largest supporters of this policy was Rafael Skasi, a deputy of Richelie, the governor of Odessa. Afterwards, this policy was also supported by Tabou de Marini, a Frenchman who was serving the Russian emperor. Friendly relations with the Adygeis were also advocated by Tilubiakin, general-governor of Kutaisi, a town in Georgia, and Nikolai Raevski, the Commander-in-Chief of the Caucasus Line in the late 1820's.

Nevertheless, the position of generals Yermolov and Paskevitch finally won out. These generals believed that the Adygeis ought to be totally crushed and exterminated. The final stage of the conquest began after the end of the Crimean War in 1856. The Czar's troops moved methodically, step by step, up to the mountains, clearing the forests, burning Adygei villages and encouraging Cossacks to settle in their place. Maykop, the current capital Adygea, was founded as a bastile-town in 1857. It became the principal base of the Russian troops during their large-scale offensive into Adygean lands. On May 21, 1864, the Russians captured the gorge of Kbaada, the last stronghold of Adygei resistance. With this, the Caucasian War formally ended. Today this area is called Krasnaya Poliana (Red Glade); and is currently the summer residence of the Russian President.

The final Russian assault on the Adygeis, which began in the early 1860s, was accompanied by the large-scale destruction of their settlements and farms. People were taken under police escort to the Black Sea coast where the Adygeis were kept in special concentration camps and prepared for deportation to Turkey. Overcrowding and lack of medicine resulted in typhus, malaria, and other diseases. The mortality rate from these deportations was extremely high. The survivors were sent to Turkey where they formed a large Adygei diaspora. A total of one and a half million Adygeis were banished to Turkey. This deportation continued on a smaller scale until 1914.

No more than 10% of the original population of Adygea remained in the northwestern Caucasus at the turn of the 20th century. The remaining Adygeis, numbering between 100,000 and 150,000 were ordered by the Russian government to be moved from the mountains to the plain, which is now northern Adygea and a part of Krasnodar krai. Military administration remained in the Adygeis' auls (villages) until the late 1880's when they were allowed to have a modicum of civil administration, which was, of course, heavily controlled by Russian officials.

Formation of Adygei Autonomy During the Soviet Period

This was the status of the Adygeis when the Russian Empire collapsed in 1917. The Gorskaya (Mountain) Republic, headed by Tapa Chermoev, a Chechen, was proclaimed in the Northern Caucasus in the fall of 1917. Some Adygeis such as Kotsoev, for example, joined this government. The republic was short-lived as it was suppressed by both the Reds and the Whites, which were equally hostile to the idea of the Northern Caucasus' autonomy from Russia.

When the communists seized power in Russia, the Adygeis launched their own national movement aiming to create an autonomous region within the newly formed Soviet state. The Bolsheviks, who regarded the Cossacks at that time as one of the greatest threats to their power in

Russia, were willing to grant this autonomy to counterbalance them. The Adygei Autonomous Province, within the Krasnodar Krai, was proclaimed on July 27, 1922. Skhancheria Khakurate, an Adygei national leader who also headed the Adygei branch of the Soviet Communist Party was the first leader of this province.

During the early years of its existence there was no capital in Adygea and the government was located in the city of Krasnodar, the capital of the Krasnodar Krai. It should be noted that the Adygeis were an overwhelming majority in the republic at that time. Adygea included only the districts that contained Adygei villages, which meant there were no large towns that could be considered as the capital of the region. Furthermore, about a dozen settlements of the Shapsug, an Adygean tribe, had not been included into the Adygea Autonomous District but were incorporated into the Krasnodar Krai as the Shapsug National Area.

In the 1930's, when Soviet authorities started to slowly to return to the old Russification policy of the czars, it was decided to mix Adygeis with ethnic Russians. This order was given under the pretext of providing the region with its own capital. First Tuapse, a port in the Black Sea, was proposed as a possible capital, but this was rejected due to Russian concerns that it would grant the Adygeis access to the Black Sea. Finally, the town of Maykop, the former fortress and the main military base of the Russian army during the war with the Adygeis, was incorporated into Adygea and became its capital. The incorporation of a purely Russian city initiated a process that eventually resulted in the current domination of ethnic Russians over the indigenous Adygeis living in Adygea.

Declaration of Sovereignty and Contemporary Development of Statehood

While the percentage of the Russian-speaking population increased in Adygea, key governing positions in the region are still occupied by Adygeis. This enabled the leaders of the autonomous republic to demand direct financing of Adygea, thereby bypassing the Krasnodar administration. These attempts finally succeeded in the early 1980's. It was recorded in the law of the Russian Soviet Federal Socialist Republic "On Adygea Autonomous Oblast" which was adopted by the Supreme Soviet of the RSFSR on December 2, 1981.

The collapse of the Soviet Union in 1991 opened a new chapter in Adygei history. On June 28, 1991, Adygea proclaimed its sovereignty, and thus broke away from Krasnodar krai. On March 10, 1995, the Constitution of Adygea was approved, which said that Adygea was a sovereign republic within Russia.

Presidential elections were held in Adygea on December 22, 1991. Just like in many other Russian regions at that time, the elections were won by the local Communist Party boss, Aslan Djarimov.

As soon as he came to power, Djarimov took several steps to strengthen the sovereignty of Adygea. He ensured the Constitution was adopted and the law on repatriates was passed which allow the descendants of those deported at the end of the 19th century to return to the republic.

Current Political Situation in Adygea

Khasret Sovmen's Rise to Power and his First Years as Governor

In 2002, Khasret Sovmen, the wealthy owner of a gold mine in Siberia, and ethnic Adyg, succeeded Aslan Djarimov as President of Adygea. During the eleven years of his administration, Djarimov had allowed his clan to own practically the entire economy of the region. As Djarimov's clan came from Koshkhebel District, there was a joke in those days in Adygea, "We used to build socialism, and now we are building Koshkhebilism."

Sovmen, an ethnic Adyg-Shapsug (an Adygei tribe which is based in Krasnodar krai, not in Adygea proper) had no effective social contacts in the republic and no clan of his own to rely upon. The new president chose different administrative principles. He built up a team loyal to him but independent of family relations. Sovmen attempted to improve the economy of Adygea and he considered economic gain as the only way to guarantee the Republic's sovereignty. He encouraged the district administrators to concentrate on economic development. He used Murat Kudaev, head of Krasnogvardeysky region, who really had revived the economic life of his region, as a reference point.

To strengthen his position, Sovmen declared war on Djarimov's clan, whose representatives continued to control the parliament and basic industry in Adygea. The first two years of Sovmen's term was an incessant struggle with parliament, with the issue of property, and more to the point, who should control the regional economy, being considered the most important. As a result, Sovmen dissolved parliament in May 2005. The president of Adygea decided to get rid of Djarimov's influence once and for all. As a pretext, he used the lawless actions of parliament during budget approval process in 2002 and the fact that parliament ignored the finding of the Constitutional Court that demanded that this process should be reviewed.

Nevertheless, it was parliament, and not the president who was supported by Moscow. First, the republic's procuracy, being submissive to the central bodies in Moscow, protested against Sovmen's order to dissolve parliament. The procuracy announced that, "this order is contrary to federal laws and is to be rescinded."[13] Afterwards, Dmitry Kozak, the Russian president's envoy to the Southern Federal District, visited Adygea to meet with Sovmen. Kozak proposed a compromise: parliament would pass some of the laws which Sovmen supported in exchange for its voluntary dissolution in the summer. Thus new parliamentary elections would be held on time, in March 2006, and not earlier as the Adygei leader wanted.

Under different circumstances, the Kremlin might have taken the side of the president, but in 2005 Moscow had already regarded Sovmen as a serious obstacle in its plan to incorporate Adygea into Krasnodar krai and was not interested at all in making the Adygei leader stronger. Also, the Russian authorities did not want Sovmen's supporters to obtain a majority in the parliament; they needed time to prepare and to

---

[13] *Politkom*, May 15, 2005

consolidate Sovmen's opposition. Moscow decided to get rid of him to clear the way towards the unification of Adygea and Krasnodar krai.

The First Attempt to Eliminate Adygeis' Autonomy

The relationship between Adygea and Krasnodar krai has not always been friendly since the declaration of Adygei sovereignty in 1991. The authorities of Krasnodar krai could not accept the idea that they had to coexist with an independent Adygea.

Almost immediately after declaration of Adygei sovereignty, the new republic faced a strong standoff with the authorities of the Krasnodar Krai. Some sections of the two main roads that run from the Krasnodar Krai to the Black Sea coast, with its ports and tourist areas, which represent the core of the regional economy, cross Adygei territory. Hence, the question of ownership of the highways resulted in the first serious conflict between Adygea and the Krasnodar Krai. The Adygei government wanted a share of the profits that the roads generated for Krasnodar, which enraged the Krasnodar authorities. However, the conflict did not last long due to good relations between Nikolai Kondratenko, then the governor of the Krasnodar Krai, and Aslan Djarimov. The Adygeis received the right to sell goods along the road, but all official profits would go back to Krasnodar. Many in Adygea believe that this friendly relationship could be explained by the weakness of the Krasnodar government at that period of time since it had little or no support from Moscow.

Ironically, in the 1990's Russian authorities were fully on the side of Adygea. On May 21, 1994, Boris Yeltsin marked the 130th anniversary of the end of the Caucasian War in a statement which declared that, "the struggle of mountain people for their freedom was just." The regional policy of the Russian government at that time was based on the principle of equal relationship between the regions and the center. Feeling strong pressure from Communists and nationalists, Yeltsin needed the support of such ethnic republics like Adygea.

In contrast, the Russian authorities under Vladimir Putin went back to the traditional Russian principle of the center talking to the regions from a position of strength. In 2001, Vladimir Putin issued a decree repealing all regional laws that contradicted federal legislation. A total of about 90 laws, clauses, and sections of the Adygei constitution were repealed. The most important of these was the one that forbade Adygea from conducting a referendum on its status. It was the Russian Procuracy's demand to cancel this law that started a campaign to change the status of Adygea so as to unite it with Krasnodar Krai.

On January 21 2004, Prikhlenko, the republican prosecutor, made an official protest to the Adygei parliament and demanded the cancellation of the Law on Referendum adopted on January 6, 1999. In the letter to the parliament, the prosecutor informed the deputies that federal law did not allow for elections on such issues as "changes in the Adygei constitution and territory" while Russian law did not allow it to carry out a referendum on the integrity of the Russian Federation. The removal of the Law on Referendum made a legislative base for further steps to eliminate Adygeia's autonomy.

In 2004, the Kremlin sped up the process to subdue the regional leaders. In autumn 2004, the law on "New Election Procedure concerning Executive Heads in Regions" was adopted by the State Duma. At the same time, a policy of enlargement of the Russian regions was initiated. Some ethnic regions in Siberia and the Urals were eliminated by incorporating them into bigger regions. Those governors who resisted this policy, like Vladimir Loginov, the governor of Korakiya, were forced to resign. Today the Kremlin regards Adygea as another perfect candidate for removal of its status as an autonomous republic, and wants to eliminate the republic altogether.

However, there is another reason for the Russian authorities to promote this. This is due to the fact that three millions Adygeis live in 50 different countries around the world. Many of them would like to return to Adygea or at least visit it from time to time. Many even have their own businesses in the republic. The Russian authorities as well as the authorities of Krasnodar krai are not happy with the possible return of millions of Adygeis to the land from which their ancestors were deported. From the early days of their sovereignty, the Adygei government has been encouraging Circassian descendants to return to their homeland. In fact, local authorities in Adygea have created a special holiday, Day of the Repatriate, to celebrate this. The Adygei authorities have always welcomed any step to strengthen the economic and cultural ties between the region and the Circassian diaspora. The diaspora is also involved in the political process inside Adygea. The diaspora can influence Adygei policy through public organizations such as Adyge Khase, the Circassian Congress, and others.

It is clear that if Adygea disappeared, there would be no so-called Circassian problem. If there were no Adygea, the Cossacks who live in the Krasnodar krai could get rid of the psychological discomfort now live with. The existence of Adygea reminds them that it is the Adygeis and not the Cossacks who are the original residents Krasnodar krai. It is such a painful problem for the Krasnodar authorities that the Adygeis-Shapsugs who inhabit two districts of the krai are not even mentioned as one of the aboriginal ethnic groups of the Krasnodar krai in the official list. Last year there was a proposal of the Immigration Department of the krai to deport all the Shapsugs (10,000 persons) to the United States. Such discussions reveal a hidden fear of the Krasnodar residents that one day the Adygeis who live outside of Russia may come back and demand their right to Krasnodar territory.

Thus, both Moscow and Krasnodar have reasons to eliminate Adygei autonomy. The only thing needed is to work out a strategy to suppress Adygei resistance to the merger.

On December 29, 2004, Alexander Tkachov, governor of the Krasnodar Krai, said at a press conference that it would be economically feasible to unify Adygea and Krasnodar Krai. This was the first move against the autonomy.

This statement immediately aroused strong protests from the Circassian Congress and Adyge Khase, civic organizations with deep roots in Adygea. Circassian Congress Chairman Murat Berzegov declared that his group was going to appeal to the large Adygei communities in Turkey, Jordan, and the Middle East to help block any proposed unification. The Adygean authorities in turn backed these activities. Khasret Sovmen, for example, declared that abolishing Adygea would be "a political mistake" which would lead to further destabilization in the Caucasus.

This strong response silenced unification advocates for a while. However, on April 1, 2005, Murat Akhedjakh, Krasnodar Krai's Vice-Governor for Domestic Policy, who is Adygei himself, said that the polls conducted by a "Social Research Center" indicated that up to 80% of Adygean residents favored unification with Krasnodar, including 50% of Adygeis and 90% of Russians. His statement fanned the flames of the dispute. Then on April 19, *Izvestiya Yug* published an interview with Anatoly Odeychuk, a federal inspector for Krasnodar Krai and Adygea. Odeychuk previously had been an inspector for Krasnodar Krai until that previous January, when Adygea was added to his jurisdiction. Some observers regarded this move as the first step towards a possible forced unification. In the interview Odeychuk not only supported the idea of a merger, but he sharply criticized the situation in the republic. Odeychuk called Adygea, "an ethnic republic where only force, cruelty, and strong authority are respected."[14] In addition, Alexander Veshnyakov, chairman of the Russian Central Election Committee, said accidentally that he also heard of consultations on the Adygea-Krasnodar issue despite the fact that no such consultations had ever taken place.

Facing such a massive onslaught, Adygea struck back. The government of the republic appealed to Dmitry Kozak, Putin's envoy, asking him to withdraw Odeychuk. Adyge Khase and the Circassian Congress also issued a statement demanding that the federal inspector resign. The Adygei diasporas backed their demands. Kuban Khatukai, leader of the diaspora in the Netherlands, sent a letter to the president of Adygea expressing his support for the sovereignty of the republic. Abrek Chich, spokesman for the President of Adygea, warned of escalated

---

[14] *Izvestiya-Yug*, April 19, 2005

unrest in the region. "The situation is getting more and more complicated every day. There are meetings and protest actions. There are young people riding around Maikop in cars waving Adygei flags." Chich also disavowed Vesnyakov's statement about ongoing unification consultations between Adygei authorities and Krasnodar officials. At the same time, various independent sources were conducting their own surveys to find what people in Adygea really thought of the proposed merger. According to the poll organized by the *Caucasus Times* in Maykop, 39% said that they would vote against the unification; 22% supported this idea; 21% were "likely to support it"; and 12% were "likely not to." The sum of the negative responses in this survey indicated that 51% of the residents of the Adygei capital opposed the merger. This result contradicted the numbers cited by Akhedjakh.

The stiff resistance from the Adygeis forced both Krasnodar and federal authorities to back down. On April 21, Svetlana Zhuravleva, a spokesperson for the Krasnodar governor, declared that, "No concrete steps have been taken by the administration of Krasnodar Krai towards developing the idea of unification."

Thus the direct attempt to unify Adygea and the Krasnodar Krai failed due to the firm resistance of the Adegeis. The Kremlin had to pull back; the Krasnodar governor stopped talking about possible unification, and some time later Odeychuk was dismissed from his post. However, the struggle continued, as Moscow turned from open statements to secret consultations. The idea was to persuade the Adygei governing elite, especially Khasret Sovmen, to agree with the elimination of autonomy.

The Circassian Congress, Adyge Khase, and the Union of Slavs

The unification problem made the Circassian Congress, an organization that nobody had heard of before, a very influential body in the Adygei community. The quickly rising strength and popularity of the Congress became possible because of the full support received from the republican authorities who were interested in its activity. Together with another organization, Adyge Khase, the Congress mobilized the Adygei diaspora during the December 2004-January 2005 crisis.

398

In 2005, the Circassian Congress became the main organization that openly struggled against the attempts to merge Adygea with the Krai. The Circassian Congress was found by a group of Adygei intellectuals and former Adygei volunteers who had taken part in the war in Abkhazia in 1992-93 on the Abkhaz side. Since the foundation, Murat Berzegov, an Adygei painter, and Almir Abregov, Director of the Adygei National Museum, have been the main leaders of the Congress.

The Circassian Congress did not stop its attempt to defend Adygei once the winter 2005 crisis passed. Moreover, the leaders of the Congress started to look for ways to guarantee that that status of the republic would not change. On July 1, 2005, the Circassian Congress appealed to the Russian State Duma with a request to officially recognize the genocide of the Adygeis in the 19th century. The idea was that the recognition of the genocide would give the Adygeis official status as an oppressed nation which would make the elimination of their autonomy a much more difficult task.

The Duma failed to respond. Following the raid in the city of Nalchik, the capital of Kabardino-Balkaria, the Circassian Congress decided to appeal to the Russian president with the same request. In October 2005, in a letter addressed to Vladimir Putin, Murat Berzegov, Chairman of the Congress, openly threatened (or warned) the Russian leader with war in Adygea if the genocide was not recognized or if the Kremlin tried to fulfill the merger.

> "The most active part of the Adygeis – the young people, both in Russia and abroad, might reconsider their attitude to the Russian policy in the North Caucasus, and the events in Nalchik indicated this. We regard this raid as an act of despair and a protest on the p[art of the youth in the region because of their inability to realize their promise in economic or political sphere."[15]

---

[15] From a letter sent to President Putin from Murat Berzegov currently owned by the author.

Murat Berzegov's letter also protested against attempts to adopt the new Law on Referendum in Adygea that could result in the liquidation of the republic. "With 24% of the aboriginals [Adygeis] the result of this referendum could be easily predicted," Berzegov concluded.

The Russian authorities finally responded to this request in March 2006. On March 17, 2006, Berzegov received a letter from the State Duma which said the genocide of the Adygeis could not be recognized since this nation was not mentioned as an oppressed one in the "Law to Rehabilitate the Oppressed Nations" adopted by the Russian parliament in 1991 which only concerned those nations which had been deported to Siberia and Central Asia under Stalin.

The Circassian Congress was ready for such an answer. This time they appealed with a similar request to the international community at large, and specifically to the Council of Europe, to recognize the genocide and to protect their status. Thereupon Murat Berzegov told this author that if Russia did not recognize their rights they would appeal to the European Union and the United States for support.

Today the Circassian Congress continues to use this strategy but tries to avoid being too involved in Adygea's domestic politics. The Congress supports Khasret Sovmen in his standoff with the Kremlin, but only because they regard the Adygei president as a consistent defender of the Adygea's sovereignty. Sovmen needs the Congress because, unlike any other official body of Adygea, the Congress appeals to the international community not to mention the Adygei diaspora.

Adyge Khase is a close ally of the Circassian Congress, but this organization, or at least its leadership, is more closely associated with the Adygei authorities. Unlike the Congress, Adyge Khase has a well-developed network in Adygei villages, as well as in the diaspora.

After Tkachev's statement in December 2004, Adyge Khase organized a Committee to Defend the Adygei Constitution and in May 2006 the organization together with the Circassian Congress held an Assembly of the Adygei People in Maykop. The Assembly adopted a resolution that declared that the Adyegis would boycott a referendum on the status of Adygea.

Nevertheless, Adyge Khase is not as consistent and united in the struggle for the Adyegi sovereignty as the Circassian Congress. The issue of the 450th anniversary of the voluntary unification of Adygea revealed differences between the organizations on how to deal with the Russian authorities. While the Adygeysk town branch of the Adyge Khase strongly condemned the idea of celebrating this, "voluntary unification," Askhad Chirg, Chairman of the Executive Committee of Adyge Khase, declared that, "the anniversary should be celebrated."[16]

Despite some differences, both Adyge Khase and the Circassian Congress are close allies in defending Adygei sovereignty and they have the same opponent, the Union of Slavs. The Union of Slavs of Adygea was established in 1991 as an organization to protect the rights of the Russian-speaking segment of the population. The two principal leaders of this movement, Nina Konovalova and Vladimir Karataev, were deputies in the first Adygei parliament. Konovalova ran for Adygea's presidecy in 2002 and received 10% of the votes.

The chief aim of the Union of Slavs is to reunite Adygea with Krasnodar Krai since the Adygei government, as the organization claims, ignores the interests of the local Russians who constitute the majority in the region. In the 1990's, the Union had already some support among the local Russians, but this was not enough to obtain significant results. The situation started to change after Vladimir Putin became president and Alexander Tkachev became governor of Krasnodar Krai. With this development the Union of Slavs launched an aggressive campaign against Adygei authorities.

The most dedicated supporters of the organization have always been those who have no deep roots in the region, do not know its history and do not understand the reason why Adygea should exist. These are largely pensioners who have moved to the republic from the North,

---

[16] *Regnum*, August 8, 2006

retired military, and some Russian radical youth groups. In 2005, on the eve of the upcoming parliamentary election, the Union and its leaders launched a large-scale propaganda campaign directed towards the Russian population of the region. The rhetoric of the Union leader was very aggressive as the group stressed the idea that all problems of the Russians in Adygea would be solved if the autonomous republic were incorporated into Krasnodar Krai. Nina Konovalova's speeches were meant to inspire anti-Adygei feelings among the Russian voters. For example, in one of her speeches she declared that, "the Adygeis teach us, govern us, care for us in hospitals, try us in court and bury us. If only they did all this successfully, we would not have such sad mortality rate."[17]

The Union of Slavs mobilized and became as well-organized as the Adygei community. In fall 2005, Konovalova and Karatev wrote a letter to Moscow to their possible ally Gennady Raikov, Chairman of the right wing Narodnya Partiya with a request to finance their election campaign. The letter from the Slav Union leaders said that, "aggravating the social and interethnic tensions in the republic with the help of our propaganda and agitation will dramatically increase the number of citizens who are discontented with the acting regime."[18]

Raikov, Chairman of the People's Party and a deputy to the State Duma, proposed that the Union should unite its forces with the Adygei branch of the Party of Manufacturers and Entrepreneurs who also support the idea of the unification. Nikolai Pivovarov, the Mayor of Maykop, as well the Adygei branch of the Communist Party are two other allies of the Union.

During the last parliamentary election that was held on March 2006, candidates who were associated with the Union of Slavs were included into the Party of Manufacturers and Entrepreneurs candidates list. Despite some progress, Natalya Konovalova was the only leader of the movement who was elected to the Adygei parliament. All in all, the

---

[17] From a shorthand report of Nina Konovalova's speech given to the author.
[18] From a copy of a semi-classified document owned by the author.

supporters of unification and the Party of Manufacturers and Entrepreneurs received, together with the Communist Party (who also argue for unification), only 33% of the seats in the parliament. It was not enough to adopt a new Law on Referendum that would allow holding a plebiscite on the republic's status. Still, the tactics of the PME and the Slav Union include navigating this bill through parliament and promoting a referendum that will almost surely bring them a success.

There are many supporters of unification in Adygea, but they are not as active as the Adygeis who have strong organizations like the Circassian Congress and Adyge Khase. The Slav Union and other political forces of Adygea who stand for the unification with the Krasnodar krai expect support from the Russian authorities to achieve their goal and most likely will soon get it. In this case the Slav Union will get a chance to play a special role in the Kremlin's plans.

The Second Attempt to Unify Adygea and Krasnodar Krai.

By the end of the spring of 2005, Russian officials practically stopped publicly mentioning the possibility of unification. Meanwhile, in Adygea discussions continued on this issue. In 2005, the Circassian Congress asked the Council of Europe, "to immediately intercede in the situation in Adygea to help preserve its sovereignty." They also appealed to the State Duma with a request to recognize the genocide of the Adygeis. On January 2006, some Adygei activists organized a protest, where protesters picketed in front of government buildings in Maykop in order to preserve and strengthen the status of Adygea as an independent entity in the Russian Federation.

This event made it clear to the Kremlin that something needed be done to calm the Adygeis, otherwise the issue would come up in the international arena and complicate Moscow's plan to unify the region with Krasnodar. In early March 2006, Alexander Tkachev paid a surprise visit to Adygea to meet with Sovmen. The leaders of two regions held a press conference where they discussed the possible unification of the two regions. The possible unification was deemed baseless at that time. However, this declaration did not stop the

403

Circassian Congress from appealing to the international community. That March, immediately after receiving a negative response from the Russian parliament, the Congress sent a letter requesting the Council of Europe to recognize the genocide. Murat Berzegov told the *Kommersant* newspaper that real guarantees were needed, not just empty declarations like the one Tkachev made in Maikop.[19]

After the meeting in Maykop between Tkachev and Sovmen, some sources from Tkachev's entourage told the Russian newspaper *Kommersant* that it was too early to say that Tkachev had completely rejected the idea of the region's dissolution. The same source said that, while talking with Sovmen in private, Tkachev did not exclude the possibility of unification. By this time the Kremlin had changed tactics. Instead of declarations, Kozak and Tkachev were having private discussions with Sovmen to persuade him to give up the republic's autonomy. On the same day of Tkachev's visit to Adygea, Dmitry Kozak said that the question of unification was a domestic issue of the two regions and it should be decided by referendum, which in practice meant a merger through referendum.[20]

The only problem was that despite the presence of many deputies supporting unification, the new Adygei parliament did not hurry to adopt a new law concerning this referendum. The Adygei branch of the United Russia party achieved a majority in the legislature and Sovmen continued to control the party. It became clear that the Law on Referendum would not be adopted until the Adygei leader sanctioned it.

In April, Putin's envoy to the North Caucasus, Dmitry Kozak became increasingly aggressive and started to call Sovmen regularly in an attempt to force him to resign. Finally, on April 4, the Adygei president issued a demarche announcing his resignation during the second session of parliament. In his speech Sovmen said that, "Moscow does not understand me. Even if I step down from the presidency, I will

---

[19] *Kommersant*, March 3, 2006
[20] *Kommersant*, March 3, 2006

provide the republic with economic and social help." Sovmen wished the parliament good luck and recommended several possible successors, including Adam Zhane, Minister of Health, and Murad Kudaev, the head of Adygea's Krasnogvardeisk district.

It should be noted that initially Ruslan Khadzhibiekov, the new Chairman of the parliament and a member of United Russia, refused to allow the Adygei leader to speak. Sovmen the handed the speaker a written statement. Instead of reading it aloud, Khadzhibiekov said that the statement would first be reviewed by the Political Council of United Russia. Khadzhibiekov, who is now one of the two main candidates to become the next Adygei president, was loyal to the Kremlin. Nevertheless, Sovmen's dramatic move was a bluff. This declaration inspired mass rallies in support of the Adygei president.

On April 11, Sovmen was invited to the Kremlin to meet with Kozak and Sergei Sobyanin, the head of Putin's administration.[21] Putin's formal meeting with the Adygei president on April 17, during which he asked Sovmen to remain in power, was the result of this meeting between Sovmen, Kozak, and Sobyanin.

Sovmen had demonstrated his popularity to the Kremlin, and the Russian authorities had to retreat again. Most likely Moscow decided against taking any radical steps for fear not of angering the Adygei president so much as angering the Circassian Congress. During protest rallies in Maykop the leaders of the Circassian Congress predicted a, "second Nalchik," in the republic if Sovmen was forced to resign and the region was forcibly united with Krasnodar Krai. Given Russia's loss of control throughout much of the North Caucasus, the Kremlin understood that it needed to exert more caution in dealing with Adygea.

Nevertheless, it became clear to the Kremlin that a replacement for Sovmen should be found as quickly as possible. On April 17 Putin also met with Ruslan Khadzhibekov who had tried to prevent Sovmen from

---

[21] *Kommersant*, April 17, 2006

delivering his resignation to the local legislature. The Russian authorities had already regarded Khadzhibekov as a person who, unlike Sovmen, could be easily manipulated from the center and who would not oppose any shift in Kremlin policy toward the region. Furthermore, the Russian authorities needed Khadzhbiekov to adopt the Law on Referendum, but it soon became clear that even Khadzhibiekov's assistance would not be enough while Sovmen remained president of the region.

Dmitry Kozak made attempts to begin negotiations with Adygei civic organizations to discuss Sovmen's possible successor which also failed. Everybody, even many Russian organizations, refused to discuss possible successors while the president was still in power. For example, Svetlana Doroshenko, a leader of Otchizna party, said that consultations on Sovmen's successor would destabilize the republic, and Nurbiy Gutchetl, a leader of Adyge Khase, said, "It is improper to discuss who will be the next president when the current president is still alive."[22]

Finally there was nothing left for Kozak to do but to declare that Sovmen would remain in office until the end of his term next February. However, Kozak warned that, "We will support all his positive steps, but if there are any destructive actions, we will stop him," adding that, "there are no grounds for a 'second Nalchik,'" in Adygea."[23] By making this assertion Kozak made sure that people understood that he would not let Adygea use the threat of possible military resistance to protect Adygea's sovereignty.

Although they failed to topple Sovmen, Russian authorities decided to weaken his position in the republic through economic pressure by creating a blockade around the republic which would provoke mass protests of Russians who live in Adygea and to make Sovmen more compliant. According to Regnum news agency, Adygea did not receive any of the 400 million rubles (approximately $15 million) that Moscow

---

[22] *Kavkazki Uzel*, April 28, 2006.
[23] *Interfax*, April 20, 2006

was supposed to invest into the republic's agriculture this year as part of the National Projects program.[24]

In addition to funding problems, Adygei factories such as the Maikop Beer Brewery or Giagin Sugar Mill have found it hard to sell their products outside of Adygea to Krasnodar Krai. At the same time, all attempts of the Circassian (Adygei) Diaspora to invest in Adygea face firm resistance from the Russian authorities. On May 30, 2006, border guards in the Krasnodar airport stopped and sent back to Turkey a famous Turkish businessman of Adygei origin, Muzaffar Avdzhi (Dzyiba). He wanted to visit Adygea to discuss the possibility of future investments in the local economy.[25] It should be noted that this was not the first time the Russian authorities blocked the attempts of the Adygei government to attract investments from the Circassian diaspora. In March 2005, Asfar Khagur, the then-prime minister of Adygea, visited Turkey where, along with the Turkish prime minister, he met with local businessmen of Adygei origin, including the owners of such companies like Elisman, Ulker, and Uki. The Adygei prime minister and the businessmen agreed that entrepreneurs would come to Maykop next year to discuss possible investment projects, but all discussions stopped immediately when the Adygei prime minister informed Kozak about this.[26]

The Kremlin believes that hurting Adygea's economy will help to weaken Sovmen's influence in the region. It will also help to intensify the process of unification with Krasnodar Krai since economic bankruptcy is a favorite excuse given by the Russian authorities for the unification of elimination of other regions. Moreover, the Kremlin is not at all interested in investments from Adygeis who live abroad, especially in the Middle East.

Thus the Kremlin is attempting to weaken Sovmen and his popularity among the Adygeis by provoking protests among the local Russian

---

[24] *Regnum*, July 15, 2006
[25] *Regnum*, June 1, 2006
[26] *Regnum*, July 27, 2006

populace. They are attempting to do this by weakening the regional economy, hence making it easier to get rid of Sovmen, who is an obstacle to the Kremlin's plans to incorporate Adygea into Krasnodar Krai.

Due to these economic problems, Sovmen found himself in a difficult position and tried to find a way to reconcile his differences with the Kremlin. Some people from the republican government managed to contact Murat Khapsirokov, an Adygei who is an aide to Igor Sechin, a deputy head of the Russian Presidential Administration, and asked for monetary assistance for celebrations in 2007 for the 450th anniversary of the voluntary unification of Adygea, Karachaevo-Cherkessia, and Kabardino-Balkaria with Russia. In Soviet times the marriage between Kabardinian Prince Timruk 's daughter and the Russian Czar Ivan the Terrible in 1557 was celebrated as the official date of voluntarily unification of the Adygeis with Russia.

Sovmen had evidently decided to use the upcoming anniversary to demonstrate his loyalty to the federal government. Yet Adygei society was enraged when the plans for this celebration became public. The Executive Committee of the Adygeysk town branch of the Adyge Khase, an organization that is quite influential in Adygea, issued a special statement stating that,

> "To hold such a celebration would mean justifying the actions of the Russian Empire in Circassia in the 19th century. It would look [as though] that Adygeis did not defend their freedom during the Russian-Caucasian war that, but were 'separatists' who revolted against legitimate authorities. This celebration would mean that there was no war of free Circassiania against the aggressor, but would be [redefined as] 'a counterterrorist operation.'"[27]

---

[27] *Regnum*, August 8, 2006

The Circassian Congress supported this statement. Murat Berzegov, Chairman of the Circassian Congress, told Kavkazky Uzel, "Our position is clear on this issue; one should not celebrate a date in history that does not exist."

On September 9, Vladimir Putin signed three decrees to commemorate the anniversary in Adygea, Karachaevo-Cherkessia, and Kabardino-Balkaria. It is evident that he approved of the idea, but it is unlikely that this would help Sovmen to remain in power. Furthermore, celebration of such a provocative anniversary could actually only weaken Sovmen's position due to the strong opposition to this idea in Adygei society.

It seems that Sovemen's attempts to appease the Kremlin and obtain some financing from the center were made too late to influence Moscow's decision to choose a new leader that could be better controlled by them.

According to the new Russian law "New Election Procedure Concerning Executive Heads in Regions" discussions on a new regional leader should be started three months before the old governor's term has expired. Since Sovmen's term is set to expire in February 2007, Dmitry Kozak announced that he would visit Adygea in November 2006 to discuss possible future candidates. However, the Kremlin was so impatient about eliminating Sovmen, that Kozak came a month earlier to make the process move faster. On October 2, Dmitry Kozak began his trip to Adygea. However, ten days before arriving, Sovmen suffered a major setback to his succession plans which seriously marred discussions about his hand-picked successor.

Understanding that he had little chance to stay in power, Khasret Sovmen had already made plans to select his future successor. But this plan failed when the person he had selected was suddenly murdered. On September 25, the head of Krasnogvardeisk district, Murat Kudaev, whom Sovmen named his successor during the April standoff, was assassinated on his way home by a group of people dressed in police uniforms. When Kudaev came up to Adamy, his native village in

Krasnogvardeisk district, a fake police patrol pulled him over to check his identification papers. A uniformed assassin examined Kudaev's driver's license and then pumped two bullets into Kudaev's chest and a third into his head.

Kudaev was the principal protégé of Khasret Sovmen and the leading candidate to succeed him. Moreover, Kudaev was very popular within the republic; under its leadership Krasnogvardeisk district became one of the most developed and prosperous areas of the republic. The Adygei president had always held up Kudaev as an example of a good manager. Both Sovmen and the local parliament could support Kudaev. The parties and organizations that advocated the unification with the Krasnodar Krai could not object to Kudaev either because of his established reputation as a successful manager.

Undoubtedly, both the leaders of civic organizations and parliamentary deputies, especially members of the Adygei branch of the pro-Kremlin United Russia party, whose members are still loyal to Sovmen, would have nominated Kudaev as the new Adygei president if he had not been killed. However, neither the Kremlin nor Kozak would dare trust a popular candidate nominated by the maverick Sovmen, because it would violate the vertical power principles of Putin and Kozak. A quick survey of the new North Caucasus leaders appointed by Putin this year reveals a string of weak, unpopular puppets totally controlled by Moscow, such as Mukhu Aliev in Dagestan, Murat Zyazikov in Ingushetia, or Arsen Kanokov in Kabardino-Balkaria.

Despite the prevailing opinion in Adygea, Kozak's entourage is unlikely to discover any political motives in Kudaev's case. A source in Kozak's administration told *Kommersant*, "According to preliminary data there is no political background to the District Chief's assassination." The same source also told *Kommersant*, "We will not accept any candidate nominated by Sovmen." On October 2, Kozak visited Maykop to discuss the possible candidates to replace Sovmen. On the eve of his visit, supporters of unification initiated a popular campaign against Sovmen. On September 15, Nina Konovalova declared that the Union of Slavs had already collected 20,000 signatures to support the new Law

410

on Referendum. Grigory Senin, the head of the Adygei branch of the Communist Party called for Sovmen's resignation. He blamed Sovmen for all economic troubles of the region.

According to sources in the republic, most civic leaders support another term for Sovmen, but these demands are likely to be ignored by Moscow. Russian media sources report that among the seven candidates mentioned at the meeting, Aslan Tkhakushinov, president of the Adygei Institute of Technology, and Ruslan Khadzhibiekov, who was proposed by United Russia were the only genuine contenders. It is still unclear which of these two candidates will be chosen by Putin. On one hand, the Kremlin has been courting Khadzhibiekov for a long time, but on the other hand, it needs a president who would navigate the Law on Referendum through the local parliament. However, Tkhakushinov would not oppose the unification thanks in part to his close ties with Krasnodar business circles. Moreover, it appears that the main criterion for the Kremlin to appoint either Khadzhibiekov or Tkhakushinov, will be which one is more ready to promote unification without any resistance.

Despite some weak protests from the Circassian Congress and Adyge Khase, these organizations have almost completely capitulated to Kozak. Most probably, the leaders of these organizations just do not know what to do when even Sovmen himself is not strong enough to resist. Following Kozak's visit, the Adygei president gave an interview to the republican TV and said the Adygei population was on his side.

Military Resistance in Adygea: Reality or Simply a Threat

Today the principal question is whether the threat of another Nalchik in Adygea is real or not. It is common knowledge that the rebels who assaulted the law enforcement offices in Nalchik were mostly Kabardinians (Circassians), and were dedicated Muslims. It was religious persecution that made them take up arms. When considering the risk of armed resistance in Adygea, the Muslim factor should come first. It is no secret that despite a plethora of reasons for being a member of antiauthority and anti-Russian military groups in the North

Caucasus (excluding Chechnya), it is dedicated Muslims who are usually at the forefront of this phenomenon.

The Adygeis living in Adygea are also largely Muslim, but Muslim traditions there are not as strong as in Kabardino-Balkaria or Karachaevo-Circassia. The Western Adygeis (those who had always inhabited the Black Sea coast) converted to Islam mostly as a method of resistance against the imperial policy of Russia of conquering the northwestern Caucasus. During Soviet times, Islam was nearly forgotten by Adygeis but with Adygea's sovereignty being proclaimed in 1991, some people began to return to their beliefs. Ironically, Djarimov, the first president of Adygea, and an ex-communist leader, encouraged re-Islamizing. His wife headed the Adygei section of the world Muslim charity organization "Islam Invitation" and Djarimov himself ordered a Collegiate Mosque built in the center of Maykop. Djarimov probably saw Islam something that would help to create a new identity in the sovereign republic.

As long as nothing threatens the sovereignty of Adygea, the majority of Muslims in the republic are unlikely to become heavily politicized. Furthermore, their numbers are constantly growing, albeit not very rapidly. On the one hand, many Adygeis have left to study at religious institutions in the Middle East; meanwhile refugees and immigrants began to arrive from other North Caucasus regions with deeper Islamic traditions such as Chechnya and Dagestan. Currently Adygea is estimated to have a total of around 20,000 practicing Muslims, although no more than a thousand regularly go to the mosques which can be found in the two major cities, as well as in every mountainous valley in Adygei (40 in all). The imam of the Maykop mosque, Anzor Djeukozhev, told the author that, at most, 300 believers gather in the main mosque to attend Friday prayers.

It should be noted, however, that many Muslims are afraid to visit mosques in order to avoid being noticed by law enforcement agencies. This is especially true with repatriated Adygeis and newcomers from other regions of the Caucasus.

412

The situation for the Muslim community in Adygea turned sharply worse after the Nalchik attack in October 2005. Spot-checks by police in mosques, detentions and beatings of believers, and police interrogations have become more frequent. Some repatriate imams were even deported. All these excesses have not yet radicalized the local Adygei Muslim community, but this can change if Adygea is forced to become part of Krasnodar Krai. Even now many Muslims are united in jamaats (Muslim communities) closed to strangers because their members are afraid of persecution and prosecution by law enforcement agencies. It is likely that the pressure imposed on the Muslims in Krasnodar Krai will be similar to the problems the Adygei Muslims will face if their autonomy suddenly disappears. This could then lead to the emergence of an armed underground movement in the republic.

Nevertheless, Islam may not be the only driving force of resistance. Many more Adygeis would rise up in arms to protect their sovereignty. The true reason for the centuries-old resistance of the Adygeis to Russian expansion was their love for freedom, not the struggle with infidels. History could very well repeat itself in Adygea because for many Adygeis the Caucasian war never really ended. The fact that they at least had some modicum of sovereignty always seemed to soothe tensions with Moscow. But if they lose their autonomy, there will be no barriers to preventing them from renewing their resistance once again. What complicates this for Moscow is the fact that the general situation in the Northern Caucasus also fuels this hunger for freedom. Support from Chechen and other Caucasian separatists means that Adygeis are quite capable of one-day transforming Adygea into yet another front of the Caucasian War. The Adygei resistance will have an Islamic shell but it will be nationalistic at its core.

Conclusion

With the retirement of Khasret Sovmen now set for February 2007, his departure from the scene will mark the end of federalism in Russia as he is the last independent regional politician in the country. When Sovmen leaves, the Russian Federation will finally become an empire once again where there will be no place for a peaceful political

413

opposition. This only leaves the option of armed opposition. Sovmen's departure will prompt the Kremlin to appoint some new protégé to be the head of Adygea. One can only suspect what impact this will have on the Adyge Khase and the Circassian Congress as they will interpret this as the imposition of Putin's vertical power. They will no longer have the support provided to them by Sovmen and they will remain alone against a repressive machine controlled from Moscow, which will try to knock them down as soon as possible.

The Kremlin will try to intimidate the Adygei population and in every possible way attempt to stoke the anti-Adygei mood of the Russian-speaking population in order to finally achieve its treasured goal – to destroy the republic by dissolving it into Krasnodar krai. When this happens, it will be the Russian authorities who will bear the weight of responsibility for any war that may break out in the Northwest Caucasus.

A Survey of Political Trends in the Northwest Caucasus: Krasnodar, Adygeia, and Stavropol

Matthew A. Light, J.D., Ph.D.

Introduction: The Other Caucasus

Russia's Northwest Caucasus is often overshadowed by the more colorful, multiethnic, and troubled republics that border it to the east. Unlike the Northeast Caucasus, the three provinces that comprise the Northwest—Krasnodarskii Krai, the Republic of Adygeia, and Stavropolskii Krai—have by and large escaped major political violence in the post-Soviet period.[1] While the Northeast Caucasus republic have non-Russian majorities and have experienced a major decline in their ethnic-Rssian population, the people of the Northwest Caucasus (with the partial exception of Adygeia), are predominantly ethnically Russian (or at least Slavic) in origin. Indeed, in the 1990s, the three provinces served as a haven for ethnic Russians from other parts of the Caucasus.[2] Perhaps for these reasons, the Northwest Caucasus generally has not received the extensive Western media coverage devoted to Chechnya, Dagestan, or the other Northeast Caucasus republics. Nonetheless, the Northwest Caucasus is of major importance to the Russian Federation. It contains two of the country's leading resort areas (the Black Sea littoral in Krasnodar and the Caucasian Mineral Waters spa towns in Stavropol), as well as Russia's major remaining Black Sea port (Novorossisk). The Northwest Caucasus also possesses strategic

---

[1] The three regions will henceforth be referred to by the simplest English versions of their names: Krasnodar, Stavropol, and Adygeia. Whenever it is necessary to disambiguate the capital cities of Krasnodar and Stavropol from their regions, the terms "Krasnodar City" and "Stavropol City" will be used.

[2] See Mayrbek Vachagaev, "The Continuing Exodus of Ethnic Russians from the Caucasus," *Chechnya Weekly*, Volume 8, Issue 30 (July 26, 2007).

significance for Russia as a relatively calm and loyal outpost in a turbulent frontier region.

This survey reviews recent political developments and trends in the Northwest Caucasus region and analyzes how the area fits into the political plans of President Vladimir Putin and his administration. As will be argued, the Northwest Caucasus now seems to be assuming greater importance for the Kremlin than at any time in the recent past. President Vladimir Putin and his envoy in the North Caucasus, Dmitrii Kozak, have been moving to integrate the region's political life into their plans for a more centralized federation. In particular, Putin appears to be according greater power and privileges to the governor of Krasnodar, Aleksandr Tkachev, than to the chief executives of the other two provinces. The next section provides a brief overview of the Northwest Caucasus region and its three provinces. Then, in the following three sections, the major political issues in each province will be assessed in turn. Finally, a brief conclusion summarizes the results of the survey and argues that the Northwest Caucasus may be entering a period both of greater salience on the national political scene, and also possibly of greater instability.

A Brief Sketch of the Northwest Caucasus

The three provinces in this survey share a similar history. All were incorporated relatively late into the Russian state, from the 18th to the 19th centuries, as a result of years of war between the forces of the Russian Empire, often assisted by Cossacks, and indigenous peoples, notably the Circassians (see below, footnote 6). The conquest included a component of ethnic cleansing and massacre of the indigenous inhabitants, which has resulted in a population that is predominantly ethnically Russian. Today, the populations of Stavropol and Krasnodar are each around 85 percent ethnically Russian, and even Adygeia has an ethnically Russian majority. More recently, during the post-Soviet period, Russian observers have noted the gradual appearance of a political bifurcation within the provinces of the North Caucasus. In the western provinces, the Russian state's authority is regarded as relatively intact, albeit threatened. The eastern, ethnic republics, in contrast, have "de facto fallen out of Russia's sovereignty," as a result of the ramifications of the conflict in Chechnya (Sukhov 2005).[3] Stavropol occupies an ambiguous position in this dichotomy. It is the easternmost of the western, "Russian" provinces, and borders not only Chechnya but other ethnic republics as well. Stavropol has been described by a prominent local academic as Russia's strategic linchpin in the North Caucasus. This is usually taken to mean that Stavropol is the ethnically Russian region that is most threatened by the violent ethnic conflict in its immediate proximity.[4] Thus, to one degree or another, all three provinces can be viewed as an outpost of Russia in the Caucasus.

The region's exposure to the troubles of the Caucasus is also evident in post-Soviet population movements. Both Stavropol and Krasnodar were major destinations for so-called "forced migrants," that is, internal refugees (predominantly ethnic Russians, but also including many other ethnic groups, notably Armenians) who left other regions of the Caucasus (in particular Chechnya) or other former Soviet republics for broadly political reasons during the 1990s and early 2000s. According to different estimates, Stavropol holds between 200,000 to 700,000 such persons, out of a total population of 2.7 million. Many "forced migrants" continue to experience extreme material hardship years after their resettlement, and migrant organizations often express dissatisfaction with what they perceive as official indifference to their plight.[5] This influx of forced migrants has also meant that ordinary residents of Stavropol and Krasnodar are much more acutely aware of the fate of ethnic Russians in the Northeast Caucasus than are most people in other parts of Russia.

---

[3] Ivan Sukhov. 2005. "North Caucasian Map of Threats." *Russia in Global Affairs* 3 (4):150-59.

[4] V.S. Belozerov. 1997. "Regional'nye faktory migratsii i etnicheskaia struktura migratsionnogo potoka na Severnom Kavkaze." In *Problemy rasseleniia: istoriia i sovremennost'*, edited by S. Artobolevskii, et al. Moscow: Instititut geografiii Rossiiskoi Akademii nauk.

[5] Svetlana Biryukova. "NGOs of Stavropol Territory: authorities ignore migrants' problems," *Caucasian Knot*, April 28, 2007.

417

Despite their commonalities, there are significant differences between the regions. Krasnodar is the largest and richest, with a population of over 5 million and a booming economy. Stavropol, with a population of around 2.7 million, is somewhat less prosperous, and has also suffered more from its proximity to Chechnya. (There were several terrorist incidents in the province during the 1990s.) Finally, tiny Adgyeia, with approximately 450,000 inhabitants (around one third of whom live in the capital, Maikop), stands out from the other two regions in a number of respects. It is an enclave of Krasnodar, which entirely surrounds it, and to which, until 1991, it belonged. In the post-Soviet period, Adygeia received the status of "republic," which was supposed to offer substantial autonomy to the indigenous Adyg ethnic group, although the latter actually represent a small minority (between 20 and 25 percent) of the total population.[6] Adygeia is also the most economically depressed of the three provinces. Its unemployment rate has been unofficially estimated at around 50 percent.[7]

Certain commonalities can also be detected in the provinces' political life. In the 1990s, both Stavropol and Krasnodar were considered to belong to the so-called "Red Belt" of strong support for the Communist Party of the Russian Federation (KPRF). Here is a quick review of the political leadership of each province, as of 2006.

Krasnodar's first post-Soviet governor was the Communist Nikolai Kondratenko, who was known as a major regional opponent of President Boris Yeltsin and also as Russia's leading anti-Semitic politician. In 2000, possibly under pressure from the new Russian President, Vladimir Putin, Kondratenko announced that he would not be seeking reelection. Instead, Kondratenko backed the candidacy of his close associate, Aleksandr Tkachev, likewise a Communist. Despite Putin's lack of enthusiasm for Tkachev,[8] he was duly elected, and then

---

[6] The Adygs are closely related to other ethnic groups of the North Caucasus, the Cherkess and the Kabardin; the name "Circassian" is often applied in common to all three groups.

[7] Paul Abelsky, "Adygeya Seeks to Maintain its Identity," *Russia Profile*, August 1, 2007.

[8] "Kremlin is Main Loser in Regional Election Marathon," *Jamestown Foundation Monitor*, December 5, 2000.

reelected in 2004, on both occasions winning by a huge margin. Most recently, following the transition to appointed regional governorships, he received Putin's nomination to serve a third term and was confirmed by the Krasnodar legislature in April 2007.[9] Tkachev initially continued his predecessor's tradition of chauvinist populism, shifting the focus of official hostility from Jews to other minority ethnic groups, primarily those with a large immigrant component, such as the Armenians and the small Meskhetian Turkish community. Eventually, Tkachev's abuse of the Armenians led to President Putin's intervention on their behalf, and the mistreatment of the Meskhetian Turks led to their mass departure to the United States as refugees beginning in 2004. While Tkachev attempted to depict his conflict with these minority ethnic groups as emanating from popular sentiment among the Russian population, in fact it appears to have been a deliberate and strategic campaign undertaken by Tkachev for political purposes.[10] Since the Meskhetian Turks' exodus, Tkachev appears to have been somewhat chastened and has mostly abandoned his political use of the ethnic theme,[11] although many of Krasnodar's abusive migration practices persist. He has also mended fences with the Kremlin, and indeed now belongs to the United Russia Party.

Alexander Chernogorov is the governor of Stavropol. As candidate for the KPRF, he defeated his predecessor Petr Marchenko in 2006, and has held office continuously since then. Chernogorov is a weaker and less popular figure than Kondratenko and Tkachev. He has avoided their populist excesses and has maintained more correct relations with the Kremlin, eventually leaving the Communists for United Russia.

Adygeia's chief executive holds the formal title of "President" because of Adygeia's republic status. The first President of Adygeia was Aslan Dzharimov, who was defeated by Khazret Sovmen in 2002. Sovmen had spent most of his career outside Adygeia and was better known as a

---

[9] RFE/RL Newsline, April 24, 2007.

[10] The present author has described these events in greater detail in his doctoral dissertation, *Regional Migration Policies in Post-Soviet Russia*, Department of Political Science, Yale University, 2006.

[11] Abelsky, *supra*, note 7.

mining magnate than as a politician. He was elected partially on the strength of hopes that he could revitalize Adygeia's flagging economy. Adygeia is also notable for the activities of competing ethnic organizations: the Slavic Union, which has advocated the republic's merger with its neighbor, Krasnodar; and the Adygeia branch of the Cherkess Congress, a nationalist organization promoting the autonomy of Adygs (Circassians).

With this brief background completed, we now turn to a survey of recent political developments in the three provinces.

Krasnodar: From a Kremlin Headache to a Kremlin Ally?

Three major related developments have dominated the news from Krasnodar in 2007: the planned Sochi Winter Olympics of 2014, the province's ongoing economic boom and the planned improvements in its infrastructure; and the rise to national political prominence of Governor Tkachev.

The undoubted sensation of the year for Krasnodar has been the International Olympic Committee's decision, announced in July, to award the 2014 Winter Games to Sochi. Sochi's candidacy was considered something of a long shot, and its narrow victory over the South Korean ski resort of Pyeongchang has been attributed in large part to the President's personal commitment to the Olympic project, which included a personal appearance at the IOC deliberations in Guatemala City. As visitors to Sochi can attest, despite the region's natural beauty, its physical infrastructure and tourism facilities are not yet up to international standards.[12] To secure the Olympics for Sochi, Putin promised the IOC to invest $12 billion in infrastructure improvements for the region. The announcement of Sochi's win has been treated in the media as a significant boost to Russia's international

---

[12] A recent investigative report by a Russian newspaper found major problems with the disposal of waste, the road network, and rail connections. "Gateway to the Future," *gazeta.ru*, August 17, 2007.

image, and of course to Putin's own standing.[13]   Although the Sochi Olympics will not take place until after Putin is scheduled to leave the Presidency, the President is said to see the success of the games as the crowning glory of his two terms in office.[14]

However, despite the understandable pleasure many Russians take in the country's first Olympiad since the 1980 Summer Games in Moscow, the euphoria surrounding "Sochi 2014" has not kept observers, including Russian ones, from asking certain pointed questions about the Sochi Games.   Who will benefit from them, and what effects will they have for ordinary residents of Krasnodar?

The Sochi Games are to be planned and organized by a newly created corporation under mixed public and private ownership.   This entity's official budget is given as $12 billion, of which the state is committed to providing $8 billion, with private investors (including both Russian and foreign sources) invited to contribute the balance.   However, some observers already expect total outlays for the Sochi Olympics to reach $30 billion.   With such huge sums at stake, chairmanship of this new state corporation was immediately viewed as a plum appointment that would be given to a close ally of Putin.   True form, the President eventually named former Transneft CEO Semyon Vainshtok, a major architect of Putin's energy policy.[15]   There are also concerns that the funds allocated for Olympic construction may not all be used for their intended purpose.   The newspaper gazeta.ru quotes an unidentified source as saying that tensions with the IOC have already emerged, and that Russia has been warned that it could lose the right to hold the 2014 winter games if it fails to fulfill its promises of infrastructure improvements.[16]

---

[13] Pavel K. Baev, "Russia Wins Olympic Bid, Now Must Realize Ambitious Plans,"
Jamestown Foundation, *Eurasia Daily Monitor*, July 9, 2007.
[14] "Gorod-preemnik," *gazeta.ru*, August 8, 2007.
[15] Business-Ukraine, "Russian Pipeline Tsar Departs for Sochi Olympics," September 24,
2007, available at http://www.businessukraine.com.ua/russian-pipeline-tsar-departs.
[16]Ekaterina Mereminskaia and Oksana Novozhenina, "Goskapitalicheskie igry," *gazeta.ru*,
August 16, 2007.

There is also the question of how construction in Sochi is being carried out. The IOC's decision accelerated a process that was already underway before the announcement of the Sochi games, namely, a transformation of the ownership structure of hotels and other tourist sites on the Black Sea littoral. Even before the announcement, and even more so after it, smaller private owners are being edged (or forced) out of the tourism business, and being displaced by much larger corporate structures, often with political connections. In an article under the heading "Demolition for the Olympiad," The Russian internet news source gazeta.ru suggests that the city government of Sochi is engaged in the selective demolition of buildings (such as privately owned hotels), ostensibly for building code violations, but in fact to make way for more powerful investors.[17] Ordinary people are unlikely to benefit from the boom: Sochi rents are skyrocketing, having risen by 30 percent just in the week following the IOC announcement.[18] While public works and real estate market skullduggery are hardly unique to Russia, what is gradually emerging from the post-IOC news coverage is that in contemporary Russia, it will be difficult to carry out a major infrastructure project in a transparent manner and to the satisfaction of international (as opposed to Russian) stakeholders. It remains to be seen whether the 2014 Olympics will be remembered as a triumph for Russia, or primarily as a triumph for politically connected institutional investors.

Moreover, alongside the question of how the Sochi Games are being planned, there is also the question of whether they should take place at all. Perhaps surprisingly, there is not total unanimity on this point in Russia. Environmentalists have expressed alarm about the impact of Olympic construction on the fragile ecology of the Black Sea littoral, which includes a major national park.[19] An even more pointed analysis by an exiled Russia journalist of Circassian origin points to two further objections. First, given the ongoing political turmoil in the Caucasus,

---

[17] Valerii Perevozhikov and Natliia Eremina, "Snos pod Olimpiadu," *gazeta.ru*, August 16, 2007.

[18] Marina Ivanova, "TSenovaia olimpiiskaia eiforiia," gazeta.ru, July 14, 2007.

[19] "Ekologi schitaiut olimpiiskii uspekh Sochi 'Pirovoi pobedoi,'" *Kavkazskii Uzel*, July 11, 2007/

including what could be described as a low-level civil war in Chechnya and other republics, Russia's capacity to provide adequate security in Sochi is open to question. Second, Cirassian activists have reacted with anger to the choice of Sochi. Many Circassians believe that Sochi should not be awarded an Olympiad until Circassians' claims on their historic territory have been addressed. There have also been accusations that Olympic construction is already resulting in the destruction of important historical sites, including mass graves containing the bodies of Circassians who were massacred by Russian troops during the nineteenth century.[20] The holding of the Olympic Games in Sochi may be used by Circassian organizations to draw attention to their grievances.

Whatever the fate of the Sochi Olympiad, the award of the games to Sochi undoubtedly fits in with a larger trend toward the enhanced importance of Krasnodar within Russia. This process has both economic and political aspects. As noted above, the Black Sea coastal area is now experiencing an economic boom, whose effects are spilling over to other regions of the province. Like Sochi, real estate prices in Krasnodar City are skyrocketing, and the city is undergoing massive urban redevelopment that is expected to completely transform its appearance.[21] In addition, the Russian government is devoting major attention to improving the province's transport infrastructure. This concerns not only Sochi, but also the port of Novorossisk. The latter is to be expanded for both civilian and military uses: in addition to being a major commercial hub for the trade in oil and other commodities, Novorossisk is also expected to become the new home of Russia's Black Sea Fleet when Russia's lease of Sevastopol (in the Crimea, part of Ukraine) expires in 2017.[22]

---

[20] Fatima Tlisova, "The Challenges of the Sochi Olympics and Russia's Circassian Problem," Jamestown Foundation, *Chechnya Weekly*, August 16, 2007. Tlisova also points to concerns about the disposal of radioactive waste at industrial sites near the planned Sochi Olympics.

[21] Timothy Post, "Real Estate in Krasnodar: Kubano Naberezhnaya," Discovery Institute, Real Russia Project (accessible at http://www.russiablog.org), August 8, 2007.

[22] Vladimir Socor, "Russia Launches Massive Program to Develop Black Sea Ports," Jamestown Foundation, *Eurasia Daily Monitor*, July 13, 2007.

Finally, the rising profile of Tkachev's province also appears to be lifting the governor's own political fortunes. Despite his history of tension with the Kremlin, Tkachev now seems to have developed a successful political relationship with Putin. No less than for Putin, the Sochi Olympiad is a major coup for Tkachev. One can infer that Tkachev either must be on good terms with the Kremlin, or must be powerful enough to demand such a reward for his allegiance to Putin— or both. He has even been mentioned as a "dark horse" candidate for the Presidency in 2008.[23] Further evidence of Tkachev's rise can be gleaned from the distinctly less encouraging turns taken by the careers of his counterparts in the neighboring provinces of Adygeia and Stavropol, which will be addressed in the following two sections.

Adygeia: The Limits of Autonomy

If recent events in Krasnodar suggest the increasing power and prestige of the province and its leadership, the news from Adygeia suggests after years of being ignored, this tiny republic has come to the attention of powerful people in Moscow. Unfortunately, in practice, this appears to mean that the tenuous autonomy that Adygeia gained in the 1990s has now become unacceptable for the Kremlin. Several recent news events and trends indicate a desire on the part of the Moscow leadership to bring Adygeia more tightly under its control, both directly and (through the agency of Tkachev) indirectly. This section will examine three such stories: the creeping annexation of Adygeia by Krasnodar, the departure from power of President Khazret Sovmen, and tensions between the government and the republic's organized Muslim community.

The years 2006 and 2007 saw the climax and apparent failure of Kremlin efforts to incorporate Adygeia into Krasnodar. The annexation proposal was never formally identified as official Kremlin policy. Nonetheless, indirect efforts to promote merger of the two regions began in 2004 when both central government officials and

---

[23] Brian Whitmore, "Russia: Dark Horses Emerge In Presidential Transition," RFE/RL, August 9, 2007.

424

provincial officials, including Tkachev, began suggesting in public that Adygeia would be better off as part of its larger and more economically dynamic neighbor. However, the reaction to the merger among the Adyg political elite was far more negative and vigorous than the Kremlin expected. Both Sovmen and Adyg groups (including the local branch of the Cherkess Congress, headed by Murat Berzegov, as well as Circassian organizations abroad) furiously denounced the proposal.[24] By late 2006, after their mass protests began to attract media attention, both Kozak and Putin had been forced to distance themselves from the merger, and it was officially no longer on the agenda.

However, the Kremlin's retreat was only tactical. Putin's government was by no means finished with its plans for modification of Adygeia's political institutions. These plans appear to have two important components. First, Sovmen left office in 2007 and was replaced by the former academic Aslan Tkhakushinov. Before Sovmen's departure, the Russian press had reported that both Putin and Kozak found him unduly independent.[25]

The installation of Tkakhushinov, therefore, appears to signal a desire to impose a more pliant leader on Adygeia.[26] Moreover, Sovmen's departure and his replacement by Tkhakushinov are only part of a more general process involving the ongoing quiet transfer of powers from the government of Adygeia to the government of Krasnodar. In the most important instance of such jurisdiction-stripping, Adygeia's separate customs and transport ministries were abolished and incorporated into their Krasnodar counterparts; there are rumors that the migration service may follow. This de facto loss of power over the republic's internal affairs has led one observer to refer to Adygeia's autonomy as merely "virtual."[27] As expected, President Tkhakushinov's approach on relations with Krasnodar has been far

---

[24] Andrei Smirnov, "Russian Authorities Press Ahead with Plans to Combine Adygeya and Krasnodar Krai," Jamestown Foundation, *Eurasia Daily Monitor*, April 29, 2005.
[25] EDM, April 10, 2006; Regnum, April 20, 2006.
[26] Kavkazky Uzel, May 1, 2007.
[27] EDM, May 17; Andrei Smirnov, "Kremlin Lets Adygeya Keep Its Virtual Autonomy," EDM, January 16, 2007.

more accommodating than was Sovmen's. The two regions recently entered into a "cooperation" agreement that Tkhakushinov enthusiastically praised.[28] It is also unlikely that Tkakhushinov will press the issue of repatriation of Circassians living abroad (which has been a major priority for Cirassian nationalists throughout the Caucasus, including the Cherkess Congress), thus marking a further departure from the official nationalism of the Dzharimov and Sovmen years.

What conclusions can be drawn about the Kremlin's views of the Northwest Caucasus from its handling of the annexation issue? First, despite Adygeia's relative poverty, it would be a mistake to conclude that the Russian government's motivations for the merger are primarily concerned with administrative efficiency or economic development. Nor did the merger proposal emanate from a desire to please the Slavic majority within Adygeia. As the present author has argued elsewhere, the merger proposal, while nominally supported by most Slavs in Adygeia, was not a major priority for most of them.[29] Therefore, it is unlikely that Putin was responding to pressure from within Adygeia. Instead, the Kremlin is motivated by a desire to reduce the power of the government of Adygeia. Or rather, it might be more accurate to say that the Kremlin is motivated by a desire to reduce the power of the Adyg community within the republic's political life. In his eagerness to secure this objective, Putin showed himself prepared to alienate broad swathes of the Adyg population. The latter have good reason to fear rule by Tkachev. As noted above, Tkachev is already notorious for his numerous xenophobic statements and his sometimes-brutal mistreatment of the Armenian and Meskhetian Turkish communities in Krasnodar Krai. The non-Russian population of Adygeia is well aware of Tkachev's poor record as the governor of a multiethnic region.[30] Either these considerations did not weigh very heavily with

---

[28] *RFE/RL Newsline*, June 1, 2007.

[29] Matthew A. Light, "The Proposed Merger of Adygeia and Krasnodar Krai: Who Wants it, Why and What Would Be the Consequences?", Jamestown Foundation, *Chechnya Weekly*, July 19, 2007.

[30] Kavkazky Uzel, February 12, 2006.

Putin's administration, or the President and his staff were simply unaware of them.

In addition, as should be obvious, the de facto incorporation of parts of the government apparatus of Adygeia into Krasnodar empowers Tkachev. Indeed, both the merger proposal and the subsequent creeping merger make sense when understood as being part of the Putin administration's plans to solidify control over the North Caucasus by means of strategic alliances with selected local politicians, such as Ramzan Kadyrov in Chechnya.[31] What appears to be unfolding in the Northwest Caucasus is a similar process of transforming Krasnodar's executive into the Kremlin's main regional ally. Such an interpretation would be consistent both with the merger proposal and with the Russian government's strong support for the Sochi Olympics.

While superficially not related to the political maneuverings of high-ranking officials, a series of events involving the Muslim community of Adygeia also helps elucidate the Kremlin's attitude toward this republic. Adygeia's Muslims are overwhelmingly secular in outlook, there has never been organized Islamist extremism in the republic, and such Muslim institutions as exist were largely created with official sponsorship in the 1990s. Nonetheless, the republic's organized Muslim community and practicing Muslims are now finding themselves under official scrutiny and suspicion. In one incident in early 2006, Nadzhmudinnu Abazi, the Yugoslav-born imam of Adygeisk (the republic's second-largest city) was removed from office. Abazi also was targeted for prosecution for alleged extremism.[32] In an interview that the present author conducted with him in Maikop in July 2007, Abazi claimed that his dismissal violated the community's charter and was instigated by public officials. Other respondents in the Muslim community of Adygeia attributed his removal from his post to the local government's desire to replace him with a less independent figure (author's field notes).

---

[31] Regnum, April 18, 2006; World Politics Review, March 28.

[32] "Imamu Adygeiska mozhet byt' pred"iavleno ovbinenie," Regnum, April 19, 2006.

Meanwhile, in late 2005, following disturbances in Nalchik (Kabardino-Balkaria), the imam of Maikop and other worshipers leaving the main mosque of Maikop were arrested, held overnight, and allegedly tortured until they confessed to extremist activities.[33] The case against them was later dropped. According to one respondent in the Maikop Muslim community, interviewed in June 2007, efforts to bring charges against the police involved were thwarted (author's field notes). Taken together, both these incidents suggest increaing official suspicion of organized Muslim religious life—perhaps because the North Caucasus is less fully pacified than the Kremlin publicly claims. In turn, this suspicion is apparently leading the Kremlin to wish to fully dominate Muslim religious institutions, even in a relatively tranquil region such as Adygeia. In other words, like the merger with Krasnodar, the treatment of Adygeia's Muslims' indicates an assault on the republic's nominal autonomy. As the next section will argue, the Kremlin is making a similar foray into local politics in the final province of the Northwest Caucasus, Stavropol.

Stavropol: Weakened Governor, Political Ferment, Simmering Tensions

Recent political events in Stavropol have garnered an unusual degree of national and international media coverage for the province. First, the provincial legislative elections of March 2007 resulted in the country's only victory for the official "opposition" party, A Just Russia, over the United Russia Party. Second, and possibly as a result of A Just Russia's victory, Chernogorov may be about to lose his gubernatorial post. Finally, the outbreak of ethnic riots in Stavropol City has tarnished the province's image as an oasis of relative ethnic calm in the North Caucasus.

The most sensational political event of 2007 in Stavropol has undoubtedly been the elections to the provincial legislature, or duma. In common with thirteen other provinces, legislative elections were

---

[33] "Kabardino-Balkaria Cracks Down on Muslims," Jamestown Foundation, *Chechnya Weekly*, October 27, 2005.

held in Stavropol on March 11. Among all regions holding elections, only in Stavropol did the largest pro-Kremlin Party, United Russia, fail to receive the most votes. In Stavropol's election, A Just Russia received 37.7 percent of the votes, while United Russia received slightly below 24 percent. At the same time, all is not lost for United Russia in Stavropol, as the Party actually received more seats in the provincial duma than did A Just Russia (15 versus 12) because of United Russia's better performance in the single-member districts.[34]

Against the backdrop of United Russia's presumed dominance of the Russian political scene, even this modest victory for A Just Russia elicited widespread comment within Stavropol and throughout Russia. There were numerous allegations of fraud and misconduct in the Stavropol legislative elections. Governor Chernogorov hinted at improprieties, describing the election campaign as "Orange" in its inspiration, an allusion to the so-called Orange Revolution in Ukraine.[35] In addition, both independent observers as well as opposition parties, notably the Communists, also claim that fraud took place. The KPRF won only 14 percent of the vote in this formerly heavily Communist province. Communist leaders allege that both fraud and competition from ostensibly "socialist" A Just Russia played a part in the KPRF's defeat.[36] However, another opposition party, the SPS (Union of Right Forces) does not appear to share this assessment. Boris Obolonets, head of the provincial SPS, did claim that the pro-Kremlin parties had used "administrative resources." Like the Communists, he also claimed that there is hardly any difference between the two pro-Kremlin parties. At the same time, he attributed

---

[34] Jonas Bernstein, "Russia: Kremlin 'Parties of Power' Sweep Regional Ballots," RFE/RL, March 13, 2007.
[35] "A. CHernogorov: v Stavropol'skom krae oprobovana 'oranzhevaia' model' vyborov," Kavkazskii Uzel, March 13, 2007. Presumably, the governor's comparison was meant to cast A Just Russia as the counterpart of the "Orange" forces in Kiev.
[36] "V Stavropol'skom krae zaiavliut o massovykh narusheniiakh v khode vyborov," Kavkazskii Uzel, March 3, 2007; "Kommunisty nedovol'ny vyborama v Stavropol'skom krae," Kavkazskii Uzel, March 13, 2007.

A Just Russia's victory primarily to its broader support and better organization in the province, rather than to outright fraud.[37]

It is difficult to assess the actual significance of A Just Russia's victory in Stavropol and its strong showing other provinces. As might be expected, "Putin's deputy chief of staff, Vladislav Surkov, pointed to the competition between Unified Russia and A Just Russia—and the March 11 elections more generally—as evidence that political pluralism is alive and well in Russia," while opposition leaders alleged that A Just Russia is essentially a pro-Kremlin party without any significant policy differences from the current Presidential administration.[38] (As noted above, this is certainly the view of both the Communists and the SPS.) A further question is why A Just Russia won an outright victory only in Stavropol. It is certainly possible that the province's traditional support for the Communists has been transferred to the supposedly left-leaning A Just Russia. Following this line of interpretation, one might infer that A Just Russia is now tacitly authorized to compete with United Russia in at least some parts of Russia, and just happened to succeed in Stavropol. A more cynical, although admittedly highly speculative, interpretation would be that an election victory for A Just Russia in at least one provincial legislature was necessary to preserve the appearance of pluralism to which Surkov refers; and that Stavropol, for some reason, was chosen as the venue for A Just Russia's victory. As to what that reason might be, it is certainly a noteworthy coincidence that United Russia's apparent defeat[39] in the province coincided with serious political difficulties for Stavropol Governor Chernogorov.

As noted above, Chernogorov emerged out of the KPRF, and he has never been seen as a particular favorite of either President Yeltsin or President Putin. But unlike his counterparts in Krasnodar,

---

[37] "SPS: na vyborakh v Stavropol'skom krae ispol'zovalsia adminresurs," *Kavkazskii Uzel*, March 13, 2007.

[38] See Bernstein, *supra*, note 4.

[39] United Russia's defeat in Stavropol is a highly qualified one. As noted above, the Party actually won more seats than A Just Russia. It also appears that a member of United Russia will chair the province's electoral commission (*tsentrizbirkom*), possibly at the Kremlin's insistence. "Kraevoe prezidentskoe pravlenie," *Kommersant*, August 11, 2007.

430

Kondratenko and Tkachev, Chernogorov has avoided conflict with Moscow. He duly joined the United Russia Party when governors came under pressure to do so, and he has headed the Party's list in elections to the provincial legislature, most recently in March 2007. Now, however, recent indications suggest that official displeasure with Chernogorov emanating from the Kremlin may cost the governor his job. One such indication is the outbreak of an embarrassing scandal involving the governor and his ex-wife, Irina Chernogorova, who has accused him of abusive behavior, failure to make alimony payments, and corruption. Pointing to his possession of an expensive Bentley automobile, Mrs. Chernogorova has suggested that her ex-spouse enjoys a standard of living not consistent with his official salary. (During the campaign for the March elections, an opposition poster displayed in Stavropol City read, "Sell the Bentley and pay the alimony!") In the run-up to the March elections, Mrs. Chernogorova even went to the length of addressing a personal appeal to President Putin, with a plea to protect her from her allegedly abusive ex-husband.[40]

In today's largely tamed Russian media, the private misdeeds of public figures are mostly off limits to press scrutiny. Therefore, the fact that this tawdry affair has been given broad coverage strongly suggests that Chernogorov is out of favor. There are also more directly political indications that Chernogorov's tenure as governor may be drawing to a close. Following United Russia's relatively poor showing the March election (discussed above), the Party's national committee voted to expel him.[41] There then ensued a curious drama in which Chernogorov publicly announced that he would not resign, and then apparently received the backing of Putin against A Just Russia's delegation to the provincial duma, who were said to wish to oust him.[42] More recently, there has been renewed speculation in the press that President Putin

---

[40] "Eks-supruga glavy Stavropol'skogo kraia prosit zashchitit' ee ot Chernogorova," *Kavkazskii Uzel*, March 29, 2007.

[41] RFE/RL Newsline, March 16, 2007.

[42] "Gubernator Stavropol'skogo Kraia v otstavku ne sobiraetsia," *Kavkazskii Uzel*, March 16, 2007; "Politekhnolog: Kreml' poprosil 'SR' ne trebovat' otstavki gubernatora Stavropol'skogo Kraia," *Kavkazskii Uzel*, March 23, 2007.

may soon exercise his power to dismiss Chernogorov, among several other provincial governors.[43]

While Chernogorov's future is still in question, there does not seem to be much doubt that he is out of official favor. The official explanation for the President's dissatisfaction is Chernogorov's failure to secure an election victory in March. This explanation raises some questions, however. Given the possibility that the March elections were rigged (or could have been rigged had the government wished), it is not clear why Putin should be concerned about Chernogorov's lack of charisma or ineffectiveness as a campaigner. In addition, the fact that Chernogorov's wife began her public campaign against him before United Russia's election defeat further suggests that official displeasure with Chernogorov predates the election. Another possible explanation for Chernogorov's fall from grace could be a more generalized desire on Putin's part to replace 1990s pre-Putin holdovers such as Chernogorov with figures closer to the current President. In any case, the recent humbling of Stavropol's governor, especially when viewed against the backdrop of Putin's increasingly close ties with Tkachev, is a further indication that Moscow wishes to turn Krasnodar's chief executive into its main ally and lieutenant in the Northwest Caucasus.

The other news highlight of 2007 from Stavropol has been a serious of violent ethnic clashes in Stavropol City. While Stavropol remains an overwhelmingly ethnically Russian province, in recent years there has been a rapid rise in the population belonging to ethnic groups indigenous to neighboring Caucasus republics such as Chechnya and Dagestan.[44] The troubles in Stavropol City began in a violent clash between Chechens and Russian skinheads on May 24, in the course of which a Chechen student was killed. A Chechen witness (who was a friend of the deceased) claims that the police on the scene actually facilitated the skinheads' attack. The witness also states that instead of arresting the assailants, the police detained both him and his injured

---

[43] Natalya Krainova and Svetlana Osadchuk, "Governors Risk Loss of Party List Places." *Moscow Times*, August 13, 2007.

[44] See Vachagaev, *supra*, note 2.

friend, whom they prevented from receiving medical assistance. On June 3, two Russian students were stabbed to death. Many Russian residents immediately attributed their deaths to a revenge killing by Chechens, although prosecutors promptly identified a Russian as the suspect in their murder.[45] Nonetheless, hundreds of Russians took part in a "Slav Rally" on June 5, during which the crowd shouted chauvinistic slogans such as "Russia for the [ethnic] Russians!"[46] Governor Chernogorov and other regional officials initially claimed that the disturbances were not ethnic in nature, a denial that was met with widespread derision among local residents.[47]

As with the troubles of Chernogorov and the provincial duma elections, the actual significance of the Stavropol riots is unclear. Since last year's anti-Caucasian riot in Kondropoga, Karelia, hate crimes and racist organizations in Russia have received substantial media attention, both within the country and abroad. It is certainly true that there is extensive public hostility to ethnic groups from the Caucasus with the Slavic population of Russia, and that organized xenophobic organizations flourish there. Moreover, the number of hate crimes appears to be rising. "Sova," a monitoring organization, recently claimed that "37 people have been killed so far this year in racist attacks—22 percent more than for the same period last year."[48] Seen in this light, the outburst of ethnic violence in Stavropol is certainly not unique and does not necessarily herald a general breakdown of public order in the province. It is not even clear that ethnic tension in Stavropol is more severe than in many other provinces. On the other hand, when such incidents take place in Stavropol, they unavoidably attract more public attention, probably because they feed into both official and mass doubts about the province's long-term stability—and,

---

[45] Natalya Krainova, "Police Detain 51 at Stavropol Protest," *Moscow Times*, June 7, 2007.
[46] "Russia: Ethnic Tensions Mounting In Restive Stavropol," RFE/RL, June 7, 2007;
"'Slavianskii skhod' v Staropole: besporiadkov ne bylo," www.svoboda.com, June 6, 2007.
[47] "Krasulia: naselenie Stavropolia v strakhe I gotovo k 'sotsial'nomu vzrysu,'" Kavkazskii Uzel, June 6, 2007.
[48] Claire Bigg, "Russia: Seven Sentenced in Killing of Antiracism Campaigner," RFE/RL, August 7, 2007.

indeed, the possibility of creating a peaceful multiethnic milieu in the contemporary North Caucasus.

Conclusion: Finally on the Kremlin's Radar Screen

This survey has revealed several patterns and general trends in the political developments of the Northwest Caucasus. First, the Russian government is giving the region's political life increased attention, and is more determined than ever to manage it closely. This was clearly indicated by the government's undermining of provincial chief executives in both Stavropol and Adygeia. Second, the Putin administration appears to be pursuing a strategy of building up Krasnodar's economy and infrastructure, in an effort to turn the province's political leadership into the main ally and regional power base of the Kremlin in the Northwest Caucasus. This can be seen in the government's avid pursuit of the Sochi Olympics, its major capital investments in the province, and its attempt to hand over control of Adygeia to Krasnodar's Governor Tkachev.

Krasnodar's growing preeminence within the region can be explained by a variety of factors. First, it is clearly the most economically dynamic of the three provinces, and may simply appear the most appealing for substantial investments. Second, it provides (in Novorossisk) a military alternative to unreliable bases in Ukraine. Finally, it is less exposed than the other two regions to factors the Kremlin could regard as destabilizing: proximity to Chechnya (in the case of Stavropol) and the presence of a large and politically mobilized non-Russian population (in the case of Adygeia).   Under this interpretation, one way to understand the significance of the Northwest Caucasus for the Russian government is that the region serves as a kind of buffer zone, sheltering central European Russia (home to the bulk of the country's population and economic activity) from turmoil in the Northeast Caucasus (whose leaders' adherence to the state is tenuous at best). As a major strategic asset for Russia, the Northwest Caucasus can no longer be left to its own devices. In each region, the Kremlin has

434

begun to take matters into its own hands. In Krasnodar, Putin has both strengthened Tkachev and integrated him into Putin's "power vertical." In Stavropol, Putin has deliberately weakened Chernogorov. And in Adygeia, Putin has removed Sovmen altogether. In other words, the increasing political tension in the provinces of the Northwest Caucasus is not internal to the region. Rather, it is the Kremlin's own political machinations that are leading to instability there.

AUTHOR BIOGRAPHIES

Dr. Pavel K. Baev
Norwegian Peace Research Institute

Pavel K. Baev is a research professor at the International Peace Research Institute, Oslo (PRIO). He is also affiliated with the Centre for the Study of Civil War at PRIO. After graduating from the Moscow State University (MA in Political Geography, 1979) he worked in a research institute in the USSR Defence Ministry and then in the Institute of Europe, Moscow before joining PRIO in October 1992. In 1995-2001 he was the editor of PRIO's quarterly journal *Security Dialogue*. His research interests include the transformation of the Russian military, the energy dimension of Russian-European relations, and the post-Soviet conflicts in the Caucasus and the greater Caspian area.

Marie Bennigsen
Specialist on the North Caucasus

Marie Bennigsen has spent many years studying and writing about the region. She was the editor of *Central Asian Survey* for 25 years, and is currently planning to launch a new journal focusing on the Caucasus within the next year. She is also the co-author with Alexandre Bennigsen of The Islamic Threat to the Soviet State.

Dr. John B. Dunlop
Senior Fellow, Hoover Institution

John B. Dunlop is a senior fellow at the Hoover Institution. He is an expert on Russia's two wars in Chechnya, nationalism in the former Soviet Union, Russian cultural politics, and the politics of religion in Russia. His current research focuses on the conflict in Chechnya, Russian politics since 1985, Russia and the successor states of the former Soviet Union, Russian nationalism, and the politics of religion

436

in Russia. He has testified on the subject of the current war in Chechnya before the Helsinki Commission in Washington (November 1999) and the Senate Foreign Relations Committee (July 2001). He also made a presentation on the subject at the U.S. State Department in March 2002. He was the editor of the Jamestown Foundation's *Chechnya Weekly* from 2000–2002. His most recent books are: Russia Confronts Chechnya: Roots of a Separatist Conflict (1998) and The 2002 Dubrovka and 2004 Beslan Hostage Crises: A Critique of Russian Counter-Terrorism (2006).

Dr. Moshe Gammer
Senior Lecturer in Middle Eastern and African History at Tel Aviv University

Moshe Gammer (PhD, the London School of Economics and Political Science, University of London) is a senior lecturer at the Department of Middle Eastern and African History, Tel Aviv University. He is the author of Muslim Resistance to the Tsar: Shamil and the Conquest of Chechnya and Dagestan (London: Frank Cass, 1994) and The Lone Wolf and the Bear: Three Centuries of Chechen Defiance of Russian Rule (London: Christopher Hurst and Pittsburgh: the University of Pittsburgh Press, 2005) as well as numerous articles and chapters on the modern and contemporary history of the Caucasus, Central Asia and the Middle East.

Paul Goble
Vice Dean for the Social Sciences and Humanities at Audentes University, Tallinn and a Senior Research Associate at the EuroCollege of the University of Tartu in Estonia

Paul Goble is the publisher of the blog, Windows on Eurasia. He is the former director of research and publications programs at the Azerbaijan Diplomatic Academy in Baku. Prior to joining that institution but after retiring from the U.S. government in 2004, he was vice dean for the social sciences and humanities at Audentes University in Tallinn and a senior research associate at the EuroCollege of the University of Tartu in Estonia. Earlier, he served in a variety of

437

capacities in the U.S. government, including at the Department of State and Central Intelligence Agency; at U.S. international broadcasting institutions like Radio Free Europe/Radio Liberty and the Voice of America, and at various think tanks, including the Carnegie Endowment for International Peace, the Potomac Foundation, and the Jamestown Foundation. The editor of five volumes on ethnicity and religion in the former Soviet space, he continues to prepare daily commentaries on these issues, posting his articles at:www.windowoneurasia.blogspot.com or on request by e-list (paul.goble@gmail.com). Trained at Miami University in Ohio and the University of Chicago, he has been decorated by the governments of Estonia, Latvia and Lithuania for his work in promoting Baltic independence and the withdrawal of Russian forces from those formerly occupied lands.

Glen E. Howard
President, The Jamestown Foundation

Glen Howard is the President of The Jamestown Foundation. Fluent in Russian and proficient in Azerbaijani and Arabic, he is a regional expert on the Caucasus and Central Asia. Mr. Howard was formerly an analyst at the Science Applications International Corporation (SAIC) Strategic Assessment Center. His articles have appeared in publications including *The Wall Street Journal*, the *Central Asia-Caucasus Analyst* and *Jane's Defense Weekly*. Mr. Howard has also served as a consultant to the private sector and to governmental agencies, including the U.S. Department of Defense, the National Intelligence Council and major oil companies operating in Central Asia and the Middle East.

Dr. Matthew A. Light, J.D., Ph.D.
University of Massachusetts, Amherst, Department of Political Science

Dr. Matthew A. Light is a Visiting Assistant Professor of Political Science at the University of Massachusetts at Amherst. He conducted field research on the politics of Adygeia in Maikop from May to July

438

2006 while holding an Independent Advanced Research Opportunity fellowship from IREX.

Dr. Andrew McGregor
Director, Aberfoyle International Security, Toronto

Andrew McGregor is the director of Aberfoyle International Security, a Toronto-based consultant group, and previously worked as a research associate at the Canadian Institute for International Affairs. He earned his Ph.D. from the Department of Near and Middle Eastern Civilizations at the University of Toronto. Dr. McGregor has published widely on Islamic movements in the North Caucasus and Middle East.

Dr. Mikhail Roshchin
Senior Lecturer and Specialist on Islamic Movements in the North Caucasus, Institute of Oriental Studies, Russian Academy of Sciences.

Mikhail Roshchin is a specialist on the role that Islamic groups play in the North Caucasus. He was trained in Muslim Studies at the Moscow State University and holds a doctorate in contemporary Arabic history from the Institute of Oriental Studies of the Russian Academy of Sciences. From 1997 to 1998 he was a William Paton Fellow of Selly Oak Colleges in Birmingham, United Kingdom. His publications include Socio-Cultural Problems of Arab Youth (1992), Garamantide (1994), and Dagestan: Village Hushtada (1995). He also recently completed a collaborative research project on Badahshan, completing fieldwork among the Ismailis in this region straddling Tajikistan and Afghanistan.

Abdurashid Saidov
Correspondent, *Dagestanskaia Pravda*

Abdurashid Saidov writes for *Dagestanskaia Pravda* under pseudonym Abdul Malikov. He also writes for such Dagestani newspapers as

Novoye delo, *Chernovik*, and *Dagestantsy*. He is a member of the Russian PEN-center and the International Association of Writers.

Murad Batal-al-Shishani
Independent Writer & Researcher on Islamic Movements in the North Caucasus & the Middle East

Murad B. al-Shishani is a Jordanian-Chechen writer and researcher who is a specialist in the Islamist movement of the Middle East and Chechnya. He is a regular contributor to newspapers, journals, and internet publications, including *Terrorism Monitor*, *Central Asian Caucasus Analyst*, *Prague Watchdog*, as well as the Jordanian dailies *al-Ghad*, *al-Siyasah*, *al-Dawlih*, and others. He is also the author of several books, including The Islamic Movement in Chechnya and The Chechen-Russian Conflict: 1990-2000 (Amman: 2001). He has participated in several conferences on Islamist movements, terrorism, and North Caucasus issues. He has appeared in other media such as Radio Free Europe/Radio Liberty, al-Arabiya and others.

Andrei Smirnov
North Caucasus Correspondent, Jamestown Foundation

Andrei Smirnov is an independent journalist and expert covering the Islamic movements in the North Caucasus and an expert on Chechnya. He is a frequent contributor to Jamestown Foundation's publications *Chechnya Weekly* and *Eurasia Daily Monitor*. From 2002 to 2006 he was a coordinator of The Yalta Initiative for Peace in Chechnya (YIPIC), a coalition of Chechen and Russian peace-building non-governmental organizations. He is also a coordinator of the Viktor Popkov Informational and Analytical Center, which conducts studies on Chechen war issues. He is based in Russia.

Fatima Tlisova
North Caucasus Correspondent, Regnum News Agency

Fatima Tlisova is the Editor-in-Chief of the North Caucasus desk at the Regnum News Agency. She is also a staff correspondent for the Associated Press in this region. Her duties carry her every week across the North Caucasus from Adygea to Dagestan. She is a native of Karachaevo-Chersekiya and currently resides in Nal'chik.

Mairbek Vachagaev
Ph.D. Candidate, L'École des Haute Études en Science Sociales, Paris

Mairbek Vatchagaev is a doctoral candidate at the School for Advanced Studies in Social Sciences in Paris. A former spokesperson for separatist Chechen President Aslan Maskhadov, his research examines the historical relationship between indigenous Islamic practices in the North Caucasus and Chechen resistance to Russian colonial rule.

441

Index

445